A Short History of Parliament

A Short History of Parliament is a comprehensive institutional history, not a political history of parliament, though politics is included where, as frequently occurred, institutional changes resulted from particular political events.

It covers the English parliament from its origins, the pre-1707 Scottish parliament and the pre-1800 Irish parliament, the parliament of Great Britain from 1707 and the parliament of the United Kingdom from 1801, together with sections on the post-devolution parliaments and assemblies set up in the 1990s and on parliaments in the Isle of Man, the Channel Islands and the Irish Republic.

It considers all aspects of parliament as an institution: membership of both the Lords and the Commons; constituencies, elections and franchises; where the Lords and the Commons met; how business was arranged and managed, including Speakers, the use of committees, the development of parties, lobbying and voting procedures; legal cases in the House of Lords; official recording of and reporting of business and debates; the conflict and balance of power between the two Houses; and the position of the monarch in parliament.

Each section contains a chronology listing key events, suggestions for further reading and 'inserts' – short anecdotes or accounts of particular figures or episodes which provide lively illustrations of parliament at work in different periods.

A Short History of Parliament

ENGLAND, GREAT BRITAIN,
THE UNITED KINGDOM,
IRELAND & SCOTLAND

Edited by Clyve Jones

THE BOYDELL PRESS

© Contributors 2009

All Rights Reserved. Except as permitted under current legislation no part of this work may be photocopied, stored in a retrieval system, published, performed in public, adapted, broadcast, transmitted, recorded or reproduced in any form or by any means, without the prior permission of the copyright owner

The right of the contributors to be identified as the authors of this work has been asserted in accordance with sections 77 and 78 of the Copyright, Designs and Patents Act 1988

First published 2009
The Boydell Press, Woodbridge
Reprinted in paperback 2012

ISBN 978-1-84383-717-6

Transferred to digital printing

The Boydell Press is an imprint of Boydell & Brewer Ltd
PO Box 9, Woodbridge, Suffolk IP12 3DF, UK
and of Boydell & Brewer Inc.
668 Mt. Hope Avenue, Rochester NY 14620-2731, USA
website: www.boydellandbrewer.com

The publisher has no responsibility for the continued existence of accuracy of URLs for external or third-party internet websites referred to in this book, and does not guarantee that any content on such websites is, or will remain, accurate of appropriate

A CIP record for this title is available
from the British Library

This publication is printed on acid-free paper

Contents

List of Inserts, Tables and Figures vii
Notes on Contributors x
List of Abbreviations xiv

1 Prologue
   Clyve Jones 1

Parliament of England to 1307

2 Origins and Beginnings to 1215
   John Maddicott 3
3 The Development of Parliament, 1215–1307
   Paul Brand 10

Parliament of England, 1307–1707

4 The House of Lords, 1307–1529
   Chris Given-Wilson 16
5 The House of Lords, 1529–1629
   David L. Smith 29
6 The House of Lords and the 'Other House', 1640–60
   Jason Peacey 42
7 The House of Lords, 1660–1707
   Robin Eagles 54
8 The House of Commons, 1307–1529
   Simon Payling 75
9 The House of Commons, 1529–1601
   Alasdair Hawkyard 86
10 The House of Commons, 1603–29
   Paul M. Hunneyball 100
11 The House of Commons, 1640–60
   Stephen K. Roberts 110
12 The House of Commons, 1660–1707
   Paul Seaward 126

Parliament of Great Britain, 1707–1800

13 The House of Lords, 1707–1800
   Clyve Jones and Stephen Farrell 147
14 The House of Commons, 1707–1800
   Bob Harris 170

Parliament of the United Kingdom since 1801

15 The House of Lords, 1801–1911
   Richard W. Davis   193

16 The House of Lords, 1911–49
   William Frame   211

17 The House of Lords since 1949
   Peter Dorey   226

18 The House of Commons, 1801–1911
   Philip Salmon   249

19 The House of Commons, 1911–49
   Philip Norton   271

20 The House of Commons since 1949
   Paul Seaward   283

Other Parliaments and Legislatures of the British Isles

21 The Parliament of Scotland to 1707
   Julian Goodare   301

22 The Parliament of Ireland to 1800
   Charles Ivar McGrath   321

23 The Northern Ireland Parliament and Assembly at Stormont
   Graham Walker   339

24 Other Legislatures within the British Isles
   Clyve Jones   352
      Isle of Man
      Channel Islands
      Irish Parliament

25 The Post-Devolution Legislatures
   Clyve Jones   358
      Scottish Parliament
      National Assembly for Wales

26 Epilogue
   Clyve Jones   363

   Index   365

Inserts, Tables and Figures

4 **The House of Lords, 1307–1529**
  Parliamentary Proxies *18*
  A Child Attends the House of Lords *19*
  Rank and Precedence among the Peerage *19*
  Parliaments at Westminster and Elsewhere *20*
  The 'Fane Fragment' of 1461 *22*
  The Language of Parliament *25*

5 **The House of Lords, 1529–1629**
  Mitred Abbots in the House of Lords *30*
  The King of Naples and Jerusalem Attends the House of Lords *31*
  Parliamentary Diaries *37*
  Petition of Right *39*

6 **The House of Lords and the 'Other House', 1640–60**
  The Oxford Parliament *44*
  Uniting the Two Houses *48*
  The Cromwellian 'Other House' *50*

7 **The House of Lords, 1660–1707**
  The Restoration of the Bishops *57*
  Provisional Government and Convention 1688–9 *59*
  Philip, 4th Lord Wharton *62*
  Oaths, Proxies and the 7th Earl of Huntington *64*
  Obesity and Voting in the House of Lords *65*
  Trials and Impeachments *67*

8 **The House of Commons, 1307–1529**
  The Frequency and Duration of Parliaments *75*
  The Meeting Place of the Commons *76*
  The Origins of Divisions *79*
  Parliamentary Elections *81*

9 **The House of Commons, 1529–1601**
  The Union with Wales *87*
  The Northern Palatinates *88*
  The Earl of Hertford's Letter of 1541 to the Isle of Jersey *88*
  The Royal Assent *93*
  Sir Simonds D'Ewes *96*

10 **The House of Commons, 1603–29**
    Freedom of Speech and the Protestation of 1621   *104*
    The Great Contract of 1610   *106*

11 **The House of Commons, 1640–60**
    Writ to Summon a Member to the Nominated Assembly 1653   *112*
    The Oxford Parliament   *113*
    Sir Simonds D'Ewes and Thomas Burton   *115*
    Example of Ephemera Printed for Parliament 1643   *116*
    Commons Declaration of 4 January 1649   *117*
    A Stranger in the Commons 1659   *119*
    Heaven, Hell, Paradise and Purgatory   *122*

12 **The House of Commons, 1660–1707**
    The Bill of Rights   *127*
    Poll Books   *129*
    Election Entertainment   *131*
    Parliamentary Tactics   *134*
    Reporting the House   *142*

13 **The House of Lords, 1707–1800**
    The Royal Veto   *148*
    The Election of the 16 Scottish Representative Peers   *150*
    The Creation of the 12 New Peers by the Earl of Oxford   *152*
    Peerage Bill of 1719   *153*
    Dissenting and Protesting   *157*
    A Public Spectacle   *159*
    Fox's India Bill   *162*
    'The thanes, high priests and household cavalry'   *165*

14 **The House of Commons, 1707–1800**
    Hastings Impeachment   *180*
    Middlesex Election Crisis   *188*

15 **The House of Lords, 1801–1911**
    When did the Spiritual Side of the House become the Government Side?   *194*
    Irish Representative Peers   *197*
    George IV   *201*
    The Wensleydale Life Peerage of 1856   *205*
    The 3rd Marquess of Salisbury and the Referendal Theory   *207*

16 **The House of Lords, 1911–1949**
    Maundy Gregory and the Sale of Honours   *215*
    The House of Lords and the Approach of War   *219*
    The Trial of Lord de Clifford   *220*

17 The House of Lords since 1949

Table 1 Allocation of House of Lords' time (main activities), 2006–7 228
Table 2 Increased activity in the House of Lords, 1950–1 to 2006–7 230
Table 3 Examples of inquiries conducted by the key House of Lords' select committees since 1997 232
Table 4 Government defeats in the House of Lords since 1959 234
Table 5 Hereditary and life peers in the House of Lords, 1949–2007 (excluding *ex officio* peers) 237
Table 6 Party membership in the House of Lords, 1970–2007 (excluding *ex officio* peers) 237
Table 7 Occupational background of life peers, 1958–2007 238
Table 8 Peers with professional or occupational backgrounds in higher education who spoke in the House of Lords' second reading debate on the Higher Education Bill, April 2004 240
Table 9 Party affiliation of life peers created 1958–2007 241

18 The House of Commons, 1801–1911

Murder in the Commons' Lobby 250
Bellamy's Kitchen 251
Bellamy's and the 'Rage for Speaking' 252
Table 1 Procedural reforms associated with the growth of ministerial control 254
Hansard and the Printed Parliamentary Debates 260
Table 2 UK electors and constituencies 1801–1911 262
Figure 1 Cross-party votes cast in double-member seats, 1818–1910 264
Figure 2 Divisions with cross-party voting in House of Commons, 1836–1903 266

19 The House of Commons, 1911–1949

University and Double-Member Seats 273
Electoral Systems 274
Party Leaders and Leaders of the Opposition 276

21 The Parliament of Scotland to 1707

Attendance at Some Scottish Parliaments 305

23 The Northern Ireland Parliament and Assembly at Stormont

Sir James Craig 341
Sir Norman Stronge 342
A Painting of the Battle of the Boyne 342
Éamon de Valera 346

Notes on Contributors

Paul Brand is senior research fellow at All Souls College, Oxford. He has edited the first two volumes of the *Parliamentary Rolls of Medieval England* (1995), the first four volumes of the *Earliest English Law Reports* (1996–2007) for the Selden Society, and volume 6 of *Plea Rolls of the Exchequer of Jews* (1992). He has written *Origins of the English Legal Profession* (1992), *The Making of the Common Law* (1992), and *Kings, Barons and Justices: The Making and Enforcement of Legislation in Thirteenth-Century England* (2003).

Linda Clark was co-editor with J. S. Roskell and Carole Rawcliffe of *The History of Parliament: The House of Commons, 1386–1421* (4 vols, Stroud, 1992). She is currently editor of the House of Commons section of the History of Parliament, covering the period 1422–61.

Richard W. Davis is emeritus professor of history at Washington University in St Louis. Among his books are: *Dissent in Politics, 1780–1830: The Political Life of William Smith MP* (1971); *Political Change and Continuity, 1760–1885: A Buckinghamshire Study* (1972); *Disraeli* (1976); *The English Rothschilds* (1983); *A Political History of the House of Lords, 1811–1846: From the Regency to Corn Law Repeal* (Stanford, CA, 2008). He is a fellow of the Royal Historical Society and in 1981–2 he was distinguished visiting professor at Christ's College, Cambridge. He was the 2002 Wellington lecturer at the University of Southampton and received a two-year Andrew W. Mellon Emeritus Fellowship in 2005.

Peter Dorey is reader in British politics at Cardiff University. He has published widely on aspects of post-1945 British politics, public policy and constitutional reform. His most recent books are *Policy Making in Britain: An Introduction* (2005), *Developments in British Public Policy* (editor, 2005), *The Labour Governments, 1964–1970* (editor, 2006), *The Labour Party and Constitutional Reform* (2008), *British Conservatism and Trade Unionism, 1945–64* (2009), and *House of Lords Reform since 1911* for publication in 2010. He is currently completing (with Alexandra Kelso) a monograph on House of Lords reform since 1911.

Robin Eagles is a senior research fellow in the House of Lords 1660–1832 section of the History of Parliament. His previous publications include *Francophilia in English Society, 1748–1815* (2000), entries in the *Oxford Dictionary of National Biography* and 'Unnatural Allies? The Oxfordshire Élite from the Exclusion Crisis to the Overthrow of James II', *Parliamentary History*, xxvi (2007).

Stephen Farrell is editorial controller for the History of Parliament Online project. He contributed extensively to *The History of Parliament: The House of Commons, 1820–1832*, edited by D. R. Fisher (forthcoming), particularly on Irish MPs and constituencies. He completed his Cambridge PhD thesis on the Rockingham whigs and the House of Lords in 1993, and has since published articles on related subjects in *Parliamentary History*. With Melanie Unwin and James Walvin, he edited *The British Slave Trade: Abolition, Parliament and People* (Edinburgh, 2007).

Contributors

William Frame is curator of modern historical papers in the Department of Manuscripts at the British Library, with particular responsibility for 20th-century and contemporary archives. He wrote his PhD on politics and unemployment in Britain in the 1930s and has since published a number of articles on 20th-century history.

Chris Given-Wilson is professor of late medieval history at the University of St Andrews. He has published several books on the political and social history of late medieval England, including *The Royal Household and the King's Affinity: Service, Politics and Finance in England, 1360–1413* (1986) and *The English Nobility in the Late Middle Ages* (1987). More recently, his research interests have focused on historical writing and on the history of the English parliament. He is the author of *Chronicles: The Writing of History in Medieval England* (2004) and has edited a number of chronicles. He is also the general editor of *The Parliament Rolls of Medieval England, 1275–1504* (16 vols, 2005; also available in CD-Rom and on-line). He is a member of the council of the Royal Historical Society and the editorial board of the History of Parliament.

Julian Goodare is a reader in Scottish history at the University of Edinburgh. He is the author of *State and Society in Early Modern Scotland* (Oxford, 1999) and *The Government of Scotland, 1560–1625* (Oxford, 2004), and editor of *The Scottish Witch-Hunt in Context* (Manchester, 2002). He is co-editor (with Michael Lynch) of *The Reign of James VI* (East Linton, 2000) and (with Lauren Martin and Joyce Miller) of *Witchcraft and Belief in Early Modern Scotland* (Basingstoke, 2008). He has been publication secretary of the Scottish History Society (1989–2002), and director of the ESRC-funded Survey of Scottish Witchcraft which went online in 2003. He is an associate editor of the *Oxford Dictionary of National Biography*.

Bob Harris is a fellow and tutor in Modern History at Worcester College, Oxford. Before 2006 he was professor of British History at the University of Dundee. His latest book is *The Scottish People and the French Revolution* (2008). His other books include *Politics and the Nation: Britain in the Mid-Eighteenth Century* (2002) and *Politics and the Rise of the Press: Britain and France, 1620–1800* (1996). He has also published many chapters and articles on British 18th-century politics and political culture. He is currently leading a collaborative project on Scottish towns in the age of enlightenment.

Alasdair Hawkyard is a fellow of the Royal Historical Society. For 14 years he was co-editor and principal research assistant under S. T. Bindoff on the House of Commons 1509–58 section of the History of Parliament. He is currently completing the introductory survey to the volumes entitled *The History of Parliament: The House of Commons, 1509–1558*, ed. S. T. Bindoff (3 vols, 1982).

Paul M. Hunneyball is a senior research fellow at the History of Parliament, working on the House of Commons 1604–29 section. His publications include a monograph, *Architecture and Image-Building in Seventeenth-Century Hertfordshire* (Oxford, 2004). He is currently working on the architectural patronage of Oliver Cromwell and his circle.

Clyve Jones is an honorary fellow of the Institute of Historical Research. He has been the editor of the journal *Parliamentary History* since 1986. Previously he was reader in modern history in the University of London and collection development librarian in the Institute of Historical Research. He has published extensively on the history of the house of lords and of the peerage in the early 18th century. His main publications are editions of *The London Diaries of William Nicolson, Bishop of Carlisle, 1702–1718* (with Geoffrey Holmes) (Oxford, 1985), and *Tory and Whig: The Parliamentary Papers of Edward Harley, Third Earl of Oxford, and William Hay, MP for Seaford, 1715–1754* (with Stephen Taylor) (Woodbridge, 1998). He has also edited a festschrift for his mentor Geoffrey Holmes (1987), and essays in memory of his friends Philip Lawson (Woodbridge, 1998), John A. Phillips (Edinburgh, 2005) and, again, Geoffrey Homes (Oxford, 2009).

Charles Ivar McGrath is a lecturer in the school of history and archives, University College Dublin, and a committee member of the Irish Historical Society. He is the author of *The Making of the Eighteenth-Century Irish Constitution: Government, Parliament and the Revenue, 1692–1714* (Dublin, 2000), and articles in *The English Historical Review*, *Irish Historical Studies*, *Parliamentary History*, and *Eighteenth-Century Ireland*. He is co-editor (with Michael Brown and Thomas P. Power) of *Converts and Conversion in Ireland, 1650–1850* (Dublin, 2005) and, with Christopher Fauske, of *Money, Power, and Print: Interdisciplinary Studies on the Financial Revolution in the British Isles* (Newark, DE, 2008).

John Maddicott retired recently after 37 years as fellow and tutor in medieval history at Exeter College, Oxford. An undergraduate and postgraduate at Worcester College, Oxford, he completed his DPhil in 1967 on Thomas of Lancaster, Edward II's chief baronial opponent. This was published in 1972. A second biography, *Simon de Montfort*, was published in 1994. His main interests lie in English political and social history in the 13th and 14th centuries, and in the Anglo-Saxon economy. In addition to his two biographies he has published on Anglo-Saxon trade and industry, Edward the Confessor, the English peasantry, the history of parliament, and the politics of the reigns of Henry III and Edward I. In 2004 he gave the Ford Lectures at Oxford on 'The Origins of the English Parliament', and he is currently preparing these for publication.

Philip Norton (Lord Norton of Louth) is professor of government and director of the centre for legislative studies at the University of Hull. His publications include 27 books, among them *Dissension in the House of Commons* (1975), *Parliament in British Politics* (Basingstoke, 2005) and as editor *Parliaments in Western Europe* (3 vols, 1996). He has served as president of the British politics group in the USA and the politics association in the United Kingdom. He edits *The Journal of Legislative Studies*, and he chaired the Conservative Party's commission to strengthen parliament (1999–2000). He was elevated to the peerage in 1998 and has served as chairman of the Lords select committee on the constitution.

Simon Payling is a senior research fellow at the History of Parliament. He is the author of *Political Society in Lancastrian England: The Greater Gentry of Nottinghamshire* (Oxford, 1991) and a series of articles on late medieval legal and parliamentary history.

Contributors

Jason Peacey is lecturer in history at University College London. He is the editor of *The Regicides and the Execution of Charles I* (2001), co-editor of *Parliament at Work* (2002), and editor of *The Print Culture of Parliament, 1600–1800* (2007). He is also the author of *Politicians and Pamphleteers: Propaganda in the Civil Wars and Interregnum* (2004), and recent articles include 'Cromwellian England: A Propaganda State?', *History*, xci (2006), and 'The Protector Humbled: Richard Cromwell and the Constitution', in *The Cromwellian Protectorate, 1653–9*, ed. P. Little (Woodbridge, 2007). He is currently writing a book upon popular participation in parliamentary politics during the mid-17th century.

Stephen K. Roberts is editor of the House of Commons 1640–60 section at the History of Parliament. He is also joint-editor of the journal *Midland History* and general editor of the Worcestershire Historical Society. His first published book was *Recovery and Restoration in an English County: Devon Local Administration, 1646–1670* (1985) and was co-editor in 1986 of a festschrift for Ivan Roots entitled *Politics and People in Revolutionary England*. Since then he has published widely on aspects of government in mid-17th-century England and Wales, and contributed 36 articles to the *Oxford Dictionary of National Biography*. He has written chapters for county histories to be published for Cardiganshire and Monmouthshire.

Philip Salmon is the editor of the 1832–1945 History of Parliament project. His publications include *Electoral Reform at Work: Local Politics and National Parties, 1832–1841* (Woodbridge, 2002) and articles in *Parliaments, Estates and Representation* and *Parliamentary History*. He co-edited *Partisan Politics and Reform in Parliament and the Constituencies, 1689–1880* (Edinburgh, 2005). He is currently completing a book on the impact of the 1835 Municipal Corporations Act and a two-volume edition of the diaries of Henry Grey, 3rd Earl Grey.

Paul Seaward is the director of the History of Parliament. He is the author of *The Cavalier Parliament and the Reconstruction of the Old Regime, 1661–1667* (Cambridge, 1989), *The Restoration* (Basingstoke, 1991) and (with Mark Goldie and Tim Harris) *The Politics of Religion in Restoration England* (Oxford, 1990). He also contributed 'The House of Commons' in *The British Constitution in the Twentieth Century*, ed. Vernon Bogador (Oxford, 2002).

David L. Smith has been a fellow of Selwyn College, Cambridge, since 1988, where he is currently director of studies in history and tutor for graduate students, and he is also an affiliated lecturer in the Cambridge History Faculty. He has won the Royal Historical Society's Alexander Prize and Cambridge University's Thirlwall Prize for Historical Research. His publications include *Constitutional Royalism and the Search for Settlement, c. 1640–1649* (1994), *A History of the Modern British Isles, 1603–1707: The Double Crown* (1998), *The Stuart Parliaments, 1603–1689* (1999), and (with Patrick Little) *Parliaments and Politics during the Cromwellian Protectorate* (2007).

Graham Walker is professor of political history at Queen's University, Belfast. He has published extensively in the fields of British and Irish history and politics. His latest book is *A History of the Ulster Unionist Party: Protest, Pragmatism and Pessimism* (Manchester, 2004), He has also co-edited *A Biographical Dictionary of British Prime Ministers* (1998). He is currently working on a comparative study of devolution in Scotland and Northern Ireland.

Abbreviations

Initials appended to inserts
- AH   Alasdair Hawkyard
- CJ   Clyve Jones
- LC   Linda Clark
- SF   Stephen Farrell

Bibliographical citations
- APS   *Acts of the Parliaments of Scotland*, ed. T. Thomson and C. Innes (12 vols, Edinburgh, 1814–75)
- CJ   *Commons Journal*
- HMC   Historical Manuscripts Commission
- LJ   *Lords Journal*
- ODNB   *Oxford Dictionary of National Biography* (61 vols, Oxford, 2004)
- PA   Parliamentary Archives (formerly the House of Lords Record Office)
- PP   *Parliamentary Papers*
- PROME   *The Parliament Rolls of Medieval England, 1275–1504*, ed. C. Given-Wilson *et al.* (16 vols, Woodbridge, 2005)
- PRONI   Public Records Office of Northern Ireland
- RO   Record Office

Note: Place of publication of books shown in the notes and 'Further Reading' is London unless stated otherwise.

1 Prologue
Clyve Jones

It is a commonly held misconception that the Westminster parliament is the 'mother of all parliaments'. This may have come about as a result of Westminster-type parliaments that have appeared around the world in the wake of the British empire. The phrase 'the mother of all parliaments', however, originated with the radical politician John Bright, who on 18 January 1865 made a speech in Birmingham in which he stated that '*England* is the mother of all parliaments.' Presumably he meant that the parliament of England (or by then the United Kingdom) at Westminster was proving the model for assemblies and legislatures around the largest empire the world had seen. But in terms of age, Westminster is easily outstripped by the Althingi – the parliament of Iceland established on 23 June 930 – which claims to be the oldest parliament in the world (perhaps we might call it 'the grandmother of all parliaments').[1] Even within the British Isles, the Tynwald – the parliament of the Isle of Man – is much older than Westminster, claiming to be the oldest unbroken parliamentary institution still in existence in the world, having been established by 979.[2] (The Althingi was abolished in 1800, not to be refounded until 1843–5.) The Isle of Man is, however, not part of England or even part of the United Kingdom, being crown property (as are the Channel Islands). But Westminster can at least lay claim to be the oldest existing parliament on the mainland of Great Britain, if not within the British Isles. The first known act of the English parliament is from 1229, while from the Irish parliament it is from 1216.

In some sense the Scottish parliament in Edinburgh, first recorded in 1235 and in existence until 1707, might be able to lay claim to be a mother of a particular type of parliament which is uncommon in the modern English-speaking world: the Scottish parliament was unicameral unlike those of England and Ireland which were bicameral, with an upper and lower house. Even the Tynwald and the states of the Channel Island, which govern and legislate for small territories and populations, are bicameral (though there is an argument that Tynwald is in fact tricameral). The Althingi, again responsible for a small population, is also bicameral.

---

[1] The Faroese 'Logting' may well be older, being established as early as the 9th century with annual assemblies being recorded in the 10th century. It was abolished in 1816, to be reconstituted in 1852 not as a legislative assembly but as an advisory body.

[2] However, the claim has been disputed, as between the 11th and 15th centuries Tynwald was a judicial court, and did not create legislation.

In the latter part of the 20th century, historians, whether through political correctness (possibly not wishing to offend the Irish) or through trendiness, started to call the British Isles 'the North Atlantic archipelago'. This volume will have none of that nonsense. Its subject is a short institutional history of the parliaments of the British Isles: those of England to 1707, Ireland up to 1800, Northern Ireland since 1922, Scotland to 1707, Great Britain, 1707–1800, and the United Kingdom since 1801, with nods towards the assemblies of the Isle of Man and the Channel Islands, the new Scottish parliament and Welsh assembly, and the post-1922 parliament of Ireland. By 'institutional' is meant a history of how these bodies started, developed and worked; it is not a political history, though politics have not been totally excluded for such bodies grew and changed as a result of political crises and out of politicians fashioning their proceedings to suit their times.

The history of the parliaments in this volume are arranged with the English parliament coming first, though it was some time before the institution permanently established itself at Westminster, often meeting elsewhere in England to suit the necessity or convenience of the monarch, the last meeting outside Westminster being as late as 1681 when, to avoid the heated political atmosphere of the capital, parliament meet in Oxford. This section of the book starts with the origins and beginnings of the English legislative before the Norman Conquest and continues to the present day. It is followed by a section on the parliament of Scotland from its origins to its abolition with the Anglo-Scottish union in 1707. Next comes the parliament of Ireland, also from its origins in the 13th century to its abolition with the Anglo-Irish union in 1801. Upon the dissolution of this union in 1922 the legislature for Northern Ireland was established at Stormont. The penultimate chapter takes a brief look at Tynwald, the Channel Island assemblies, the new parliament in Scotland and the assembly in Wales, and the present Irish parliament.

2 Origins and Beginnings to 1215

John Maddicott

The origins of parliament can be traced back to the great national councils which emerged in early 10th-century England. It was then, during the reigns of Edward the Elder (899–924) and Athelstan (924–39), that the areas of Scandinavian settlement in the east and north of the island were conquered by the West Saxon monarchy and a new kingdom of England came into being. Earlier kings, ruling smaller kingdoms, had made use of assemblies of their great men, but had governed mainly through itineration, travelling around their lands to provision their courts, distribute patronage and supervise their subjects. But with the emergence of a larger kingdom, government by itineration became much less practicable, and in fact the late Anglo-Saxon kings confined their travels mainly to England south of the Thames. In these circumstances assemblies of the witan, the king's 'wise men', began to do the work which itineration could no longer do.

The numbers, names and status of those 'wise men' are recorded in the witness-lists attached to the royal charters whose publication almost invariably took place at assemblies. From the witness lists two particular characteristics of these gatherings stand out: they were often very large, and they included men from distant parts. Athelstan's charters and those of his successors Edgar (959–75) and Æthelred (978–1016) sometimes had as many as 80 to 100 witnesses, indicating a good many more attenders than the 40 to 80 present at most 13th-century parliaments. In both periods magnates and churchmen predominated. Under Athelstan they sometimes included prominent Danes from eastern England and the princes and kinglets of the far north and west over whom Athelstan claimed lordship; under Edgar, some of the leading nobles of Northumbria. Via assemblies, regions of doubtful loyalty which the king was unable to visit in person could thus be drawn vicariously into the orbit of royal government and royal authority.

More so than in later parliaments, that authority was sometimes asserted through charismatic display, for which great assemblies provided the necessary stage and setting. From the mid-10th century onwards royal crown-wearings were used to demonstrate the transcendent nature of the king's power and the God-given quality of his kingship. Their religious aura was enhanced by their particular association with the great feasts of the church, Christmas, Easter and Whitsun, whose growing linkage with major assemblies was beginning to create a regular rhythm of meetings and to mark out their increasingly institutional character. But most assembly business was more mundane, and closely resembled that of later parliaments. Legislation, including 19 of the 22 law codes issued between 899 and 1022, was almost always made and published in assemblies. State trials, such as that of Ealdorman Ælfric for treason in 985, took place there, initiating a practice which would last until the impeachment of Warren Hastings and beyond. Political decision-making was a regular and central function, and even in the dark days of the uncounselled Æthelred most of the major decisions affecting war and peace with the Danes emanated from assemblies. Only perhaps in the concentration within assemblies of land grants made by charter did their business differ markedly from that of later parliaments, whose royal convenors dispensed their patronage more evenly through the year.

The bringing of so much business before these meetings promoted the consensual relationship between the king and his great men on which political stability ultimately depended. If assemblies allowed magnates to participate in royal government, the eating, drinking and general socializing which was another of their features worked to the same consensual end. They were great social occasions, usually located on royal estates in southern England – at Andover in Hampshire, for example, or Amesbury in Wiltshire – where such entertainment was possible; though by the reign of Edward the Confessor (1042–66) towns like Oxford and London had become more prominent as meeting places. Despite their geographically peripheral and often rural setting, and their lack of the regular venue such as Westminster which distinguished later parliaments, these assemblies as they developed between c. 925 and 1066 were truly national, not only in the range of their business and of their participants but in the way in which contemporaries regarded them. Their meetings were often described as those of 'the witan of the English people' or something similar:[1] those attending could be seen as standing for the whole realm. In this way too they resembled later parliaments.

In 1066 this conciliar apparatus passed into Norman hands without much change. In William the Conqueror's own duchy large councils had been unusual and had lacked both the regularity and the set functions of their long established English counterparts. Secular legislation, for example, whether made at councils or elsewhere, was unknown in Normandy. William adopted the conciliar traditions of the vanquished because he found them useful. Like Anglo-Saxon assemblies, their Anglo-Norman successors brought together large numbers of men, such as the 40 witnesses to a charter from the Whitsun assembly of 1081 who included two archbishops, 13 bishops, six abbots and 15 magnates. They provided a similar forum for public discussion of what William of Malmesbury called 'the vital business of the realm',[2] such as the planning of the Domesday survey

---

[1] E.g. *Die Gesetze der Angelsachsen*, ed. F. Liebermann (3 vols, Halle, 1903–16), i, 374 (Ordinance for the Dunsaete, c. 935).

[2] William of Malmesbury, 'Vita Wulfstani', in *William of Malmesbury, Saints' Lives*, ed. M. Winterbottom and R. M. Thomson (Oxford, 2002), 82–3.

at the Christmas council of 1085, and they continued to be associated with legislation, of which the famous ordinance removing ecclesiastical pleas from the hundred courts is perhaps the best known example. There was perhaps an increased stress on crown-wearing at the great festal councils, now held with more (though by no means perfect) regularity at particular places: Gloucester for Christmas, Winchester for Easter, Westminster for Whitsun. But this was a mark of the need felt by a former duke to demonstrate his new and transcendent royal status, to impress his magnates and to overawe his opponents, rather than of anything essentially new.

The main changes to conciliar conventions after 1066 affected attendance rather than agenda. They sprang from feudal obligations unknown to pre-conquest England. Throughout the post-Carolingian west it was the vassal's duty to render 'counsel and aid' to his lord,[3] and in England from about 1090 this obligation to give counsel was translated into an obligation to attend councils. In practice this meant that those summoned to councils were the king's tenants-in-chief, who held land from him. By the 1120s, and quite probably earlier, the greater tenants-in-chief were being summoned individually, through writs addressed to them in person, while the lesser tenants-in-chief, whose names may often have been unknown to the government, were summoned through the sheriffs of the counties where they resided. In Anglo-Saxon England no principle beyond the king's will seems to have determined attendance at assemblies, but now tenure provided the basis for a summons, as it continued to do into the age of parliaments. Long before the days of the elected knights of the shire, this principle brought the smaller landholders, who formed the majority of the lesser tenants, to at least some royal councils. When Roger of Howden tells us, for example, that 'knights' were present when the assize of Northampton was made at the council there in 1176, he is probably referring to these men.[4]

Throughout the 12th century councils continued to deal with affairs of state. Momentous political decisions, such as the settlement of the crown on Henry I's daughter Matilda at the Christmas council of 1126; legislation, such as the Constitutions of Clarendon, produced at the Clarendon council of 1164; and state trials, such as that of Becket at the council of Northampton in 1164: matters of this sort continued to form their staple diet. The council's charismatic functions, on the other hand, declined, as crown-wearing was largely abandoned after Henry I's early years. By Henry II's time there was a more general loosening of what had formerly been conciliar conventions. Councils no longer tended to coincide with the great feasts of the church, and they met as often at royal hunting-lodges in the countryside, such as Brampton in Huntingdonshire and Geddington in Northamptonshire, as at Westminster. Henry II's own predilections,

---

3 E.g. *The Letters and Poems of Fulbert of Chartres*, ed. F. Behrends (Oxford, 1976), 92–3.

4 *Gesta Regis Henrici Secundi Benedicti Abbatis*, ed. W. Stubbs (2 vols, Rolls Series, 1867), i, 107.

and the perturbations of routine brought by his frequent absences abroad, do much to explain these changes. Yet the tone of councils remained essentially the same. They continued to be largely consensual occasions, where the king sought counsel from his great men, and the great found honour and prestige in giving it. One negative point helps to explain the harmony which usually prevailed: as yet taxation formed no part of the council's business. Geld, the traditional land tax, needed no conciliar sanction and was in any case abandoned after 1162, while the crown mainly depended for its financing on land revenues, feudal aids and incidents, and the profits of justice, which were similarly free of any need for consent.

Between the death of Henry II in 1189 and Magna Carta in 1215, consensus broke down and the council began to metamorphose into a less manageable body and one recognizably closer to the parliaments of the mid-13th century than to the Anglo-Saxon witan. The essential cause of this change was the novel fiscal pressure applied by the crown to finance Henry II's projected crusade of 1188, Richard I's ransom of 1189, and, above all, the Anglo-French wars which ran throughout the period. Not only did these pressures create new political tensions, but they also brought about the revival of general taxes, in the form of levies on movables, which fell on the whole realm. The first such levy, Henry II's Saladin tithe of 1188, set a precedent through its concession by the magnates assembled in council. The council thus assumed, at first insensibly, a more representative role: in making their grant the magnates spoke for the nation's taxpayers. When, a little later in 1205, another council at Oxford forced John to swear to preserve 'the rights of the kingdom of England',[5] those present acted more self-consciously as the representatives of the realm, and this time in opposition to the crown.

Behind this tension lay John's oppressive government, of which his attitude towards councils and counsel formed a part. Although much national business still came before magnate councils in the traditional way, John increasingly relied for private counsel on an intimate circle of *familiares*, his friends and confidants. Twelfth-century kingship provided plenty of precedents for such reliance, but in John's case his *familiares* were often aliens, set against a body of magnates who were becoming assertively English in outlook. John's use of the inner bureaucracy of the exchequer rather than the more public forum of the council to judge and punish recalcitrant magnates was another breach with tradition: state trials were being privatized. There are signs too that the counsellors themselves were subjected to pressure. The granting of the heaviest tax of the reign, the 13th of 1207, supposedly conceded freely by the magnates in council, was probably obtained only after a measure of manipulation and double-dealing. This may account for the demand made in Magna Carta that no future general taxes should be granted 'without the common counsel' of all the

---

[5] *The Historical Works of Gervase of Canterbury*, ed. W. Stubbs (2 vols, Rolls Series, 1879–80), ii, 97–8.

tenants-in-chief. Though this clause was dropped from the charter's reissues, in practice its prescription was followed, so in effect making direct taxation dependent on the counsel which could be given only in council. A feudal duty to advise had become a right to consent.

The charter itself marked a significant stride forward in the transformation of the old council, the lineal descendant of the witan, into the parliament of the 13th century. Though negotiated by the magnates, it took the form of a grant made by the king to 'all the free men of our realm',[6] whom the magnates could now be considered as representing not only in the granting of taxes but also in the securing of liberties. In making taxation dependent on consent and in consolidating the position of a few great men as representatives of the rights of a much wider political public, the charter opened the way for the parliamentary debates which were to characterize Henry III's reign. It was perhaps no more than a terminological anachronism when, in 1244, one of Henry's clerks wrote of the Magna Carta assembly of 1215 as 'the parliament of Runnymede'.[7]

---

[6] J. C. Holt, *Magna Carta* (2nd edn, Cambridge, 1992), 450–1.
[7] *Close Rolls, 1242–7*, 242.

Chronology

924
Accession of Athelstan, the first ruler to be styled 'king of Britain'

949
King Eadred wears his crown at a meeting of the witan at Somerton, Somerset, the first known public crown-wearing

957
Accession of Edgar as ruler of the Mercians

959
Accession of Edgar as ruler of all England

978
Accession of Æthelred 'the Unready'

1016
Death of Æthelred and conquest of England by Cnut of Denmark

1020–1
Cnut's law code, the last pre-Conquest legislation, issued at a Christmas meeting of the witan at Winchester

1051
Earl Godwin of Wessex, Edward the Confessor's father-in-law and enemy, is put on trial at a meeting of the witan in London

1066
Deaths of Edward the Confessor and his successor Harold, Battle of Hastings and accession of William the Conqueror

1085
The Domesday survey is planned at a Christmas meeting of the king's council at Gloucester

1100
Accession of Henry I

1126
Matilda, Henry I's daughter, is nominated as his heir at a Christmas meeting of the council

1135
Accession of Stephen

1139
Civil war

1154
Accession of Henry II

1188
Henry II is granted a crusading tax, the Saladin tithe, at a meeting of the council at Geddington, Northamptonshire

1189
Accession of Richard I

Origins and Beginnings to 1215

1189–94
During Richard I's absence on crusade and in captivity a magnate council helps to govern the country

1199
Accession of John

1204
John loses Normandy to Philip Augustus, king of France

1215
Magna Carta

Further Reading

G. B. Adams, *Council and Courts in Anglo-Norman England* (New Haven, 1926)

T. H. Bisson, 'The Politicising of West European Societies (c. 1175–1225)', in *Georges Duby: L'écriture de l'histoire*, ed. C. Duhamel-Amado and G. Labrichon (Brussels, 1996), 245–56

J. A. Green, *The Government of England under Henry I* (Cambridge, 1986)

J. C. Holt, *Magna Carta* (2nd edn, Cambridge, 1992)

S. Keynes, *The Diplomas of King Æthelred 'the Unready', 978–1016* (Cambridge, 1980)

T. Reuter, 'Assembly Politics in Western Europe from the Eighth Century to the Twelfth', in *The Medieval World*, ed. P. Linehan and J. L. Nelson (2001), 432–50

W. L. Warren, *Henry II* (1973)

P. Wormald, *The Making of English Law: King Alfred to the Twelfth Century*, I: *Legislation and its Limits* (Oxford, 1999)

3 The Development of Parliament, 1215–1307
Paul Brand

The period of just under a century which begins with the granting of Magna Carta by King John in 1215 and ends with the death of Edward I in 1307 is a significant one in the early history of parliament. It is the period when the term 'parliament' first comes to be used for the special occasional meetings of the king's council to which a larger group of the king's subjects were summoned. It is the period when representatives of the counties, of towns and cities, and of the lower clergy were first summoned to attend such meetings. It is the period which first saw the submission of petitions to the king and council in parliament. Finally, it is also the first period from which any official records of parliament survive.

The term 'parliament' (*parliamentum* in Latin, *parlement* in French) was not used before the 13th century for the occasional special meetings of the king's council to which a wider group of participants was summoned to provide general advice to the king and to give consent on behalf of a wider national community to royal taxation and legislation. The word (like its analogues in other western European languages) refers to the act of having a conversation or to a general meeting where discussion took place. It is initially used in England, as elsewhere, in a variety of different contexts. Its earliest appearance in official records bearing what was later to become its primary meaning is in a legal record of 1236. This records the adjournment of a litigant in the court of king's bench to 'parliament' at Westminster early the following year. Initially the term 'parliament' was only one of a number of words that might be used in official records for such sessions. By the reign of Edward I (1272–1307), however, it had become the normal, if still not the invariable, term for such meetings.

Meetings of 'parliament' (to use a partially anachronistic but useful single term for these meetings) in the reigns of Henry III and Edward I were almost always attended by the king, members of his council and a wider group of magnates, both lay (earls and barons) and ecclesiastical (bishops, abbots and priors). Very occasionally, a parliament might be held in the king's absence. It was, for example, on two occasions in 1254 while Henry III was in Gascony and once in 1297 while Edward I was campaigning in Flanders. Only very exceptionally (as in Lent 1297, when Edward I had withdrawn his protection from the clergy) might a parliament meet without any major prelates being summoned. It seems not improbable that some of the king's justices and the senior officials of chancery and the exchequer were also regularly present at parliament in Henry III's reign. It is, however, only in Edward I's reign that we begin to get evidence of their being summoned to meetings or of their attendance. The earliest evidence of knights being summoned to attend parliament as representatives of individual counties comes from 1254; the earliest evidence of burgesses being summoned to attend as representatives of their towns or cities only from 1265. Since the presence of such representatives seems initially to have been required primarily in order to give consent to taxation no such representatives were summoned when taxation was not under discussion, and before the mid-1290s their attendance seems to have been relatively uncommon. Such representatives might also be sent home once they had given their consent and parliament continued in session for the transaction of other business. It was also primarily to give consent to taxation that representatives were summoned from the lower clergy. The earliest evidence for this comes from 1254, but the experiment was not repeated until 1295. During the reign of Edward I special summonses were also on occasion sent out for the attendance of particular individuals or representatives for specific purposes. In 1296 the cities of London and Canterbury and other towns were instructed to send representatives to the November parliament for consultation by the council on the planning of a new town at the newly conquered Berwick upon Tweed; in 1301 the commissioners appointed to make perambulations of the boundaries of the royal forests and the justices of the forest were summoned to the Hilary parliament for discussions on the extent of the forests, the universities of Oxford and Cambridge were told to send experts in the learned law to help in drawing up the king's response to a papal mandate instructing him to withdraw from Scotland, and religious houses and cathedral chapters were required to send messengers with any information they could glean from chronicles in their possession on the king's rights over Scotland.

There seem to have been meetings of parliament in most years, and it was quite rare for more than two years to elapse between meetings. The main exceptions seem to have been between 1286 and 1290 while Edward I was in France, and between 1302 and 1305 while he was campaigning in Scotland. As many as three parliaments a year were held between 1232 and 1234, in 1236, 1244, 1254, 1262, 1268, 1269, 1278, 1290 and 1297, and as many as four a year in 1255, between 1258 and 1260, and in 1267, 1270 and 1292. The frequency seems generally to have been determined by the amount of business that was to be dealt with, but for a brief period beginning in the summer of 1258 there was a positive requirement imposed by the reforming Committee of Twenty-Four (with 12 nominees of the king and 12 of his baronial opponents appointed at the parliament of Oxford) as part of a general reform of governmental institutions that parliament meet three times a year and at specific times in early October, early February and around 1 June. Parliaments in general seem not to have lasted long. In Edward I's reign (when our information about their length becomes fuller and more satisfactory) parliaments might last as little as one or two weeks, but more commonly lasted for three or four. It was quite exceptional for parliaments to last as long as nine or even ten weeks, though this was the case with the Easter parliament of 1290 (albeit with a short break), the mid-Lent parliament of 1305 and possibly with the Hilary parliament of 1307.

The most common meeting places for sessions of parliament during this period were Westminster and London. We also know of sessions held close by at Lambeth in 1232 and at Stepney in 1299. A majority of parliaments which met elsewhere met in the south of England. Oxford was the venue of meetings on six occasions between 1227 and 1264; Winchester on five occasions between 1236 and 1270; Northampton on four occasions between 1229 and 1268; Gloucester on four occasions between 1216 and 1278. Shrewsbury was also the venue on four occasions between 1220 and 1283, but in all these the decision to choose this location was evidently related to specific Welsh business which was being dealt with at parliament, where proximity to Wales was an advantage. The wish to be close to Scotland for Scottish business likewise explains most of the meetings held north of the Trent: at York in 1237 and 1298; at Newcastle-upon-Tyne in 1244; at Norham and Berwick in 1291–2 and at Carlisle in 1307. Most sessions of parliament held outside Westminster and London were held in towns but the relatively small size of parliament also allowed sessions to be held at non-urban locations: at Merton in Surrey (in 1217, 1236 and 1255), at Kenilworth in Warwickshire (in 1266), at Clipstone in Nottinghamshire in 1290 and at Ashridge in Hertfordshire in 1291.

The most important kind of business dealt with by or at parliaments was the 'great business of [the] kingdom and of [the king's] foreign lands', as it was put in 1280 in a memorandum dealing with the disposition of petitions submitted to parliament.[1] It was at parliament that Henry III and Edward I took advice on matters such as the arrangement of truces or peace treaties with the kings of France and Welsh princes or on arrangements for military campaigns against the same rulers and against the Scots. It was there that kings took advice and made arrangements for the governance of their lands in Gascony and (under Edward I) Ponthieu, and took major decisions on the governance of the king's lands in Ireland. It was there that kings consulted their subjects on responses to papal diplomatic and other initiatives. It was at parliament that Henry III was declared of age and that arrangements were made for the governance of England during the absence of Henry and Edward. Meetings were also arranged to coincide with such events as royal coronations or the marriages of members of the royal family. Parliament was the venue for some, if not all, major state trials including those of Hubert de Burgh in 1239, Simon de Montfort in 1256, David of Wales in 1283, the justices of the common bench in 1290, and Nicholas Segrave in 1305. It was also the venue for the hearing of the earl of Gloucester's claim to the town and castle of Bristol against the king in 1276. Parliament was also the normal venue throughout the 13th century for the making of all major legislation: where that legislation was discussed and, where necessary, amended, and

---

[1] *Calendar of the Close Rolls, Edward I* (5 vols, 1900–8), ii, 56–7.

consent given to its enactment and subsequent proclamation. It was also, certainly in the second half of the century, the place to which significant legal problems (including problems about the interpretation of existing legislation) were referred for discussion and resolution. Parliament was the place where the king sought the agreement of his subjects to the levying of extraordinary taxation and where that consent was given or withheld. It was therefore also the place where the king might have to make specific concessions to his subjects before such consent was granted. A new addition to the business of parliaments as from the beginning of the reign of Edward I was the consideration of individual petitions submitted to the king and council asking for favours or justice. These were submitted both by the king's English subjects and also (at some parliaments at least) by his subjects in Ireland, Gascony, the Channel Islands and (in the early 14th century) Scotland. Closely related to these were the collective complaints submitted to parliaments by the clergy in 1280, 1285 and 1300; and the collective complaints submitted to the king by the laity at the 1258 parliament of Oxford and at the 1300 parliament at Lincoln.

Most of the legislation of this period survives. Much of it survives in official copies, either free-standing or as enrolled by chancery or copied by the exchequer. This is in some sense the earliest and most complete surviving record of at least some of the business done by parliament. No official record of other business done there survives before the reign of Edward I. The earliest surviving records of parliament from 1279 and 1283 are no more than brief and scrappy memoranda. The first surviving rolls of parliament begin only in 1290. The earliest rolls are heterogeneous in nature. Some record only petitions submitted and their responses. Others include petitions but also record some litigation, administrative decisions and legislation. Some contain extracts from business done at two or more parliaments, often parliaments for which no more complete roll survives. Many original petitions survive and their endorsements are also an original record of decisions made at parliament. Much of the more important business transacted at parliament relating to matters like peace and war or discussions about the granting of taxation was apparently not recorded at all. The official records of parliament are, therefore, a misleading guide to what was discussed or done there, but if they are read with care and an awareness of their limitations they are much better than having no record at all.

The 13th century was a formative period in the history of parliament. Parliament was taking on new functions and beginning to incorporate a representative element. It begins to be possible to see something of its workings through the survival of some official records, though only of some of its activities and only at some of its meetings. But parliament was still developing and changing. It was no longer an infant but by 1307 parliament had only just entered adolescence.

Chronology

1215
Magna Carta granted by King John

1216
Henry III succeeds to the throne

1227
Henry III declared of age at parliament

1236
Statute of Merton; first occurrence of 'parliament' in an official document

1239
Trial of Hubert de Burgh at parliament

1254
Two parliaments held in the absence of Henry III in Gascony; first summons of knights to parliament on behalf of counties, and of representatives of the lower clergy

1258
Parliament of Oxford, at which the committee of 24 establishes a requirement for three regular sessions of parliament at specific times of the year and collective grievances voiced in the 'Petition of the Barons'

1265
First summons of burgesses to parliament on behalf of towns and cities

1272
Succession of Edward I

1276
Hearing of earl of Gloucester's claim to Bristol against Edward I at parliament

1279
Easter parliament for discussion of administration of Ponthieu and terms of Treaty of Amiens

1283
Trial of David of Wales at Shrewsbury parliament; enactment of the statute of Acton Burnel

1290
Hilary parliament: conviction of the justices of the common bench; first surviving rolls of parliament

1296
Summons of town representatives to assist in planning of new town at Berwick-upon-Tweed

1297
Lent parliament held in absence of clergy; Michaelmas parliament held in name of the king's son while Edward I is in Flanders

1300
Lincoln parliament: collective demands submitted to the king at parliament

1301
Hilary parliament to which special summons of those involved in forest perambulations and experts in learned law and those able to provide information on Scotland from chronicles

1305
Mid-Lent parliament; discussion at parliament of arrangements for governance of Scotland; re-establishment of law and order in England; trial of Nicholas Segrave

1307
Death of Edward I

Further Reading

P. Brand, 'Petitions and Parliament in the Reign of Edward I', in *Parchment and People: Parliament in the Middle Ages*, ed. L. Clarke (Edinburgh, 2004) [special issue of *Parliamentary History*, xxiii/1], 14–38

J. H. Denton, 'The Clergy and Parliament in the Thirteenth and Fourteenth Centuries', in *The English Parliament in the Middle Ages*, ed. R. G. Davies and J. H. Denton (Manchester, 1981), 88–108

G. Dodd, *Justice and Grace: Private Petitioning and the English Parliament in the Late Middle Ages* (Oxford, 2007)

G. L. Harriss, 'The Formation of Parliament, 1272–1377', in *The English Parliament in the Middle Ages*, ed. R. G. Davies and J. H. Denton (Manchester, 1981), 29–60

J. C. Holt, 'The Prehistory of Parliament', in *The English Parliament in the Middle Ages*, ed. R. G. Davies and J. H. Denton (Manchester, 1981), 1–28

M. McKisack, *The Parliamentary Representation of English Boroughs during the Middle Ages* (Oxford, 1932)

J. R. Maddicott, 'The Earliest Known Knights of the Shire: New Light on the Parliament of April 1254', *Parliamentary History*, xviii (1999), 109–30

—— 'Parliament and the Constituencies, 1272–1377', in *The English Parliament in the Middle Ages*, ed. R. G. Davies and J. H. Denton (Manchester, 1981), 61–87

The Parliament Rolls of Medieval England, 1275–1504, I: *Edward I, 1275–1294*; II: *Edward I, 1294–1307*, ed. P. Brand (2005)

H. G. Richardson and G. O. Sayles, *The English Parliament in the Middle Ages* (1981)

G. O. Sayles, *The Functions of the Medieval Parliament of England* (1988)

—— *The King's Parliament of England* (1975)

4 The House of Lords, 1307–1529

Chris Given-Wilson

The Emergence of the Parliamentary Peerage

Although the term 'House of Lords' did not come into use until the 16th century, the essentially bicameral structure of the English parliament was in practice well established by the middle of the 14th century. Following the first parliament to be so called, that of January 1237, it remained usual for a further 70 years or so to summon only 'lords' to parliaments; during the reign of Edward II (1307–27), however, the 'commons' (the knights and burgesses) came to be summoned with much greater frequency, and after 1325 no assembly which excluded representatives of the Commons was described as a parliament. It was at least in part as a result of this inclusion of representatives of lesser status that the Lords came increasingly to insist upon their exclusiveness as a separate 'estate' in parliament: it was in 1317, for example, in a letter to the king from the earl of Lancaster, that the phrase 'peers of the land' was first used.[1] Within a few more years the peers, or lords, would be claiming the collective right to pass judgment in 'state trials', as they did against the Despensers and the earl of March in 1321 and 1330 respectively, and in 1341 the right of peers to be tried by their own peers in parliament was enshrined in statute form (not to be revoked until 1948). As the case of Archbishop Stratford of Canterbury (which gave rise to this statute) demonstrated, the 'peers of the land' included the lords spiritual as well as the lords temporal, sitting as one 'estate', in contrast to several of the continental European assemblies of this period in which clergy and nobility were regarded as separate estates.

Such claims to privilege and exclusivity were based not simply upon inherently superior status, but also upon the fact that whereas the Commons were elected by their shire or borough constituents, the peers were summoned individually to parliaments by personal writ from the monarch. The number summoned varied considerably, but tended to decrease with time. The lords spiritual comprised the 21 bishops of England and Wales plus a number of abbots of religious houses. In 1295 no fewer than 99 abbots were summoned, but this was unusually high; around 50 was a more normal figure under Edward I (1272–1307). By the mid-14th century a standardized list of some 25 abbots (in addition to the 21 bishops) had emerged, which remained more or less unchanged until the Reformation.

---

[1] J. E. Powell and K. Wallis, *The House of Lords in the Middle Ages* (1968), 284.

The lords temporal were less easy to define by rank. Those who held earldoms were naturally included, but the number of earldoms in England hardly ever exceeded 20 during the middle ages and was not infrequently less than ten, while the number of lords temporal summoned to parliaments sometimes passed the 100 mark. Those who were not earls were generally referred to as 'barons', and one criterion which was used by the king in determining whom to summon was whether or not the landholder in question held his lands by the form of feudal tenure known as barony. On the other hand, the king always retained the freedom to summon 'new men' to parliament – those, for example, who had served him well in war: those who were summoned without holding land by barony were sometimes referred to as 'bannerets', although by the 15th century the distinction between barons and bannerets had fallen into disuse, and all were now known simply as 'lords' or 'peers'. By this time, too, the number of lords temporal normally summoned had steadily fallen, from between 80 and 100, which was by no means unusual around 1300, to around 70 by the mid-14th century, and to not much more than 50 during the 15th century. What is more, the lists of those summoned had become increasingly standardized, so that by about 1370 it was becoming unusual for a lord to be summoned unless his ancestor(s) had been, and correspondingly likely that, should he leave an heir, his heir would be summoned after (or even before) his death. Membership of the Lords, in other words, was becoming progressively more hereditary, and thus more exclusive and more jealously guarded. One consequence of this was that kings no longer had the same latitude to summon whomsoever they wished to their parliaments – although they always retained a certain degree of freedom to do so; another was that 'nobility' in England (or at least 'high' nobility) came increasingly to be equated with the right to be summoned to parliament.

Attendance and Seating at Parliaments

During the 15th century, therefore, the parliamentary peerage – or 'House of Lords' – consisted of about 100 persons, roughly equally divided between lords spiritual and lords temporal. Of course, they did not all attend every session. The abbots in particular were notoriously lax about attendance: it was far from uncommon for only a quarter or fewer of those summoned to turn up, although their habitual absence was to some extent mitigated by their being allowed to send proxies to represent their views (as, indeed, were all peers, although they were frequently exhorted by the king to attend in person). The attendance record of the 'barons' was somewhat better, although it was still far from uncommon for half or more of them not to come. The bishops, earls and dukes – more intimately involved, by reason of their status, in the 'great business of the realm' – were more assiduous, although in time of war the ranks of the temporal lords were liable to be seriously depleted, as was the case, for example, in several of the parliaments of Henry V's reign.

Rank and status within the peerage were naturally reflected in seating arrangements. Although these arrangements were not illustrated in detail before the early 16th century, there can be little doubt that the system described then was based on well-established tradition. When parliament met at Westminster – as more than 80% of parliaments did during the 14th and 15th centuries – the opening session would almost invariably

Parliamentary Proxies

Peers unable to attend parliaments were allowed to send proxies to represent their views, and records of the nomination of such proxies survive from 1263. In the late 14th century concern about absenteeism sometimes prompted a royal prohibition of the appointment of proxies, and insistence on personal attendance; only such infirmity as prevented travel would excuse absence. The abbots in particular were notoriously lax about attendance: it was far from uncommon for only a fraction of those summoned to turn up, and no fewer than 19 abbatial letters of proxy survive for the parliament of 1406. Less often, prelates, particularly from Wales and the marches, also named proxies, but lay peers rarely did so, a notable exception being Edward, earl of Devon, who, having gone blind, was a permanent absentee from 1401.

Although the proxies nominated by the abbots were often members of their monastic communities, sometimes laymen were named, and not infrequently these laymen were people with experience of the workings of parliament gained from sitting in the House of Commons. Significantly, those actually serving as MPs in the parliament in question might be chosen. Seven members of the parliament of 1406 were authorized to be proxies in the other house; and at the parliament at Bury St Edmunds in 1447 the four MPs so nominated included both the shire knights for Huntingdonshire (asked to act on behalf of the abbot of Ramsey). Intriguingly, William Tresham, who was often named as a proxy and for more than one abbot, served as such in the parliaments of 1439 and 1442 when he was Speaker of the Commons. The practice of members of the Lords naming MPs as their proxies raises a number of questions relating to the ability of MPs to discover what was going on in the other house, and as to how the two houses communicated. While evidence about what proxies actually did is difficult to find, it should be noted that the now famous 'Thomas Haxey's bill', which excited Richard II's ire by criticizing the cost of his household, was introduced while Haxey was attending the parliament of January 1397 as proxy for the abbot of Selby.

LC

Sources: The History of Parliament: The House of Commons, 1386–1421, ed. J. S. Roskell, Linda Clark and Carole Rawcliffe (4 vols, Stroud, 1992), i. 27–9, 32, 34, 80–1; National Archives, SC10 – Special Collections: Parliamentary Proxies

A Child Attends the House of Lords

Half-way through the parliament of 1423 the 23-month-old King Henry VI was brought into the House of Lords by his mother, Catherine de Valois. This fulfilled a promise made by Bishop Langley in his sermon at the opening. Presumably he sat in his mother's lap. Speaker Russell made a loyal address to him on behalf of the House of Commons. The timing of the king's appearance had been postponed a day as he had cried and screamed so much several days earlier that he could not be persuaded to travel towards London then.

AH and CJ

Sources: The Parliament Rolls of Medieval England, 10: *Henry VI, 1422–1431* (2005), 202; *The Chronicles of London*, ed. C. L. Kingsford (Oxford, 1905), 280–1.

Rank and Precedence among the Peerage

As membership of the peerage became more closely defined, so too did rank and status, especially among the lay contingent. Immediately below the king came the dukes: the first English dukedom was created by Edward III in 1337 when he made his eldest son, Edward the Black Prince, duke of Cornwall. Below the dukes came the marquesses (a title introduced to England by Richard II in 1385), then the earls (a title dating from Anglo-Saxon times), then the viscounts (first introduced to England in 1440), and finally the rest of the lords. As these ranks proliferated, promotion within the peerage tended to become an ever more delicate matter: Richard II's promotion of the unpopular earl of Oxford, Robert de Vere, firstly to a marquessate in 1385, and then in the following year to a dukedom (a title usually, though not invariably, restricted to members of the royal family), aroused considerable protest, and when in the parliament of September 1397 the same king created five new dukes on one day, one contemporary chronicler gibed that they were popularly referred to as the *duketti* (little dukes). Precedence disputes within the various grades of the peerage also became more common: thus a meeting of the royal council in 1405 was required to pronounce on three separate disputes, between the earls of Warwick and Norfolk, the earls of Kent and Arundel, and Lords Beaumont and Grey, 'as to which of them should have precedence in their sitting in parliaments and councils'.* The first of these erupted again in the parliament of 1425, while in 1449 the then earl of Arundel was once again claiming precedence over a fellow earl, this time of Devon.

* J. E. Powell and K. Wallis, *The House of Lords in the Middle Ages* (1968), 437.

be held in the Painted Chamber, a long, narrow room of some 82' × 28' situated towards the southern end of the medieval palace of Westminster, so called because of its unusually lavish murals dating from the 13th century, when it had served as Henry III's private chamber. In front of the king, who sat on his throne at one end of the chamber, sat the chancellor and judges on woolsacks, a custom probably dating from the reign of Edward III (1327–77) and symbolic of the importance of the wool trade to the English economy. The clergy sat on the king's right – the 'spiritual side' – with the archbishop of Canterbury immediately below the king; to the king's left sat the laity, although they were headed by the archbishop of York and his two suffragan bishops (thus enabling the king to be flanked by his two archbishops), followed by the dukes, marquesses, earls and remaining peers.

However, the Painted Chamber was used only for the plenary opening and closing sessions of parliaments. Once the opening speech

Parliaments at Westminster and Elsewhere

Of the 179 assemblies held between 1300 and 1529 which were officially designated as parliaments, only 32 (18%) were summoned to meet elsewhere than at Westminster. Twenty of these occurred between 1300 and 1335 and the other 12 between 1378 and 1459; between 1459 and 1529, parliaments were always held at Westminster (although parts of two sessions were summoned to Blackfriars in London in both 1523 and 1529). This pattern chiefly reflects the decreasing itinerancy of the major departments of the royal administration and their eventual anchorage, largely accomplished by the mid-14th century, at Westminster Palace. The king, accompanied by his household and his private secretariat, naturally continued to spend long periods of time away from the London area, and might still decide to summon a parliament to wherever he happened to be, as Henry V did in the spring of 1414 when he was undertaking a judicial tour of the midlands and called a parliament to meet at Leicester. More commonly, however, parliaments were summoned to meet away from Westminster for one of two circumstances. The first was when the king was campaigning elsewhere in Britain and needed advice and/or money urgently; for example, the series of parliaments held at York between 1332 and 1335, when the Scottish war dominated Edward III's agenda, or the Gloucester parliament of 1407, as the Glyn Dwr revolt in Wales reached a critical phase. The second was when the government's unpopularity made it inadvisable to summon a parliament to the politically volatile capital: this was probably the case in 1378, when parliament met at Gloucester, and more certainly so in 1459, when, with the eruption of the Wars of the Roses, the Londoners were suspected of sympathizing with the Yorkists, so that Henry VI summoned parliament to meet at Coventry in the Lancastrian-dominated midlands.

(usually given by the chancellor, whose directive role in the Lords was not dissimilar to that of the Speaker in the Commons) had been delivered, and triers and receivers of petitions appointed, the Lords retired to the White Chamber (immediately south of the Painted Chamber) while the Commons made their way across the palace yard to the abbey. For a short period in the 14th century, they met in the abbey's chapter house; during the 15th century, in the monastic refectory. Thus the two 'houses' largely deliberated separately, until coming together again in the Painted Chamber for the closing session – which normally consisted of the formal grant of taxation and answering of petitions followed by the dissolution.

The Role of the Lords in Parliamentary Business

Yet if separate deliberation by Lords and Commons was, ostensibly, the normal procedure, in practice there was naturally a considerable amount of consultation between representatives of each group during the course of a parliament. Sometimes this was done formally, through the appointment of an 'intercommuning' committee of a dozen or fewer lords to 'advise and treat' with the Commons in relation to their 'charge' (request from the king for taxation) and other matters. These meetings took place in the Painted Chamber. The first parliament during which formal intercommuning is recorded on the parliament roll was that of 1352, although similar informal processes are attested at least a decade earlier. In its early stages, intercommuning probably involved discussions with 20 or 30 members of the Commons, but as time went on this number fell: at the parliament of 1378, for example, it was suggested that 'six or ten' lords be appointed to intercommune with the same number of commons; as the authority of the Speaker grew from the late 14th century onwards, there were times when these discussions in effect took place between him alone and the Lords' committee. Indeed, this may be why, after 1407, formal intercommuning was no longer recorded on the roll, even though similar, less formal procedures undoubtedly continued during the 15th century, as demonstrated by the 'Fane Fragment' of a lords' journal in 1461.

The matters upon which these representatives of the Lords and Commons intercommuned were, broadly speaking, those which constituted the chief business of parliaments – that is, finance, legislation and justice. On the question of finance (which often meant taxation, but might also involve the raising of loans or the apportionment of resources), the Lords had to be circumspect. Since the mid-14th century, it had come to be accepted that responsibility for determining the amount of taxation granted to the king lay with the Commons, and any attempt by the Lords to usurp their role in this process was liable to provoke protests from the knights and burgesses. In 1407, for example, the parliament roll records an 'altercation' between Lords and Commons after the Lords had unilaterally advised the king as to the level of taxation which ought to be granted. When 12 members of the Commons were summoned and told the amount

> ### The 'Fane Fragment' of 1461
>
> The 'Fane Fragment' – so called because it was discovered among the papers of Francis Fane, 1st earl of Westmorland (1624–9) acquired by the British Museum in the 19th century – is the earliest substantial fragment of a Lords journal. These journals, which were probably first compiled 12 or 15 years earlier, were kept on loose quires of paper on each side of which was written a list of the lords present at each sitting of parliament and brief notes about the business done at that sitting. The 'Fane Fragment' preserves this information for days 22–5 and 30–3 of the parliament of November 1461: that is, 28 November to 2 December and 8 to 11 December. (Lists of the lords present on 5 and 12 December have also been found in British Library, Harleian MS 158, fol. 129r–v, but these quires lack any description of the business done on those days.) The Lords journals are valuable not only as a record of attendance but also for illuminating procedure: for example, the 'Fane Fragment' describes the lords carefully scrutinizing, article by article, bills sent up to them from the Commons, adding their comments, and then going through the bill a second time and making further amendments. It also describes one instance of informal intercommuning between a group of senior lords and 'a notable number of the substance of the [lower] house', although it carefully points out that this occurred 'without the bar' – that is, beyond the rail which formally marked off the parliament chamber.

that was demanded of them, they declared themselves to be 'greatly perturbed' by this procedure, saying that it was 'to the manifest prejudice and derogation of their liberties' – for they were, in effect, being presented with a *fait accompli*.[2] In the event, they granted what was asked of them, but only in return for a promise from the king that in future he would not pre-empt the right of either the Commons or the Lords, in bilateral discussions, without the intervention of the king, to decide the level of taxation. It was an important point of principle, ensuring that the accepted way of voting supply would continue to be 'by the Commons, with the advice and assent of the Lords'.[3] As this incident demonstrates, the Lords certainly had (and continued to have) a say in the granting of taxation, but that did not encompass making unilateral deals with the king.

Legislation and justice were to some degree connected. Edward I had actively encouraged his subjects to submit petitions to his parliaments, and many thousands of them did so – to such an extent, indeed, that by the early 14th century it was becoming necessary to siphon off the majority of these private petitions to the king's other courts, while parliament

---

[2] *The Parliament Rolls of Medieval England, 1275–1504* [hereafter *PROME*], ed. C. Given-Wilson *et al.* (16 vols, Woodbridge, 2005), viii, 426.

[3] *PROME*, viii, 418.

proper increasingly restricted itself to the consideration of petitions brought forward by communities (towns, shires, guilds and so forth) or by the Commons as a whole (the 'common petition', upon which legislation would in future be based). Yet private petitions, especially from great persons, continued to be dealt with in parliament, and the task of deciding which of them would be heard was entrusted to the 'triers of petitions', two committees of whom (one for the British Isles, one for the crown's overseas territories) were appointed at the beginning of each parliament. These committees were almost invariably composed of the great prelates and magnates of the realm; their job of sifting and prioritizing was a sensitive and intensive one, carried out during the first few days of each parliament in specially assigned rooms such as the Chamberlain's Chamber (close by the entrance to the Painted Chamber) and the Marcolf Chamber, which was apparently situated underneath the east end of the Painted Chamber. It was in the White Chamber, however, where they sat together as a body, that the Lords undertook their clause by clause scrutiny of the 'common' bills sent up to them by the Commons; and, although the Commons had a major role in initiating legislation, the Lords retained the right unilaterally to amend the bills which the Commons passed to them, whereas the Commons rarely amended bills sent down to them by the Lords.

The 'High Court of Parliament'

The Lords thus retained, throughout the 15th century, a decisive role in the framing of legislation, as they did in the dispensing of justice. It was during the 14th century that the notion of a 'High Court of Parliament', distinguished from other royal courts by its omnicompetence, began to take root. During the first half of the century, as noted above, the 'peers of the land' were already claiming the collective right to act as judges in state trials. In the 'Good' Parliament of 1376, when the first parliamentary impeachments took place, this process was taken a step further: these impeachments – initially of the king's chamberlain William, Lord Latimer, and the financier Richard Lyons – involved collective prosecution by the Commons before the Lords, who in turn collectively passed judgment, with both 'houses' claiming to be acting on behalf of the realm. Twelve years later, in the 'Merciless' Parliament, such claims had inflated to the extent that when five dukes and earls (the 'lords appellant') brought an appeal of treason against five of Richard II's supporters (including a duke, an archbishop and an earl) and the judges objected that such a process did not conform with either the common or the civil law, the Lords replied that:

> in the case of so high a crime as that alleged in this appeal, which touched the person of our said lord the king and the estate of all his kingdom, perpetrated by persons who are peers of the realm

and others, the case should be conducted nowhere other than in parliament, and that it pertained to the lords of parliament and to their franchise and liberty of the ancient custom of parliament to be judges in such a case, and to adjudge such a case with the assent of the king.[4]

It was the most explicit statement yet of the judicial supremacy not just of parliament but of the Lords in parliament. Nevertheless, lingering doubts about the validity of the process of appeal meant that it would only be used on one further occasion in parliament (in 1397, when Richard II took his revenge on the lords appellant), although the process of impeachment was used on a number of occasions during the subsequent decades, until replaced during the Wars of the Roses (1455–85) by the act of attainder. This involved the reading of a bill of attainder before the Lords and Commons, their (often silent) acquiescence, and the royal assent. There was no trial as such, no opportunity for defence, and judgment resulted not merely in the death of the individual concerned but also in the forfeiture of his estates and the disinheritance of his heirs ('tainting of the blood'). As a summary procedure for the eradication of political opponents, attainder continued to be found useful under the Tudors and Stuarts. One point to note about these various forms of state trial is that if they involved the death sentence, the prelates among the Lords would withdraw from the chamber, since clergy could not partake in sentences leading to bloodshed.

The 14th and 15th centuries also witnessed the depositions of no fewer than five English kings, from Edward II in 1327 to Richard III in 1485. That parliament had a role to play in these is undeniable: to seek the broadest possible assent for such acts was only natural. This does not mean, however, that parliament as an institution had acquired the right to depose kings. For an incoming king to acknowledge that parliament had the power to replace him would have been political folly. Royal depositions were engineered by magnate factions, and what was sought from parliament was the ratification of a *fait accompli*. Indeed, it has been argued that these 'deposition parliaments' were not really parliaments at all but extraordinary assemblies of the 'estates of the realm' convened for this specific purpose. Nevertheless, by the end of the 15th century the involvement in deposition proceedings on a number of occasions of what some people chose to describe as parliaments meant that parliamentary approval had come to be seen as a necessary act of validation in the making and unmaking of kings. Both Richard III, in 1484, and Henry VII, in 1485, induced the Commons to submit bills affirming their right to the royal title, to which they duly assented.[5]

Yet if it was the Commons who ostensibly petitioned both Richard III and Henry VII to assume the crown, we can rest assured that

[4] *PROME*, vii, 99–100.
[5] *PROME*, xv, 13, 97.

contemporaries would not have been taken in by such acts of political theatre. It was the Lords, not the Commons, who dominated political life in the middle ages – at court and in the council chamber no less than in parliament. Unfortunately, the records of medieval parliaments do not convey this impression very adequately. The 'rolls of parliaments' (*rotuli parliamentorum*), the official 'minutes' of parliaments compiled by clerks of the crown, which run to some 4 million words and cover the period 1275–1504, focus on the formal business transacted between the Commons and the government rather than the informal discussions between the government and the Lords at which, we may be sure, most of the decisions which really mattered were taken. They do, naturally, include certain formal items relating to the Lords – promotions, state trials, the apportionment of great inheritances – but for those occasional but instructive glimpses of the Lords engaged in debate (usually in relation to trials or personal disputes), we learn more from chronicles and newsletters than from the official record. And although the journals of the House of Lords (as they are now called) were being compiled from the middle of the 15th century, those few which survive before 1510 are fragmentary, and they only survive in a continuous series from 1554. Only thence are we in a position to understand in detail the parliamentary role of England's politically dominant estate.

The Language of Parliament

The day-to-day language used in parliament at its inception was Norman French, although many of the documents submitted to it were in Latin. Nevertheless, English may have been spoken in parliament as early as the late 13th century. In 1362 a statute enacted that all pleas in the law courts should henceforth be in English, although they were still to be enrolled in Latin, and a year later English became the daily language of parliament too. The reason given for this change was that French was not understood by the majority of people who had dealings with parliament. In 1399 the abdication of Richard II was announced in parliament first in Latin and then in English. Even so, the language of record in the *rotuli parliamentorum* was French from 1331 until 1425 when it became Latin, with the triers of petitions still named in French and a growing proportion written in English, largely because an increasing number of petitions entered in the rolls in the 15th century were in that language. The 'Fane Fragment' of the draft proceedings in the Lords in the parliament of 1461, drawn up by the clerk of the parliaments probably for use in the compilation of the parliament roll, has the heading for the day and the lists of lords in Latin, with triers of petitions named in French, and the minutes themselves in English.

The transition to English as the sole language of business was long drawn out. Even as late as the 16th century both Latin and French remained in occasional use. The sermon given at the opening of each parliament by the lord chancellor was delivered in a mixture of tongues until 1523, when on behalf of the sick Chancellor Wolsey, Bishop Tunstal spoke in Latin and English. For certain proceedings at the formal opening of parliament, the presentation of the Speaker, and the prorogation or dissolution, the chancellor addressed the assembly in Latin or French. But the Speaker answered him in English. The surviving records are open to interpretation as to when these multi-lingual exchanges came to an end.

From the mid-13th century until 1489 statutes and acts were written in French, although some passages were in Latin. The single exception to this was the statute of labourers of 1349 which was in Latin throughout. Private acts until then, to judge from the extant summaries of their contents, may have been largely written in English. After 1489 all acts were drafted and approved in English. There were occasional phrases or passages that were not in English, the most notable instance being in 1555: the entire text of the Latin dispensation issued by Cardinal Pole which appears in chapter 11 of the act restoring first fruits and tenths to the Catholic Church. However, the clerical annotations denoting various stages in the passage of bills or their enactment remained in French.

At the ceremony granting the royal assent, the clerk bowed to the monarch and then indicated approval, saying '*Le Roi le veut*' for public acts, '*Le Roi Remercie*' for acts raising money and '*Soit fait comme il est desire*' for private acts. In the absence of Charles I from London during the civil wars in the 1640s, the measures agreed in parliament were published as ordinances to distinguish them from acts with royal assent. For four years following the king's execution in 1649 the ordinances similarly lacked any form of assent. Following the establishment of the protectorate in 1654 the Lord Protector adopted the English formula 'We do consent.' At the Restoration the traditional formulae were revived, and these have remained in use until the present day.

The writs summoning people to parliament or ordering parliamentary elections were issued in Latin until the mid-17th century. During the interregnum they were written in English. At the Restoration the previous practice was revived, and it continued until 1731–3 when in a series of measures parliament declared English the official legal language. The election returns for MPs were traditionally made in Latin, but from the 16th century onwards this seems to have been increasingly at the discretion of the returning officer. During the interregnum the language used was English. For just over 70 years from 1660 Latin enjoyed something of a comeback although never to the same extent as before the civil wars.

Between 1510 and 1540 the Lords journal was written entirely in Latin, but during the course of the first session of the parliament of 1542 the bills under consideration were noted in English, with only the rank and title of members of the peerage and the episcopacy, the note of their attendance, the dates at the beginning of each day's proceedings, and the stages in a bill's passage eventually remaining in Latin. Similarly, the proxy deeds drawn up by the clerks, and filled out by lords wishing in their absence to give their vote to another, remained in Latin, until the suspension of the use of proxy voting in 1868. The Commons journal originating in 1547 followed the same practice as the Lords journal. During the interregnum the Commons journal was composed throughout in English, but at the Restoration the original practice was reinstated.

LC, AH and CJ

Sources: R. Butt, *A History of Parliament: The Middle Ages* (1989), 324–5; J. E. Powell and K. Wallis, *The House of Lords in the Middle Ages* (1968), 234, 361, 424, 512; 4 Geo. II, c. 26; 5 Geo. II, c. 27; 6 Geo. II, c. 4

Chronology

1237
First English assembly described as a parliament

1317
First use of the phrase 'peers of the land'

1321
'Peers' pass collective judgement on the Despensers

1327
Deposition of Edward II

1341
Statute affirming right of peers to be tried by their peers in parliament

1352
First record of formal intercommuning between Lords and Commons

1376
'Good' Parliament; first parliamentary impeachments

1388
'Merciless' Parliament; first appeal of treason in parliament

1399
Deposition of Richard II

1407
'Altercation' between Lords and Commons on the question of taxation

1449
First surviving fragment of a Lords journal

1461
Usurpation of Edward IV; 'Fane Fragment'

1483
Usurpation of Richard III

1485
Usurpation of Henry VII

1509
Death of Henry VII; accession of Henry VIII

Further Reading

R. Butt, *A History of Parliament: The Middle Ages* (1989)

L. Clark, 'Magnates and their Affinities in the Parliaments of 1386–1421', in *The McFarlane Legacy: Studies in Late Medieval Politics and Society*, ed. R. H. Britnell and A. J. Pollard (Stroud, 1995), 127–53

The English Parliament in the Middle Ages, ed. R. G. Davies and J. H. Denton (Manchester, 1981)

The Fane Fragment of the 1461 Lords' Journal, ed. W. H. Dunham (New Haven, 1935)

The History of Parliament: The House of Commons, 1386–1421, ed. J. S. Roskell, L. Clark and C. Rawcliffe (4 vols, Stroud, 1992)

K. B. McFarlane, *The Nobility of Later Medieval England* (Oxford, 1973)

The Parliament Rolls of Medieval England, 1275–1504, ed. C. Given-Wilson et al. (16 vols, Woodbridge, 2005)

J. E. Powell and K. Wallis, *The House of Lords in the Middle Ages* (1968)

J. S. Roskell, 'The Problem of Attendance of the Lords in Medieval Parliaments', *Bulletin of the Institute of Historical Research*, xxix (1956), 153–204

5 The House of Lords, 1529–1629
David L. Smith

The 100 years from the assembling of the so-called 'Reformation' Parliament in 1529 to Charles I's dissolution of another parliament and the beginning of his personal rule in 1629 were a period full of significance for parliament in general and the House of Lords in particular. Throughout the 16th and early 17th centuries it remained the more socially prestigious, politically influential and procedurally sophisticated of the two houses. Yet by 1629 the House of Lords was only 20 years away from its outright abolition as 'useless and dangerous to the people of England'.[1] The intervening years are thus of considerable interest and repay careful investigation.

Membership and Attendance

To attend the House of Lords in this period required a personal summons from the monarch. This was normally extended to three categories of people. First, there were the lords spiritual, who comprised the archbishops of Canterbury and York, the bishops, and (until 1540) a number of abbots and priors. In 1529 there were 19 bishoprics. Henry VIII created six new ones in 1540–2, two of which (London and Westminster) were merged in 1550, leaving a total of 24 that thereafter survived for the remainder of this period and beyond.[2]

Second, there were the lords temporal, who consisted of the peers, together with the greatest officers of state, the lord chancellor (or lord keeper) who presided over the Lords, the lord treasurer, the lord president of the council, and the lord privy seal. The peerage, consisting of the dukes, marquesses, earls, viscounts and barons, remained remarkably stable in size under the Tudors. In all, they numbered 54 in 1529, and 55 on Elizabeth I's death in 1603. The highest total they attained at any stage in between was 62 in 1559. The early Stuart period, by contrast, saw a steady expansion of the peerage, to 81 in 1615, and then to 104 by James I's death in 1625. Charles I continued this trend, until by 1629 the total stood at 126.

The third category, who were not members of the House, comprised

---

[1] *The Constitutional Documents of the Puritan Revolution, 1625–1660*, ed. S. R. Gardiner (3rd edn, Oxford, 1906), 387.

[2] Under the duke of Northumberland the bishoprics of Gloucester and Worcester were merged, and that of Durham suppressed, but both these changes were reversed during Mary I's reign.

> ### Mitred Abbots in the House of Lords
>
> Twenty-eight abbots from the greater monasteries and the prior of the hospital of St John of Jerusalem received writs of summons to the House of Lords for the parliament of 1529, and another abbot was summoned during its course. The same group was summoned again in 1536. Following the suppression of the less well off monastic houses, only 19 abbots were summoned in 1539. These men were present for the passage of the bill for the dissolution of the greater monasteries and witnessed Henry VIII giving the royal assent to it. A year later when the Knights Hospitallers were suppressed by act (32 Hen. VIII, c. 24) the only spiritual peers remaining in the House of Lords were bishops.
>
> During the Marian reaction Mary I inaugurated a programme of monastic restoration. The recently appointed abbot of Westminster and the prior of St John were summoned to the parliament of 1558, and Elizabeth I summoned the pair again in 1559. Abbot Feckenham helped spearhead resistance to the Elizabethan church settlement, but Prior Tresham's deteriorating health kept him largely away. No heads of monastic houses or of religious orders were summoned again.
>
> AH

the senior judges and legal officers of the crown, such as the masters in chancery, the judges of king's bench and common pleas, the attorney general, the solicitor general, the master of the rolls, the chief baron of the exchequer, and the king's serjeants at law. The members of this third group attended the Lords as 'assistants': they provided legal expertise that was invaluable in guiding the Lords' conduct of judicial and legislative business, but they could neither speak unless invited to do so, nor vote.

By the 1530s a summons to the Lords was increasingly regarded as an attribute of noble status rather than as the result of territorial possession. Although it was usual for the royal summons to be withheld from a few peers on the grounds that they were minors, or impoverished, or overseas, or insane, the normal expectation was that the monarch would summon all the others. By the early 17th century, such a royal summons was generally regarded as a right – what Henry Elsynge (clerk of the parliaments, 1621–35) called 'an essential point of inheritable honour'[3] – rather than as a matter of royal discretion. When, in 1626, Charles I attempted to withhold a writ of summons on political grounds from the earl of Bristol and Bishop Williams of Lincoln, the House protested against this as a breach of privilege by refusing to transact any business until eventually the king relented and issued the writs.

The Lords journal, unlike the Commons journal, includes lists of those present in the House each day it was sitting. We are thus able to gain a much more precise idea of attendance rates in the upper House than

---

[3] Henry Elsynge, *The Manner of Holding Parliaments in England* (1768), 54.

for the lower. It seems that the numbers present in the Lords fluctuated considerably during this period. There was also a marked tendency for the proportion of those present to tail off the longer a session lasted, as other concerns and priorities crowded in to distract members from parliamentary business. Relatively low attendances, especially by the abbots and priors, had apparently been endemic during the middle ages and the early 16th century. From the 1530s onwards, however, attendance rates for the Lords as a whole seem to have improved somewhat. Under Edward VI the average attendance was as high as 82%, although the proportion who attended three-quarters or more of the sittings was only 51%. During Mary I's reign the percentage of members who attended the Lords varied between 54% and 86%, although the proportion present at three-quarters or more of the sittings was in the much lower range of 23–44%. These rates were generally maintained in the Elizabethan parliaments. For example, daily attendance in the parliament of 1571 averaged 54, but during the last week it fell to 45. The corresponding figures in 1572 were 48 and 37; in 1584, 42 and 35; in 1593, 45 and 39; and in 1597, 43 and 33. In the first four sessions of James I's first parliament (1604–10) attendance in the Lords never fell below 50%, and was often higher. It seems that there was then a slight tailing off in the parliaments of 1621–9, when attendance was rarely over 60, and often considerably less. Nevertheless, even these figures represented attendance rates that were considerably higher than those normally seen in the Commons.

The Lords met in the Queen's Chamber, also known as the White Chamber, which lay at the south end of the medieval palace of Westminster.

The King of Naples and Jerusalem Attends the House of Lords

Prince Philip, the son of Emperor Charles V, married Mary I at Winchester in July 1554. On the eve of the marriage the emperor created him king of Naples and Jerusalem so as to be of equal status with his bride. After their marriage he was styled king of England and Ireland, though he was never crowned. As such, in the parliament of November 1554 he accompanied his wife on four occasions, occupying a throne beside her on the dais at the southern end of the Lords' chamber. The pair were described in the Lords journal as 'Rex et Regina'. The first occasion was on 12 November for the formal opening of parliament. He returned three days later for the presentation of the Speaker and a week later to consent to the repeal of Cardinal Pole's attainder. Later, on 16 January 1555, at the dissolution, 'in the Parliament Chamber, the King's and Queen's Majesties gave their Royal Assent to Twenty one Acts'.

AH and CJ

Sources: LJ, i, 465–6, 469; CJ, i, 41.

This was a room of 80' × 28'. At the south end was a throne for the sovereign, flanked by chairs for the consort and the prince of Wales. On the monarch's right sat the archbishops and bishops in order of appointment, while on the left sat the peers by rank (dukes, marquesses, earls, viscounts, barons) and thence by date of creation. In the centre of the chamber, the clerks, judges and legal assistants sat on large woolsacks. The lord chancellor, who acted as the 'Speaker' of the Lords, sat on the woolsack immediately below the throne. Until Inigo Jones's alterations during 1623–4 the room was lit by four windows in its side walls, a small round window high above the throne, and a triple lancet at the north end. Jones blocked the side windows and inserted four dormer windows into the new ceiling he had designed. The walls were hung with tapestries, and matting covered the floor. Off the south end, concealed by one of the tapestries, opened the Prince's Chamber, available for the prince of Wales's use when he took his seat as a member of the Lords (within this period only done by Prince Charles in the parliaments of 1621 and 1624).

Committees and Conferences

Not all of the Lords' business was actually conducted within the House itself. In particular, committees were an essential feature of the procedure of both Houses, and can be divided into several categories. First of all, *ad hoc* committees were set up to discuss particular matters, such as bill committees which over the course of this period were created with growing frequency to discuss and amend bills after their second reading in the House. During Henry VIII's last four parliaments (1536, 1539, 1542, 1545), less than 20% of bills read in the Lords were committed. The proportion fluctuated between 59% and 10% in the parliaments of Edward VI and Mary I, and as late as 1601 only 44% of bills were committed after their second reading in the Lords. The proportion appears to have increased further in the early Stuart period, but the committing of bills was still by no means universal: for example, in the parliament of 1624, 75 of the 110 bills read in the Lords were committed.

When a committee was appointed in the Lords, members were named from each 'bench' in turn (bishops, earls, barons and so forth). In the early 17th century, up to 1629, it became quite common for committees to be composed of an equal number of earls and bishops, and double that number of barons, but this rather rigid practice appears to have been declining by 1628–9, and it was abandoned entirely in 1640. Once appointed, members of the committee would then determine exactly when and where they met, usually at eight o'clock in the morning and/or two o'clock in the afternoon. Lords committees usually met in the Painted Chamber or the Prince's Chamber, and in this period they were chaired by the peer who was first in order of precedence.

In the Lords it was established practice that no member who was absent from the House could be appointed to a committee unless his role as an officer of state directly impinged on the committee's business. Appointment to committees thus tended to fall to a core of regular, active members. For example, in the parliaments of 1621–9 only 14 peers were appointed to more than 30% of the committees created during those sessions in which they participated. At times there was also a connection between activity and political alignment, as for instance during the 1620s, when certain peers hostile to Buckingham, such as Southampton, Saye, Bedford and Essex, were disproportionately likely to attend the House and therefore to be appointed to committees.

A second category of committees were the standing (or 'grand') committees, which first came into general use in the Lords in 1621. These were appointed at the start of each session, continued to meet until the end of that session, and handled any business that arose within a broad subject area. The two most important Lords standing committees were the committee for privileges and the committee for petitions. The latter in effect took over the role of a medieval body known as the receivers and triers of petitions, who continued to be appointed but ceased to serve any real purpose.

From 1606 an increasing amount of discussion in both houses of parliament took place under a new procedure called the committee of the whole House. This procedure was first recorded in the Lords journal on 1 December 1606; it was certainly used in the Commons by the spring of 1607, but may have been adopted as early as April 1606. Either House could vote to discuss a matter as the committee of the whole House, which meant that it then followed the procedure of committees rather than the usual rules of debate. The practical consequences of this were that the normal restriction that no member could speak more than once on the same subject in any given day was lifted, and that the proceedings were not recorded in the journal (although evidence of them can be found in the manuscript minutes from 1621 onwards). It seems that the procedure for the committee of the whole House was introduced on the initiative of privy councillors who wished to have more opportunity to answer questions and challenges to their proposals. Once established, however, the procedure offered considerable advantages to those members who found themselves in a minority, and who could use it to exert pressure on the crown and its advisers.

From time to time, joint committees comprising members of both Houses were created to handle a range of business. Either house could request that a joint committee be appointed to discuss matters of mutual concern, and by the reign of James I the established practice was for the Commons to nominate twice as many representatives as the Lords. These joint committees were always chaired by a peer, and they usually met in the Court of Wards. The meetings were very formal and emphasized the social inequality between the two houses, with the peers seated and wearing their hats while the members of the Commons stood in their presence, with their hats off.

In addition to these joint committees, members of the Lords and Commons sometimes also met in conferences of the two houses. These could be either formal conferences (at which information was exchanged) or free conferences (at which free debate and discussion took place), and they were normally held in the Painted Chamber. Either House could request a conference. When such a request was agreed each House appointed 'managers' to represent them and, as at joint committees, the Commons appointed twice as many representatives as the Lords. Similarly, as at joint committees, the convention at conferences was that the peers sat with their hats on, while members of the Commons stood bareheaded in front of them. Most conferences were concerned with legislation, but sometimes other matters such as judicature or privilege were considered as well, and conferences thus offered another useful channel of communication between the two houses.

Privileges, Judicature and Legislation

One of the privileges that was particular to the Lords and not shared by the Commons was the custom whereby a peer who was unavoidably absent was entitled to appoint another to act as a proxy. It cost £2 to register a proxy with the clerk, who recorded it in the proxy book. There appears to be no evidence from Tudor parliaments that proxies actually exercised absentees' votes, with the sole exception of a tied vote on 1 March 1581 when proxies were called for. The main role of proctorial representation in the 16th century seems to have been symbolic: it affirmed the absentee's right to sit in the Lords and associated him, in his absence, with all decisions taken by the House. The issue of proxies only really became politically contentious during the 1620s, culminating in the parliament of 1626 where the duke of Buckingham held no fewer than 13 proxies. This prompted the House to pass a standing order that no peer could hold more than two proxies. This order also confirmed a longstanding custom that lords spiritual should give their proxies to other lords spiritual, and lords temporal to other lords temporal.

During its sessions the Lords received a large number of petitions from various individuals or interest groups requesting legislative, administrative or judicial action to redress some grievance or remedy some alleged miscarriage of justice in a court of law. The earliest petition in the Lords' archive dates from 1531, but few survive from before 1621. In that year, the situation changed dramatically with the revival of the private party judicature of the Lords. This revival embraced both first instance judicature (in response to petitions) and appellate judicature (the adjudication of appeals against the decisions of inferior courts). It developed in response to the growing frustration of litigants with the chronic delays and high costs of the central law courts, and the inability of the privy council to cope with the ever increasing volume of petitions submitted to it. The appellate judicature of the Lords, which had fallen into disuse during the later middle ages and under the Tudors, was therefore revived in 1621, and from then onwards the Lords functioned very effectively as the highest court of appeal. The number of petitions and appeals that the Lords accepted for review increased rapidly, from 14 in 1621 to 86 in 1626. In all, during the parliaments of the 1620s the Lords adjudicated some 207 cases, of which the largest single category (74 cases) related to matters of property. Indeed, by 1629 judicial business was taking up more of the Lords' time than any other subject.

The Lords proved to be both willing and well equipped to handle this upsurge in judicial business, which in a sense grew out of parliament's earliest origins as an extension of the king's council. Indeed, much of the Lords' judicial activity was conducted in co-operation with the privy council, and the overlap in their membership assisted such collaboration. The Lords took their duties as a high court very seriously, and derived invaluable expert guidance from the legal 'assistants' who sat in the House. During the 1620s the Lords re-established itself as a vital element within the legal system, which could provide a speedy and authoritative ruling on cases and help to resolve jurisdictional conflicts between the common-law courts (king's bench and common pleas) and the equity courts (chancery and exchequer). The fact that the Lords brought together senior judges and legal officers of both the common-law and equity courts as 'assistants' in the upper House was very helpful in sorting out disputes over jurisdiction between the two.

The modern separation between judicature and legislation was quite alien to early modern England, and contemporaries regarded parliament's judicial and legislative functions as part of a single process in which the houses collaborated with the crown to redress grievances and solve problems. The effectiveness and efficiency of the Lords were as evident in its handling of legislation as in its exercise of judicature. Fewer bills were initiated in the Lords than in the Commons; indeed, the proportion of bills that began life in the upper House remained remarkably similar throughout this period: 35% in 1547–58; 38% in 1571–97; 35% in 1603–25. However, although they were fewer in number, bills that originated in the Lords consistently stood a better chance of actually becoming acts. In the parliaments of Edward VI and Mary I, 59.5% of bills initiated in the Lords became acts, compared with only 25% of those that originated in the Commons. Between 1571 and 1597, 43% of bills initiated in the Lords became acts, but only 18% for the Commons. For the period 1603–25, the equivalent figures were 39% and 18%. These figures reflect the more orderly and efficient nature of the Lords and also that it was less deluged by proposals for bills than the Commons.

Primary Sources for the Lords

The judicial and legislative work of the Lords can be reconstructed in detail because of the extensive records that survive for the House in this period. These can be divided into two categories: the official, comprising principally the Lords journal and the main papers, which are rather fuller than those which survive for the Commons, and the unofficial, consisting of a small number of diaries, which are much sparser than those for the lower House. As in the Commons, the journal developed as a working tool of the clerks which enabled them to keep track of parliamentary business, the appointment of committees, the progress of bills and so on. The Lords journal survives from 1510 but only continuously from 1554: no journal survives for the second and third sessions of the parliament of 1512, the parliament of 1523, all but one session of the parliament of 1529 or for Mary I's second parliament (April 1554). The Lords journal achieved a settled format from 1536 onwards which – unlike that for the Commons – includes very helpful lists of those who were present on each day.

The Lords journal for 1510–1649 was published in a printed edition by 1771, but, although convenient, this version cannot entirely take the place of the manuscripts from which it is derived. The printed edition sometimes introduces lay-out, capitalization and punctuation not found in the manuscript journal; even more problematically, paragraphing is changed in places, with the result that certain items of business are broken up while others are merged. For the Lords from 1621–8 (and also 1640–2 and 1661–90) we also have the draft journals, from which the manuscript journal was prepared, and an even earlier stage known as the manuscript minutes (sometimes called 'scribbled books') which survive from 1610 onwards and are the notes that the clerks compiled either while the Lords was actually sitting or immediately afterwards. These earlier stages can sometimes be very helpful in giving a clearer idea of the order in which business was taken, and in places they also contain material that was deleted in the subsequent versions of the journal.

The survival of the Lords' draft journals and manuscript minutes comes about because from at least the 1590s the archives of the upper House were stored in the 14th-century Jewel Tower across Old Palace Yard. The House of Lords' archive thus escaped the disastrous fire that destroyed most of the old Palace of Westminster in 1834, and with it much of the corresponding archive for the Commons. This also explains the survival of the large collection of sessional and judicial papers used by the Lords, or arising from its proceedings, that are known as the House of Lords main papers. Arranged in a vast chronological sequence, the main papers are particularly valuable for the light that they throw on the Lords' activities as a court of law, and they have only recently begun to receive the scholarly attention that they deserve.

Whereas for this period the surviving official sources for the Lords are much fuller than for the Commons, when we turn to unofficial sources the situation is reversed. We have only a very small number of private diaries compiled by members of the Lords, of the kind that exist in much larger quantities – sometimes as many as eight or more by the later 1620s – for the Commons. No such manuscript diaries have survived for the

Lords during the 16th century, and, for the 17th century up to 1629, only three appear to be extant. These are the diaries of Henry Hastings, earl of Huntingdon (covering the sessions of 1610, 1614 and 1621); Edward, Lord Montagu of Boughton (1621, 1624, 1625, 1626 and 1629); and John Egerton, 1st earl of Bridgwater (1628).[4]

> ### Parliamentary Diaries
>
> The private diaries kept by members of the Lords and Commons are the most important surviving source for what was actually said in each House during the 16th and 17th centuries. They survive in much greater quantity for the Commons than the Lords: very roughly a ratio of five to one for much of the Tudor period, rising to something more like eight to one by the 1620s. Most of the Commons diaries have now been printed, but for the Lords the picture is much more patchy and incomplete.
>
> These diaries do not contain accurate transcripts of what members said on a given day. Their accounts of the same speech sometimes differ dramatically, and there is often no simple way of determining which of the available accounts is closest to what was actually said. Members kept diaries in a variety of different ways and for a range of reasons. Sometimes we have the actual notes that they made during proceedings, often in very cramped conditions. Other diaries are fair copies that were written up at a later date. Some members kept diaries as records which they could then share with their patrons and friends, while others apparently took down only such details as seemed interesting and useful to them. Some members wanted to compile a record for their own subsequent use, whereas still others seem to have been motivated primarily by sheer fascination with the business and workings of parliament.
>
> Each diary thus reflects the particular biases, motives and concerns of the member who compiled it, as well as their attitudes and working methods. There is not even any guarantee that all the speeches recorded in a diary were necessarily delivered. Provided that proper scholarly precautions are exercised, however, the diaries can still offer a better insight into what members said than any other source.

The Lords and Politics

In using these various official and unofficial sources, historians have stressed the Lords' significance as an institution that assisted the crown by means of its legislative, conciliar and judicial functions. Equally, it is important to recognize that those roles could give rise to political debate – even conflict – and the nature of political groupings within the Lords in

---

4 For a detailed and authoritative account of the surviving sources for the Lords in this period, see M. F. Bond, *Guide to the Records of Parliament* (1971), 3–196.

this period therefore merits some discussion. Such groupings were generally so fluid in the 16th and early 17th centuries that they do not really deserve the name 'factions' except during certain specific periods when they temporarily hardened around a blend of political, religious and personal allegiances. The most notable of these periods were the early 1530s to the late 1550s, the 1590s and the later 1620s.

The first of these periods was characterized above all by divisions over religious policy and especially over how far the reformation should be promoted or resisted. Conservatives led by the Howards and Bishop Stephen Gardiner vied with reformers such as Archbishop Cranmer, the Seymours and Lord Paget in a series of bitter confrontations, especially during the reigns of Edward VI and Mary I. The situation gradually stabilized after 1559 as the Elizabethan settlement helped to reduce (but not eliminate) religious controversy. For much of Elizabeth I's reign, politics within the Lords was less factional, and although members put pressure on the queen (for example, to marry, to name a successor, and to execute Mary, queen of Scots), it is difficult to identify anything approaching factions until the last decade of the reign, when the intense rivalry between Sir Robert Cecil and the 2nd earl of Essex produced an abrasive and competitive style of politics that spilled over into the Lords. This largely died down after Essex's execution in 1601, and factional politics only resurfaced in the parliaments of 1625–9, when resentment of Buckingham's influence and concerns over the direction of royal policy under Charles I led some peers to support the attempted impeachment of Buckingham in 1626 and the Petition of Right in 1628. Although there was still no organized 'opposition' as such, it is possible to identify certain peers – Pembroke, Saye, Essex, Southampton and Bedford prominent among them – who were forthright in their hostility to the crown's 'new counsels' and policies.

Two features of these political groupings are worth stressing in particular. First, they represented an extension of politics within the court and the privy council that spilled over into the Lords. The considerable overlap in personnel between these three institutions facilitated this process. Secondly, peers very often collaborated with like-minded allies and clients in the Commons to promote particular policies or measures. Relations between the two houses were generally harmonious, and bicameral groupings of members were able to co-ordinate strategy both formally, in joint committees and conferences of both Houses, and more informally, through personal connections. Such bicameral co-operation rested not only on shared political and religious beliefs but also on the close links that bound many members of the two houses to each other. In Tudor and early Stuart parliaments, between a quarter and a third of members of the Commons were nominees of noble patrons, relatives or allies. These links did not make members of the Commons tame lackeys of the Lords, but they did foster the pursuit of shared goals through bicameral collaboration: this was often quite fluid but it could at times assume forms that were more organized and co-ordinated.

One such time was the later 1620s. The monarch's power to appoint bishops and create peers gave him a direct influence over the membership of the Lords, and this meant that he should generally have been able to rely on the support of the upper House. It was therefore a very disturbing sign that the parliaments of 1625–9 saw a steady deterioration in the relations between Charles I and the Lords, culminating in the latter's passing of the Petition of Right in May 1628. For any monarch to have lost support within the upper House to the extent that Charles had done by 1628–9 was a very worrying development and a warning sign of major troubles ahead.

The Petition of Right

After lengthy debate during April and May 1628, the houses of parliament presented the Petition of Right, written by the Commons, to Charles I. The petition reflected the houses' deep unhappiness with the policies that Charles had pursued over the previous 18 months in the course of his wars against Spain and France. Specifically, the petition cited Magna Carta and a series of medieval statutes to demonstrate that non-parliamentary taxation, the imposing of martial law, billeting of troops on civilians without their consent, and imprisonment without cause shown were all contrary to the 'laws and statutes of this realm'.

The petition was a very practical document that grew out of mistrust of one particular monarch and his policies during 1626–7. The framers of the petition went out of their way to assert that they were not seeking to make new laws but rather to enforce existing ones and to spell out the statutory safeguards against abuse of royal discretionary powers. They did not seek to abrogate those powers but to ensure that Charles I did not misuse them by deploying them in non-emergency situations.

When the petition was presented to Charles, he initially gave an evasive answer that reserved his prerogative powers (2 June 1628). However, five days later, in order to secure a parliamentary grant of supply, Charles gave a second answer using the traditional formula of assent for such a petition: '*Soit droit fait comme est désiré.*' The houses were delighted and shortly afterwards voted Charles five subsidies, believing that the petition now had the force of a statute. However, when the petition was printed at the end of the session, the king instructed that its statute number be erased and that both his answers be printed. He thereby caused uncertainty over the petition's statutory status and strengthened his own growing reputation for duplicity.

Chronology

1529–36
'Reformation' Parliament

1539–40
Abbots and priors cease to sit in the Lords

1540–2
Henry VIII creates six new bishoprics (two later merged in 1550)

1547
Death of Henry VIII; accession of Edward VI

1553
Death of Edward VI; accession of Mary I

1558
Death of Mary I; accession of Elizabeth I

1559
Elizabethan church settlement

1601
Trial and execution of earl of Essex

1606
Procedure of committee of the whole House first used in the Lords

1621
Impeachment revived; revival of first instance judicature and appellate judicature of the Lords

1621–35
Henry Elsynge is clerk of the parliaments

1625
Death of James I; accession of Charles I

1626
Charles I attempts to withhold writ of summons from earl of Bristol and Bishop Williams of Lincoln; attempted impeachment of duke of Buckingham; standing order that no peer can hold more than two proxies

1628
Petition of Right

1629
Charles I dissolves parliament; beginning of his personal rule (until 1640)

Further Reading

D. Dean, *Law-Making and Society in Late Elizabethan England, 1584–1601* (Cambridge, 1996)

G. R. Elton, *The Parliament of England, 1559–1581* (Cambridge, 1986)

E. R. Foster, *The House of Lords, 1603–1649: Structure, Procedure, and the Nature of its Business* (Chapel Hill, NC, 1983)

M. A. R. Graves, *The House of Lords in the Parliaments of Edward VI and Mary I: An Institutional Study* (Cambridge, 1981)

—— *The Tudor Parliaments: Crown, Lords and Commons, 1485–1603* (1985)

J. K. Gruenfelder, *Influence in Early Stuart Elections, 1604–1640* (Columbus, Ohio, 1981)

J. S. Hart, *Justice upon Petition: The House of Lords and the Reformation of Justice, 1621–1675* (1991)

J. Loach, *Parliament under the Tudors* (Oxford, 1991)

Parliament at Work: Parliamentary Committees, Political Power and Public Access in Early Modern England, ed. C. R. Kyle and J. Peacey (Woodbridge, 2002)

C. Russell, *Parliaments and English Politics, 1621–1629* (Oxford, 1979)

D. L. Smith, *The Stuart Parliaments, 1603–1689* (1999)

6 The House of Lords and the 'Other House', 1640–60

Jason Peacey

The period from 1640 to 1660 was one not merely of profound political upheaval within England, but also of significant constitutional innovation, and the House of Lords was at the centre of some of the most striking developments and most significant controversies. These involved the power of parliament within the constitution, the relative authority of the two houses and the relations between them, and the very legitimacy of bicameralism. They resulted in important changes in the internal make-up of the House of Lords, its usurpation and abolition by the Commons, and eventually its revival as part of constitutional experimentation during the Cromwellian protectorate.

Membership

The Lords witnessed change from the very start of the 1640s, most obviously in relation to membership. In November 1640, at the opening of the 'Long' Parliament, the upper House comprised 150 members, including two archbishops and 24 bishops, but the majority of these owed their places to the early Stuart kings, and the sense that the chamber reflected the crown's political and religious views prompted calls for change as part of a process of 'further reformation'. Membership of the Lords thus became a political football between parliamentarians on the one hand, and the king on the other, and revealed tension between both Houses.

This battle focused initially upon the bishops, and began with the impeachment and imprisonment of Archbishop William Laud. In the aftermath of a widespread petitioning movement for 'root and branch' church reform, moreover, the Commons introduced a bill to prevent bishops from interfering in state affairs, the Lords' rejection of which merely provoked a bill for the complete abolition of episcopacy in May 1641, which was quickly rejected by the peers. The Commons responded by impeaching 13 bishops and demanding their removal from the Lords, but peers again refused to co-operate, while the king raised the stakes by signalling his intention to make five new episcopal appointments. When 12 bishops issued a protestation regarding their treatment by the London mob, they were accused of breaching parliamentary privilege and sent to the Tower. Although some of their colleagues remained active in parliament in subsequent weeks, the episcopal presence eventually came to an end when the king accepted the bishops' exclusion bill.

Scarcely less controversial were initiatives to alter the lay membership of the House. Initially, this involved attempts by the Commons to remove Catholic peers in late 1640, and although the Lords again resisted such interference, the lower House continued to exert pressure on this issue, although the matter was finally settled by the outbreak of war, and the withdrawal of men whose allegiance naturally lay with the king. Charles I, meanwhile, demonstrated his willingness to create new peers in 1641, not least in an attempt to save the earl of Strafford (see below). This was one area, however, where parliament was determined to undermine the royal prerogative, and an ordinance was eventually passed in 1646 declaring invalid all titles conferred since May 1642. By this stage, deaths and expulsions had reduced the number eligible to vote in the House to a mere 29, and the Commons subsequently sought to guarantee their influence over the upper House by demanding permanent veto powers over new creations (December 1647).

Attendance

In terms of the practical working of the Lords during the 1640s, such formal changes were probably much less significant than absenteeism, which ensured that the House became dominated by a tiny group of active parliamentarian peers.

Before the outbreak of war attendance patterns were affected most obviously by the threat from London apprentices, who demanded the sentencing of the earl of Strafford in May 1641 and the removal of the bishops later in the year. Intimidatory crowds certainly drove some peers and clerics away, and may also have influenced the decisions of those that remained, perhaps accelerating the decision to formally purge the episcopal benches. Other peers withdrew in the aftermath of the king's departure from London in January 1642, and in response to his summons to attend the court at York, and by May 1642 the House had been deprived of its Speaker, lord keeper Littleton, who took with him the great seal. By the time that fighting commenced later in the year only around 30 peers remained at Westminster.

As with the lower House, the Lords was subsequently thinned further by the involvement of individual peers in military campaigns, but more striking was the impact of parliamentarian factionalism. Most obviously, the failure of proposals for peace negotiations with the king in the summer of 1643 prompted six peers to defect to the king, and another to retire to his country estate. Although the peers were willing to look favourably upon those who subsequently sought readmission, the Commons refused to agree, and an ordinance subsequently prohibited the return of any deserters until both Houses had agreed.

By the time that the royalist Oxford parliament was summoned in January 1644, the king was able to count on the support of around 50 peers, perhaps double the number regularly attending at Westminster.

> ### The Oxford Parliament
>
> Peers known to have been present on 27 January 1644 (in order of signatures appended to letter sent to the earl of Essex, parliamentarian lord general):
>
>> Prince Charles (prince of Wales), Prince James (duke of York), duke of Cumberland, Lord Littleton, Lord Cottington, duke of Richmond, marquess of Hertford, earls of Lindsey, Dorset, Shrewsbury, Bath, Southampton, Leicester, Northampton, Devonshire, Carlisle, Bristol, Berkshire, Cleveland, Rivers, Dover, Peterborough, Kingston, Newport, Portland, Viscount Conway, Lords Digby, Mowbray and Maltravers, Wentworth, Cromwell, Rich, Paget, Chandos, Howard of Charlton, Lovelace, Savile, Mohun, Dunsmore, Seymour, Percy, Wilmot, Leigh, Hatton, Jermyn, Carrington.
>
> Peers who attended at some later point:
>
>> Viscount Campden, Lords Abergavenny, Arundel, Capel and Newport.
>
>> Source: *A Catalogue of the Names of the Knights, Citizens and Burgesses that have Served in the Last Four Parliaments*(1656), 20–5

Although attendance by parliamentarian peers improved slightly after the end of fighting in 1646, heightened political tension during 1647 and 1648 merely emptied the benches once again, not least as a result of renewed popular agitation. The 'forcing of the houses' by a crowd of apprentices in July 1647 certainly targeted those 'independents' who sought a harsh settlement with the king, nine of whom fled to the army for safety. Of the eight peers who remained until the army restored order in early August, seven were quickly impeached by the Commons. By the time of 'Pride's Purge' in December 1648, indeed, there were only half a dozen peers in regular attendance, and in the following weeks this number was reduced to a mere three or four.

Procedure

Changing patterns of attendance were arguably of far greater significance than alterations in procedure, which changed much less dramatically during the 1640s than in earlier decades, and scarcely at all in terms of legislative powers. Nevertheless, some important developments did take place, above and beyond the general air of disorderliness and tension that was frequently apparent, as tempers frayed within a politically and religiously divided chamber.

First, the House exercised greater control over its officers, and after the flight of its first (impeached) Speaker, Lord Finch, and the defection of his successor, Lord Littleton, the peers claimed the authority to fill the post for the first time, although they merely rotated the task amongst themselves. Second, changes were made to procedures for undertaking and recording votes, and from 1640 minority peers were able to register not only their dissent from particular decisions, but also their protest. Thus, when peers responded to MPs' September 1641 decision to suppress religious innovations, by merely reissuing their earlier order justifying existing practices, six peers issued a formal statement of their desire to work more closely with the Commons.

Third, new procedures emerged for conducting business between the two Houses. In terms of joint conferences, the most obvious developments involved the 1641 decision that no peer should speak contrary to the general sense of the House, and the subsequent trend towards 'adhering' to an original position, in the face of MPs' amendments. More significant was the tendency to appoint joint committees, which were less bound by procedural formalities, and which enabled informal and private co-ordination between peers and MPs. Having sought to ensure that each House was fairly represented on such bodies (1645), this became the Lords' procedure of choice (1647). Indeed, many joint committees became powerful standing bodies, designed to undertake executive responsibilities, most obviously the committee of both kingdoms (1644–9), which contained seven members of the Lords, and which was virtually independent of parliament.

One final area of procedural interest relates to the use of proxies. The ability of peers to deploy the votes of absent members was clearly not new, but it took on much more significance in a smaller House, and as factional divisions hardened. The most dramatic evidence of this relates to the earl of Mulgrave's proxy, which was deployed decisively by Viscount Saye in 1645, in order to secure the passage of controversial votes regarding the New Model Army, but which was subsequently switched to the earl of Essex in 1646, thereby giving effective control of the chamber to Saye's presbyterian rivals.

Judicial Proceedings

One very noticeable trend during the 1640s related to peers' judicial workload. In part this involved a much larger number of petitions and private cases, as well as writs of error, being brought before them, which probably explains the highly unusual decision to allow the committee for petitions to sit beyond the dissolution of the 'Short' Parliament in 1640. Such demands upon peers' time were entirely natural, because the king's inability to dissolve parliament after 1641 made it a more permanent, identifiable and reliable avenue for the redress of grievances, and because of the weight of public business being undertaken by the Commons. There were also far fewer alternative routes through which to pursue private matters, after the impeachment of the judges, the abolition of the privy council's judicial powers, and the removal of star chamber and high commission (1641), as well as the suspension of the court of requests (1642), and the disintegration of the ecclesiastical courts.

Somewhat more dramatically, the Lords were also increasingly preoccupied by impeachment proceedings, powers regarding which had been revived in the 1620s. Theoretically, this meant the trial of individual peers by the Lords after charges were brought by the Commons, although few cases were ever completed. Strafford was executed following an act of attainder, and Finch fled to France, and although Laud was finally executed after a protracted trial, he was no longer a lord of parliament by this time, even if he had been when he was impeached. Moreover, it is striking how often the Commons sought to participate in such legal proceedings, and how often intra-parliamentary tension emerged as a result. Only in the case of the seven presbyterian peers impeached in 1647 were the Lords expected to conduct their own trial, and on this occasion the factional balance of power ensured that they refused to do so, despite pressure from MPs.

Conflict between Lords and Commons

Analysis of institutional, procedural and judicial developments during the 1640s reveals, therefore, a number of instances when friction emerged between the two houses. There were areas where activities failed to be coordinated, as with the treatment of petitions, and many more occasions when the houses failed to agree on matters of substance. Tension was most obvious over measures which were perceived to enhance the power of the Commons at the expense of the Lords, such as the Self Denying Ordinance (1645) (which barred peers and MPs from holding either civil or military office), and over infringements of the royal prerogative. There were also occasions when disagreements forced one or other House to act independently, as with the passage of the Grand Remonstrance in 1641, the creation of the new great seal in 1643, and the issuing of the justification for breaking off negotiations with the king in 1648, all of which involved the Commons acting without backing from peers. Peers were probably less inclined to act independently, although they did so by reissuing orders regarding religious practice (see above), and by granting reprieves to individuals, such as Sir John Hotham, who had been sentenced to death by courts martial (January 1645).

It is no longer feasible, however, to view such difficulties merely in terms of a reforming lower House being confronted by a conservative upper chamber. There were plenty of occasions when differences managed to be resolved, such as when the Lords eventually joined the Commons in demanding control of the militia in 1642, and in passing the bishops' exclusion bill. Indeed, recent research has emphasized that factional divisions existed within both chambers, that political interest groups were bicameral, and that certain MPs acted like 'men of business' for aristocratic patrons. Members of competing factions certainly worked through whichever House was most likely to prove most effective, and initiatives such as the creation of the committee of both kingdoms and the creation of the New Model Army may actually have begun in the Lords rather than the Commons.[1]

Nevertheless, from the early 1640s at least some peers resented the growing power of the Commons, and grumbled that the country's political 'head' was being governed by its 'tail', while at least some people began to formulate ideological opposition towards the constitutional position of the Lords. In order to justify acting without joint agreement in late 1641, therefore, some MPs effectively claimed political superiority by virtue of being the representative body of the kingdom, and when the Houses disagreed over how to deal with a defeated and captive king in May 1646, at least one member argued that the Commons not only could but should act alone.

Before the late 1640s such comments represented only momentary outbursts of frustration, and intra-parliamentary tension was generally overcome by strong personal connections between peers and MPs, and by the overwhelming desire to maintain the constitutional *status quo*. Nevertheless, there can be little doubt that those who were frustrated by the perceived backwardness of the Lords, both inside and outside Westminster, grew in strength and political importance as the 1640s progressed, or that these local difficulties provide part of the background to the eventual abolition of the Lords in January 1649.

Concerted opposition to the Lords developed in part as opposition to the electoral influence of particular peers gave way to general attacks upon aristocratic patronage, but by 1643 challenges were also being made to the judicial power of the upper House, not least by commoners such as Clement Walker, who faced imprisonment for accusations levelled against individual nobles. Walker was followed by many other individuals from the mid-1640s – including the Leveller John Lilburne – who demanded to be tried by their own peers, rather than by members of the aristocracy.

Such attacks also became focused upon peers' immunity from prosecution. The invocation of parliamentary privilege had been important in response to the king's decision to search the houses of leading lords after the Short Parliament, and in response to Charles I's attempted arrest of Lord Mandeville in January 1642, and the peers were probably even more concerned than the Commons to appeal to privilege in response to the

[1] J. S. A. Adamson, 'Parliamentary Management, Men-of-Business and the House of Lords, 1640–49', in *A Pillar of the Constitution: The House of Lords in British Politics, 1640–1784*, ed. C. Jones (1989), 21–50; J. S. A. Adamson, 'Of Armies and Architecture: The Employments of Robert Scawen', in *Soldiers, Writers and Statesmen of the English Revolution*, ed. I. Gentles, J. Morrill and B. Worden (Cambridge, 1998), 36–67; J. S. A. Adamson, 'The Triumph of Oligarchy: The Management of War and the Committee of Both Kingdoms, 1644–1645', in *Parliament at Work: Parliamentary Committees, Political Power and Public Access in Early Modern England*, ed. C. Kyle and J. Peacey (Woodbridge, 2002), 101–27.

mass lobbies of parliament by London crowds, and to prevent the reporting of their proceedings. In 1644, however, privilege was denied to peers who had deserted parliament, and the mid-1640s also witnessed a number of attacks upon the abuse of privilege by peers, not least from political radicals who began to demand fundamental constitutional reform, and unicameral parliaments.

The eventual decision by the Commons to abolish the upper House followed peers' opposition to the king's trial in 1649, but was probably not the inevitability that historians used to suggest. It is certainly true that the Commons responded by claiming sole legislative authority, but the Lords nevertheless continued to sit, and their future remained uncertain even after the Commons' refusal to acknowledge a messenger from the Lords (1 February 1649). Debates in the lower House during the days that followed revealed that many MPs – including Oliver Cromwell – wanted to preserve the Lords, even if only as a court of judicature, while others probably favoured a plan that had first been mooted in 1645, and which advocated uniting the two houses in one chamber. The case for retaining the upper House was finally lost, however, on 6 February, when the Commons resolved that the Lords was 'useless and dangerous, and ought to be abolished', and an act to this effect was passed on 19 March.[2]

[2] *CJ*, vi, 132.

Uniting the Two Houses

In January 1645 it was reported that a plan had been devised to unite the two houses in one chamber, according to a model familiar from the Scottish parliament. This plan, knowledge of which springs from comments made by the Venetian ambassador, would have had the effect of removing the peers' veto, while preserving the positions of those lords who were loyal to the parliamentarian cause, or to the independents. It emerged at a time when the peers were reluctant to agree to the execution of William Laud or to pass the Self Denying Ordinance, and seems to have been provoked by their refusal to renew ordinances regarding martial law. It may be regarded as a threat by the Commons, and as having had the desired effect, in terms of weakening the resolve of the upper House. The idea is alleged to have been revived in January 1649, perhaps in order to threaten those peers who opposed the trial of Charles I.

Sources: S. R. Gardiner, *History of the Great Civil War* (4 vols, 1886), ii. 106; C. H. Firth, *The House of Lords during the Civil War* (1910), 210.

The Cromwellian 'Other House'

Individual peers were not entirely absent from parliament after 1649. Three were elected to the 'Rump' House of Commons (4th earl of Pembroke, 2nd earl of Salisbury, and Lord Howard of Escrick), and four were returned to the Cromwellian parliaments (the 2nd earl of Salisbury, 1st earl of Stamford, 14th Baron Dacre, and Lord Eure), while others sat on the council of state and the protector's council. Eventually, in 1657, a bicameral constitution was restored. This is often seen as evidence of a swing towards conservatism and monarchism, not least since it coincided with the offer of the crown to Cromwell. The change actually emerged from opposition to the Commons' assumption of judicial power, in debates over the punishment of the quaker blasphemer, James Nayler. Cromwell was evidently worried by the absence of any constitutional check upon the power of the Commons, and feared that Nayler's case presaged parliamentary tyranny. A second chamber formed part of the proposals made to Cromwell for constitutional reform in 1657, and parliament quickly resolved to restore bicameralism, specifying that the new House should contain between 40 and 70 members, with a quorum of 31. It also outlined its somewhat proscribed judicial powers, which ensured no involvement in criminal causes, other than upon impeachment proceedings instigated by the Commons, and no participation in civil causes, other than upon writs of error or referral from lower courts, or in relation to their own privileges. The Commons also ensured that proxies were not to be used, and demanded parliamentary oversight of nominations, although the latter proviso was eventually dropped, leaving the protector with ultimate control over the new body's composition.

Procedurally, the new House was fairly conventional: Nathaniel Fiennes was chosen as Speaker; committees were nominated, and generally met in the Prince's Chamber; divisions had two tellers; dissents and protestations were allowed; and there was a committee of the whole House. The real novelty was that the 62 men who were summoned to appear for the second session of the 1656 parliament were mostly new creations, styled 'lord' even though they were not peers. Of the seven existing English (together with one Scottish) peers named by Cromwell, only two appeared, including his son-in-law, Viscount Fauconberg, although they were joined by an Irish peer, Lord Broghill.

In practice, the nomination of new lords from within the Cromwellian political elite undermined the government's ability to control the Commons, and the absence of 'old' peers in both 1658 and 1659 had important repercussions in terms of parliamentary expertise. More worrying may have been the intensity with which debate soon raged over the very desirability of a second chamber, and about the new institution's name and powers. The decision not to call it the House of Lords (which seems to have been ignored by Oliver Cromwell

The Cromwellian 'Other House'

Those summoned to attend by writs dated 10 December 1657:

Richard Cromwell; *Henry Cromwell; Nathaniel Fiennes; John Lisle; Henry Lawrence; Charles Fleetwood; *†Robert, earl of Warwick; *†Edward, earl of Manchester; *†Edmund, earl of Mulgrave; *‡John, earl of Cassills; *†William, Viscount Saye and Sele; †Thomas, Lord Fauconberg; ¶Charles, Viscount Howard of Morpeth; Philip, Viscount Lisle; Sir Gilbert Pickering bt; †George, Lord Eure; *†Philip, Lord Wharton; ‡Roger, Lord Broghill; *William Pierrepoint; John Cleypole; Sir Bulstrode Whitelocke; John Disbrowe; Edward Montagu; *George Monck; John Glynn; William Lenthall; *Oliver St John; *William Steele; Sir Charles Wolseley; William Sydenham; Philip Skippon; Walter Strickland; *Francis Rous; Philip Jones; John Fiennes; Sir John Hobart; *Sir Gilbert Gerrard; *Sir Arthur Hesilrige; Sir Francis Russell; Sir William Strickland; Sir Richard Onslow; Edward Whalley; *Alexander Popham; *John Crew; *Sir William Lockhart; Richard Hampden; Sir Thomas Honywood; Sir William Roberts; Sir Archibald Johnstone of Wariston; Richard Ingoldsby; Sir Christopher Packe; Sir Robert Tichborne; John Jones; Sir Thomas Pride; Sir John Barkstead; Sir George Fleetwood; Sir Mathew Tomlinson; Sir John Hewson; Edmond Thomas; James Berry; William Goffe; Thomas Cooper.

Additional peer encouraged to sit in 1659:

*†Algernon, earl of Northumberland

Key:
* * Did not take seat
* † 'Old' English peerage
* ‡ Non-English peerage
* ¶ Hereditary peer created by Oliver Cromwell. The other such peer, Edmund, Lord Dunch of Burnell, created in April 1658, was apparently not entitled to sit.

Sources: G. E. C., *Complete Peerage*, iv, 589–93, 614–15; C. H. Firth, *The House of Lords during the Civil War* (1910), 270.

himself)[3] did little to placate republicans, however, who argued during Richard Cromwell's parliament that the old peerage now lacked sufficient landed property to justify co-ordinate power, and who also ensured that it was two months before the decision was taken to 'transact' business with the 'other House', and that no agreement was ever reached on its composition or powers.[4]

---

3 HMC, *Lords MSS*, new ser., iv, 514.
4 *CJ*, vii, 621.

Although such opponents of the protectorate were not diametrically opposed to the idea of a second chamber, they were certainly determined that any bicameral parliament should involve two representative chambers. A second chamber was demanded by the army a week after the reassembly of the Rump in May 1659, perhaps influenced by the ideas of James Harrington, and the 'seven fundamentals' of government prepared by the army council in the following December included the idea that 'both the assemblies of the Parliament shall be elected by the people of this commonwealth duly qualified'.[5] Along with many of the procedural innovations witnessed during the 1640s, however, such ideas quickly disappeared from view with the recall of the Long Parliament in December 1659, and the subsequent Stuart restoration in 1660.

[5] *Mercurius Politicus*, 598 (8–15 December 1659), 956.

Chronology

1640
April	'Short' Parliament of three weeks, called by Charles I
November	'Long' Parliament summoned to address the persistent crisis in the north

1642
4 January	Charles I's unsuccessful attempt to arrest five members of the Commons and one of the Lords
August	Outbreak of civil war in England and Wales

1644
January	Royalist rival parliament meets at Oxford

1645

Self-denying ordinance, required members of either House to lay down military or civil office acquired since 1640

1645–7

'Recruiter' elections to Long Parliament

1647
July	Some 58 members, including Speaker Lenthall, flee presbyterian-inspired violence around Westminster

1648
6 December	Purge by New Model army of up to 231 members of the Commons

1649
4 January	Declaration by the Commons that undivided sovereignty is vested in itself by both houses of parliament on behalf of the people
January	Trial and execution of Charles I
March	'Commonwealth' Parliament abolishes House of Lords. The Commons, a sovereign unicameral parliament, is later known as the 'Rump' Parliament.

1653

20 April	On behalf of the army, Oliver Cromwell forcibly dissolves Rump Parliament.
July–December	Nominated Assembly (also known as 'Barebones' Parliament or 'Barebone's Parliament')
December	Inauguration of protectorate of Oliver Cromwell; Instrument of Government provides England, Wales, Scotland and Ireland with their first written constitution

1654

September	Meeting of first Protectorate parliament under Lord Protector Oliver Cromwell; no legislation passed

1656

September	Meeting of second Protectorate parliament; despite exclusions by the Lord Protector's council, at least 36 public acts passed
December	Case of James Naylor judged by parliament

1657

25 May	The Humble Petition and Advice, a revised written constitution, provides that a second house of parliament should be restored, and guaranteed that parliaments should not be interrupted or purged
26 June	The Additional Petition and Advice clarifies and amplifies the Humble Petition and Advice

1659

January	Third protectorate parliament (Lord Protector Richard Cromwell) elected on the pre-1653 franchise, but no legislation passed
April	Rump Parliament revived

1660

February	Return to Commons of members secluded in December 1648
16 March	Members of the Long Parliament finally and, in their eyes, legitimately dissolve the assembly

Further Reading

J. S. A. Adamson, 'Of Armies and Architecture: The Employments of Robert Scawen', in *Soldiers, Writers and Statesmen of the English Revolution*, ed. I. Gentles, J. Morrill and B. Worden (Cambridge, 1998), 36–67

—— 'The English Nobility and the Projected Settlement of 1647', *Historical Journal*, xxx (1987), 567–602

—— 'Parliamentary Management, Men-of-Business and the House of Lords, 1640–49', in *A Pillar of the Constitution: The House of Lords in British Politics, 1640–1784*, ed. C. Jones (1989), 21–50

—— 'The Triumph of Oligarchy: The Management of War and the Committee of Both Kingdoms, 1644–1645', in *Parliament at Work: Parliamentary Committees, Political Power and Public Access in Early Modern England*, ed. C. R. Kyle and J. Peacey (Woodbridge, 2002), 101–27

P. Christianson, 'The Peers, the People and Parliamentary Management in the First Six Months of Long Parliament', *Journal of Modern History*, xlix (1977), 575–99

C. H. Firth, *The House of Lords during the Civil War* (1910)

E. R. Foster, *The House of Lords, 1603–1649: Structure, Procedure and the Nature of its Business* (Chapel Hill, NC, 1983)

J. S. Hart, *Justice Upon Petition: The House of Lords and the Reformation of Justice, 1621–1675* (1991)

—— *The Rule of Law, 1603–1660* (Harlow, 2003)

G. F. T. Jones, 'The Peers' Right of Protest in the Long Parliament', *Bulletin of the Institute of Historical Research*, xxxi (1958), 211–15

'The Journal of the Protectorate House of Lords', HMC, *Lords MSS*, new ser. iv (1908), 503–67

I. Roots, 'The Debate on "the Other House" in Richard Cromwell's Parliament', in *For Veronica Wedgwood These: Studies in Seventeenth-Century History*, ed. P. Tudor-Craig and R. Ollard (1986), 188–230

—— '"The Other House": Bicameralism in the Protectorate Parliaments', in *Bicameralisme*, ed. H. W. Blom, W. P. Blockmans and H. De Shepper (The Hague, 1992), 249–60

M. P. Schoenfeld, *The Restored House of Lords* (The Hague, 1967)

D. L. Smith, *The Stuart Parliaments, 1603–1689* (1999)

A. Swatland, *The House of Lords in the Reign of Charles II* (Cambridge, 1996)

7 The House of Lords, 1660–1707
Robin Eagles

On 25 April 1660 after a break of a dozen years ten peers re-entered the House of Lords[1] signalling its restoration following the House's suppression in 1649. The earl of Manchester was appointed temporary Speaker and their first order was for a day of fasting to be appointed for the following Monday (30 April). The same afternoon three more peers (Dorset, Middlesex and Rivers) were added to their number, immediately throwing into confusion General Monck's intention that former cavaliers and their sons should be excluded from the restored House. Thus the resumption of their seats by a cadre of former Cromwellian peers proved the catalyst for the remaining peers to return to their places, such that by June 1660 the House (barring the bishops) was fully restored and in November 1661 the bishops were also permitted to return. Until the opening of the new parliament of Great Britain in 1707 this remained the model for the House.

Membership

1. Peers

By the time of the Restoration, most of the peers entitled to a seat in the House of Lords held titles of relatively recent creation. Few truly ancient peerages remained, and of those that did (among them the de Vere earldom of Oxford, the Nevill barony of Abergavenny and the Berkeley barony of Berkeley) many had been crippled by confiscations and fines during the interregnum. During the reign of Charles II, the peerage was boosted with a number of new creations, though most came from at least the fringes of noble society and many served merely to replace peerages that had become extinct. Some of Charles's new creations represented promotions promised by his father during the civil war and which made no impact on overall numbers (such as the earldom of Cardigan to Lord Brudenell) and several of the new lords were near relatives of peers already sitting (such as Edward Montagu, earl of Sandwich, who was a cousin of Edward Montagu, Baron Montagu of Boughton as well as of Robert Montagu, earl of Manchester). A number of prominent former Cromwellians who were instrumental in bringing about the Restoration were rewarded. Sandwich was one of these; as were Anthony Ashley Cooper, Lord Ashley (later earl of Shaftesbury), and the most prominent of them all, George Monck,

---

[1] Manchester, Northumberland, Lincoln, Suffolk, Denbigh, Saye and Sele, Wharton, Hunsdon, Grey of Warke and Maynard.

duke of Albemarle. While peerages were not strictly speaking for sale, on occasion they do appear to have been made available in return for large sums of money. In 1682 the countess of Lichfield (one of Charles II's illegitimate daughters) was reported to have an 'earldom to sell for £8,000'[2] while John Fell, bishop of Oxford, was said to have been granted a patent for an earldom, which he intended to bestow on one Luttrell to raise funds for his building projects at Christ Church.

In 1660 147 peers were eligible to sit in the House of Lords. During his reign of 36 years Charles II created 103 new peerages. His successor, James II, on the throne for just three years created 10 more, while William and Mary (and later William alone) created a further 43. Despite this apparent largesse, by the time of William III's death the overall number of those eligible to sit had hardly grown at all. In 1702 there were 162 peers, which by the winter of 1703 had fallen to 161 (excluding females, Catholics, exiles and minors), only 14 more than at the Restoration. Before the Act of Union brought the addition of 16 Scots representative peers into the British House of Lords, Queen Anne presided over the creation of a further 21, including a mass creation of 11 peerages in the winter of 1706 (though only four of these constituted additions to the House, the remaining seven being promotions). Thus, although the period from 1660 to 1707 saw some 177 peerages created, there was a net gain of just 35 new lords in parliament. The reason for this was not necessarily a cataclysmic inability of families to survive. Several of the new peerages were promotions (66), which made no difference to the number of peers in the House, while others (10) represented the granting of peerages to females, who were barred from sitting in parliament. There were also some additional honours, which conferred no alteration in the grantee's rights in the House. One example of this was the barony of St Liz, which was awarded to Basil Feilding, earl of Denbigh, in 1665. Something that did increase membership temporarily was the practice of occasionally calling up the eldest sons of peers in their fathers' baronies. Beneficiaries of this practice were the 2nd and 3rd earls of Berkeley, each of whom was summoned as Baron Berkeley while their fathers were alive.

As well as peerage creations there were, following the revolution of 1688-9, several cases of peers either being disabled from their right to sit or stripped of their peerages through outlawry as adherents of the exiled King James. Those unwilling to take the oaths to the new regime, the so-called non-jurors, lost their seats (for example, Theophilus Hastings, earl of Huntingdon and Henry Hyde, earl of Clarendon), but an example of a peer deprived of his title was Edward Griffin, James's last creation before his flight, who sat briefly as Baron Griffin before also fleeing to the Continent following implication in a series of plots. Griffin's very admission to the House was controversial, taking his seat for the first time in the convention without being formally introduced. His irregular

---

[2] HMC, *Rutland*, ii, 67.

presence attracted the notice of the earl of Berkeley while others complained that, 'this was no parliament, and that they could not be introduced but in parliament'.³ Although several peers called on Griffin to withdraw, he was rescued by Lords Delamer and Lovelace, initially among the most vocal of those demanding that he be removed, who introduced him in summary fashion, according to some to distract attention from Lord Carteret, who had also been admitted without formal introduction. Griffin continued to attract trouble after this episode and in his dotage he was one of those captured during the abortive Jacobite invasion of 1708. He passed the remainder of his life in the Tower of London awaiting execution. It was not until the reign of George II that his grandson, another Edward Griffin, petitioned successfully to be recognized as 3rd Baron Griffin.

2. Bishops

The removal of the bishops from the House before the final abolition in 1649 meant that at the Restoration they were initially not included in the restored House of Lords. By early 1661, though, it was being debated whether the lords spiritual should be restored to their places. One peer who argued strongly in favour was Richard Sackville, earl of Dorset, who penned a lengthy argument on the necessity of their attendance. Others took a different view, Pepys noting that during the elections for parliament in London in the spring of 1661 a common cry heard in the streets was 'No bishops, no bishops' and Pepys himself reckoned that 'the bishops are so high, that few do love them'.⁴

The readmission of the bishops in November 1661 increased the numbers eligible to sit to 170 and provided the court with 26 members who could normally be counted on to be sympathetic to the court line (though not invariably so) and were consequently on occasion referred to disparagingly as being 'dead weight' within the House.⁵ Although the bishops were very far from acting *en bloc*, they were certainly a separate element in the House from the peers: their very position in the House was not that of peers after all, but spiritual lords of parliament. For most of this period the bishops took a less prominent part in the administrative business of the House than the peers: none was appointed to high office of state, and while some such as Cosin of Durham and Henchman of Salisbury did chair a number of committees, the vast majority were presided over by lay lords. The reason for their failure to take a more prominent role may have been simply a result of the consecutive meetings of convocation, which meant that when not in the House, the bishops were fully occupied with business there. Their presence, though, did cause controversy

---

³ Alan Simpson, 'Notes of a Noble Lord, 22 January to 12 February 1688/9', *English Historical Review*, lii (1937), 87–98 at 92.

⁴ *The Diary of Samuel Pepys*, ed. R. Latham and W. Matthews (11 vols, 1970–83), ii, 57

⁵ K. H. D. Haley, *The First Earl of Shaftesbury* (Oxford, 1968), 375.

on occasion, most notably over the question of whether they should be permitted to vote on matters of blood. Following numerous heated discussions, the bishops, as a rule, vacated the chamber before sentence was passed against those found guilty of capital offences.

The Restoration of the Bishops

Although the readmission of the bishops excited initially relatively little comment, their restoration soon provoked re-examination of their status within the House. Within a week of their readmission, the committee for privileges was requested to consider a standing order of the House that declared the bishops to be lords of parliament rather than peers and to determine whether the standing order should be overturned. Eighteen years later, the prospective trials of the earl of Danby and the impeached Catholic lords precipitated further parliamentary scrutiny over whether the bishops should be permitted to participate. Viscount Dursley, sitting in the Commons, hoped that the Lords would see sense and remove the bishops for the duration of the trials.* The question of the bishops' place in the House was covered in a variety of treatises, notably those by Edward Stillingfleet, Lawrence Womock and Thomas Hunt (in their favour) and by Thomas Barlow and Lord Holles (against). A less well-known commentator was the 5th earl of Dorset, who as chairman of a number of key committees took a particular interest in the regulation of the House. For Dorset, the bishops' place in the House was of crucial importance, 'a[s] aunciently temporall peeres, and members of the Lords howse, as any sitting there', whose exclusion would bring into question the very validity of the assembly, 'It being clear, that the Lord[s] spirituall are one of the three estates: it must necessarily follow that they cannot be excluded by the king and the other two estates; the consequence of that being the inevitable destruction of the Parliament.'†

The result of such musings was, perhaps inevitably, a compromise. Without any formal resolution to that effect, the bishops as a rule maintained their places until conviction and then withdrew before sentence of death was imposed. It was not until the 19th century, though, that their place in the House was formally defined, when it was concluded that although lords of parliament there was no sense in which bishops were ennobled: a bishop's temporalities did not 'render him noble; they do not make him a peer of the realm'.‡

* Gloucestershire RO, Smyth of Nibley, vol. 2, fol. 108.
† Centre for Kentish Studies, Sackville MSS, U269/O36.
‡ *Reports from the Lords Committees touching the Dignity of a Peer of the Realm* (3 vols, 1820), i, 393.

Major Legislation

During the period from the Restoration to the Act of Union, the House oversaw a wide variety of legislation. Much of the House's time was taken up with private bills, but it was also responsible for the final scrutiny of major national legislation, such as settling the militia and the Restoration religious settlement. Other less well-known acts affected relations between the kingdoms of England, Ireland and Scotland. The Navigation Act of 1661 specifically protected English, Welsh and Irish shipping to the Indies from competition from that of Scotland, which threatened (like that of France) to undercut the industry of the other three. From 1664 Ireland came under assault as the Lords passed a series of bills prohibiting the importation of 'foreign' Irish cattle into England in an attempt to shore up English agriculture, though these measures provoked great jealousies in all three kingdoms. The Scots feared they would be comprehended within the term 'foreign', while many English peers possessed extensive Irish estates, which were affected, and many of those that did not relied upon the importation of cheap lean Irish cattle to be fattened up on their pastures in England before slaughter. Despite such opposition, in 1681 it was determined to make the act perpetual.[6] Of far greater significance to the country as a whole, though, were the measures that constituted the Test Acts, which from 1673 barred non-Anglicans from holding a variety of office. After 1678 Catholic peers were deprived of their seats in the House, with the exception of the duke of York (later James II) who committed himself to overturning the legislation during his brief reign. Of great importance too was the Triennial Act, introduced into the House in 1694 by its champion, the duke of Shrewsbury, which provided for regular meetings of parliament and elections every three years.

Although it was usual for the king (or queen) to be present to grant the royal assent to bills being passed, in the case of the king's absence this was done by commission. In these circumstances, the great officers sat apart from the rest of the House and the formula '*Le Roy le veult*' (the king wishes it) was spoken by the clerk of the parliaments. Sometimes the royal assent was withheld. On six occasions between the Restoration and the overthrow of James II and on five occasions between 1692 and 1696, monarchs exercised their veto, most controversially in 1693 over the Triennial Bill, though it was eventually passed the following year. Although it was common for the majority of bills to be presented *en masse* at the close of a session, from the Restoration onwards the king (or queen) routinely attended the House mid-session to assent to individual bills presumably to speed the dispatch of business.

---

[6] C. A. Edie, 'The Irish Cattle Bills: A Study in Restoration Politics', *Transactions of the American Philosophical Society*, new ser., lx part 2 (1970), 5.

Where the House Sat

For most of the period the House sat in the former Queen's Chamber in the old palace of Westminster to which they had moved from the Painted Chamber in the early 16th century. There were, however, occasional exceptions. Twice in the period (1665 and 1681) sessions of parliament were held in Oxford, when the Lords were housed in the Geometry School, and following James II's flight gatherings of peers constituting the provisional government met variously at the Guildhall in the City of London, at offices in Whitehall and latterly in the Queen's Presence Chamber in St James's Palace before resuming their deliberations in the House of Lords before the summoning of the 'Convention' Parliament. The peers' gathering in the House of Lords in advance of the Convention was controversial and

The Provisional Government and Convention, 1688–9

Although the revolution of 1688–9 affected a broad swathe of society, the role of the Lords at the head of the movement was vital. Following news of the king's flight, on 11 December an assembly of 27 lords temporal and spiritual gathered in the gallery of the Guildhall to take charge of affairs in London. On the following day the meeting was convened at Whitehall, where further assemblies were held on 13, 14 and 15 December before matters were complicated by the king's unexpected return to London on 16 December. On 21 December the peers assembled once more in the Queen's Presence Chamber in St James's Palace before returning to the House on 22 December, where subsequent meetings were held on 24 December and on Christmas Day.

The meetings of the provisional government and the subsequent Convention Parliament that met from 22 January 1689 revealed the deep divisions within the peerage and the keen struggle that was waged between the various interest groups in an effort to resolve the crisis. In essence, there were three options. First, the return of the king under severe limitations; second, the establishment of a regency; and third, the replacement of James II either with his daughter Mary or with a joint monarchy of Mary and her husband William of Orange. During the meetings the early dominance of those eager to reach some kind of accommodation with the king (led by his brothers-in-law, Clarendon and Rochester) was overtaken by those determined to limit or even replace him. Debate in the convention altered things further, as the more hard-line elements forced the Lords to accept that James' flight constituted not just a desertion of his post but an abdication of his kingship, leaving the way clear for the proclamation of an alternative monarch, made possible by the Lords' acceptance that the throne was vacant on 6 February 1689, ironically enough, the fourth anniversary of James II's accession to the throne.

at least one peer (Clarendon) voiced his opposition to their making use of the chamber for an irregular assembly.

The House's committees met in a variety of locations. Most were held in chambers within the palace, usually in the Prince's Lodgings, but occasionally the Lord Keeper's Lodgings or offices in Whitehall were also employed. Conferences between Lords and Commons usually took place in the Painted Chamber.

Management

At one level, management of the House necessitated a logistical balancing act reflecting the various responsibilities of a number of prominent members of the House who doubled as ministers, court officials and legal officers. It has already been noted that the bishops' attention was divided between convocation and parliament, and similar conflicts of interest could be caused by overlapping business in the law courts. In May 1679 Colonel Edward Cooke reported to the duke of Ormond how the day's business had been curtailed by the late arrival of the lord chancellor, busy overseeing the court of chancery, and by the need to rise early to allow the privileges committee to finalize arrangements for the anticipated trial of the five peers then imprisoned in the Tower. As a result little business was conducted that day.[7]

Aside from such practicalities, political issues also affected the House's management. The most dominant figure of the first years of the reign in both government and the House was the lord chancellor, Clarendon, loyally assisted by the lord treasurer, the earl of Southampton. Even before the king's return, Sir Alan Brodrick informed Clarendon how he met each evening with Southampton in the latter's chambers in the Temple to receive his instructions for the Commons for the following day, and it seems reasonable to assume that similar informal meetings were convened to co-ordinate the Lords' business.[8] By the late 1670s management had become both more organized and more polarized as the earl of Danby emerged as a loyal counterpoise to Shaftesbury who headed the opposition. Danby was in turn succeeded by Robert, 2nd earl of Sunderland, and by the revolution of 1688–9 the emergence of the 'tory' and 'whig' parties was as influential in the Lords as in the Commons, perhaps more so, as many of the most prominent leaders were in the upper chamber. Having returned to England from exile in 1690, Sunderland was employed by William III to establish a court party, largely whig in character but embracing figures such as Marlborough and Godolphin whose loyalties were more ambiguous, in an effort to curb the excesses of the more extreme whigs and more implacable tories. The admission of a number of peers who had previously sat in the Commons towards the end of the reign

---

[7] HMC, *Ormond*, new ser., v, 109–10.
[8] *Calendar of Clarendon State Papers*, v, 20.

of William III and during Queen Anne's reign, such as Thomas, Lord Wharton, Charles Montagu, Lord Halifax, and Charles Spencer, 3rd earl of Sunderland, threatened to alter the character of the House. Wharton and Halifax in particular brought with them a more familiar and aggressive style of debate, which was noted by contemporaries with some unease, but their admission may also have contributed to a strengthening in the management of parties within the House.

Although high politics dictated the business of parliament, managers were also presented with more fundamental difficulties such as ensuring a reasonable turnout at certain periods of the year. In July 1661, in his speech proroguing the current session, the king noted the extreme thinness of both Houses, while in August 1699 James Vernon wrote of the forthcoming meeting of parliament at the close of September that, although it would have been preferable to delay meeting for a further two weeks, it would have interfered with a meet at Newmarket 'at which time there will be fewer in town'. As it was, he complained that it was 'with all the difficulty in the world that six are got together to make a council'.[9] One way in which the problem of low turnout could be combated was by the use of proxy votes. Absent peers were coaxed into nominating peers to hold their proxies so that their voices were not lost. The period from 1688 onwards saw an increasing sophistication in the way in which parliament was managed leading to a number of politicians drawing up reliable forecasts on the likely outcome of divisions.

Parties

It has long been acknowledged that even by the end of the period it is too simplistic to speak of just 'whigs' and 'tories'. In 1660 even these umbrella terms did not exist. The efforts of Philip, Lord Wharton to categorize the state of the peerage on the eve of the Restoration resulted in the compilation of various categories of those who had been royalist, those who had sat with the parliamentarians, those who had 'withdrawn a little' and neutrals as well as the sons of the cavalier nobility of the civil war, many of whom continued their fathers' royalist traditions. Within these groupings there were further substrata based broadly on religious affiliations: presbyterians, independents and Catholics. Most of the last were royalist, but the presbyterians comprised both men of parliamentarian stamp, like Manchester, as well as thoroughgoing royalists like Lord Craven. Early attempts at parliamentary management were pioneered by Wharton, who assigned particular members of both Houses, who he conceived to be his 'friends', to various individuals to be managed on certain issues, and by the earl of Bristol in his efforts to bring down the lord chancellor, Clarendon.

---

9 University of Nottingham Library, Portland MS, PwA 1500: James Vernon to earl of Portland, 22 August 1699.

Philip, 4th Lord Wharton

Wharton had come to the fore in the years running up to the outbreak of the civil war as a member of the opposition to the court. After serving ingloriously at Edgehill, he took no further part in the conflict, but was prominent in parliament and was prized by Cromwell. Despite this, he refused to participate in the king's trial and after 1649 seceded from parliament and refused to accept Cromwell's offer of membership of his Other House.

By the Restoration, Wharton had reconciled himself to the king's return, though he remained an object of suspicion and was implicated in a series of plots against the new regime. It was perhaps in response to his decidedly precarious position that Wharton set out to categorize the members of both Houses making a systematic attempt to martial those members who he considered to be sympathetic to him under the guidance of a variety of 'managers'. Several of those whom Wharton counted among his friends appear to have been identified as such by mistake: a number were solid cavaliers with whom he appears to have had little in common. But the vast majority appear to have been selected for good reason and the resulting lists compiled by Wharton serve as a useful guide to the likely disposition of a number of peers and members of the Commons on issues in the early years of the Restoration.*

By the 1670s, Wharton was closely associated with the opposition coalescing around Shaftesbury that was to prove the foundation of the later whig party. In February 1677 Wharton joined Shaftesbury, Buckingham and Salisbury in the Tower for asserting that parliament was dissolved by the long prorogation of more than a year. The experience appears to have cooled his ardour for opposition somewhat, though in December 1678 he was again called to account in the House for failing to kiss the Bible when taking the oaths. Claiming that he had never done something that he conceived to be idolatry, Wharton was teased by Shaftesbury who 'hoped kissing was no idolatry for then they must forbear kissing their wives'.† By the time of the Oxford parliament of March 1681, Wharton and Shaftesbury's friendship had cooled noticeably and when Wharton's servant arranged rooms for his master close to those of his former associate, Wharton requested that they be changed. Wharton remained associated with opposition well into old age and was one of the peers to participate in the provisional government formed in December 1688, though by that time his zeal had largely been overtaken by that of his heir, 'Honest Tom' Wharton, the future 1st marquess of Wharton.

* Bodleian Library, MS Carte 81, fols. 63, 78–82.
† British Library, Verney MS, M636/32: John Verney to Sir Ralph Verney, 5 December 1678.

During the 1670s the issue of exclusion brought to the fore a new grouping dominated by Shaftesbury and Charles II's bastard, James, duke of Monmouth, which ultimately proved the foundation for the whig party. In response to this, prominent figures loyal to the established order coalesced into what was effectively to become the 'tory' party. (Both terms were originally labels of abuse, the former a reference to the rebellious Scots whiggamores and the latter to the Catholic thieving 'tories' of Ireland.) By 1680 at least one commentator (John Potenger) describing the 'great ferment' of the nation noted the existence of three broad groupings: 'whig', 'tory' and 'trimmer' (the most notable exponent of the last being the marquess of Halifax) and by the 1690s these had further fragmented with the addition of 'court' and 'country' interests.[10]

Committees and Lobbying

Undoubtedly, peers, bishops and interested parties in legislation before the House employed their influence where matters concerned them. On occasion, this gave rise to concern that committees were being 'packed' by adherents or opponents of a measure, but at the revolution, perhaps to prevent this from happening, it became customary to name everyone present in the House at the time the committee was formed. This did not mean, of course, that all would necessarily attend it, while those who had not been nominated were free to attend and speak but were proscribed from voting. The size of a committee might also be boosted by the nomination of additional lords after the committee was established. Committees had previously been made up of lords nominated by other members and it seems likely that it was those with a special knowledge of a case or interest in it that were included in the list. It was also a requirement that there should be a balance of barons, earls and bishops, but this does not always appear to have been adhered to strictly.

In the early years of Charles II's reign a few peers came to the fore as the most regular chairmen. Richard Sackville, earl of Dorset, John Egerton, earl of Bridgwater, and Antony Ashley Cooper, earl of Shaftesbury, proved particularly assiduous, dominating the committees in the first half of the reign. Towards the end of William III's reign, Viscount Longueville was far and away the most frequently nominated chairman of both select committees and committees of the whole House, while under Queen Anne the 2nd earl of Stamford and the earl of Rochester shared the majority of select committee work. Committee chairmen enjoyed great influence. In February 1665 Charles II made it known to Dorset, chairman of the Yarmouth Fishery Bill, that he would not prorogue the current session until the bill was passed; the extent of the chairman's influence was further highlighted during the ongoing debates over the Popish Plot, when one

---

[10] H. Horwitz, *Parliament, Policy and Politics in the Reign of William III* (Manchester, 1977), 2.

> ### Oaths, Proxies and the 7th Earl of Huntingdon
>
> On 15 February 1673, the 7th earl of Huntingdon, having succeeded his father in 1656 as a minor, 'sat first as a Peer in Parliament, by Descent, by his Proxy', registered with the duke of York (an arrangement engineered by the duke's chaplain). Normally a peer would have been expected to have sat in the Lords in person before they would issue a proxy. Huntingdon, however, may be the only case where a lord who had not sat before 'sat first' by reason of his proxy. With the Test Act of 1678 lords were required to take the oaths of supremacy, of allegiance, and of abjuration at each new parliament before they could sit in the House, and consequently before they could register a proxy. Before 1678 peers and bishops appear not to have taken any oaths upon their first appearance in the Lords, at least since 1628. This is despite the Standing Order no. 43 of 1625 which required 'All the Lords shall once every Parlyament take the oath of Allegiance'. In 1675 Standing Order no. 67 stated 'That noe Oath shall be imposed by any Bill or otherwise upon the Peeres with a penaltie in case of Refusall to loose their Places and Votes in Parliament or liberty of Debates therein'. This was clearly overruled by the Test Act.
>
> CJ
>
> Sources: LJ, xii, 532; HMC, Lords MSS, new ser., x, 8, 15; Bodleian Library, MS Carte 77, fols. 536–7: Benjamin Woodroffe to Huntingdon, 8 February 1673; PA, HL/PO/JO/13/5 (proxy book vol. 5).

witness claimed to have testified on oath before the 2nd earl of Clarendon, chairman of the committee investigating the plot, to information concerning an attempt to assassinate Shaftesbury, Titus Oates and various others, which Clarendon had then failed to pass on to the rest of the committee. Clarendon denied that the witness had provided such detailed evidence, but his omission demonstrated the important part played by the chairman in determining what information came to the committee's attention.

Contentious measures were often referred to a committee of the whole House. One of the earliest examples of this concerned the earl of Danby's bill to prevent dangers which might arise from persons disaffected to the government, which bore a close resemblance to the earl of Clarendon's abortive non-resisting Test Bill. Danby's bill was opposed by a motley alliance of differing interest groups and having been introduced on 15 April 1675 was finally thrown out on 2 June after some of the most bad-tempered debate the House had witnessed since the Restoration.

Voting

The House of Lords enjoyed certain privileges peculiar to its members. Several concerned the manner in which the Lords voted. In the case of known absence, peers and bishops were permitted to sign a certificate granting their proxy vote to another member of the House. The only restrictions were that bishops could only give their proxies to other bishops and peers to other peers. (There was nothing to prevent an earl registering his proxy with a baron for example.) No peer could hold more than two proxies at any one time; and a peer holding a proxy could not exercise

> ### *Obesity and Voting in the House of Lords*
>
> On 27 May 1679, during the passage of the Habeas Corpus Bill through the House of Lords, a vote for a free conference with the House of Commons was passed, the vote in the division being 57 to 55. According to Gilbert Burnet's *History of My Own Time*, the vote
>
>> was carried by an odd artifice of the House of Lords. Lord Grey and Lord Norris were named to be the tellers. Lord Norris, being a man subject to vapours, was not at all times attentive to what he was doing: so a very fat lord coming it [in?], Lord Grey counted him for ten, as a jest at first, but seeing Lord Norris had not observed that, he went on with his misreckoning of ten for one: so it was reported to the House, and declared that they who were for the bill were the majority, though it indeed went on the other side: and by thus means the bill passed.
>
> There is no other record of this 'artifice', and an examination of the manuscript minutes does not confirm the story as far as the numbers voting is concerned: the record of the lords present in the House on that day in the minutes numbers 107, not the total of 112 if Burnet's story is to be believed. However, the minutes were the rough workings of the clerks of the Lords taken down during the proceedings of the House. They are inevitably subject to human error, and there are many examples throughout the minutes where its evidence does not tally with other records concerning proceedings. Often it is impossible to decide which piece of evidence is correct. So Burnet's story may be the truth. Indeed, it may not be the only instance in which the tellers got the figures wrong, either deliberately or not. On 19 May 1712 a division over the commitment of the Land Grants Bill necessitated a second count, after the tellers, Carteret and Masham, failed to agree the tally, while in 1799 Henry Cowper, the clerk assistant to the House, reported to the prince of Wales that on a vote on 14 July in a division on a bill to limit the slave trade, a mistake in the telling had occurred because both tellers, Lords Kinnoull and Holland, were 'unus'd to that office'.
>
> CJ
>
> Sources: *Burnet's History of My Own Time: The Reign of Charles II*, ed. O. Airy (2 vols, Oxford, 1897–1900), ii, 264; *The Later Correspondence of George III*, ed. A. Aspinall (5 vols, 1962–70), document no. 1983; HMC, *Lords* MSS, new ser., ix, 242.

his vote while withholding the proxy. Proxies were vacated by the death of either peer, when a session ended or with the resumption of his seat by the absent member. It was also possible for a peer or bishop to withdraw the proxy from the current holder and make it over to another.

Divisions in the House, could take several forms. In most instances a vote was taken by a simple calling of 'aye' or 'no', but where a vote was too close to determine in this fashion, the Speaker (normally the lord chancellor or lord keeper) might order that a division should be held. Any member of the House might also move for a division, which would be allowed if the motion were seconded. Initially, the form appears to have been for peers in favour of the motion to stand, while those in opposition remained seated, but by the time of the Restoration this was already a cause of confusion, as attested by an order of 15 December 1660 that the committee for privileges should consider ways of improving seating, 'the better to prevent disorder in the House when they come to voting, for want of seats'.[11] Dissatisfaction with this method of voting led to a refinement enshrined in standing order 22 of 25 November 1691, whereby those in favour of the motion processed out below the bar of the House and were then counted as they filed back in, while those opposed remained in their seats. As in the Commons, the counting was overseen by tellers, though, unlike the Commons, the Lords nominated only two, and in their case the tellers' votes also counted towards the overall tally. It is not at all clear whether tellerships were in any way 'political', but at times tellers do appear to have been selected on a partisan basis.

In more formal divisions, including trials, the Lords voted by 'individual voice': each peer or bishop standing in turn and declaring himself content or not content. In the question of a trial the declaration was guilty or not guilty 'upon mine honour'.

Legal Cases

From the outset, the Lords was closely involved in the judicial aspects of the Restoration, notably over the question of how best to deal with those who had been involved in the trial and execution of Charles I. The Lords defended jealously their right to try their own members and in 1667 this was put to the test with the efforts to impeach the lord chancellor, Clarendon. The Popish Plot and its aftermath found other members of the House in jeopardy: five Catholic peers and the earl of Danby, though of these only one, Viscount Stafford, was found guilty, attainted and executed. Following the Glorious Revolution, the House oversaw several other high-profile trials. In December 1696 a bill of attainder was passed against Sir John Fenwick and on two occasions the hot-headed Charles, Lord Mohun, was tried for murder (1693 and 1698). Mohun, was fortunate to count a number of powerful members of the whig junto among his friends and

---

[11] *LJ*, xi, 211.

was saved from execution on both occasions, his punishment for the second murder being limited to being 'branded in the hand with a cold iron'.

Besides such high profile trials, the Lords was also the venue for the settlement of marital discord, which occasionally resulted in divorce cases in a period when the only means of achieving a formal separation was by act of parliament. Many saw the efforts of Lord Roos to achieve a divorce from his wayward spouse in 1667 as a 'stalking horse' for a possible royal divorce once it was apparent that Queen Catharine of Braganza would be unable to bear the king an heir, but quite as important in legal terms were cases such as that between Lord and Lady Leigh, an explosive case involving Leigh's imprisonment and 'chastisement' of his wife in response to her wayward living, which involved among other things an affair with John Wilmot, earl of Rochester, and a rumoured attempt to have Leigh assassinated.

Trials and Impeachments

Unsurprisingly, the Lords were always reluctant to turn on one of their own. The example of the earl of Strafford in the previous reign cast a long shadow over the House under Charles II, but the hysteria generated by the Popish Plot, commencing in the late summer of 1678, led to the execution of another noble scapegoat, William Howard, Viscount Stafford, who was attainted in December 1680 and put to death the following month. During the remainder of this period a number of trials and attempted impeachments of peers were conducted in Westminster Hall, including those of Morley and Monteagle, Delamer, Mohun (twice), Portland, Halifax, Orford and Somers as well as the controversial trial and condemnation of the commoner Sir John Fenwick. Others were fortunate to escape the same fate, among them Danby, Shaftesbury and both the 1st and 2nd earls of Clarendon, while the duke of Monmouth was condemned and executed without recourse to a formal trial at all.

The example of Viscount Stafford also demonstrates the Lords' reluctance to inflict the grisly sentence prescribed for high treason on their fellows. Although Stafford was found guilty by a clear majority, enquiries were made by the lord steward whether it was within the competence of the House to ameliorate the sentence to be imposed. The lawyers' advice was that to interfere would call into question his attainder, leaving the lord steward with no choice but to impose the full rigours of the law: hanging, castration, drawing, beheading and quartering. In the event, the king demonstrated a degree of clemency by restricting Stafford's sentence to simple beheading – a courtesy normally (but not always) granted to someone in acknowledgement of his (former) noble status. The same mercy was granted to Fenwick.

Conflict between the Houses

There were three particular areas of dispute between the two Houses in the period. First over the right of the Lords to initiate and amend money bills; second over their right to a say in electoral contests (*Ashby v. White*); and third over questions of judicature: particularly with reference to appeals from the lower courts. Shortly after the Restoration, a potential dispute between the two Houses over the proceedings against King Charles I's judges was only averted when the Commons decided not to contest the point, but by the following decade the lower House was less willing to give ground. In April 1675 a seemingly innocuous case between Dr Thomas Shirley, royal physician, and Sir John Fagg, MP for Steyning, over a disputed sale of lands, which had progressed through the courts of chancery and exchequer found its way to the Lords on Shirley's appeal. Having read his petition, the Lords duly ordered Fagg to put in an answer, thereby triggering an extremely bad-tempered struggle with the Commons that rumbled on for the ensuing 18 months. Although Fagg seems to have been willing enough to comply, other members of the lower House argued robustly that the Lords' summons had infringed Fagg's privilege as an MP, but when Shirley was summoned to the Commons' bar to answer the charge, the warrant was seized by Lord Mohun and presented to the Lords as a breach of the peers' privilege. As the dispute between the two Houses escalated, the division acquired a political edge by the actions of the earls of Shaftesbury and Danby, the former in defence of the privileges of the Lords, the latter of those of the Commons. By fomenting division, Shaftesbury hoped to derail Danby's Test Bill and his actions had the required effect as the session ended in stalemate. When Shirley attempted to renew his suit the following November, the result was the same. A later case that excited similar resentments between the two Houses was the ongoing suit of Thomas Skinner versus the East India Company, the cause of the latter being championed by the Commons, a number of whose members were directors of the company implicated in Skinner's appeal. The Commons' attempt to dictate in matters of impeachments also provoked spirited resistance from the Lords, while the Lords' efforts to acquire a say in disputed electoral contests provoked quite as lively defence from the lower House. Similarly provocative was the Lords' throwing out of the attempted impeachments of Lords Somers, Portland, Halifax and Orford that originated in the Commons.

Officers of the House

Although the office of Speaker in the House was usually taken by either the lord chancellor or (where there was none) the lord keeper (who was not a member of the House), on occasion the role was assumed by someone else. In the early days of the convention of 1660 the position was normally occupied by the earl of Manchester (the lord chamberlain), but the diary kept by Humphrey Henchman, bishop of Salisbury, demonstrates that in the first five years after the Restoration, the role of Speaker was fulfilled by a number of members of the House including the lord chief justice, the lord privy seal and the archbishop of Canterbury.[12] On 4 August 1685 the earl of Rochester acted as Speaker by commission during the incapacity of the then lord keeper, Lord Guilford, and during the 1689 convention, the marquess of Halifax was appointed as Speaker *pro tempore* after the archbishop of Canterbury declined the position. In the 29 years that had elapsed since the last irregular meeting of the House, certain conventions had been forgotten, necessitating Halifax to request that one of the clerks investigate whether Manchester had had a mace when he was Speaker in 1660. Between 1689 and 1694 Sir Robert Atkyns acted as Speaker in his capacity as chief baron of the court of exchequer. His appointment occurred at a time when the chancellorship was in commission, but he retained the post even after a new lord chancellor had been put into office. On the occasions when the Lords adjourned themselves into a committee of the whole House, the Speaker left the woolsack and abrogated his responsibility to the chairman of the committee, who presided over the business for the duration. Once the House was resumed, it was usually this peer or bishop who reported the committee's findings.

When necessary, the Lords were able to call on the expertise of a number of senior lawyers, who were not members of the House, but might attend to give legal counsel while the House was in session or at committees. On occasion, additional advice or assistance might be sought. At the time of the Popish Plot, an order of 19 March 1679 required that the clerk of the parliaments should provide two clerks to assist the committee examining the plot and on 25 March, the House was acquainted with the appointment of John Sheldrake and Culverwell Needler to undertake these duties.

Responsible for overseeing the ceremonial of the House was the lord great chamberlain, an hereditary post that was held at the time of the Restoration by Montagu Bertie, 2nd earl of Lindsey. Lindsey's father had secured the right to the great chamberlaincy during Charles I's reign, but at the Restoration Lindsey's title was again challenged by Aubrey de Vere, 20th earl of Oxford, as well as by the earl of Derby and Baron Windsor. Following the narrowest of votes in the House, Lindsey's right was again acknowledged. At times disputes also arose between the lord great chamberlain and the lord chamberlain of the household over jurisdiction within the palace of Westminster and during the second and third exclusion parliaments the office was executed by a number of different peers on account of Lindsey's absence from both sessions.

Officers attendant on the House expected to be paid for their services, which was reflected in a scale of fees depending on the post and occasion. Peers wishing to pass a private bill were expected to disburse fees

[12] Bodleian Library, MS Rawlinson A130.

amounting to £25 including £10 to the lord chancellor, £7 to the clerk of the parliaments and £5 to black rod. In April 1662 the House voted £200 to be divided between the 16 serjeants at arms and the knight marshal's men, who had guarded the Lords since their restoration.

Reporting Business and Publishing Proceedings

Day-to-day events of the House were recorded by the clerks in the Lords journals. Minutes of the day's proceedings were edited in a first draft that was later refined into the manuscript journal, which was then in turn eventually produced in printed form in the late 18th century. During this period the journals were only recorded in manuscript form, but the survival of fragments of particular days' proceedings in the papers of a number of peers suggests that copies of all or part of the records of a session were commonly made available to members of the House. Francis Godolphin excused himself for not reporting parliament's business to the earl of Essex, who was away at his post as lord lieutenant of Ireland, supposing that 'the journals of both houses are transmitted to you weekly'.[13] Scrutiny of the record was entrusted to the Lords' committee for the journal (a sub-committee of the committee for privileges), which, unlike the other standing committees of the House was a select group of usually fewer than a dozen peers and bishops, of whom about half a dozen appear to have met regularly to sign off the manuscript journal which had been collated by the clerks. Division lists were not published, though unofficial accounts do exist for particular issues. On occasion, lists of protesting lords were also published unofficially, something that was frowned upon by the House. The first exponent of this was the earl of Shaftesbury, and by the end of this period the practice was a relatively common occurrence, although standing order 77 of 27 February 1698 declared it to be a breach of the House's privilege for anyone to publish 'anything relating to the proceedings of this House' without permission.[14]

[13] *Essex Papers*, ed. C. E. Pike (Camden Society, 3rd ser., xxiv, 1913), 30.
[14] HMC, *Lords* MSS, new ser., xii, 18.

Chronology

1660
25 April	Restoration of the House
14 May	Charles II proclaimed king
29 August	Act of Free and General Pardon, Indemnity and Oblivion
6 November	Opening of second session of Convention
29 December	Convention dissolved

1661
8 May	Opening of 'Cavalier' Parliament
November	Restoration of the bishops

1662
Act of Uniformity

1663
First cattle act limiting Irish exports to England

1664
Triennial Act, Conventicle Act

1665
Five Mile Act

1667
30 August	Clarendon resigns as lord chancellor
October	Attempted impeachment of Clarendon
29 November	Flight of Clarendon to France

1670
Second Conventicle Act

1672
20 January	Stop of the exchequer
15 March	Second Declaration of Indulgence
17 November	Shaftesbury appointed lord chancellor

1673
29 March	First Test Act
30 March	Duke of York fails to take Anglican communion
15 June	York resigns as Lord High Admiral
19 June	Viscount Latimer (later earl of Danby) appointed lord treasurer
9 November	Shaftesbury dismissed as lord chancellor

1675
April	Beginning of the dispute between the two Houses over *Shirley* v. *Fagg*; Danby's non-resisting test bill introduced into the House

1678
13 August	First news of the Popish Plot
29 September	Titus Oates appears before the privy council
17 October	Sir Edmundbury Godfrey found murdered
November	Second Test Act deprives Catholic peers of their seats in the House of Lords
19 December	Commons votes to impeach Danby

1679

24 January	'Cavalier' Parliament dissolved
6 March	Opening of first 'Exclusion' Parliament
26 March	Danby resigns and is sent to the Tower
15 May	Exclusion Bill receives its first reading in the Commons
12 July	Parliament dissolved
19 November	Lawrence Hyde (later earl of Rochester) appointed first lord of the treasury

1680

26 June	Shaftesbury attempts to charge York with recusancy
21 October	Opening of 'Exclusion' Parliament
December	Attainder of Viscount Stafford

1681

10 January	Exclusion Bill defeated in the Lords
18 January	Parliament dissolved
21 March	Opening of the Oxford parliament
28 March	Parliament dissolved
2 July	Shaftesbury arrested for treason

1683

28 January	Sunderland appointed secretary of state
12 June	First news of the Rye House plot
21 July	Lord Russell executed

1685

6 February	Death of Charles II; accession of James II
19 May	Opening of parliament
June-July	Monmouth's rebellion
15 July	Monmouth executed
9 November	Opening of second session of parliament
20 November	Parliament adjourned

1687

2 July	Parliament dissolved

1688

29–30 June	Seven Bishops' trial
5 November	William of Orange lands at Torbay
11 December	Provisional government dominated by the Lords meets at Guildhall

1689

22 January	Opening of 'Convention' Parliament
14 February	William III and Mary II proclaimed king and queen

1690

27 January	Bill of Rights
20 March	Opening of parliament

1691

25 November	Standing Order 25 stipulates new voting arrangements in divisions whereby those in favour of a motion process out below the bar of the House and are counted back in

1693

12 January	Lord Mohun submits petition to the House to be bailed and tried for murder (bail is denied him)
31 January	Mohun tried for murder
4 February	Mohun acquitted by 69 votes to 14

1694

Triennial Act; death of Mary II

1696

Trial of Sir John Fenwick

1697

Fenwick executed

1698

27 February	Standing Order 77 declares in a breach of privilege for proceedings of the House to be published without permission
October	Mohun indicted again following involvement in a second murder

1701

June	Attempted impeachments of Portland, Somers and Orford

1702

8 March	Death of William III, accession of Queen Anne
8 May	Godolphin appointed lord treasurer

1703

Second Occasional Conformity Bill defeated in the Lords

1704

Writ of error moved in the House in the cause of *Ashby* v. *White* (case continues until 1705)

1706

22 July	Draft Treaty of Union complete
9–30 December	Mass creation of 11 peerages

1707

24 April	Parliament prorogued
29 April	Proclamation continuing parliament as the first parliament of Great Britain

Further Reading

R. Beddard, *A Kingdom without a King: The Journal of the Provisional Government in the Revolution of 1688* (Oxford, 1988)

A. Browning, *Thomas Osborne, Earl of Danby and Duke of Leeds, 1632–1712* (3 vols, Glasgow, 1951)

The Correspondence of Henry, Earl of Clarendon, and his Brother Laurence Hyde, Earl of Rochester, with the Diary of Lord Clarendon from 1687 to 1690, ed. S. W. Singer (2 vols, 1828)

The Diary of Samuel Pepys, ed. R. Latham and W. Matthews (11 vols, 1970–83)

K. Feiling, *A History of the Tory Party, 1640–1714* (Oxford, 1924)

K. H. D. Haley, *The First Earl of Shaftesbury* (Oxford, 1968)

The History of Parliament: The House of Commons, 1660–90, ed. B. D. Henning (3 vols, 1983)

The History of Parliament: The House of Commons 1690–1715, ed. E. Cruickshanks, S. Handley and D. W. Hayton (5 vols, Cambridge, 2002)

G. Holmes, *British Politics in the Age of Anne* (rev. edn, 1987)

H. Horwitz, *Parliament, Policy and Politics in the Reign of William III* (Manchester, 1977)

G. F. T. Jones, *Saw-Pit Wharton: The Political Career from 1640 to 1691 of Philip, Fourth Lord Wharton* (Sydney, 1967)

J. R. Jones, *The First Whigs: The Politics of the Exclusion Crisis, 1678–1683* (1961)

J. P. Kenyon, *Robert Spencer, Earl of Sunderland, 1641–1702* (1958)

D. R. Lacey, *Dissent and Parliamentary Politics in England, 1661–89: A Study in the Perpetuation and Tempering of Parliamentarianism* (Brunswick, NJ, 1969)

Party and Management in Parliament, 1660–1784, ed. C. Jones (Leicester, 1984)

A Pillar of the Constitution: The House of Lords in British Politics, 1640–1784, ed. C. Jones (1989)

M. P. Schoenfeld, *The Restored House of Lords* (The Hague, 1967)

P. Seaward, *The Cavalier Parliament and the Reconstruction of the Old Regime, 1661–1667* (Cambridge, 1988)

V. Stater, *Noble Government: The Stuart Lord Lieutenancy and the Transformation of English Politics* (1994)

A. Swatland, *The House of Lords in the Reign of Charles II* (Cambridge, 1996)

[Ebenezer Timberland], *The History and Proceedings of the House of Lords from the Restoration in 1660, to the Present Time* (7 vols, 1742)

A. S. Turberville, 'The House of Lords under Charles II', *English Historical Review*, xliv (1929), 400–17; xlv (1930) 58–77.

8 The House of Commons, 1307–1529
Simon Payling

During the later middle ages the Commons emerged as an important, perhaps even indispensable, facet of English government. It secured and defended the crucial right of assent to the levy of taxation and the making of new law; it developed an established composition and nurtured the notion that it was a body to which special privileges attached; and it was the arena before which some of the great events of the period were enacted, most notably the depositions of Edward II in 1327 and Richard II in 1399. Its rapid institutional development can be summarized under five heads: taxation, legislation, composition, institutional identity and political role.

Taxation

According to the *Modus Tenendi Parliamentum*, a unique and, in places, somewhat fanciful parliamentary manual of the 1320s, 'two knights who come to Parliament for the shire have a greater voice in the granting and denying [of taxation] than the greatest earl in the kingdom' because they are the representatives of the 'whole community' where the earls and lords

---

The Frequency and Duration of Parliaments

Fourteenth-century parliaments were generally brief, consisting of a single session of no more than a few days to a few weeks, and summoned frequently. Some 80 parliaments met between in the 72 years between the accession of Edward III and the deposition of Richard II, and sometimes they were held in quick succession (as many as six parliaments met between May 1382 and December 1384). By marked contrast, only 15 parliaments met between 1461 and 1509, Henry VII convening only one in the last 12 years of his rule. Yet, although parliaments were summoned less frequently as the period advanced, they tended to last longer, sometimes over several sessions. At first long assemblies were indicative, as in 1406 (the first parliament to last over three sessions), of tension between crown and Commons, but later, as in 1472–5 and 1529–36, they betoken something very different: a king reluctant to dissolve a compliant assembly, preferring instead to prorogue it from session to session.

> ### The Meeting Place of the Commons
> From the 1340s, the first date for which reliable evidence is available, the Commons generally met in the Painted Chamber of the Palace of Westminster, next to the White Chamber, the meeting place of the Lords. From the 1370s, however, the two Houses became more physically separate, with the Commons moving first, for a brief period, to the chapter house of Westminster Abbey and then, from 1383, to the abbey's refectory, where they continued to meet until the mid-16th century. When parliament was summoned away from Westminster, the Commons were assigned a separate meeting place: in 1380, for example, they met in the dormitory of the Cluniac abbey of St Andrew in Northampton, and, in 1407, in the refectory of Gloucester Abbey.

represent only themselves.[1] This 'voice' was endowed with an immense and lasting political significance by the military ambitions of Edward III, which could be funded only by a considerable augmentation of the crown's traditional revenues. In the 1350s the Commons, already secure in its right of assent to direct taxation (which generally took the form of a levy on movables, known as the 15th and 10th), succeeded in extending that right to the lucrative customs' revenues, principally an export duty on wool. This right of assent was an obligation as well as a privilege: subjects had a duty to support the crown with their bodies and their goods in the defence of the realm, and hence the Commons was under little short of an obligation to respond positively to royal requests for taxation. Indeed, in practice, the wool subsidy and other customs duties became a permanent levy; the Commons continually renewing its assent so that the ordinary charges of national defence could be maintained. Importantly, however, this preserved the concept that direct taxation could be justified only by urgent and exceptional need, and there was thus room for negotiation over its granting. At the beginning of each parliament, the chancellor or another senior royal servant set before the Lords and Commons the basis of the king's necessity; and, in making a judgment on the extent and timing of the taxation warranted by this plea, the Commons was drawn into a dialogue with the crown over matters of royal policy, at least in so far as concerned expenditure. Hence the crown had to measure its demands to avoid exciting criticism of its government. The consequences of its failure to do so are exemplified most clearly by two parliaments: in the 'Good' Parliament of 1376, the Commons, in seeking to legitimate the extreme step of refusing to grant direct taxation, alleged misgovernance, accusing certain courtiers of misappropriating royal revenue; and, in 1406 they

---

[1] *Parliamentary Texts of the Later Middle Ages*, ed. N. Pronay and J. Taylor (Oxford, 1979), 39, 89–90.

delayed their grant of taxation to force important, albeit short-term, concessions from Henry IV, who promised to rule under the supervision of a council nominated in (but not by) parliament.

The other context of taxation was the local: in making grants, the Commons had to balance the king's requirements against the resources of its constituents. In the parliament of October 1339, nervous of the massive war expenditure to which Edward III, was committed, it requested time to consult locally before increasing its grant. This practice was a contravention of the *plena potestas* with which election endowed MPs (that is, the power to bind their constituents to the decisions of parliament) and was only repeated once more (in the wake of the Peasants' Revolt of 1381). None the less, the threat of opposition in the shires was sufficient to impede tax collection or, on the terrible lesson of that revolt, to provoke serious disorder. This gave the crown reason to temper its demands upon the Commons and the latter an incentive to find means of justifying its grants before the bar of public opinion. Herein, in part, lies the origin of the doctrine of redress before supply, in other words, of making a grant of taxation conditional on concessions from the crown. In the parliament of March 1340 the Commons made its grant dependant upon the appointment of a baronial council to supervise the expenditure of taxation and to answer for that expenditure before parliament; and, in the assembly of January 1401, they asked Henry IV for an undertaking to answer their petitions in advance of any grant. Although they failed to establish this principle – Henry IV repudiated it as against custom – the fact of its assertion illustrates an awareness on the Commons' part of its bargaining power.

None the less, the relationship between crown and Commons over taxation cannot be properly understood by concentrating on those occasions when the Commons proved uncooperative. At times of successful warfare and strong kingship, it responded to royal requests for taxation with a generosity that enhanced monarchical power and funded aggressive warfare, most notably under Henry V, that would have been impossible without its co-operation. But, even when royal government was weak and without direction, its obligation to aid the crown in time of need ensured that grants continued to be made, although they became a matter of prolonged negotiation. Even so, in one important sense, the Commons proved surreptitiously obstructive: it was resistant to the replacement or supplementation of the ancient 15th and tenth, levied on a fixed quota system from as early as 1334, with a form of taxation that more accurately reflected the social and geographical distribution of wealth. As a result, the chief restraint on a strong monarch's ability to exploit direct taxation was not a reluctance on the part of the Commons to grant it, but the failure of that taxation to tax the nation's real wealth. This, in turn, encouraged the crown to develop non-parliamentary sources of income, the so-called 'fiscal feudalism' of the Tudors, and so threatened to diminish the importance of the Commons' right of assent to taxation. Not until the subsidy acts of the early part of Henry VIII's reign, which instituted directly assessed taxes on incomes and goods, was parliamentary taxation established on a more tax-efficient basis, and even then the new system was soon undermined by collusive under-assessment.

Legislation

Although the making of new law was already theoretically established as consensual between king and subjects, in the reign of Edward I legislation arose solely out of royal initiative and was drafted by royal counsellors and judges. In the course of this period, however, the assent of the Commons became an indispensable part of the legislative process. The first stage of this important transformation was a fundamental change in the pattern of petitioning. In the early 14th century, in what was a natural elaboration of parliament's well-established role as the forum for the presentation of petitions of individuals and communities, the Commons began to present petitions in its own name, seeking remedies, not to individual wrongs, but to general administrative, economic and legal problems. The king's answers to these petitions became the basis of new law. Later there was further important procedural elaboration: from the late 14th century, private petitioners increasingly came to address their petitions not to the king but to the Commons in the hope that the lower House would add weight to their requests by endorsing them; and, from the early 15th, the king began to send private petitions, to which he was ready to assent, to the Commons for its approval. The latter development explains the unhistorical assertion made by the Commons in 1414, that 'it has ever been their liberty and freedom that neither statute nor law should be made unless they have given their assent thereto'.[2] This wishful thinking on its part soon found a constitutional fulfilment. From the early 1450s legislation, hitherto described as having been made 'at the request of the Commons' came to be described as having been made 'by assent of the Commons' and, by 1489, the judges had ruled that legislation was invalid without the Commons' assent. With the benefit of hindsight, the transformation of the Commons from a mere petitioner for new law to an assenter to its enactment was of fundamental importance. Yet the crown's legislative initiative was not threatened, at least in the hands of a monarch determined enough to employ it: by the simple means of introducing its own bills among the common petitions the government was able to steer its own legislative programme through the Commons, while retaining the power to veto any bill it found displeasing. Here there was a parallel with earlier developments in taxation, the crown's financial resources were expanded by the system of parliamentary taxation, so later was its legislative force and reach extended by the Commons' endorsement of the initiatives of a strong monarch, a fact strikingly demonstrated by the legislative break

---

[2] *The Parliament Rolls of Medieval England, 1275–1504*, ed. C. Given-Wilson *et al.* (16 vols, Woodbridge, 2005), ix, 52.

with Rome during the long-drawn-out parliament of 1529. Thus, although in the late medieval period, the Commons was drawn increasingly into the legislative process, that greater involvement did not come about at the expense of royal power. What had changed since the reign of Edward I was the degree of consultation involved in an increasingly sophisticated legislative process, not the fundamental balance of initiative between crown and subject.

> ## *The Origins of Divisions*
>
> Innovations in procedure can be detected in virtually every parliament. In that of 1523 there were two striking changes. One, the two estates of the knights (*miles*) and the burgesses (*burgenses*) which until then had agreed to taxation separately ceased to do so and consented to a single money grant from both social groups. Two, acclamation was recognized to be an unsatisfactory method of deciding the outcome of a vote when it was a close-run thing. Under the direction of Speaker More the House of Commons divided on the wording of the money grant, that is those in agreement went to one side of the debating chamber while those in opposition went to the other. The chronicler Edward Hall, almost certainly as a member witnessed this innovation, and later described it.* This innovation had a sinister aspect, as it was intended to identify opponents to a measure so that they could then be dissuaded of their recalcitrance. Henry VIII recognized the advantages of this innovation when in 1532 he repeated it, making clear when he did so that those voting against the bill under consideration were disloyal subjects to him.
>
> AH
>
> * *Hall's Chronicle*, ed. J. Johnson, F. and C. Rivington, and T. Payne (1816), 657

Composition

The representative element became a defining feature in the institution of parliament early in the 14th century. No parliament after 1325 met without local representatives, and, even before that date, they were summoned frequently if not invariably. A crucial development in this formative period was the exclusion of the proctors of the lesser clergy. Although, in the early 14th century, it was the crown's preferred option to gain assent, in the same assembly, to the valuable tax on clerical income that paralleled the direct taxation of the laity, the church was reluctant to concede the principle that secular authority had the right to compel clerical attendance at what was a lay court. By 1340 the church had won its case: it was established that the convocations of York and Canterbury were the proper fora for negotiation between crown and clergy over clerical taxation, and, from thenceforward, the proctors of the lesser clergy no longer took their place in the Commons. The lower House thus became, with later unfortunate consequences for the church, an exclusively lay assembly composed of the representatives of the shires, described as 'knights of the shire', and a greater number of borough MPs, known as burgesses. Those called from the shires quickly assumed a standard form: two MPs were elected from each of 37 shires (Durham and Cheshire, as county palatines, were not represented). These 'knights of the shire', a declining proportion of whom were belted knights, came predominantly from the wealthiest county gentry, the same pool of men who provided the sheriffs, escheators and JPs upon which county administration depended. This, at least, was the case by the late 14th century, by which date men saw election to parliament as an expression and vindication of their local status. Whether this was so earlier in the century is not certain. Some county studies suggest that there was a period, in the 1320s and 1330s, when men of lesser standing were routinely returned, implying perhaps a reluctance to serve on the part of more substantial gentry.[3] However this may be, this disinclination did not persist: growing competition for seats is implied by an interest, evident even before the electoral legislation of the early 15th century, on the part of chroniclers and Commons alike in the exclusion of external interference from the electoral process.

The story of borough representation is more complex than that for the counties. A standard list of parliamentary boroughs was slow to develop, the number of boroughs represented fluctuating from parliament to parliament. The general pattern of the early 14th century was for the number to decline as smaller communities failed to return MPs, but, between about 1350 and 1450, an average of over 80 boroughs was represented in each parliament, the list become increasingly standardized over time with each borough electing two MPs (with the exception of London which, from 1355, returned four). Thereafter the figure began to rise as new parliamentary boroughs were created, at first infrequently but with a quickening pace after 1500. The curious distribution of these seats is one of the great mysteries of parliamentary history. Even as the map was being drawn in the 14th century, it bore only a passing relationship to one based on the size and wealth of towns. The greatest distortion was the massive over-representation of the south-west: the five south-western counties of Cornwall, Devon, Dorset, Somerset and Wiltshire, contained 36 parliamentary boroughs at the beginning of the 15th century and over 40 at its end, compared with only three in the four northern parliamentary shires of Cumberland, Lancashire, Northumberland and Westmorland. This uneven and illogical distribution of seats had important consequences from the late 14th century onwards. While the larger boroughs continued to be represented by their merchants and tradesmen, representation of the many small boroughs fell into the hands of minor gentry, lawyers

---

[3] N. Saul, *Knights and Esquires: The Gloucestershire Gentry in the Fourteenth Century* (Oxford, 1981), 120–2.

and royal servants not significant enough to command county seats. Problems of definition make precise figures hard to equate, but this process had begun by the late 14th century. Some 7% of MPs in the 'Merciless' Parliament of February 1388 were non-residents, and thereafter the proportion increased progressively. In the parliament of 1422 nearly a quarter of borough MPs may have fallen into this category, and, in that of November 1449, nearly a half. Statutes of 1413 and 1445, which laid down that all members should be resident in the constituency they represented on the day of the writ of summons, identified the problem, but were not employed as a remedy.

Institutional Identity

A long-enduring composition established with shire and borough MPs forged together, the Commons quickly developed a sense of institutional identity. Particularly notable here was the period between 1376, when it was, for the first time, represented by a Speaker, chosen from the MPs, to communicate their views to crown and Lords and to preside over their own deliberations (although this latter role may only have been established later), and 1430, when legislation regulating the election of knights of the shire culminated in the famous statute (8 Hen. VI, c. 7) defining the franchise. These were manifestations of a self-awareness on the part of the Commons that it was a body to which special privileges attached, not only corporately but also individually.

Parliamentary Elections

By the 1330s the right of election had come to be seen, at least in the counties, as an important local privilege. Thereafter, as the Commons grew in political weight, this freedom was, on the one hand, challenged by crown and peers anxious to secure the return their own men and, on the other, compromised by a growing competition for seats and a wider clamour or participate in elections. This is the context of the electoral legislation, which in 1406 established formal election indentures as insurance against fraudulent returns, and in 1430 famously defined the county franchise as freeholders with annual incomes of 40s. and over. This franchise was a comparatively broad one, extending beyond the ranks of even the most poorly endowed gentry and implying that yeoman and husbandman, as contributors to taxation and parliamentary wages, were considered to have a legitimate interest in the electoral process. In practice, however, most county elections went uncontested, the MPs informally agreed between the leaders of county society to avoid the inconveniences and potential disturbance of a mass poll. The franchise in borough elections was not fixed in 1430, and electoral practice in individual boroughs was determined by varying local custom.

A statute of 1404 instituted penalties against those who assaulted MPs that went beyond the common-law penalties for assault; and, although the right was not enshrined in statute, MPs enjoyed the privilege of freedom of arrest for debt and other civil pleas during the course of a parliamentary session. More tentative was their assertion of the right to freedom of speech. At least one MP believed in 1455 that it was the 'old liberty' of he and his fellows to speak as they saw fit without fear of punishment, but the Commons is not known to have made any formal request for such freedom until 1523.

Political Role

An older tradition of scholarship maintained that the institutional development of the Commons in this period was not translated into an independent political role. On the one hand, it is argued, its bargaining with the crown over taxation and the redress of grievances equated with real political weight only when anachronistically viewed from the perspective of a later age; on the other, MPs subservience to the Lords, to which they were individually bound by ties of clientage, was so complete that they could offer opposition to the executive only as the tools of baronial faction.[4] Modern scholarship presents a more nuanced view. Undoubtedly, the Commons looked to the Lords for leadership in matters of high politics, yet in lesser matters it was capable of maintaining an independent line. In the fields of local government and the administration of justice, it consistently espoused a view very much at odds with that of the upper House. In the 1320s it complained bitterly about baronial maintenance and abuses of the law; in the reigns of Richard II and Henry IV it sought to restrain the unbridled distribution of livery badges by peers; and the electoral legislation it successfully sought in the early 15th century was designed to limit baronial (as well as royal) influence on parliamentary elections. This independence of mind could extend further. Even though the baronial opposition to Richard II and Henry VI was able to orchestrate the hostility of the Commons to the government, it was not it that called that opposition into being. Indeed, on occasion, the Commons was the more radical, as in the impeachment of William de la Pole, duke of Suffolk in 1450 and, arguably, also in that of the duke's grandfather, Michael de la Pole, earl of Suffolk, in 1386.

More difficult to refute is the idea that the Commons' rights of assent to taxation and legislation was yet to be translated into independent political power: the redress of its grievances, despite its occasional attempts to assert the contrary, remained a matter of royal grace, yet it was under an obligation to grant taxation as necessity demanded (a necessity largely interpreted by the crown); and its right means of assent to new law was a theoretical rather than a practical restraint on the king's freedom of

---

[4] G. O. Sayles, *The King's Parliament of England* (1975), 109–36.

legislative action. Nor can there be any doubt that the crown, in most circumstances, had the reserves of power to bend the Commons to its will. Not only could it call and dismiss the Commons, but it could also choose its place of assembly. A summons away from Westminster was a occasional means of securing a compliant Commons: in 1459, for example, the Lancastrian regime called parliament to its stronghold at Coventry to secure the attainder of their Yorkist opponents.

A more routine means of asserting control was through royal servants among the members. In the early 14th century relatively few MPs were royal officials or members of the royal household, but in many of the parliaments of the 15th century, such men came to form a significant minority in the Commons. In the parliament of 1453, to take an admittedly extreme example, as many as 61 of the 278 known MPs were royal servants. This process of control was taken a step further by Edward IV and the first two Tudor kings: their easy relations with the Commons were facilitated in part through the Speaker, usually an experienced lawyer in royal service.

Nevertheless, the fact remains that the Commons could be a place of serious confrontation between king and subjects. When the executive was weak, the Commons took up itself the responsibility for correcting what it saw as royal misgovernance, as it did, for example, in 1376, 1386 and 1450, resorting to the novel process of impeachment to remove royal ministers it saw as corrupt. In doing so, its voice gained an additional force, as it did in the field of taxation, because it was the representative of communities in the way that the Lords was not. Further, the new techniques evolved under the Yorkist and early Tudor kings for royal supervision of its deliberations can itself be read as testimony to its political independence. It would, however, be wrong to create the impression that a naturally fractious Commons was restrained only by royal management, or to conceptualize it only in terms of its ability to restrain monarchical power or to mould government policy. Medieval MPs would not have seen themselves as engaged in the pursuit of either of these aims. Consensus rather than conflict was the normal state of their relations with the crown: by granting taxation and enacting legislation they extended the power of an able king. Yet, on occasion, they could bring home forcefully to a failing one the grievances of the realm.

Chronology

1325
Last parliament to which the Commons are not summoned

1339
October Commons asked to consult their constituents before making a grant of taxation

1340
March Commons make their grant of taxation conditional on the appointment of a baronial council to supervise its expenditure

1376
'Good' Parliament, the first recorded occasion on which the Commons are represented by a Speaker; impeachment of court clique

1381
Peasants' Revolt

1401
January Commons request that their petitions be answered before they make a grant of taxation

1404
Statute (5 Hen. IV, c. 6) imposing penalties for those who assaulted MPs

1406
'Long' Parliament

1414
Commons claim that legislation is dependant upon their assent

1430
Statute (8 Hen. VI, c. 7) establishing the 40s. franchise

1489
Judges rule that legislation is invalid without the assent of the Commons

1529
'Reformation' Parliament

Further Reading

S. B. Chrimes, *English Constitutional Ideas in the Fifteenth Century* (Cambridge, 1936)

L. Clark, 'Magnates and their Affinities in the Parliaments of 1386–1421', in *The McFarlane Legacy: Studies in Late Medieval Politics and Society*, ed. R. H. Britnell and A. J. Pollard (Stroud, 1995), 127–53

J. G. Edwards, *The Second Century of the English Parliament* (Oxford, 1978)

The English Parliament in the Middle Ages, ed. R. G. Davies and J. H. Denton (Manchester, 1981)

G. L. Harriss, *King, Parliament and Public Finance in Medieval England to 1369* (Oxford, 1975)

Historical Studies of the English Parliament, ed. E. B. Fryde and E. Miller (2 vols, Cambridge, 1970)

The House of Commons, 1386–1421, ed. J. S. Roskell, L. Clark and C. Rawcliffe (4 vols, Stroud, 1992)

M. McKisack, *The Parliamentary Representation of the English Boroughs during the Middle Ages* (Oxford, 1932)

Parchment and People: Parliament in the Middle Ages, ed. L. Clark (Edinburgh, 2004) [special issue of *Parliamentary History*, xxiii/1]

Parliamentary Texts of the Later Middle Ages, ed. N. Pronay and J. Taylor (Oxford, 1979)

The Parliament Rolls of Medieval England, 1275–1504, ed. C. Given-Wilson *et al.* (16 vols, Woodbridge, 2005)

J. S. Roskell, *The Commons and their Speakers in English Parliaments, 1376–1523* (Manchester, 1965)

—— *The Commons in the Parliament of 1422* (Manchester, 1954)

N. Saul, 'The Commons and the Abolition of Badges', *Parliamentary History*, ix (1990), 302–15

G. O. Sayles, *The King's Parliament of England* (1975)

9 The House of Commons, 1529–1601
Alasdair Hawkyard

Meeting Places

Under the Tudor dynasty the House of Commons ceased to use the London Blackfriars (1529) and the refectory at Westminster Abbey (1529–44) as a meeting place and acquired a permanent meeting place of its own in the chapel of the recently dissolved college of St Stephen at Westminster in the late 1540s. The inner chapel of St Stephen's measuring 57' 6" long by 32' 10" wide provided the debating chamber while the outer chapel was adapted as a lobby (28' × 32'), a committee room, various chambers for the staff and a lavatory called the bog house. In the roof there was a purpose-built muniment room. The chamber's poor acoustics provoked complaints from members unable to follow proceedings clearly.

Membership

During the same period the Commons underwent considerable expansion. In 1529 there were 310 members (or 155 constituencies represented). By 1586, when Elizabeth I brought the process to a temporary hiatus, there were 462 members (or 243 constituencies). As early as 1579 the queen had refused to enfranchise Newark on the grounds that there were 'over many' members.[1] Between 1604 and 1629 the total rose to 493 members (or 259 constituencies). This enlargement, particularly after the arrival of Welsh members in 1542, resulted in every region within the kingdom becoming represented in the House.

Recognition of the social and economic modesty of some of the new additions, against the power of ancient, much more vibrant communities such as Bristol, Exeter, London and Norwich, meant that an increasing number of the new creations had only one member. Some of the additions did not last long, Calais barely 22 years until its capture by the French in 1558, and the three constituencies in County Durham less than a year in 1553. In 1549 Newborough on Anglesey was demoted on account of its poverty in favour of the more prosperous nearby Beaumaris. But the general principle of rationalizing representation by transferring the franchise to other places lacking membership seems not to have found favour, and was not repeated.

---

[1] *The History of Parliament: The House of Commons, 1558–1603*, ed. P. W. Hasler (3 vols, 1981), i, 55.

The Union with Wales

From the mid-13th century the four Welsh bishops (Bangor, Llandaff, St Asaph and St David's) were regularly summoned to parliament. Unlike their English counterparts, no abbots were summoned from the Welsh monasteries. Apart from the parliaments of 1322 and 1327, no members sat for Wales in the House of Commons in the middle ages, with the names of those for North Wales extant from the second occasion.

The Act for the Administration of Justice in Wales (27 Hen. VIII, c. 26) passed in 1536, more commonly known as the Act of Union, formed part of the Tudor dynasty's programme of rationalizing administration in the localities. The act allowed for parliamentary representation, both of the shires and group-borough constituencies, allocated a single person each, and the payment of wages to the Welsh members. On account of its poverty Merioneth was allowed a knight of the shire, but its boroughs no burgess. Monmouthshire was finally separated from the rest of the region and formally incorporated into England; in recognition of its greater prosperity it was allocated a higher representation than the Welsh counties. Delays in the work of reorganization meant that the administration necessary for the holding of elections was not in place until 1541. The first returns by Wales and Monmouthshire were to the parliament of 1542, when to mark the occasion Henry VIII elaborated the opening with honouring a selection of members with knighthoods and Speaker Moyle delivered a memorable speech. Further problems arising from the execution of the Union led in 1543 to another act (34 and 35 Hen. VIII, c. 26), sometimes called the Second Act of Union, resolving these issues, and also making Haverfordwest a parliamentary borough.

According to contemporary regulations and custom members were expected to be residents in their constituencies. Departure from these expectations was officially frowned upon, notably by Mary I, and in response to her clearly stated preference for burgesses there was an upsurge in the number of townsmen with municipal experience during the mid-1550s and in 1604. However, if one accepts an ostensibly less clear-cut notion of residency, that is men well-known in the locality, with property and interests there, there is no significant change in the nature of the membership throughout the period beyond a modest fluctuation in the precise balance between townsmen and local gentlemen. Some two-thirds of the members were familiar figures to their constituents. The local gentlemen more often than not had attended an inn of court in the capital, as part of their education, and thus had some grounding in the law. But to see them as practising lawyers seeking to advance their own careers to the exclusion of townsmen, as has been

The Northern Palatinates

Of the three palatinates in the north (Cheshire, Durham and Lancashire) in the middle ages, only Lancashire returned knights and burgesses for over two and a half centuries. In 1283 the town of Chester was summoned to send two members to the parliament to sentence David of Wales for his part in the recent Welsh insurrection. In the case of Cheshire, legislation enacted in parliament affecting the county palatine had to receive approval in the *parliamentum* of the county court before enforcement. Changes made by the Tudors in the running of the county court deprived Cheshire of any say in the measures affecting it. The enfranchisement of Cheshire with two knights and Chester with two citizens in 1543 by an act (34 and 35 Hen. VIII, c. 13) remedied the anomaly.

Taxation voted in parliament applied to the inhabitants of County Durham without their having any right of approval, however nominal. Successive bishops resisted any attempt to enfranchise the county palatine. Following the imprisonment of Bishop Tunstal for treason in 1552, the Edwardian regime took steps to reform the palatinate. The series of changes put in hand included in 1553 writs authorizing the election of a knight for the county, a citizen for the cathedral city and a burgess for an unidentified borough. After the accession of Mary I, Tunstal was released and many of the recent changes in the palatinate and the bishopric reversed, including the suspension of parliamentary representation. Repeated efforts to resecure enfranchisement came to nothing until the Protectorate when Oliver Cromwell summoned members from the county and the city. In 1673 an act (25 Chas. II, c. 10) provided for a writ to be sent to the bishop authorizing the issue of a precept to the sheriff, and the county and the city to be enfranchised, with two knights and two citizens respectively.

The Earl of Hertford's Letter of 1541 to the Isle of Jersey

Late in December 1541, the earl of Hertford in his capacity as captain of Jersey wrote to the island telling it to elect 'two of the discretist & of most experience in the state of the same Isle' to the parliament to meet in three weeks' time. Hertford undertook to ensure that the pair would be admitted as members. Whether Jersey complied with his instructions is not known, nor whether any of the captains of the other Channel Islands sent letters in a similar vein there.*

* *Actes des États de Jersey, 1524–1596* (Société Jersiaise xii, 1897), 9–10.

done,[2] is to misunderstand the facts. Nevertheless, some of the poorer boroughs, notably in Cornwall, Lancashire, Sussex, Wiltshire and Yorkshire were havens for outsiders, often from far afield.

The expectation whereby the Speaker should be a knight of the shire underwent modification although it remained the aspiration. The first Speaker who certainly did not represent a county was Sir John Baker, in 1545 a member for Lancaster, The circumstantial evidence is that following their nomination by the crown the Speaker-designate often fell victim to successful attempts by the electorate to derail the crown's plans, and they often had to look for seats other than a county which they could no longer rely upon as a prescriptive right. In 1584 John Puckering was the first Speaker to be chosen without having any previous experience of the House of Commons. This lack of experience did not prove an impediment, and two years later he was chosen for a second term in the post.

Whenever public bills were known in advance, the crown and other interested parties clearly tried to ensure that men with professional expertise relevant to these measures were members. Thomas Eynns. Prince Edward's secretary entered the Commons in 1543 in time for the discussion of the prince's Welsh patrimony, and presumably to defend it. Following the Submission of the Clergy in 1532 convocation ceased to legislate on church matters and parliament dealt with ecclesiastical business. This may have prompted clergyman to seek membership in the Commons. But in October 1553 there were challenges to the membership of John Foster and Alexander Nowell, that is two men in holy orders; and, as master of Westminster School, Nowell, at least, was ejected. This precedent was to be periodically contested, without any success.

Members remained entitled to speak freely during debates, provided they kept to the subject under discussion. However, they found ways and means to raise points close to their hearts. Thus, during a debate on fortifying the Scottish border in 1532, Thomas Temys argued that it would be unnecessary if Henry VIII was reconciled to Catherine of Aragon; the thrust of his argument was that if the king kept his wife the international situation would not deteriorate, and there would be no war between England and Scotland. Both the marriage of the monarch and the succession of the crown were repeatedly raised until 1603. The parliament of 1572 was summoned specifically to discuss the problems raised by the arrival in England of Mary, queen of Scots. This created a precedent that could not be reversed. The freedom to speak freely resulted in tumultuous debates, described laconically as 'arguments' or 'murmurings'. The bills dissolving colleges and chantries in 1545 and 1547, the Marian measures to reverse the Henrician and Edwardian ecclesiastical legislation, and the Elizabethan church settlement in 1559 were such occasions. During the 1570s and 1580s Peter Wentworth ignored the traditional limits upon free

---

[2] G. R. Elton, 'The Body of the Whole Realm': Parliament and Representation in Medieval and Tudor England (Charlottesville, VA, 1969).

speech: he argued that without untrammelled speech parliament was little more that 'a very school of flattery and dissimulation and soe a fitt place to serve the Devil'.[3] The right to freedom from arrest for members and their servants, and from seizure of goods while parliament was sitting established earlier was jealously guarded. Following George Ferrers's arrest for debt in 1542 members brought business to a complete standstill for two weeks while they discussed it. Following a brawl in St Paul's churchyard in 1573 where a man died from his injuries the House insisted upon Arthur Hall paying damages, thereby establishing the principle that it could discipline as well as protect the servants of members.

When the practice of members taking an oath before entering the premises of the House of Commons at the opening of parliament originated is not clear. It may have been established in the wake the Act of Supremacy in 1534 when Henry VIII was declared the head of the church in England. The form was set out in the Acts of Succession of 1536 and 1545. The members renounced all other foreign rulers. In 1555, under Queen Mary, the oath was repealed, but within four years it was reinstated by her sister Elizabeth. In 1563 the taking of the oath by members was made compulsory. Its effect in the long term was to preclude Roman Catholics from election to parliament.

Notwithstanding the meagreness of the evidence, it is clear that at the beginning of the period that members continued to be paid for attending parliament, or expected to be. Some of them negotiated a remission of their wages in order to ensure election. Not all the constituencies paid the full statutory rate of 4s. a day for the shires and 2s. a day for the boroughs. London and some of the wealthier constituencies also provided garments for their representatives befitting their status as well as the cost of boat hire along the Thames. Some of the poorest boroughs contributed nothing. Wages evidently continued to be paid without any significant abatement.

The Electorate and Elections

As a result of inflation in the 16th century, there was an increase in the number of those entitled to vote in the rural shires, that is the 40s. freeholders. In contrast, in the urban counties (that is the cities, towns and boroughs with shire status) the franchise remained constant, being limited to the ruling oligarchy, often to the town council varying in size between 12 and 48, with the single exception of London, where liverymen numbering 500 or more took part. During the period the right to vote was curtailed in some constituencies, often in an attempt to curb disturbances at elections. In the boroughs the size of the participating electorate varied in size from over 100 to less than ten. At Gatton the right to vote was attached to a single property owned by the Copley family.

---

[3] *Proceedings in the Parliament of Elizabeth I*, ed. T. E. Hartley (3 vols, Leicester, 1981–95), i. 426.

For the first 25 years of our period the men returned at elections were not necessarily the same as those who entered the House. Following the elections the sheriffs sent in the names of those elected. Those returned then went to the opening of parliament, where some on being approached by other interested parties decided to withdraw, or where if returned for more than one constituency they opted for which to represent. The sheriffs accordingly amended the election indentures in the light of these amicable arrangements. This was how Thomas Cromwell entered the parliament of 1529. This practice continued until November 1554. During the parliament of 1547 the Speaker had directed that the return for Sandwich be examined to ascertain the names of its members. Early in 1553 a committee was set up by the House to investigate Maidstone's right to representation, and later in the same year a pair to consider the validity of the elections at Plympton Erle and West Looe. These were the first recorded committees for returns whereby the House came to regulate its own membership. The success of these committees accounts for the ending of the earlier practice with which for a several years they ran in tandem. The Speaker, on behalf of the House, authorized the issue of writs by chancery for replacements.

Elections were sometimes disputed on account of breaches of electoral law. Traditionally these breaches were referred to the lord chancellor, the privy council, the regional councils, and the law courts. In 1586, following the disputed election in Norfolk, two returns were delivered into chancery and a complaint somewhat unusually made to the House. Notwithstanding that Elizabeth I upheld the historic right of chancery to decide the outcome of such disputes, the House insisted that it had the power to do so. Three years later it allowed that the names certified by chancery to it should be accepted, albeit with a degree of reluctance.

By-elections had originated earlier in the Tudor period to deal with the case where for some reason a member was deemed to have become physically incapacitated, and thus was unable to perform his parliamentary duties. Originally they were not seen as answers to the gaps in the membership arising from ennoblement, death, imprisonment, flight abroad or employment on embassies. This refinement was largely conceived and realized by Thomas Cromwell during 1532–3. Half a century later in 1581 the House decided that the pretext of physical incapacity had been abused and should no longer be allowed. Even so, with its habitual inability to adhere to procedural decisions, within a quarter of a century, the pretext of physical incapacity was revived. Despite its obsession with precedents, whenever it suited the members they ignored what they had previously agreed and followed.

Meetings and Procedure

The House of Commons met daily except Sunday. Until the Reformation it did not meet on the major religious festivals. The number of these was then reduced, but during the restoration of Catholicism under Mary I

Ash Wednesday was briefly reinstated. From 1559 proceedings for the day started with the under-clerk saying the litany, followed by prayers. Anyone absent was expected to pay 4d. into the poor-box. In the mid-16th century the times of business were restricted normally to the morning, committees and conferences being held in the afternoon, but from 1542, at least, the Commons met in the afternoon in order to complete as much work as possible before the prorogation or dissolution. With the single exception of the subsidy bill which it drafted and the passage of which determined the length of a session, bills were normally expedited with speed. The bill for the dissolution of the lesser monasteries in 1536 passed through the House within less than seven days. Examples of measures provoking intense scrutiny, which thus took somewhat longer, are the Militia and Musters Acts of 1558, the Act of Uniformity of 1559 and the Treasons Act of 1571.

From 1571 the Commons agreed first to meet in the afternoon three times in order to give private bills a first reading then every afternoon to allow a second. This arrangement ensured a drop in the number of bills left unfinished at the dissolution of the parliament of 1571. But the practice in later parliaments increasingly to use the afternoon session as an extension of the morning's business meant that throughout the period the total figure of unfinished bills, including those lost in passage, remained consistently in the region of 40.

The regime prepared in advance a list of bills which it hoped to see enacted. To this nucleus it added other official bills which if unfinished, that is if they had not completed their passage through both Houses by the time the subsidy bill had been agreed, the monarch and minsters were prepared to lose. When no monetary grant was involved, the two considerations determining the length of a session were the contemporary preference for short parliaments and the time that it took to approve the key items of legislation. Thus the parliament of November 1554 was dissolved once the treasons bill had passed, that is three weeks after the date originally envisaged.

Divisions had originated in the parliament of 1523 as a means for Cardinal Wolsey to ascertain the full extent of the opposition to the subsidy bill then under consideration. They evolved in the mid-Tudor period from simple divisions where literally the members divided, that is moved from one side of the House to another to denote their support (the ayes) or opposition (the noes), to a method adopted by the early 1550s whereby the supporters of a measure left the debating chamber while the opponents remained seated there. This evolution reflected the constrictions of St Stephen's Chapel, which lacked the space for the movement necessitated by divisions as originally conceived. Acclamation continued to be the means preferred for showing acceptance or rejection.

The scope and variety of committees underwent expansion. Originally their purpose seems to have been to defuse the uproar provoked in debate by identifying the key issues of contention which they then sought to resolve before returning the bill to the debating chamber. The bills under consideration were 'committed' to a select body of members for detailed evaluation and any necessary amendment at any stage during their passage. The men selected were nominated on the basis of known expertise in the relevant field, or of interest demonstrated during debate. In the Bill in Restraint of Appeals in 1533 Thomas Cromwell seems to have sought a conspectus of opinion. In this he may have been breaking with

The Royal Assent

The royal assent was customarily given to a bill on passing both houses of parliament. The monarch gave it once a session to all the bills, and immediately following the ceremony parliament was prorogued or dissolved. Any measure then left unfinished was lost. The giving of the assent defined the length of a parliament and its sessions.

In 1542 Queen Catherine Howard was attainted in parliament for adultery. To spare Henry VIII any further pain and to ensure that no other business then in hand was lost, the privy council devised a scheme whereby the king authorized a select panel of eminent figures to give the assent on his behalf. Five years later, while the king lay dying, the same expedients was adopted with the bill attainting the 3rd duke of Norfolk and his son the earl of Surrey for treason.

In the autumn of 1553 Mary I was so delighted by the speedy passage of the bill forming the cornerstone of her religious policy that she came in person to give her assent, with the result that the other pieces of her proposed legislation, no less important, and the money bill, were lost, and these had to be reintroduced in a new, second session. To prevent a similar scenario a year later arising from the reversal of Cardinal Pole's attainder, the regime persuaded parliament 'if, upon the royal assent, [it] may proceed without any prorogation'.* The following day the queen gave her assent. This was the first occasion that the royal assent was given in person without all the unfinished work being lost. Neither Mary I nor her sister Elizabeth I availed herself of this precedent, but with the development of multi-sessional parliaments spanning several years in the 17th century the Stuart monarchs came to use it with regularity.

During the civil wars in the 1640s, with Charles I and parliament in conflict, and the king away from London, the bills passed by both Houses were enforced as ordinances. The same expedient held after the king's execution in 1649 until the establishment of the protectorate in 1654 after which the Lord Protector consented to legislation. At the restoration in 1660 none of the measures passed in the previous 18 were recognized, and because they lacked the royal assent the original ordinances and acts from the period were destroyed.

* CJ, i, 38.

established custom. In 1601 it was decided that no one who had spoken against a bill could serve on its committee. Initially, only the names of the chairmen of the larger committees were noted but from 1571 the journal records the names of all those chosen. Not all those nominated chose to take part in the work. Committees were also used to draft legislation. The emergence of select committees to address specific problems, draft messages, consider petitions, or conduct enquiries is more difficult to chart as these were only rarely recorded in the journal as first conceived. In 1552 a select committee to consider the validity of certain returns was ordered.

During the 1590s the Commons devised 'general' committees which later became known as committees of the whole House. These achieved a settled form during 1606–7. The Speaker surrendered the chair to another Member, and the normal rules of debate were relaxed to allow participants to make multiple contributions. Because of the Speaker's withdrawal, the committee of the whole House has been seen as a key weapon in the Commons' effort to free itself from the crown's control. In reality, it evolved with government encouragement as a means of transacting business more efficiently. By definition, committees of the whole House met in the Commons chamber. Other committees used the committee room above the lobby in St Stephen's Chapel, Star Chamber and the Court of Wards in the old palace of Westminster, rooms in the new palace better known a Whitehall, the inns of court, Serjeants' Inn, the Savoy, the London Guildhall and elsewhere.

Management

During the 16th century the work of the House of Commons continued to be directed by a Speaker, ostensibly elected by the members, but in actuality chosen by the crown whose nominee they merely rubber-stamped. The crown's nominee was invariably a lawyer held in high regard and a man with previous experience as a member. The first Speaker to have no such experience was John Puckering in 1584. This did not prove a serious impediment to Puckering, who went on to be Speaker for a second term in 1586. From 1415 the Speaker had a serjeant at arms from the royal household attached to him, with particular responsibility for controlling access to the premises. The House was managed on behalf of the crown by the treasurer, comptroller and vice-chamberlain of the royal household backed by a handful of their closest colleagues there. These men were also privy councillors. This method held true even during the 1530s, 60s and 90s, when Thomas Cromwell, and Sir William Cecil and his son Sir Robert Cecil as secretaries dominated the Henrician and Elizabethan regimes and were sitting in the Commons. At the nucleus of every parliament was a contingent from the household who were bound by oath to do whatever the monarch and the chamberlain and his deputies told them to do. Others in the service of the crown also bound by similar oaths when combined with the men from the household provided the government with the potential means to obtain the successful passage of any legislation that it wanted. Sometimes when it came to the crunch these men voted against their consciences. Only a relatively small number of members not in the service of the crown had to be persuaded by reason or threats as to a bill's merit to ensure its acceptance. Even so, not all bills of interest to the crown were enacted. The bill to penalize Protestant exiles failed in 1555, when Sir Anthony Kingston demanded a vote and, snatching the key from the serjeant at arms, locked the outer door. Whatever the extent of the passions elicited by certain bills, any opposition was individual and particular to each bill. Groups of members with shared views or common interests existed. These joined together or disbanded as the occasion demanded. There was no continuity of purpose.

Records of Procedure

Under the aegis of the under-clerk the bureaucracy of the House underwent transformation. To the book of orders and usages and the register of leave of absence both kept by him and the lists of members compiled by the clerk of the crown but then maintained by him he added the journal from the autumn of 1547. As originally conceived and developed by John Seymour (d. 1567) this was fundamentally a record of bills and their passage. Seymour's successor Fulk Onslow (d. 1602) initially followed his model but from 1572 onwards Onslow became gradually more expansive. After 1580 the journal kept by Onslow is lost, though much of its text is preserved in Sir Simonds D'Ewes's 17th-century edition of the Elizabethan journals.

The members continued to make reports on what happened in the House to their constituents. From this period it is clear that they also kept notes on parliamentary business for their own use, the earliest known (but now lost) diary, that of Edward Hall being subsumed where appropriate in his *Chronicle*.[4] During the parliament of 1563 William Lambarde compiled a set of notes on procedures which circulated extensively in manuscript after his death in 1601,[5] and during his successor of 1571 John Hooker *alias* Vowell made similar notes on the orders and usages.[6] The transfer of Sir William Cecil to the House of Lords in 1571 as Lord Burleigh seems to have catalysed record keeping. The under-clerk provided Burleigh regularly with brief summaries on where bills had reached in their progress. Daily reporting on the activity in the House to the lord chancellor and others had long been customary, and verbally given, but after 1571 these reports seem to have been submitted increasingly in writing. From 1571 there exists a

---

4 Edward Hall, *Chronicle*, ed. J. Johnson, F. and C. Rivington, and T. Payne (1816).

5 *William Lambarde's Notes on the Proceedings of the House of Commons (1584)*, ed. P. L. Ward (House of Commons Document No. 10, n.d.).

6 V. F. Snow, *Parliament in Elizabethan England: John Hooker's Order and Usage* (New Haven, 1977).

> ### Sir Simonds D'Ewes
>
> With the encouragement of his friend Sir Robert Cotton, Sir Simonds D'Ewes formed a collection of copies of original manuscripts intended for use in his writing a history of England. In 1625 he saw 'an elaborate journal' of the parliament of 1593 which was a member's personal compilation, and not part of the Commons journal, led him to have transcribed it for the entire reign. Either he or the copyists engaged by him omitted the names given in lists of Members nominated to serve on committees and other small details thought by them to be of no or little interest. The team incorporated details from other sources, including a diary kept by Sir William Cecil, which do not appear in the extant journals. The work of transcription was largely completed by 1632 but nothing came of the study for which it had been meant, although D'Ewes's knowledge of procedure resting on it presumably stood him in good stead as a member of the Long Parliament. 'These volumes are intended chiefly for my own private use, and my Posterities.' Over 30 years after his death the copies were published in 1682 as *The Journal of All the Parliaments during the Reign of Queen Elizabeth*. Following the disappearance of the original journals between 1580 and 1603, *The Journal* provides us with the torso of the lost original manuscript. Scrutiny of the published volume against what survives of the original journal suggests that Paul Bowes who revised and published the transcription may have taken liberties with it, or even been careless in seeing it through the press, but it is more likely that the original manuscript after 1570 made available to D'Ewes was a rough version made preliminary to the final, clean copy that now survives.* His text of the journal for the first part of the reign may also derive from a variant no longer extant.
>
> * ODNB, xvi, 1–3; Sir Simonds D'Ewes, *The Journal of All the Parliaments during the Reign of Queen Elizabeth* (1682), preface.

plethora of diaries meant either as *aides-memoires* or for the reference of public figures elsewhere; for example, John Hooker, Thomas Cromwell (the grandson of Henry VIII's minister), William Fleetwood, Sir Willliam Fitzwilliam, Henry Jackman and Hayward Townshend.[7]

Legislation

Of the bills enacted the greater number started life in the House of Commons, with the single exception of the parliament of 1539, when, interestingly, Thomas Cromwell as Lord Cromwell sat in the upper House. This figure does not portend the eventual supremacy of the

[7] *Proceedings in the Parliaments of Elizabeth I*, ed. Hartley, i–iii.

Commons, only that it sat more often and for longer, and thus there were greater opportunities to introduce measures there. Analysis of the bills enacted reveals the extent of regional interest in legislation, either in measures introduced by their representatives or in response by the crown to problems referred to it by the localities. Another feature of mid-Tudor legislation is the number of provisos obtained by members safeguarding their own interests. In the 1540s the quantity noticeably fell, and after March 1553, when Sir Francis Jobson failed to obtain a personal proviso, they ceased. The House of Commons practice in how it dealt with bills was not fixed in 1529 although it had become more so a century later. The number of readings received varied between three and six until 1558. There were several occasions when a bill received four readings early in Elizabeth I's reign, but a maximum of three readings became the norm. Some bills underwent radical amendment, such as the Elizabethan church settlement in 1559. In the case of the church settlement, however, the members may have played into Elizabeth I's hands, as she had been cautioned to be temperate in how she broke with Rome. She could argue that she was merely accepting an expression of the will of her subjects, not imposing her wishes upon them.

The Monarch

Under the Tudors the monarch resided at Whitehall, or occasionally nearby at St James's, while parliament was in session, with the single exception of the first session of the parliament of 1586, when Elizabeth I stayed at Richmond in an effort to dissociate herself from the proceedings against Mary, queen of Scots. Lord Burleigh drew the queen's attention to the unnecessary stress placed on him and his colleagues by the need to keep her informed at a distance and ensuring not only that monarch and ministers remained in broad agreement over the course of action being followed but also problems were addressed and resolved promptly. The difficulties raised by Burleigh re-emerged in the next reign to face the earl of Salisbury and other Jacobean ministers when James I left Whitehall to go hunting or attend the races while parliament was in session. Residence at Whitehall ensured that Henry VIII, Edward VI, Mary I and Elizabeth I were able to keep a close watch on business there. The Speaker reported to the monarch on a regular basis and headed delegations from the lower House on given points. These meetings enabled the monarch to make known his or her observations on proceedings. Henry VIII, Mary I and Elizabeth I also summoned delegations to their presence whenever it suited them. Henry VIII, at least, also summoned individuals. In 1533 he summoned to his presence Sir George Throckmorton who opposed the bill in restraint of appeals to Rome in a vain attempt to persuade him to change. In the previous year the king had gone in person to the House to end the impasse over the bill in restraint of payment of annates and had ordered a division in his presence. Four years later he went again to deliver the bill for the dissolution of the lesser monasteries. In 1545 he returned again. In an attempt to stall the increasingly vehement criticism of Mary, queen of Scots in 1586, Elizabeth I considered visiting the House of Commons, but at the very last moment she decided against it.[8] The lord chancellor and noblemen close to the monarch also visited the House to keep the members informed on certain issues and to apply pressure for money grants.

[8] *Proceedings in the Parliaments of Elizabeth I*, ed. Hartley, ii, 102.

Chronology

1532
Submission of the Clergy

1532–53
The Reformation

1532
Act in Restraint of Appeals to Rome

1534
Act of Supremacy

1536
Act to Dissolve the Lesser Monasteries

1540
Act Suppressing the Knights Hospitallers

1542
Arrest and imprisonment of George Ferrers

1545
Act to Dissolve Religious Foundation

1547
Death of Henry VIII; accession of Edward VI; Act to Dissolve Religious Foundations

1553
Death of Edward VI; accession of Mary I

1553–8
Restoration of Catholicism; reversal of Henrician and Edwardian ecclesiastical legislation

1554
Treasons Act

1555
Act to Penalize Protestant Exiles

1558
Militia and Musters Acts; Death of Mary I; accession of Elizabeth I

1559
Elizabethan church settlement

1563
Oath of Supremacy

1571
Treasons Act

1597-1601
Monopolies agitation

1603
Death of Elizabeth I; accession of James I

Further Reading

D. Dean, *Law-Making and Society in Late Elizabethan England, 1584–1601* (Cambridge, 1996)

G. R. Elton, *The Parliament of England, 1559–1581* (Cambridge, 1986)

M. A. R. Graves, *Early Tudor Parliaments, 1485–1558* (1990)

—— *The Tudor Parliaments: Crown, Lords and Commons, 1485–1603* (1985)

T. E. Hartley, *Elizabeth's Parliaments: Queen, Lords and Commons, 1559–1601* (Manchester, 1992)

A. Hawkyard, *The House of Commons, 1509–1558: Introductory Survey* (forthcoming)

The History of Parliament: The House of Commons, 1509–1558, ed. S. T. Bindoff (3 vols, 1982)

The History of Parliament: The House of Commons, 1558–1603, ed. P. W. Hasler (3 vols, 1981)

S. E. Lehmberg, *The Later Parliaments of Henry VIII, 1536–1547* (Cambridge, 1977)

—— *The Reformation Parliament, 1529–1536* (Cambridge, 1970)

J. Loach, *Parliament and Crown in the Reign of Mary Tudor* (Oxford, 1986)

—— *Parliament under the Tudors* (Oxford, 1991)

J. E. Neale, *Elizabeth I and her Parliaments, 1559–1581* (1953)

—— *Elizabeth I and her Parliaments, 1584–1601* (1957)

—— *The Elizabethan House of Commons* (1949)

10 The House of Commons, 1603–29
Paul M. Hunneyball

In the early 17th century the House of Commons finally began to emerge from the shadow of the Lords, securing greater control over its own affairs, and gradually extending its cognizance in matters of state. Crucially, by the end of this period members were presenting themselves as the true champions of constitutional freedom. However, a substantial increase in business was not matched by improved efficiency, while the deteriorating relationship between the Commons and the crown placed the future of parliament itself in doubt.

Growth and Representation

The early Stuart period saw the first mass-produced views of the Commons in session. Except in 1625, when parliament briefly met at Oxford to avoid an outbreak of plague, St Stephen's Chapel at Westminster was now firmly established as the Commons' normal meeting place. These crude early engravings popularized a stereotypical image of the main chamber's interior, with members crammed into rows of benches around a central space dominated by the Speaker's chair and the under-clerk's desk. Some versions omit the fifth rank of seats added in 1604, and none show the gallery constructed above the entrance in 1621, but the sense of overcrowding invariably comes across clearly. Indeed, by this time the chamber could hold no more than around half the assembled House. There were 462 MPs in 1604, representing 243 constituencies, and by 1629 the enfranchisement of a further 16 boroughs had added 31 new members. James I initially encouraged this expansion, supporting the creation of seats for Oxford and Cambridge universities in 1604. Latterly, however, as his dealings with the Commons grew more fractious, he opposed further growth. In 1624 he vetoed the bill to enfranchise County Durham, arguing that decayed boroughs such as Old Sarum should first be abolished. Nevertheless, James failed to block the revival of several other boroughs which successfully staked a claim to Commons seats on the basis that they had sent representatives to Westminster at some point in the past.

The rise in the number of members did not make the Commons significantly more representative. Parliamentary franchises changed very little during this period. However, inflation continued to swell the ranks of the 40s. freeholders entitled to vote for knights of the shire. In 1624 and 1628 the Commons also widened the electorate in a handful of boroughs by settling disputed elections in favour of the candidates with the broader local appeal, and rejecting more restrictive voting customs. One such verdict, determining the dispute at Coventry in 1628, effectively abolished the time-honoured (but much abused) rule that members must be resident in their constituencies. In 1604 the king had specifically requested boroughs to elect local men, but in practice many members had only tenuous ties with the places that they represented. Smaller boroughs often stood to gain more by offering their seats to powerful external patrons who might help them in between parliaments, and outsiders were less likely to demand wages in return for serving at Westminster. That said, the larger towns in particular generally opted for local men who were best qualified to promote their constituencies' interests in the Commons.

Privileges and Organization

During this period, the Commons made significant progress towards managing its own affairs without external interference. In 1604 Sir Francis Goodwin's case established that the power to adjudicate in disputed election rested with the House, rather than with chancery. Conversely, Sir Christopher Piggott's case in 1607 established the Commons' right to expel its own members. Other long-standing privileges, such as members' freedom from arrest and from the confiscation of personal property, were also more clearly defined. These rights traditionally applied only to periods when parliament was actually sitting, with some allowance before and afterwards for members' travelling time. However, in 1629 John Rolle dramatically stretched this definition by claiming privilege for goods seized from him in October 1628. Parliament had not met then, although it had originally been scheduled to do so, and the Commons' ruling in favour of this rather hypothetical argument was therefore controversial. One sign of the Commons' greater capacity for self-government was a new emphasis on religious orthodoxy. From 1614 members were required not merely to take the customary oath of supremacy, but also to receive the Anglican sacraments at a corporate communion service in St Margaret's, Westminster. Failure to comply was punished by exclusion from the House, as the Roman Catholic Sir Thomas Gerrard discovered in 1624. While this development was doubtless partly a reaction to the fear of Catholics generated by the Gunpowder Plot of 1605, the mildly puritan ethos that it engendered also served to distance the Commons from the anti-Calvinist leanings of the royal court in the later 1620s.

The character of the early Stuart House is much easier to assess because of the relative wealth of records that survive. The Commons journal, which is no longer extant for the greater part of Elizabeth I's reign, survives again from 1604, either in draft or final version, with a brief break for the final session (October–December 1610) of the parliament of 1604. The underclerks, Ralph Ewens (1604–10) and John Wright (1614–29), recorded not just the formal proceedings but also some incidental details, such as the occasional unwelcome presence of strangers in the House. The Journal is supplemented by more than 50 contemporary private diaries, of widely varying quality and completeness. Edward Nicholas's extremely thorough notes from 1621, 1624 and 1628 were effectively informal reports for government ministers. Other authors, such as John Pym (1621, 1624 and 1625), were more selective and analytical, focusing on matters of particular interest to them. A handful of accounts, such as those of Robert Bowyer (1606–7) or Sir John Eliot (1625), also shed valuable light on the political manœuvrings that underpinned the formal business of the Commons.[1] The cumulative picture still falls well short of modern verbatim reporting, particularly with regard to debates. These were only ever summarized, and are almost entirely absent from the Journal in 1626 and 1628–9, probably because of members' concerns that their opinions were being monitored by the government. Even so, and particularly from 1621 onwards, it is possible to reconstruct events in remarkable detail.

The picture that emerges is not always edifying. The Commons' proceedings were frequently disorganized, and at moments of crisis even chaotic. Rebukes from the king typically prompted long periods of silence, while members pondered their next move. Nevertheless, there were now established protocols for the conduct of debates, such as the number and type of interventions that individuals were permitted to make during the passage of legislation, and these were generally enforced. There were few significant procedural innovations during this period. Bills normally went through just three readings and a committee stage, though exceptions to this rule were permissible. Voting was still primarily by simple acclamation. Formal divisions of the House, when those in favour left the chamber to facilitate an accurate count, remained comparatively rare. The most important procedural development was the proliferation of committees. In addition to the scrutiny of legislation, these were employed for drafting bills and other documents, the hearing of complaints, and the conduct of inquiries. As the scale and complexity of the Commons' business increased, sub-committees were more frequently used to address particular issues. The Elizabethan precedent of appointing a standing committee to deal throughout a session with privileges and elections was significantly extended, the early Stuart House establishing others to consider general grievances, trade, the courts of justice, and religion. Committees of the whole House, another late-16th-century innovation, were also more widely employed during these years. This format, which was largely perfected in 1606–7, removed many of the constraints of normal debating procedure.

[1] Edward Nicholas, *Proceedings and Debates of the House of Commons in 1620 and 1621* (2 vols, Oxford, 1766); National Archives, SP14/166 (Nicholas diary, 1624); *Commons Debates 1628*, ed. R. C. Johnson et al. (4 vols, New Haven, 1977–8), ii–iv (for Nicholas diary); *Commons Debates 1621*, ed. W. Notestein, F. H. Relf and H. Simpson (7 vols, New Haven, 1935), iv (Pym diary); Northamptonshire RO, FH 50; British Library, Harleian MS 6799; Add. MS 26639 (Pym diary 1624); *Proceedings in Parliament 1625*, ed. M. Jansson and W. B. Bidwell (New Haven, 1987) (for Pym diary and Eliot account); *Parliamentary Diary of Robert Bowyer, 1606–1607*, ed. D. H. Willson (New York, 1971).

A chairman other than the Speaker presided, and members could contribute as often as they wished. Although committees of the whole House served primarily to improve the Commons' efficiency, there is some truth in the notion that they could be exploited to limit the crown's control over events. For example, in 1628 members agreed in committee on a large tax grant requested by the government. However, they deliberately delayed reporting this decision back to the full House for a binding vote, thereby retaining a valuable bargaining counter in their negotiations with Charles I over the redress of grievances. The expansion of the Commons' committee workload had two noteworthy consequences. Hours of business lengthened, as afternoons and early mornings were increasingly assigned to committee deliberations. Also, members required extra accommodation for these meetings, and began to make greater use of other spaces around the palace of Westminster, such as Star Chamber and the Court of Wards.

Rising Confidence

From very early in the existence of parliament the country had followed the activities of MPs, with constituencies requiring reports from their representatives. Details of events and debates were frequently leaked despite the understanding that proceedings in the House were confidential. From 1621 lists of the MPs' names were published during each parliament. This innovation, apparently a private initiative, was linked to a sharp increase in lobbying, which in turn reflected the greater quantity of business that the Commons was attracting. During the parliament of 1621 in particular, the many inquiries launched by the lower House into monopolies, the legal system and other areas of grievance stimulated an upsurge in the number of petitions of complaint being received. The volume of new bills similarly soared during that session, partly because of the lack of fresh legislation in the previous decade, but also because the Commons actively promoted its image as a vehicle of reform.

Simultaneously the members displayed a growing tendency to stray into territory that had hitherto lain beyond their remit. In 1614 they offended James I by questioning the legitimacy of his recently created order of baronets, and were forced to back down. Nevertheless, during the 1620s the Commons regularly attempted to investigate matters relating to Ireland and the American colonies, largely ignoring the crown's clearly stated objections. Moreover, in that decade England's drift into war, and the government's consequent need to secure parliamentary taxation, provided the Commons with regular excuses to debate foreign policy. Despite members' initial hesitation in 1621 in broaching this previously forbidden topic, and the disastrous resultant dispute with James over freedom of speech, by 1626 the Commons was not only promoting its own alternative military strategy, but inquiring, albeit unsuccessfully, into the royal council of war's performance.

> ### Freedom of Speech and the Protestation of 1621
>
> At the start of each parliament the monarch granted the Speaker and members the liberty of speech which they increasingly interpreted as freedom of speech. It was generally acknowledged that this privilege must be exercised responsibly. Criticism of the king was unacceptable, and certain issues of state such as foreign policy or the royal succession were normally out of bounds, as they fell within the royal prerogative. Ordinarily the Commons was self-policing, anxious to avoid unnecessary wrangles with the crown. The king almost invariably came to hear of offending remarks, but members usually averted the royal wrath by claiming that he had been misinformed. In 1621, however, a major crisis developed which could not be so easily resolved. James I was seeking through diplomacy to end the Thirty Years War on the Continent, but his summoning of parliament fuelled expectations that he was preparing for military intervention. In November, confused messages from the crown's spokesmen convinced the Commons that it had permission to discuss foreign policy, whereupon a petition was rapidly prepared, which urged James to break off the current negotiations with Spain and go to war. When the king furiously condemned this infringement of his prerogative, members rushed to justify their behaviour. The ensuing war of words culminated in the Commons' protestation of 18 December, which asserted that freedom of speech to debate the vital affairs of the realm was not simply a privilege but the birthright of all members. Since the king would inevitably reject such a radical claim, the protestation was not sent to him, but instead inserted in the Commons journal as a permanent memorial. However, once the parliament was dissolved, James sent for the journal, and personally ripped out the protestation.

The significant point here is the Commons' eagerness to increase its influence, rather than the mostly minor concessions actually secured from the crown. However, some genuinely important advances were made through collaboration with the House of Lords. This was an uneasy and unequal partnership. Despite constant talk of 'good correspondency' between the two Houses, the peers rarely hesitated to assert their superior status and clout. When in 1614 and 1628 the bishop of Lincoln and earl of Suffolk insulted members, the Commons' demands for outright apologies were brushed aside. Similarly, the lower House was forced into a humiliating climbdown after it invaded the Lords' territory in 1621 by claiming the right to pass judgment on a Roman Catholic who had slandered the king's daughter. Nevertheless, the revival in 1621 of the medieval process of impeachment was possible only because the two Houses joined forces; the procedure required the Commons to prepare charges, which were then transmitted to the Lords for judgment. With this powerful weapon at their disposal, the Commons secured the dismissal of Lord Chancellor St

Albans (Sir Francis Bacon) in 1621 and Lord Treasurer Middlesex (Lionel Cranfield) three years later. Emboldened by these successes, and probably with encouragement from some peers, members tried the same tactic against the duke of Buckingham in 1626, though the impeachment hearings were eventually abandoned due to a weak case and Charles I's steadfast support for his favourite. Despite this setback, in 1628 the king was forced into accepting the Petition of Right by the combined strength of Commons and Lords. Although this triumph proved to be short-lived, it marked a significant shift in relations between the two Houses. Presenting itself as the true voice of the English people, and exploiting all the weapons at its disposal, the Commons ultimately imposed its reform agenda on the Lords, reversing the normal balance of power, and obliging the reluctant peers to choose between king and parliament. It was a foretaste of things to come.

Management Issues and Relations with the Crown

The quantity of business agreed and concluded underwent a drastic reduction, notwithstanding the overall increase in the length of sessions This contrasted sharply with the high achievement of Elizabethan parliaments with their shorter sittings. Roughly one-third of the bills introduced in James I's first four parliamentary sessions became statutes, a ratio similar to that under Elizabeth I. Thereafter, it was a different story. No bills were enacted during the second session of 1610. The 'Addled' Parliament of 1614 was similarly sterile. Just two statutes emerged from the 1621 session, representing less than 1% of the bills considered by the Commons. This trend was briefly reversed in 1624, when 42% of the 173 bills that entered the lower House passed into law. However, Charles I gave his assent to just 15 bills during his first four sessions, barely 5% of all those read in the Commons, with no additions to the statute rolls in either 1626 or 1629. Some allowance must be made for the small quantity of legislation vetoed by the king after completing its passage through both Houses, but this was a factor primarily in 1624. The general sense of failure is unmistakable, and it requires explanation.

The first issue is weak management. In 1621, for example, the Commons fell victim to its own success in attracting business. Faced with the largest influx of bills since 1604, and simultaneously deluged with petitions of grievance, the members were simply swamped by the scale of their task, tackled too much at once, and left most of it unfinished. The House was also easily distracted from its routine tasks. Proceedings in the two sessions of 1610 were dominated by discussion of the Great Contract Impeachment campaigns in 1621 and in subsequent parliaments similarly limited the time available for legislation. The proliferation of committees did not necessarily translate into action. Attendance in the House was frequently poor in this period, periodically causing the postponement of business, and this problem naturally also affected committees. In 1628 it took

> ### The Great Contract of 1610
>
> In the early Stuart period, the public finances were still structured on essentially medieval lines. The king was expected to cover routine government spending by drawing on his 'ordinary' revenues, principally the income from crown lands, feudal entitlements such as wardship and purveyance, and customs revenues. This last component was, by tradition, granted to the monarch during the first parliament of a new reign. However, all other parliamentary funding was classed as 'extraordinary' income, to be provided only in emergency situations such as war. In reality, this system was rapidly breaking down, due to the effects of inflation, the gradual erosion of the crown's own resources, and James I's extravagance. By 1610, despite strenuous government reforms, the accumulated public debt stood at £300,000, with an annual deficit of £46,000. Accordingly, when parliament met in February that year, the lord treasurer, the earl of Salisbury, proposed a radical new solution. In addition to the clearing of existing debts, he requested an annual grant of £200,000, in return for which various unpopular feudal revenues would be scrapped. The fate of this 'Great Contract' rested with the Commons, which customarily determined levels of parliamentary taxation. Although the Contract's underlying concept was not entirely novel, members were uncomfortable about bargaining with the crown, and mishandled the negotiations. Keen to secure additional government concessions, but reluctant to offer an appropriate level of financial compensation, they agreed in principle to a very favourable compromise deal in July, but then abandoned discussions in November after further wrangling. By this stage both James and the Commons had lost faith in Salisbury's scheme, but failure in 1610 to achieve political consensus over government funding condemned the crown and parliament to increasingly bitter disputes over traditional taxation during the remainder of this period.

over six weeks to draft a vital legal measure, the Bill for Continuance of Expiring Statutes, due to persistent absenteeism among those named for the task.[2]

The Commons all too often behaved like a rudderless ship. This was partly the crown's fault. The Speakers were customarily lawyers with promising careers ahead of them and considerable experience of the House behind them. However, in 1614 James I selected Ranulph Crewe, who had sat only in the parliament of 1597, and in 1621 Thomas Richardson, who was a newcomer. Richardson was the second Speaker to have lacked any previous experience. Both men struggled to command the respect of the House, let alone hold members to an agreed agenda. The government's formal spokesmen frequently fared little better during this period. As a result of James's rush to ennoble most of his leading ministers at the start

---

[2] *Commons Debates 1628*, ii, 510; iii, 175, 469; iv, 28.

of his reign, the parliament of 1604 began with just two privy councillors in the Commons, a marked reduction compared with previous parliaments. Although their numbers rose again in subsequent sessions, these spokesmen found it increasingly difficult to assert themselves, sometimes because they simply failed to impress the House, but primarily because members were becoming more inclined to challenge both the crown's policies and its authority. In 1614 the attorney general was barred from membership of the Commons, in a symbolic gesture of defiance against undue government interference. In fact, contrary to the rumours of 'undertaking' that circulated during that parliament, the crown never seriously attempted to pack the House with its supporters, with the partial exception of 1621 and 1624, when Prince Charles exploited his electoral patronage to find seats for his own candidates. On these two occasions the prince wished to promote a personal legislative programme, but this was unusual. After 1610 the crown's parliamentary agenda rarely extended much beyond requests for taxation grants, and its spokesmen therefore concentrated on defending the monarch's interests rather than actively promoting business. However, the Commons itself lacked the organization and self-discipline to exploit successfully its relative freedom of action. Although each parliament produced a small crop of leading members, opinion-formers who dominated debates, these men had their own agendas, and worked together only when their interests coincided over a particular issue. The sustained, concerted action that accompanied Buckingham's impeachment or the Petition of Right campaign was untypical.

The mounting tensions between crown and Commons were in fact the other major cause of legislative failure. Early Stuart parliaments were repeatedly disrupted by disputes over the government's finances. Members twice blocked James I's project for a closer union between England and Scotland. If events reached an impasse, the ultimate sanction lay with the monarch. The sessions of autumn 1610, 1614, 1621, 1625, 1626 and 1629 were all dissolved prematurely, with any unfinished bills automatically terminated. James even ruled that in 1614 and 1621 the sessions were merely conventions; in other words, meetings where no business had been completed, which was true of the former parliament but not of the latter.[3] Neither James nor his son could disguise their distaste for parliament, and preferred to manage without it. Between 1610 and 1621 the Commons sat for just two months. It met more frequently during the following decade only because the crown needed parliamentary taxation to fund its military adventures, and by now parliament's very future as a branch of government seemed threatened. However, while many members recognized that the Commons' own failings had contributed to this turn of events, the House was also galvanized by the mounting unpopularity of Charles I's policies. The more the king exploited his prerogative

[3] *LJ*, ii, 717; *Stuart Royal Proclamations*, ed. J. F. Larkin and P. L. Hughes (2 vols, Oxford, 1973–83), i, 534.

powers, and promoted anti-Calvinist clergy, the more the Commons seemed like a bastion of traditional liberties and true religion. That ideological divide in turn fostered more radical tactics in the House. Where James's last two parliaments had sought reform primarily through legislation, symbolized by the great bills against monopolies, the Commons in 1626 and 1628 opted for outright confrontation, attacking first the royal favourite, the duke of Buckingham, and then the royal prerogative itself. Legislation was not entirely forgotten, but it struggled for attention while the Commons played out these dramas. The session of 1629 was no different. Thirty bills were brought into the Commons, but members became engrossed in disputes over taxation, religion and their own privileges. No legislation was completed. When the king finally dissolved parliament in March, a handful of hot-headed members responded by holding down Speaker Finch in his chair while they read out a remonstrance against the government. They were duly prosecuted for rioting in the House. It would be another 11 years before the Commons sat again.

Chronology

1603
Accession of James I

1604
Goodwin's case

1605
Gunpowder Plot

1610
Great Contract debates

1614
'Addled' Parliament; no legislation completed

1621
Revival of parliamentary judicature; Protestation of the Commons

1624
Monopolies Act

1625
Death of James I; accession of Charles I

1626
Impeachment of duke of Buckingham

1628
Petition of Right

1629
Rolle's case

Further Reading

T. Cogswell, *The Blessed Revolution: English Politics and the Coming of War, 1621–1624* (Cambridge, 1989)

E. R. Foster, 'Staging a Parliament in Early Stuart England', in *The English Commonwealth, 1547–1640*, ed. P. Clark, A. G. R. Smith and N. Tyacke (Leicester, 1979), 129–46, 239–48

D. Hirst, *The Representative of the People? Voters and Voting in England under the Early Stuarts* (Cambridge, 1975)

P. M. Hunneyball, 'Prince Charles's Council as Electoral Agent, 1620–24', *Parliamentary History*, xxiii (2004), 316–35

C. R. Kyle, 'Prince Charles in the Parliaments of 1621 and 1624', *Historical Journal*, xli (1998)

R. Lockyer, *The Early Stuarts: A Political History of England, 1603–1642* (1999)

Parliament at Work: Parliamentary Committees, Political Power and Public Access in Early Modern England, ed. C. R. Kyle and J. Peacey (Woodbridge, 2002)

Parliament, Politics and Elections, 1604–1648, ed. C. R. Kyle (Camden Society, 5th ser. xvii, Cambridge, 2001)

C. Russell, *Parliaments and English Politics, 1621–1629* (Oxford, 1979)

D. L. Smith, *The Stuart Parliaments, 1603–1689* (1999)

C. C. G. Tite, *Impeachment and Parliamentary Judicature in Early Stuart England* (1974)

11 The House of Commons, 1640–60

Stephen K. Roberts

The Electorate and the Franchise

In 1640 electors in the shires continued to be the 40s. freeholders, while in the boroughs the range of local franchises persisted. The Instrument of Government of December 1653 brought in a new property qualification of £200 for votes in the counties, while leaving the borough franchise unaltered. The effects of this change are hard to disentangle from other innovations. As well as a change in franchise, there was a new pattern of increased representation for counties. The complexity of polling for the two elections held under these arrangements, in 1654 and 1656, encouraged sheriffs to compile handwritten poll books in which to record votes as they were registered, and a number of these have survived, but there is contradictory evidence as to whether the electorate was expanded.

A statute of 1640 reinforced earlier judgments against the clergy sitting. With the dismantling of the episcopal hierarchy of the Church of England during the 1640s and the opening up of various avenues by which men might become ministers of religion, clergy played an organized part as voters in the 1656 elections, and at least one minister, John St Nicholas, sat in the 1653 assembly. The Humble Petition and Advice and the Additional Petition and Advice, both of 1657, reasserted the sanction against the clergy sitting as members, but not against their voting.

The Humble Petition and Advice left the mechanics of future parliamentary elections vague, and in the hands of the Lord Protector and his council. Richard Cromwell and his advisers took advantage of the discretion allowed them to ensure that the 1659 parliament was held on the basis of 'the ancient rights of the nation in the late king's time'.[1] This meant a return to the old constituencies and the franchises as they stood in 1640.

Membership

The only immutable qualification for membership of the Commons in this period was maleness. It was a rule that parliament-men should be of full age, that is, 21, but examples can be found of exceptions. There were cases where the rule was simply ignored, as with James, Lord Compton in

---

[1] Quoted in G. Davies, 'The Election of Richard Cromwell's Parliament, 1658–9', *English Historical Review*, lxiii (1948), 488–501 at 488.

1640; or a special dispensation could be made, as in the 1654 case of Sir Richard Temple, who aged 20 was declared by the judges to be of majority age so that he could deal with massive inherited debts, and who then used that judgment to pronounce himself qualified to stand for parliament.

With the abolition of the House of Lords in 1649, the way was clear for three peers, the 4th earl of Pembroke, the 2nd earl of Salisbury and Baron Howard of Escrick, to stand for election in the unicameral 'Rump' Parliament, and they duly took seats. Other conventions were applied with little fuss. Members who held legal positions were expected to retire when they achieved high office. In the case of Sir Edward Herbert, it was acceptable that he should enter the Commons in 1640 while solicitor-general, but not that he should continue when promoted in January 1641 to be attorney-general. Other senior legal figures became assistants to the House of Lords while continuing to hold seats in the Commons, and even important politicians, such as Serjeant John Wylde, took a back seat after they became senior judges.

From the outbreak of the civil war in August 1642, the Commons regulated its own membership vigorously, on political grounds. By the time of the Nominated Assembly (or 'Barebones' Parliament) of 1653, 'godliness' (i.e. a commitment to reformed Protestantism) and loyalty to the commonwealth had become explicit qualities necessary for selection. These notions were transferred into the Instrument of Government of December 1653, which also incorporated a list of past political behaviours that would disqualify putative members from sitting in the projected new parliaments. Among the proscribed types of person were Roman Catholics, haunters of alehouses and scoffers at the word of God.

The Constituencies

Through most of the period covered in this chapter, the constituencies and their boundaries were the time-honoured ones in England and Wales. In keeping with a trend observable in the earlier parliaments of Charles I, a number of boroughs were newly enfranchised in 1640-1: Ashburton, Honiton and Okehampton in Devon; Cockermouth in Cumberland; Northallerton in Yorkshire, and Seaford in Sussex. These were enfranchisements on political grounds only, certainly not a recognition that these were populous or important places economically or socially. The Nominated Assembly departed radically from the familiar patchwork of counties and the illogical but familiar range of enfranchised boroughs. An initial proposal that the assembly should consist of 70 nominees, following the biblical model of the Jewish Sanhedrin, turned into the final quota of twice that number. The army council of officers winnowed the names of possible members suggested to Cromwell and his council, on grounds of godliness and loyalty. A summons to attend the assembly was then issued to each member in the name of Oliver Cromwell as commander-in-chief of the army.

> **Writ to Summon a Member to the Nominated Assembly 1653**
>
> Forasmuch as on the dissolution of the late Parliament it became necessary that the peace, safety, and good government of this Commonwealth should be provided for: And in order thereunto, divers persons fearing God and of approved fidelity and honesty, are by myself with the advice of my Council of Officers, nominated, to whom the great charge and trust of so weighty affairs is to be committed; and having good assurance of your love to, and courage for God, and the interest of His cause, and of the good people of this Commonwealth:
>
> I, Oliver Cromwell, Captain General and Commander in Chief of all the armies and forces raised and to be raised within this Common-wealth, do hereby summon and require you ... (being one of the persons nominated) personally to be and appear at the Council Chamber, commonly known, or called by the name of the Council-Chamber at Whitehall, within the City of Westminster, upon the fourth day of July next ensuing the date hereof; then and there to take upon you the said trust, unto which you are hereby called, and appointed to serve as a member for the county of ... And hereof you are not to fail. Given under my hand and seal, the sixth day of June, 1653. O. Cromwell.
>
> Source: *Constitutional Documents of the Puritan Revolution, 1625–1660*, ed. S. R. Gardiner (3rd edn, revised, Oxford, 1906), 405.

Members were then deemed to sit for constituencies that comprised the English shires, mostly with increased representation, London and the new constituencies of all Wales, all Scotland, all Ireland and four counties in the north of England joined as one. There were also five co-opted members.

The Instrument restored the principle of election, but redrafted the list of constituencies so that more representation was given to counties than had been customary and the franchise withdrawn from the more egregiously decayed boroughs. Durham county, Durham city, Leeds and Halifax were enfranchised, and returned members to the two parliaments held under the Instrument, in 1654 and 1656. Following the tentative precedent of the Nominated Assembly, up to 30 members each from Scotland and Ireland were included. Even so, there were 456 MPs in the 1654 'British' parliament compared with the 552 who are said to have sat for England and Wales alone between 1640 and 1642. The parliament of Richard Cromwell saw the return to the traditional constituencies, but with the retention of the Irish and Scots members.

> ### The Oxford Parliament
>
> This was a rival assembly to that which met at Westminster, and consisted of members of both Houses who adhered to the king after the outbreak of the civil war. The Commons members sat by virtue of their election to the Westminster parliament which opened in November 1640. It was convened by the king in the winter of 1643–4 as a demonstration of support for him and his cause. Some 141 members of the Commons turned up, with another 34 excused attendance by virtue of their work for the royalist cause in other spheres. Members were billeted in the Oxford colleges, and the assembly met in the hall at Christ Church. Their presence undoubtedly worsened the quality of life in the already overcrowded and disease-ridden city. The Commons elected Sir Sampson Eure, a Herefordshire lawyer, as their Speaker. Although various pronouncements were made on public morals, which paralleled the ordinances and declarations made at Westminster, the principal activities of the parliament were to make peace overtures to Robert Devereux, 3rd earl of Essex, the lord general of the Westminster parliament's main field army, and to attempt to regulate the conduct and efficiency of the regiments which fought for the king. The Oxford parliament was prorogued on several occasions, and was never officially dissolved. It simply ceased to exist when the city surrendered to the Westminster parliament in June 1646.

Speakers

Eleven men served as Speaker at one time or another between 1640 and 1660, including the oddities of Sir Sampson Eure's speakership at the Oxford parliament and that of Henry Pelham, who briefly took the chair while Speaker Lenthall and other political independents escaped from mob rule around Westminster in 1647 by fleeing to the New Model Army.

There were no deputy Speakers, and illness was met by the election of a temporary Speaker. All Speakers were lawyers, all protested their unworthiness for the office and made the traditional speeches requesting the privileges. Francis Rous, Speaker of the Nominated Assembly, was remarkable for his learning and piety, as well as for being re-elected to the chair month by month, but the outstanding Speaker of the period was William Lenthall. This was not for his personal qualities – 'obnoxious, timorous and interested' was a hostile contemporary assessment of him[2]– nor even for his uncertain control of the House, but for what he represented. He was unusual in that the king did not want him, and he had a background of unhelpfulness to the crown. The Speaker's complaints when brought to the chair, normally conventional and feigned, in Lenthall's case

---

[2] A. Wood, *Athenae Oxonienses* (2 vols, 1691–2), ii, 106.

became heart-felt and frequent, as he struggled with the enormity of his office during the period first of parliament's executive ascendancy and then its sovereignty. In this period the first glimpses are visible of a separation of the office from the person, as countless letters by MPs and others were prepared for him merely to seal before despatch, and countless letters passed through his office really destined for the Commons. There is evidence that many applied themselves to Henry Elsynge, clerk of the house, rather than to the Speaker, yet there were plenty of examples of supplicants waiting on Lenthall's personal attention. He claimed exhaustion, but he surely made more money through his office than any of his predecessors. For all the money-grubbing and whinging, he will for ever be remembered for his part in defying Charles I in January 1642 when he pronounced that he had 'neither eyes to see nor tongue to speak in this place but as this house is pleased to direct me whose servant I am'.[3]

Formal and Informal Records of the House

The official record of proceedings was the manuscript Commons journal, which occupied 31 volumes covering the period from 1640 to March 1660. In addition, eight volumes called books of ordinances have survived from 1640–9, which were intended as a conspectus of decisions by both Houses. Any supplementary material of this sort that might have been created during the parliaments of the 1650s has not survived; had it ever existed, it would probably have provided fuel for a bonfire around 1660. The journals were the private property of the House and no proposal to make them public by printing was ever mooted. Members were aware of the importance of record-keeping. In April 1640 the House asserted control over note-taking by preventing the assistant clerk from recording anything other than orders and reports, and in December it was forbidden to remove notes from the chamber. The following year, the clerk was censured for allowing members to take the journal away from the table where it lay.

It might have been considered that policing by the House of note-taking made the production of informal records difficult. In fact, the turbulence of the times stimulated the writing of journals of parliamentary proceedings, all of them by men who were present in the chamber to commit first to memory then to paper what they observed. Sir Simonds D'Ewes was the most diligent and persistent of the diarists, writing in a disciplined way, usually in his London home during the mornings, a parliamentary diary that ran from November 1640 down to 1647. D'Ewes is the fullest, if not always the most accurate, of the Long Parliament diarists. Opinionated, egotistical and often pompous, his own personality is evident on every page of his diary. The leading diarist of the Cromwellian parliaments of 1656 and 1659, Thomas Burton, is the opposite. His own views are opaque,

[3] J. Rushworth, *Historical Collections* (8 vols, 1721–2), iv, 478.

> ### Sir Simonds D'Ewes and Thomas Burton
>
> Sir Simonds D'Ewes (1602–50) was an East Anglian antiquary and lawyer who sat in only one parliament, but who recorded the proceedings of the Long Parliament in more detail and over a longer period (1640–7) than any other diarist. His main journal (1640–5) was written up at the end of each day, and he recorded the main proceedings, giving a very prominent place to his own doings and interventions. Through his record we can trace the emergence of the war party in the Commons, men he called the 'fiery spirits', and follow his own transformation from fierce critic of the government to reluctant parliamentarian as the civil war deepened. From 1644 D'Ewes also kept a parallel diary in Latin, which helps put the main diary in context and supplies details of his own 'hinterland' beyond parliament. Thomas Burton (1627–61), another lawyer, kept a different kind of diary during Oliver Cromwell's second parliament (1656–8) and that of Richard Cromwell (1659). He seems to have kept his diary openly, and wrote down speeches as they were delivered by members. His diary is therefore more immediate than that of D'Ewes, but Burton himself is virtually invisible in it, and he seems in any case not to have been interested in the great issues of the day so much as in the minutiae. What can be gained from Burton is the ebb and flow of debate in the House, which no other diarist of the 1640s and 50s ever captured so well.

but the quality of his reportage is unparalleled. His diaries record individual speeches, with all their loose ends, red herrings and infelicities, but the acuity of the diarist may owe much to the likelihood that his efforts were recognized and approved, albeit informally, by the House.

Printing and Publishing

Printing on behalf of parliament began in 1641. It is impossible to calculate accurately the number of items printed on behalf of parliament in the 1640s, still less to allocate the proportion to one House or the other. Most of the printing for the record was of acts, ordinances, orders and declarations, and in this as in so much else the Long Parliament was the pioneer. A significant volume of official publishing by the Commons was in effect propaganda, devised to combat material propagated by the king's printers at Oxford, and as the 1640s developed the presbyterians and independents proved adept at producing apparently factual material that provided readers with a highly tendentious account of some or other episode in public affairs. In a different authorial register, another form of parliamentary publishing was of fast sermons, delivered at Westminster on days set aside for spiritual reflection by ministers officially invited to the pulpit to encourage or exhort the members. The technology of printing was also used by parliament to produce printed blank forms for use

> **Example of Ephemera Printed for Parliament 1643**
>
> It is desired by the Clerks and Gentlemen belonging to the Members of both Houses of Parliament, That all Clerks belonging to any of the Inns of Court, Chancery, Guild-hall, Civil Law, Custome-house, Justices of the Peace, or any Office in and about London, would be pleased to meet them on Thursday next by Seven of the clock in the Morning, at the Piatze in Coven-Garden, with Spades, Shovels, Pickaxes, and other necessaries fit for the Digging of the Trenches, &c.
>
> Dated at Westminster the Sixt of June. 1643.
>
> Source: British Library, 669, fol. 7 (20)

by the executive committees in its dealings with parliament's friends and enemies, and could be used even more ephemerally for communications between officials. It has been estimated that in 1645, some 23% of English printing activity (nearly all of it in London) was on parliament's behalf.

No official collections of acts and ordinances were issued in this period. The nearest we have to official collections were by Edward Husbands in 1643 and 1646, and by Henry Scobell in 1658, but as commercial ventures given parliamentary approval they were at one remove from direct parliamentary printing. The Commons jealously guarded control over reporting its proceedings, but members fought a losing battle. Some fast sermons found their way into print without permission, to the fury of the Commons, and there were numerous investigations into other examples of unauthorized publication.

The Framing of Legislation, & Legislation on Parliament

Until 5 March 1642 each item of legislation passed by both Houses of parliament and approved by the king was called an act. From that date, when the Houses completed legislation on control of the militia which was not approved by the king, but which was nevertheless declared law, bills that had proceeded through the usual stages in the Commons to completion in the Lords were known as ordinances. The sovereign unicameral Rump Parliament revived the word 'act' to describe the laws it passed. After April 1653 the word 'act' was used to describe the legislative output of parliaments, while the word 'ordinance' was applied to those enactments which were issued, with the same legal effect as if they had been parliamentary, by the Lord Protector and his council.

Members of the Short Parliament challenged the right of the king to dissolve parliaments, and even asserted that the power of dissolution lay in parliaments themselves. When members met again in the second parliament of 1640, they enacted legislation on the duration of parliaments. The Triennial Act of 1641 stipulated that future parliaments should meet no later than three years after the last day of the preceding one, and prevented the king from proroguing any parliament for more than three years. The act was soon followed by another, which required the parliament then sitting to assent to its own dissolution. The legislative edifice was then in place to allow the Long Parliament to continue indefinitely, or at least while the emergency of the civil war continued. A self-approved dissolution was of course unthinkable while parliament continued first to mount a military campaign against the king and then by degrees began to run the country. The Instrument of Government of 1653 stipulated that every new parliament should sit for a minimum of five months and breathed new life into the 1641 notion of triennial elections.

Extending the Authority of Parliament

The innovations in legislative formulae were as nothing compared with the extraordinary scale of parliament's executive activity from 1642. Conrad Russell's famous dictum that before 1640 'a parliament was an event and not an institution' now loses purchase: the Long Parliament was emphatically an institution.[4] From 1643, it laid claim to the mechanism for conducting the most momentous actions of executive government, the great seal, and appointed its own commissioners of the great seal in November that year to supplant the king's lord keeper. In 1646 parliament ceremoniously destroyed the matrix for the king's great seal. The political crisis of 1648–9 has been studied from many different perspectives, but the point must be made here that the Commons' declaration of sovereignty of 4 January 1649, albeit the product of a purged parliament, could not have been conceivable without parliament's history since 1642 of extending its grip over the nation.

[4] C. Russell, *Parliaments and English Politics, 1621–1629* (Oxford, 1979), 3.

The Commons Declaration of 4 January 1649

Resolved, &c. That the Commons of England, in Parliament assembled, do Declare, That the People are, under God, the Original of all just Power:

And do also Declare, that the Commons of England, in Parliament assembled, being chosen by, and representing the People, have the Supreme Power in this Nation:

And do also Declare, That whatsoever is enacted, or declared for Law, by the Commons, in Parliament assembled, hath the Force of Law; and all the People of this Nation are concluded thereby, although the Consent and Concurrence of King, or House of Peers, be not had thereunto.

Source: CJ, vi, 110.

The sovereign Rump Parliament was well aware of the authority and dignity it was claiming. A new great seal devoid of regal symbolism was designed, and new maces were manufactured, not only for parliament itself, but for corporations up and down the land. The Rump had medals cast to commemorate its heroes, such as Colonel Humphrey Mackworth of Shrewsbury, who in 1651 had defied the forces of Charles Stuart, son of the decapitated monarch. The ceremony and symbolism disappeared with the Rump itself. Later parliaments of the 1650s for the most part laid no claim to unshared sovereignty and saw themselves as working in tandem with executive authority. The glory days of parliamentary sovereignty could not be completely effaced, however, and a loud echo of it reverberated through the case of James Nayler in 1656. Nayler was a quaker who rode into Bristol on a donkey, with a procession of followers. Against a background of general alarm among the propertied at the disruptive behaviour of this new sect, the city authorities took this to be a blasphemous re-enactment of Christ's entry into Jerusalem. Nayler was sent for trial before parliament. The exceptional nature of the case was clear both in Bristol and in parliament, where a ten-day debate ended in a sentence of savage corporal punishment followed by life imprisonment. Yet it was unclear by what authority parliament had taken on itself in effect to try Nayler and then pronounce sentence on him. Lord Protector Cromwell was evidently troubled by the proceedings, as were a number of MPs: the Instrument of Government certainly provided no justification for them.

A theme running counter to the general trend of the extension of parliamentary authority was the violence or threats of violence aimed against the House and its members. Setting aside here the various incidents that might be identified over the century as a whole when individual 'strangers' penetrated the Commons, there were orchestrated attempts to use force to interfere with the business of the House, some of which succeeded. They began with the unsuccessful attempt on 4 January 1642 by Charles I to arrest in the Commons five leading opponents of his government (and one peer), aimed at removing troublemakers rather than closing down the sitting. The last direct show of force came in April 1653, when Oliver Cromwell lost patience with the Rump, seized the mace, speaking scornfully of it as a 'bauble', and called in soldiers to clear the chamber. Exclusions of a subtler kind took place in September 1656, when an army guard prevented more than 100 members from taking their seats. Every one of these episodes contributed only to parliament's sense of self-worth and strengthened the resolve to protect parliamentary privilege, and despite them all, parliament remained open to those who came to petition, to act as men-of-business for the mighty or simply idly to observe. There was a guard set at the Palace of Westminster, but it was there to protect against organized violence, not the casual intruder or absurd impostor.

> ### A Stranger in the Commons, 1659
>
> On 5 February 1659, the eighth day of Richard Cromwell's parliament, two MPs made their colleagues aware that a man in grey clothes had sat in the Commons chamber for three days, and they had now realized he was not a member. William King was then arrested by the serjeant at arms and removed. Shortly afterwards he was brought back in to stand at the bar and explain himself. King, a London vintner, described how he had originally come to the House as a petitioner, but had been congratulated by a mischievous London alderman on having been elected a member. King was reported by a number of MPs to have distributed anti-government literature within the palace of Westminster, and the members' affront at his intrusion was compounded by their indignation at what they took to be his subversive lobbying. Argument then raged over whether the common gaol of Newgate was the best place for him, or whether the Tower of London was more appropriate for this behaviour. King was brought in again, and told members how he had left school aged 12 and had been cheated out of an estate by an elder brother. When he 'began to talk idly', it was realized that he was mentally ill, and some members shamefacedly admitted that calls for King to be imprisoned in chains had been inappropriate. The sentence of an undetermined period in Newgate seems nevertheless to have stood.
>
> Sources: *CJ*, vii, 600; *Diary of Thomas Burton, Esq.*, ed. J. T. Rutt (4 vols, 1828), iii, 68–84.

Leadership and Parties

The conventional political histories of the period stress the king's isolation in the first phase of the Long Parliament, before Charles left London, but it is apparent that there were always those in the Commons willing to support his ministers when the House divided. Equally conventionally, John Pym has been viewed as the prime mover of events in the Long Parliament until his death in 1643, but in more recent accounts he no longer figures as 'King' Pym. There was a coherent group in both Houses and with allies outside parliament who were determined opponents of the king. Puritanism, dislike of the king's foreign policy and his approach to managing his kingdoms of Scotland and Ireland were among the factors uniting them. Historians sometimes call the parliamentary elements of this opposition group the 'junto', a word that had contemporary resonance but which was used then more loosely and imprecisely than by its modern appropriators. The word 'party' can hardly be applied to Charles's opponents in parliament before the civil war, because the opposition was focused on a handful of powerful peers and their Commons allies, in a behind-the-scenes fashion that was not always evident to observers. The royalists in the Commons were drawn more to withdrawal from a hostile

London rather than to making a stand as a party in the lower House, but political factions at Westminster among those loyal to parliament then burgeoned. The most enduring of these factions were the presbyterians and independents, labels that were recognized by the press and by political commentators of every stripe. Between 1644 and 1648 the political territory disputed between them included the role of the Scots in the civil war conflict; the degree of support for the armies and the vigour and purpose of the campaign against the king; and religion, which had provided the 'parties' with their titles, and which was fundamentally over the degree of toleration that should be permitted in the state church.

Within the House of Commons, the factional conflict between independents and presbyterians can be detected in a struggle for control of important committees, by means of appointments of members of them, and particularly through appointments of chairmen; in the selection of tellers in politically sensitive divisions of the House, and in manipulation of the printing press. Behind the independents stood the army; behind the presbyterians lay the powerful financial forces in the city of London, and so like parties subsequently they drew strength from extra-parliamentary interests. Even so, it is important to sound a cautionary note. Membership of these factions was loose and informal, and was never claimed by more than a minority of MPs, most of whom were never consistently aligned to either side. The factions provided a form of political leadership, but the bulk of members owed no enduring allegiance to more than the cause of parliament itself.

Committees

These were the principal vehicle for dealing with the business of the Commons. They can be analysed in three broad categories: the standing committees, the committees named from the floor of the House, and the executive committees. The Commons appointed certain committees at the start of most parliaments. Committees for religion, for grievances, for the courts of justice and for trade were four committees of the whole House, whose meeting times were agreed in the opening days of each assembly. The Nominated Assembly, although it quickly resolved to adopt the title of parliament, did not adopt this convention. The first of the protectorate parliaments also ignored this custom, but the second revived it. Richard Cromwell's parliament merged the standing committees for grievances and the courts of justice into one. The 1654 parliament discussed the printed constitution at great length, deploying the committee of the whole House as the mechanism for doing so, and one member, Bennet Hoskins, was elected to take the chair at these proceedings on 40 occasions in little over a three month period. The privileges committee was a select committee, chosen to regulate disputed elections as well as to adjudicate on matters of privilege, and was appointed at the start of every parliament in this period, except the Nominated Assembly, which chose instead to accord comparable prominence to committees for Scottish and Irish affairs.

Committees formed to investigate matters, to devise or revise legislation and orders, or to consider petitions and communications were the bread-and-butter of Commons activity. A busy parliamentarian might be named to dozens during his career: Nicholas Lechmere was named to 138 between 1648 and 1653. There were occasions such as on 15 July 1641 when the House, evidently aware of the explosion in the number of committees and their potential for duplication of effort, competing authority and sheer muddle, tried to cull the number of committees. The frequency with which an individual appears on lists of committees recorded in the journals can be taken as a guide to his prominence in committee, but it can never be assumed that everyone named to committee actually appeared on it, or even that the committee did a significant amount of work. Between April and September 1644 Sir Simonds D'Ewes was named to six committees which were unmentioned in his private diary, a careful record of his daily schedule. For the first time in this period it becomes clearer who chaired committees, however, as the clerks began to record who was to 'take care' of a particular business.

If judged on their impact on public life, the most important committees, however, were the executive committees created by the Long Parliament. Most of these were brought into being after civil war had broken out, although a number pre-dated this, such as the committee for the navy and customs, which originated in parliamentary finance of the navy before 1642. Some of them, such as the committee for plundered ministers, which dealt with appointments of parish ministers, were composed of Commons members only; others were of both Houses. One, the committee for taking the accounts of the kingdom, made up mainly of London merchants and lawyers, was notable for having no members of either House on it at all. Appointed by parliamentary ordinance, its 25 members were brought to the Commons to swear an oath, and then attempted to exercise financial control over the plethora of committees running the war effort in the provinces. Some parliamentary committees met in and around the palace of Westminster, in places like the Treasury Chamber, the Court of Exchequer, or houses in Whitehall, but a number had offices in remote locations, such as the halls of the London livery companies in the City. These bodies were the 'clunking fist' of parliament's executive authority during the civil war, and they had a life of their own, as they employed their own staff, issued warrants and orders in their own names, and generally enjoyed much autonomy. The independents were successful in achieving control of most of these bodies, but the presbyterians used the committee for taking accounts to good effect, largely through the efforts of its leader, the indefatigable William Prynne. As a sub-category of the executive committees should be numbered the executive bodies which steered the war effort and conducted negotiations on parliament's behalf: the committee of both kingdoms and its successor, the committee of both

Houses. Few of these executive committees made much impact on procedures inside the Commons, but in terms of scope, power and originality they are the elephant in the room in any short history of parliament.

Divisions

It was established in December 1640 that those voting to preserve the existing orders of the House were to stay in while members voting for an alteration or innovation were to leave the chamber. Like the committee, the division became a much-employed tool of parliamentary procedure. There was evidently a relationship between the intensity of political struggle in the House and the number of divisions called. In periods known to have been marked by struggle between the presbyterians and the independents the number rose sharply, so that in the three years 1646–8, there were 351 divisions in all, and 1647 saw the largest number in the entire period under review: 131. The 1656 parliament, in which political antagonisms ran deep, was another in which members frequently resorted to

Heaven, Hell, Paradise and Purgatory

Among the building erected along the west wall of Westminster Hall were two open spaces or courtyards. Of these the northern Exchequer Yard became two smaller yards known jointly as 'Hell'. This yard was surrounded by the Tally Office, taverns called *Hell* and *Paradise*, and coffee houses. *Hell* was partly under and partly alongside of the exchequer. (In 1648 the MPs excluded by Pride's Purge were held there for a night. Henry Martin, MP, quipped that it was fitting for the friends of the king that they 'should go to Hell'.) Samuel Pepys drank once at *Hell* in 1660: 'At the [Westminster] Hall I met with Mr. Creed; and he and I to Hell to drink our morning draught.' *Heaven* was another eating-house at the south-west corner of Westminster Hall in the angle made by the Court of Requests and the Court of Wards. Like *Hell* it was possibly once used as part of the exchequer offices. It presumably got its name from its position on an upper story. Pepys recorded dining at *Heaven* three times in 1660: 'Thence to Westminster-hall ... and so I returned and went to Heaven.' *Purgatory*, together with *Alice's* (later *Carter's*) coffee house, stood on the east side of Old Palace Yard against the west wall of the old Court of Requests.

CJ

Sources: D. Underdown, *Pride's Purge: Politics in the Puritan Revolution* (Oxford, 1971), 148, n. 13; *The Diary of Samuel Pepys*, ed. R. Latham and W. Mathews (11 vols, 1970–83), i, 31, 303; O. C. Williams, 'The Topography of the Old House of Commons' (unpublished typescript, 1953: Parliamentary Archives, Book/61), 2, 5, 12, plate 19; 'Foundation Plan of the Ancient Palace of Westminster', by J. T. Smith (1807).

the division: between January and June 1657, 102 were held. There were always two pairs of tellers, and certain members were to be found time and again acting as tellers, which may suggest that they exercised some of the functions later associated with whips: Sir Arthur Hesilrige was a teller on 167 occasions between 1640 and 1649. In the dying days of the revived Rump, in 1659–60, he was again the leading teller, providing us with proof that republicanism went down fighting.

Chronology

1640

April — Short Parliament of three weeks called by Charles I following rebellion in Scotland, but dissolved because of the failure by king and parliament to agree how taxation could be granted and grievances met

November — Long Parliament summoned to address the persistent crisis in the north; disrupted, purged and forcibly 'dissolved' on various occasions, it continues until 1660, when it finally dissolves itself

1642

4 January — Charles I's unsuccessful attempt to arrest five members of the Commons and one of the Lords by entering the Commons chamber with an armed guard

August — Outbreak of civil war in England and Wales

1644

January — Rival royalist parliament meets at Oxford

1645

Self-denying ordinance requires members of either House to lay down military or civil office acquired since 1640

1645–7

'Recruiter' elections to Long Parliament whereby MPs expelled for supporting the king are replaced by men sympathetic to the parliamentarian cause

1647

July — Some 58 MPs, including Speaker Lenthall, flee the violence around Westminster, returning in August

1648

6 December — Pride's Purge of 231 MPs considered hostile to the New Model army's interests

1649

4 January — Declaration by the Commons that undivided sovereignty is vested in itself by both houses of parliament on behalf of the people

January — Trial and execution of King Charles I managed by both houses of parliament in the name of the people

March — Commonwealth Parliament abolishes the House of Lords, leaving the Commons a sovereign unicameral parliament, known later as the Rump Parliament.

1653

20 April	Oliver Cromwell dissolves Rump Parliament on behalf of the army, impatient with the pace of reform and controversy over plans for a successor parliament.
July–December	Nominated Assembly (known also as 'Barebones' Parliament or 'Barebone's Parliament') pursues a programme of radical religious, legal and social reform, but MPs returned their authority to Lord General Oliver Cromwell on account of irreconcilable divisions among themselves.
16 December	Inauguration of the protectorate of Oliver Cromwell; Instrument of Government, drawn up by army officers and advisers of Cromwell provides England, Wales, Scotland and Ireland with their first written constitution.

1654

September	First Protectorate parliament under Lord Protector Cromwell; no legislation enacted.

1656

September	Second Protectorate parliament; despite exclusions by Lord Protector's council, at least 36 public acts passed.
December	Case of James Naylor judged by the parliament

1657

25 May	The Humble Petition and Advice, a revised written constitution, provides for the restoration of a second house of parliament and guarantees parliaments against interruptions and purges
26 June	The Additional Petition and Advice amplifying the Humble Petition and Advice, providing for commissioners to examine if MPs are qualified to sit, and imposes an oath of loyalty on them

1658

3 September	Death of Oliver Cromwell; accession of Richard Cromwell as lord protector

1659

January	Third Protectorate parliament elected on the pre-1653 franchise; no legislation passed.
7 May	Rump Parliament revived; at least 77 public acts passed
25 May	Abdication of Richard Cromwell

1660

February	Return to Commons of MPs purged in 1648
16 March	Members of Long Parliament finally dissolve the assembly

Further Reading

M. F. Bond, *Guide to the Records of Parliament* (1971)

Constitutional Documents of the Puritan Revolution, 1625–1660, ed. S. R. Gardiner (3rd edn, Oxford, 1906)

C. Egloff, 'The Search for a Cromwellian Settlement: Exclusions from the Second Protectorate Parliament. Part 1: The Process and its Architects'; 'Part 2: The Excluded Members and the Reactions to the Exclusion', *Parliamentary History*, xvii (1998), 178–97, 301–21

P. Gaunt, 'Law-Making in the First Protectorate Parliament', in *Politics and People in Revolutionary England*, ed. C. Jones, M. Newitt and S. Roberts (Oxford, 1986)

D. Hirst, *The Representative of the People? Voters and Voting in England under the Early Stuarts* (Cambridge, 1975)

M. F. Keeler, *The Long Parliament, 1640–1641: A Biographical Study of its Members* (Memoirs of the American Philosophical Society, xxxvi, Philadelphia, 1954)

S. Kelsey, *Inventing a Republic: The Political Culture of the English Commonwealth, 1649–1653* (Manchester, 1997)

M. A. Kishlansky, *Parliamentary Selection: Social and Political Choice in Early Modern England* (Cambridge, 1986)

Parliament at Work: Parliamentary Committees, Political Power and Public Access in Early Modern England, ed. C. R. Kyle and J. Peacey (Woodbridge, 2002)

Parliament, Politics and Elections, 1604–1648, ed. C. R. Kyle (Camden Society, 5th ser., xvii, Cambridge, 2001)

J. Peacey, *Politicians and Pamphleteers: Propaganda in the Civil Wars and Interregnum* (Aldershot, 2004)

Printing for Parliament, 1641–1700, ed. S. Lambert (List and Index Society special ser., xx, 1984)

S. K. Roberts, 'The 1656 Election, Polling and Public Opinion: A Warwickshire Case Study', *Parliamentary History*, xxiii (2004), 357–74

D. L. Smith, *The Stuart Parliaments* (1999)

—— and P. Little, *Parliaments and Politics during the Cromwellian Protectorate* (Cambridge, 2007)

D. Underdown, *Pride's Purge: Politics in the Puritan Revolution* (Oxford, 1971)

A. Woolrych, *Commonwealth to Protectorate* (Oxford, 1982)

B. Worden, *The Rump Parliament, 1648–1653* (Cambridge, 1974)

12 The House of Commons, 1660–1707
Paul Seaward

A New Pace to Parliamentary Politics

It took only a little time for the restored monarchy to dismantle the constitutional legacy of the 1640s and 1650s. All legislation that had been passed by the Long Parliament without royal consent, and any legislation passed by bodies summoned other than by the king could straightforwardly be regarded as illegitimate; but the legislation to which Charles I had given his assent – including the Triennial Act – had to be dealt with more formally. The government waited three years before securing the repeal of the Triennial Act, in 1664. During the debate Secretary of State Sir William Morrice told the House that parliaments 'were the physick of the nation not the food, to be summoned but in time of sickness and want of help in affairs not at any fixed periods'.[1]

Despite the apparent return to pre-civil war institutional arrangements, something had in practice changed. The government felt it difficult to treat parliament in quite the same way as it had in the early 17th century. During the 1660s parliament met on average for more than 85 days each year, more than twice as many as in the 1620s. An apparently handsome new deal on national taxation was struck in 1660 and 1661: but as the costs of government escalated and Charles II embroiled himself in continental war he found that he could not do without regular recourse to parliament for additional taxation. As had their predecessors, Restoration kings sought to overcome this – for them – depressing logic by stepping up their search for alternative sources of revenue. For a short time in the 1680s, by abandoning their ambitions to become a regional and international power and as a result of the beginnings of a sustained period of extraordinary economic growth, they managed to balance the costs and expenses of government enough to avoid parliament for much of the time, and its meetings dwindled to an average of only 36 days a year. But in the longer term additional taxation was unavoidable, and it was ultimately more realistic to become better at dealing with parliament. Restoration politics came to centre on parliamentary management.

While Restoration kings found it hard to avoid the inexorable logic of ruling through parliaments, serious and irreversible change came with the revolution of 1688 and its aftermath. The acceptance by William III and

---

[1] Quoted in P. Seaward, *The Cavalier Parliament and the Reconstruction of the Old Regime, 1661–67* (Cambridge, 1989), 138.

> ### The Bill of Rights
>
> James II's flight from England on 23 December 1688 in the face of the occupation of London by William of Orange and his Dutch troops created the 'Glorious Revolution'. William agreed with prominent politicians to convene a 'convention', a parliament in all but name. Elections were held in January 1689, and it began work at the end of the month. By 6 February both Houses had agreed that James had in practice abdicated, and that William and his wife Mary should be declared king and queen. By the 12th they had reached agreement on the text of a statement of grievances against James II's government which they called a 'Declaration of Rights'. The declaration set out what was regarded as an acceptable constitutional relationship between crown and parliament, including that the crown had no power to suspend the law or dispense with it, to raise money by imposition on the people, or to raise a standing army in time of peace, without parliamentary consent. It was presented to William and Mary the next day, linked to the offer of the throne. Their acceptance of it, and its formal transformation in the next parliament into a statute – the Bill of Rights – made it into a fundamental document describing a new constitutional order.

Mary II of the 1689 Bill of Rights further limited monarchical capacity to rule without constant recourse to parliament. Furthermore, England was immediately plunged into the longest, most intensive and most expensive foreign war it had undertaken for centuries, under monarchs – William and Mary – whose title to power was weak and with a country intensely ideologically divided. War would guarantee parliament's continued existence and revolutionize its operations, while the party divisions which had originated in disputes over religion and the succession to the throne in the 1680s became consolidated into a new way of political and parliamentary life. Parliament's average number of sitting days per year rose to 123. In 1694 William III reluctantly accepted a reversal of the decision of 30 years before and gave his assent to a new Triennial Act, requiring a new parliament, and thus new elections, every three years. Parliament's enhanced place within the public life of the nation after 1660 meant that a seat in the House of Commons was more and more regarded as a route to influence and power. The Triennial Act and the development of party political confrontation pushed political competition in elections and in parliament itself to a level previously unheard of, bringing a new age of 'modern' politics.

Constituencies and the Franchise

After the experiments with the franchise of the 1650s, the Long Parliament reached back to the pre-revolutionary constitution when they issued writs for the Convention Parliament of 1660.[2] The 266 constituencies (39 English counties, 12 Welsh counties, 200 English and 12 Welsh borough constituencies and the two universities) sent between them a total of 507 members to the convention, in exactly the same way as they had for the Long Parliament in 1640. Apart from the addition of the Scottish and Irish constituencies under the Acts of Union of 1707 and 1800 representation remained essentially the same for the following 170 years: Durham county and city were enfranchised by act of parliament in 1673, and Newark by royal charter in the same year, the last alterations to constituencies until the transfer of Grampound's seats to Yorkshire in 1821.

The number of those legally entitled to vote is probably incalculable in this period. The number of those who did actually vote (the 'voterate') in certain constituencies is more easily accessible, for an increasing number of poll books and poll lists survive from the period. The county franchise was determined by the 1430 statute which entitled only those holding freehold property worth more than 40s. a year. Five English counties in 1660–90 had 'voterates' of more than 5,000; but the great majority of them polled between 1,000 and 5,000. During the period 1690–1715 the number of English counties with voterates of more than 5,000 had climbed to eight, no doubt because of the steady erosion of the real value of the 40s. qualification. Welsh county 'voterates' were much smaller: in half the counties fewer than 1,000 people voted.

Boroughs fell broadly into three categories: those where the right to vote went with some sort of municipal status such as membership of the corporation, or admission as 'freeman' or 'burgess'; those where it was attached to the possession of real property; and those where the qualification was permanent residence in the town concerned. Corporation boroughs had generally small electorates, commonly of 24 or 32 voters; but the large number of freeman boroughs included London, with the biggest electorate of any constituency in the country of around 8,000, as well as those with minute electorates like Queenborough, with its 19 voters in 1690. In both corporation and freeman boroughs, although the influence of local landowners was very strong, contests were relatively common, often because of conflict between opposing patrons or determined efforts by moneyed men and politicians to secure their seats, sometimes by making additional supporters from outside the borough freemen immediately before elections. Those boroughs where the right to vote was linked to the possession of property can be subdivided further into those where

---

[2] Although the large number of double returns has been taken as an indication of genuine confusion about what the franchise should be in many places: *The History of Parliament: The House of Commons, 1660–1690*, ed. B. D. Henning (3 vols, 1983), i, 106.

> ## Poll Books
>
> Lists of electors and how they voted exist in the later 17th century, often taken by one or other side at the poll and related to an attempt to challenge the validity of the election in the House of Commons. But an act of 1696 made it necessary for the returning officer in each county or borough to make a formal record of the poll; and the surviving poll books provide details of voting behaviour right down to the introduction of the secret ballot in 1872. Increasingly after 1700 they were printed and published: although the motive for publishing the first of them to be printed, that relating to the Essex by-election of 1694, appears to have been satisfying a prurient interest in its cause, the suicide of the previous member after numerous attempts through *inter alia* 'thrusting the rump of a turkey down his throat' and throwing himself downstairs.
>
> Source: G. Holmes, *Politics, Religion and Society in England, 1679–1742* (1986), 3.

the possession of freehold property conveyed the right to vote, which included very large and turbulent cities like Bristol and Norwich as well as many smaller ones; and burgage boroughs, where the right to vote was linked to the ownership of specific properties. The latter tended to be small, and contained some of the classic 'pocket boroughs', including the largely abandoned ancient city of Old Sarum, just outside Salisbury, whose bizarre status as a parliamentary borough with a mere ten voters was regularly cited as proof of the antiquity of the representative nature of parliament. The practice of selling freeholds or burgages shortly before elections and even splitting them into smaller properties which could be sold to multiply votes would become commonplace. Those boroughs where the right to vote was linked to residency used a variety of tests to determine it, including the payment of 'scot and lot' (a local tax), and being a householder or 'potwalloper', or more simply being an inhabitant. In very few places were all (male) inhabitants permitted to vote. Resident boroughs, which included the very large constituencies of Southwark (4,000 voters) and Westminster (over 7,000) were difficult and expensive to contest, and because of the poverty of their inhabitants, very open to outright bribery and corruption.

An increasing interest in electoral arrangements and local customs and laws was symptomatic of the new intensity of politics. While in many places, elections continued to be reasonably quiet affairs, with contests avoided and what has been called a process of parliamentary 'selection' – pre-election negotiation and agreement among local gentry which avoided the need for an actual poll – determining the choice of candidate, in many others the period saw a rapid growth in the number and intensity of election contests, particularly after the 1694 Triennial Act required elections to be held every three years, creating a permanent sense of expectation and political excitement. The new politics of party propagated new modes of electioneering, such as the development of a new literary sub-genre, the printed electoral advice, a sort of electioneering pamphlet that became common in the political crisis of 1679–81 and again in 1698–1701. George Savile, marquess of Halifax's *Some Cautions Offered to the Consideration of those who are to Chuse Members to Serve in the Ensuing Parliament*, first published in 1695, was regularly recycled in subsequent elections. Contests at 'general' elections rose from 50 for the elections to the Convention Parliament in 1660 to a pre-revolution peak of 107 in the fiercely fought elections to the first 'Exclusion' Parliament in early 1679, and to 110 in 1705 at the height of the 'rage of party' of Queen Anne's reign. Elections in some constituencies became routinely marked by venality and excess. Occasionally action was mooted in individual cases – the disfranchisement of Stockbridge, notorious for electoral malpractice, was discussed in 1689 and 1693–4 – and there was a spate of legislation attempting to overcome bribery and corruption in elections in 1695–6, but no constituency was disfranchised in the period, the legislation was entirely unsuccessful, and there appeared to be little appetite for or interest in a more thoroughgoing reform of the franchise and reapportionment of seats.

The poll itself did not end the election process. Arguments about the qualification of the electors or the behaviour of the returning officer frequently caused disputes over the result – or sometimes such disorder broke out at the election that the returning officer gave up and left it to the House of Commons itself to try to determine the result. The arguments were decided by the House of Commons itself. The Commons had resisted the claims of the courts to determine election disputes back in 1604, with the row over the *Goodwin v. Fortescue* case. In 1701 an argument over the Aylesbury election resulted in an appeal to the courts by one voter, sponsored by the whigs, who claimed that he had been improperly denied his vote. The eventual judgment – that election disputes could not be dealt with through the legal system – was overturned in January 1704 by a whig-dominated House of Lords, which argued that a vote was a form of property, and could therefore be defended in the law courts. The case – *Ashby v. White* – sparked a lengthy battle between the two Houses: formally it remained unresolved, but there was no subsequent challenge to the Commons' right to determine disputed elections.

Its right was exercised through the House's committee of privileges, called by MP Sir Richard Cocks 'the most corrupt court in Christendom', where the party struggle was at its most bitter.[3] The committee's judgments, normally endorsed by the House, were usually in the interests of whichever party was currently dominant. But they also reflected an overall concern to curb the unruliness and unpredictability of elections by

---

[3] Quoted in *The History of Parliament: The House of Commons, 1690–1715*, ed. E. Cruickshanks, S. Handley and D. W. Hayton (5 vols, Cambridge, 2002), i, 636.

> **Election Entertainment**
>
> In 1705 Sir Thomas Pitt grumbled to his son Robert, just elected at Old Sarum, 'When I hear in what manner you went down to Old Sarum against the election: sent a man cook sometime before, coach and six, five or six in liveries, open house for three or four months, and put me to about £500 charge. Where was the need of this? It never cost me above £10, which was for a dinner the day of the election.'
>
> Source: *The History of Parliament: The House of Commons, 1690–1715*, ed. E. Cruickshanks, S. Handley and D. W. Hayton (5 vols, Cambridge, 2002), ii, 691.

restricting the electorate: of 43 alterations to borough franchises made by the House over 1690 to 1715, 28 had the effect of narrowing the franchise.

Members, Constituents and the Distribution of Power

The satirist and MP Andrew Marvell argued that 'the very meanest commoner of England is represented in Parliament'.[4] But members found the practice of representation much more difficult and complex than the theory. Those recruited to parliament through the process belonged to a social elite: very few came from families of less than gentry status; around half emerged from titled families. For some, the effect of London's rapid growth as a trading and financial centre on recruitment to the Commons was a matter of real alarm. The 'moneyed interest' was treated with suspicion and scorn by older-established gentry, and undoubtedly the search by plutocrats such as Sir Samuel Shepheard for seats which could be easily brought was one factor in the inflation of the costs of elections. A lengthy campaign to create a property qualification for members did not bear fruit until 1711, the passage of the Landed Qualification Act, requiring county members to have an annual income of £600 a year. But although very many also benefited from employment in the professions – the law, the military forces and in government – or in business, parliament remained essentially representative of the propertied classes. Some merchants felt, indeed, that it was too much biased towards landed wealth: 'Tis well known of late years, the House of Commons has been filled with Gentlemen, whose Ignorance of, and unconcern for Trade, has by degrees brought it to the condition it is now in', wrote one of them in 1681.[5] In line with the social exclusiveness of parliament, payment of members had

---

[4] Quoted in M. Knights, *Representation and Misrepresentation in Later Stuart Britain: Partisanship and Political Culture* (Oxford, 2005), 107.

[5] *Considerations offered to all the corporations of England, well worth their observation, containing seasonable advice to them in their future election of Burgesses to Serve in Parliament, Merely in relation to, and so far forth only, as such Elections affect Trade, and are, as will appear hereby, the main cause of its present great decay* (for William Cademan, 1681).

by now almost completely fallen into disuse. Marvell was sneered at for taking a salary from his constituency (Hull) for his work in parliament, and a bill was prepared in 1677 to remove members' rights to wages, but never proceeded, perhaps because it was largely unnecessary.

Members found elections expensive, inconvenient and unpleasant, and naturally preferred to avoid them wherever possible. Governments shared that view, at least if they could find a reasonably sympathetic parliament. Charles II proved exceptionally reluctant to abandon the 'Cavalier' Parliament, which sat almost every year from 1661 to 1679, and whose early sessions at least suggested a mood of unusual support not only for the monarchy, but also for the established church. Its backing for legislation in support of religious uniformity and repressive of religious dissent evoked a sustained campaign from nonconformists and others for its dissolution and replacement. It also encouraged some to hark back to ideas of the 1640s to stress the limitations of representational power. The quaker leader William Penn wrote in the mid-1670s that

> Every representative in the world, is the *creature of the people*; for the people make them, and to them they owe their being. Here is no transsentiating or transubstantiating of being from *people* to *representative*, no more than there is an absolute transferring of *title* in a letter of attorney; the very term Representative is enough to the contrary.[6]

Penn's attitude was one which had historically been vigorously rejected by parliamentarians themselves; but politically motivated constituents became much more demanding about how they were represented. During the politically tense years of 1678–81, the practice of addressing new MPs, to impose a sort of manifesto on the elected politician, became a common political tactic. The London address of 1681, one of many, demanded that the City's MPs should 'secure the meeting and sitting of frequent *Parliaments*; to assert our undoubted Rights of *petitioning* ... to promote the happy and long-wished for Union amongst all his Majesties Protestant Subjects', as well as to repeal legislation directed against religious nonconformists.[7] Petitioning could be seen as challenging parliament's authority. Mass petitioning of parliament was outlawed by statute in 1661, and a petition from Kent in 1701 demanding that it should 'have regard to the voice of the people' created a political row when tories suspected (no doubt correctly) that the petitioners were whigs. The petition was voted to be 'scandalous, insolent and seditious, tending to destroy the constitution of parliament, and to subvert the established government of this realm', and the House ordered the arrest of the petitioners. A pamphlet in support of them warned that 'they that made you members

---

[6] William Penn, *England's Present Interest Discover'd* (1675); see also *England's Great Interest in the Choice of this New Parliament* (1679).

[7] Quoted in G. De Krey, *London and the Restoration, 1659–1683* (Cambridge, 2005), 213.

may reduce you to the same rank from whence they chose you; and may give you a taste of their abused kindness in terms you may not be pleas'd with'.[8] Threats like this did not make up a demand for political reform. But it was obvious that a more turbulent politics could help to spread participation and party well beyond the circle defined by birth, wealth and connection.

The Setting

Parliament had historically tended to meet in the winter and the early spring, omitting the uncomfortable summer months. In the 1690s this was to become a settled pattern, with a new session beginning usually in November, and an adjournment in April, May or June. The House would normally meet in the morning, with less controversial business dealt with early on, and the main political business taken in the early afternoon. It met as before in St Stephen's Chapel, Westminster, except for the two occasions in the period, in 1665 and 1681, when parliament met in Oxford, the first because of the plague then raging in the capital, the second because of the 'Exclusion crisis' and the government's fears of the effect of parliament's meeting on the already fevered political mood in London, and also perhaps in order to disrupt the strong political networks between the whig leadership in parliament and in the City. The chamber in Westminster was small, stuffy, and judging from the lowering of the ceiling in 1692, acoustically very poor. Other improvements made in the 1690s, such as the greater frequency with which the House met, made these defects no longer bearable. New galleries were added to increase the number of seats, and committee rooms were also provided. Members did begin to sit, to some extent, according to their party, though not yet in the modern manner in clear blocks on opposing sides of the House.

The fact that the House sat more frequently and more regularly than before seems to have stimulated members into trying to put the confused mass of practice and custom, precedents and orders into some sort of system. A 1667 committee, chaired by the indefatigable William Prynne, undertook some work, but although at least one procedural change resulted – one which foreshadowed a fundamental order of 1707 that grants of public money should only be considered in committee of the whole House – it seems to have made little headway. Another committee, established in 1674, with some of the same members, stimulated debate in the House, and from 1678 the House started calling some of its new resolutions and orders about its own proceedings 'standing orders'. This did not mean, though, that the House was moving in the direction of a completely systematic set of rules of procedure, for its customary rules and precedents remained (and remain) just as significant a part of the law of parliament.

[8] Quoted in Knights, *Representation and Misrepresentation*, 129–34.

> ### Parliamentary Tactics
>
> The sophistication with which parliamentary strategy and tactics could be handled by some was sketched in a 1662 description of the way some parliamentary lobby groups operated: 'They have their contrivers, their speakers, their sticklers, their dividers, their moderators, and their blancks: (their I-and-NO men) by which method and intelligence, all debates are managed to the advantage of the party, and occasion. They know when to move, when to press, when to quit, divert, put off, &c and they are as skilful in the manner of moulding their business as they are watchful for the season of timing it.'
>
> Source: Roger L'Estrange, *A Memento* (1662), 145, quoted in P. Seaward, *Cavalier Parliament, 1661–1667* (Cambridge, 1989), 94.

The Management of the House

Obtaining the desired outcome from chamber of over 500 members was an arduous and time-consuming business to which an enormous amount of effort was devoted. The crown needed above all to secure finance from parliament in the teeth of a powerful cultural resistance to any sort of non-customary taxation. At the same time it had to struggle to prevent the potential for factional conflict at court spilling out into the legislature to create factions in the country at large. All governments had recognized the difficulty and importance of parliamentary management: but as parliament loomed larger in political life, so too did the arts of ensuring its successful conclusion. From the 1660s the time and attention governments gave to management of the Commons grew steadily. In 1663 the earl of Bristol's offer with Sir Richard Temple to 'undertake' the task erupted into a huge political row; perhaps it was this that encouraged the secretary of state Sir Henry Bennet (later Lord Arlington), together with his protégé, Sir Thomas Clifford, to begin a quiet process of using government patronage to secure the consistent support of a growing group of members.

In the mid-1670s under the lord treasurer, the earl of Danby, the systematic creation of a government party reached new heights of sophistication, or to the government's many critics, degradation. Andrew Marvell alleged in 1678 that it 'is too notorious to be concealed, that near a third part of the House have beneficial Offices under his Majesty, in the Privy Council, the Army, the Navy, the Law, the Household, the Revenue both in England and Ireland, or in attendance on his Majesties Person'.[9] Marvell's figure sounds much exaggerated: in the 1690s (when the war resulted in a rapid growth in the positions available) estimates of the number of

---

[9] Andrew Marvell, *An Account of the Growth of Popery*, in *The Prose Works of Andrew Marvell*, ed. Martin Dzelzains and Annabel Patterson (2 vols, New Haven, 2003), ii, 299.

'placemen' – members of the House of Commons holding official government positions – ranged from about 90 to 110, perhaps a fifth of the House. Yet many more received secret service payments, held pensions, or were the beneficiaries of government contracts. A series of statutes – 'Place Acts' – prevented members from taking up government offices, obliging them to leave parliament on taking up certain offices, until the 1706 Regency Act required all members who took office during a session to resign their seats and undergo re-election. Yet the 'payroll vote' was never entirely reliable, and it was usually other connections, particularly party, that were of more significance in ensuring the loyalty of government employees. The continuing difficulty of dealing with the Commons was echoed constantly in the frustrations of the government's parliamentary managers: 'nobody can know, one day, what the House of Commons would do the next' complained one of them in 1692.[10]

The speakership was of critical importance in the management of business. Although formally chosen by the House, it was accepted that the government would in effect nominate the candidate to be chosen. When a new Speaker was required in 1673 the choice was discussed by the king and his most senior ministers in the foreign affairs committee (a sort of precursor to the cabinet) over two days. The man eventually chosen, Edward Seymour, was widely regarded as an ideal Speaker from the point of view of the court, responding quickly and generally ably to instructions from Danby. Following the political fire-storm of 1678, however, when allegations of popery in high places and corrupt dealings with the French government pushed an already tense situation into the 'Exclusion crisis', Danby seems to have suspected that Seymour had begun to flirt with his opponents. At the beginning of the parliament of 1679 the government forced a political row by rejecting the Commons' choice of Seymour as Speaker. After the revolution, the logic of party politics led frequently to the election as Speaker of very senior figures within the party that emerged dominant from the previous election. Paul Foley (1695–8) and Robert Harley (1701–5) were in effect leaders of their party while being Speaker. The speakership was an office of considerable profit, mainly as a result of the fees which those promoting private bills were required to pay to him – Speaker Edward Turnor (1661–70) was said always to have had his eye on private bills – but also because many groups would offer more underhand kickbacks: Turnor was 'blown in the House of Commons' according to Roger North because of a present of 50 guineas given him by the East India Company in 1666,[11] and Sir John Trevor (1685, 1690–5) was expelled from the House in 1695 for receiving bribes to promote the London Orphans Bill.

---

[10] Quoted in J. Brewer, *The Sinews of Power: War, Money, and the English State, 1688–1783* (1989), 149.
[11] Roger North, *Lives of the Norths*, ed. A. Jessop (3 vols, 1890), i, 68.

Party

The definition of party and faction has always presented a difficulty to historians in this period. At its beginning, contemporaries identified a number of different political blocs in the House of Commons. Most fundamental, though vaguest, was the old distinction between the 'court' and the 'country'. Other divisions were obvious; from the Restoration contemporaries referred to a 'presbyterian' group in the House, as well as a strongly Anglican lobby. Some prominent court politicians attempted to establish their own factions in parliament: both the earl of Bristol in the early 1660s, and the duke of Buckingham in the late 1660s and 1670s tried to do so, though neither succeeded more than marginally.

But from the early 1670s, in the hot-house atmosphere of the worries over the conversion to Catholicism of the king's brother, the duke of York (the future James II), the divisions based on religion coalesced with factional groupings and with ideas of court and country to create a new, and for some, deeply distasteful language of 'party'. One of the earliest signs of this tendency was the great meeting of MPs to co-ordinate plans against Catholicism and the French alliance in advance of the parliamentary session of 1673. The new virus was propagated by Charles II's decision shortly afterwards to identify himself, through his minister the earl of Danby, with the church 'interest', and the political crisis created by the assiduously cultivated belief in a Roman Catholic plot to assassinate the king and hasten the accession of a popish monarch. During the consequent battles over the attempt to exclude James from the throne, the parties gained their names: tories claimed the ideological legacy of royalism, and set themselves up as the defenders of the Church of England; whigs were identified with the strongest anti-Catholic feeling, and with support for religious dissent, and the civil war parliamentary past. They were labels of emotional, rather than organizational, significance, so that neither party possessed effective central leadership and control; nevertheless the labels, and the idea of party as the dominant means of understanding political battlelines, were powerful and enduring.

Enduring, but protean, as the labels could acquire subtly different meanings depending on the political and ideological context. The revolution of 1688 shook them up thoroughly. The events of the reign of James II, and its ignominious conclusion, had broken a bond between toryism and loyal support for the crown while whigs, the natural beneficiaries of the revolution, found that the oppositional language of liberty and property they had taken up during their struggle against James and popery was now strained as they tried to defend the new regime against a series of internal and external threats. Nevertheless, the complex divisions that emerged after the revolution between the parties over their attitudes to strategy in the continental war, to the toleration of dissenters, and to the growth of a powerful financial industry, echoed the preoccupations of the late 1670s and early 1680s.

The aftermath of the revolution also encouraged the development of formidable political machines which could convert party ideologies into parliamentary programmes. The regularity with which parliament was meeting in the 1690s made a systematic approach to parliamentary management both possible and essential. It took some time to achieve: the junto whigs – the composite leadership of the whig party built initially in 1693–4 around Sir John (later Lord) Somers, Charles Montagu, later Lord Halifax, Lord Wharton, and Admiral Russell, later earl of Orford – established themselves by the reign of Anne as the most effective exponents of the arts of management, spreading messages on strategy and tactics to their party followers through a series of meetings and dinners. Party demanded a greater number of organizers than before: the tories created a system of 'whips', derived from the hunting phrase 'whippers-in', on a regional basis. Like-minded groups gathered as clubs, like the whig Kit-Cat Club, founded in 1700, and in coffee houses or taverns which became colonized by one side or the other. Though the whigs, especially, had by the end of the 17th century secured a remarkable degree of control over their party, it was never absolute, and always tempered by radical spirits or independents of a determined 'country' persuasion. The tories, nursing the tradition of the bloody-minded independent squire, could never match them in cohesion, and proved much more difficult to manage when in government – but were regularly formidable when opposing a whig government.

Government Finance

Fundamental to the relationship between parliament and the crown was the former's status as the gateway to legitimate taxation. Key to the viability of the Restoration regime was the creation of a new deal on its public finance, a settlement initially made by the Convention Parliament in 1660 and based on the exchange of ancient customary revenues, in particular those of the court of wards, for some of the new fiscal initiatives of the revolutionary years, especially the excise. The estimates on which this settlement were based, it was subsequently argued, had been over-optimistic both as to yield of existing revenues and the limits of expenditure, and the shortfall left the government struggling with a constant deficit. Meanwhile the Restoration government's acceptance and development of the interregnum's expansion of state activity – most notably a large state-of-the-art navy – meant that its expenses would continually grow.

The government's options for finding money without parliamentary finance were minimal. It implicitly accepted the limits imposed by the Petition of Right on its ability to raise money without parliamentary consent. It worked hard on improving the yield of its ordinary revenue, and with the expansion of trade in the years of peace in the 1680s, the customs and excise revenue did start to become productive enough to allow it to avoid parliament for much of the decade. But expensive foreign wars could not be managed without it, and the conflicts with the Dutch republic in 1665–7 and 1672–4 and preparations for the war with France in the late 1670s brought government into a constant state of reliance on parliament. Parliamentary finance, though essential, was not enough for waging war: bridging finance was always required, and a key innovation in public finance was the statutory guarantee of loans to government through the credit order system, initiated in 1665: its aim was to create a type of government security with guarantees of repayment. Although this was an innovation which would form part of the basis of future management of government finance it did have the drawback of removing the flexibility on which the sometimes hand-to-mouth process of government finance depended: it had to be withdrawn for a time in 1672 under the stop of the exchequer, a huge blow to the government's reputation for financial integrity.

Traditionally, grants of taxation originated with a request from the king at the beginning of a parliamentary session. Extracting supply from the House of Commons was a long-winded and exceptionally difficult process, and governments approached the task with careful preparation – the time-honoured technique being for a back-bench member to be primed to propose a specific sum for a grant. In the 1660s the House assimilated some of the more systematic processes which had developed in the 1640s, particularly the use of a committee of the whole House to consider the sum to be granted (a procedure confirmed by a resolution in 1668), although the formal distinction made between the committee of supply (which determined the amount of the grant) and the committee of ways and means (which determined how it would be raised) seems to have emerged rather later. Government was increasingly willing to provide information to back up its requests. In 1661 the treasury secretary presented a report explaining the deficiencies in the ordinary (non-parliamentary) revenue. Parliamentarians had sometimes in the past tried to establish some sort of accountability mechanism for the expenditure of voted taxation. Widespread suspicion that the phenomenal sums of money voted for the second Anglo-Dutch war in 1664–7 had been misspent was behind the establishment of a statutory commission of accounts in 1667, which reported to both houses of parliament in 1669, although most of its teeth were pulled by the king's studied indifference to its results. Subsequent events made even clearer, at least to the system's supporters, the necessity for some form of parliamentary control over expenditure: there was outrage when additional customs impositions voted in 1671 in order to strengthen the navy against the growing sea power of France turned out to have been used for preparations for another war with the Dutch republic – with France as an ally – a development which considerably worsened the problem of extracting money from parliament subsequently. Appropriation, the practice of specifying within law the purposes for which supply was granted, was one response to the expectation that money voted would be diverted to other purposes; but it was also a valuable way for a treasury bureaucracy growing in sophistication to establish a firm handle on government expenditure.

The experience of the reigns of Charles II and James II helped to ensure that after the revolution the Commons insisted on under-funding the ordinary expense of government, and voting taxes on a relatively short-term basis. During the 1690s, with heavy taxes voted on almost annually, the House was forced to adopt a much more systematic approach to the whole fiscal process, and perhaps more important, governments were forced to be more effective in preparing their own proposals. The House came to expect estimates to be presented before consideration in the committee of supply, and an annual cycle developed for the presentation of estimates (in November or December) and the subsequent voting of supply. An order of 1706 (subsequently a standing order) gave the initiative in presenting money bills to the government. The creation of a national debt took one step further the system of lending on the credit of statutory taxation pioneered in the 1660s. The device of a statutory accounts commission was revived: the first was set up in 1691, and it was continued, after a brief lapse in 1692, each year until 1697. In its early years it was a powerful instrument of scrutiny; as it proceeded, however, the presence of government officials and courtiers within its ranks blunted its attack. A new commission was appointed by the tories at the beginning of the reign of Queen Anne, although it lapsed in 1704, discredited by its use as a party-political weapon.

The Grand Inquest of the Nation

If, from the point of view of the crown, taxation was the chief and historic role of the House of Commons, from the point of view of its subjects it was the investigation and redress of grievances. Pre-civil-war parliaments had used grand or general committees to consider the grievances of the country, but such a general approach to the problems of the country at large did not survive the war. Discussion and resolution of grievances was pursued instead through various different channels. One was the highly political and confrontational process of impeachment, used regularly by court factions against their rivals. The earl of Bristol botched his attempt to impeach the king's chief minister, the earl of Clarendon, in 1663; a set of charges presented by the Commons against Viscount Mordaunt in late 1666 paved the way for a full-dress impeachment attempt against Clarendon in the session of October 1667, after his dismissal from office. An extended investigation into the miscarriages of the Second Dutch War in 1667–8 resulted in a series of impeachments and expulsions in April 1668. In 1669 charges were brought against the recently dismissed lord lieutenant of Ireland, the duke of Ormond, and his rival, the earl of Orrery. In April 1675 an attempt to impeach the earl of Danby failed at the first hurdle. Impeachments were difficult to manage, as they required the Lords to accept the case presented by the Commons; it proved frequently simpler to address the king to secure the removal of an unpopular minister – though with no better ultimate result. Addresses were presented in 1674 calling for the removal of several prominent ministers. Despite their lack of success, the potential of such attacks to disrupt the processes of government were considerable and made ministers exceptionally wary. The continuing attack on Danby in 1677 and 1678 eventually forced Charles II to strike a deal with the whigs for a dissolution of the 'Cavalier' Parliament, although contrary to the agreement an impeachment was relaunched in the new parliament of 1679, and the king found no other way to overcome the problem but to issue a highly controversial pardon.

After the revolution the intensity of partisan feeling and political competitions made the pursuit of political opponents a constant preoccupation of the Commons. The 1689 Convention Parliament's committee on the state of the nation, revived many times over the ensuing years, in 1691–2, 1694, 1696, 1700 and 1701, provided a means for the government's opponents to pursue individual ministers for failures during the war. The earl of Danby, now duke of Leeds, was still a target, impeached again in April 1695. The attempts of the Jacobite conspirator Sir John Fenwick to implicate the whig leaders Godolphin, Shrewsbury and Russell in charges of treasonable correspondence with James II at St Germain in 1696 ended in his own attainder and execution. The threat of an impeachment forced the earl of Sunderland out of government in 1697; whigs followed this by turning tory-inspired criticism of the management of the exchequer under Montagu into a counter-attack on one of the tory officials previously responsible for it. After the 1698 election a vigorous response by tory and country politicians forced the earl of Orford, one of the junto, out of office by means of an investigation into corruption in navy administration, and after the 1701 election impeachments were mounted against the main junto whig leaders, Lords Somers, Halifax and the earl of Orford, although they were cleared by the House of Lords. Following their accession to power under Anne, jubilant tories used the commissions of accounts to bring down whig targets, including Lord Ranelagh, expelled from the Commons in 1702.

These titanic struggles may have been of consuming interest to politicians and to some electors who were increasingly aware of the political dramas taking place at Westminster. But just as much time and energy was occupied on grievances that were of more direct interest to the world beyond England's political village: specific problems, often general concerns about trade, industry or the administration of or access to justice. Many such issues were dealt with through select committee inquiries – 247 of these were appointed for this purpose over the period 1690 to 1715 – and would often result in legislation. Yet the vast majority of legislation passed – in some sessions over 70% – was made up of private acts, aimed at resolving the legal problems of private individuals or corporations. Demand for legislation of this kind grew phenomenally, as many found it the best way of securing watertight legal title to land or money. In the

1660s the 'Cavalier' Parliament passed a total of 334 acts. As parliament met less in the 1670s and the 1680s its productivity declined; there were 197 in the 1670s and 106 in the 1680s – many of which passed during the Convention Parliament of 1689–90. But after the revolution, legislative activity boomed. In the 1690s parliament passed 671 acts, rising to 740 in the first decade of the 18th century.

Some people's legislative opportunities were other people's legislative threats, and while industries and other groups continued to use parliament in the time honoured manner to seek protection from external competition, they had to become more alert to the threats and more canny in seizing the opportunities. The attempt to prohibit cheap imports of cattle from Ireland in the mid-1660s was determinedly, though unsuccessfully, opposed by the Irish farming industry. A powerful lobby was gathered to fight against the leather duty in 1697–9; the woollen manufacturers struggled hard to oppose competition from imports from Ireland and the East Indies. But legislation was not only the product of purely economic interest. Bills for the reformation of society, the tightening of the laws against immorality of various kinds, were popular especially in the 1690s, as part of a widespread movement for the 'reformation of manners'. The defence of the church and the protection of religious nonconformity were subjects of intense political concern. A lobbying industry began to grow up, as promoting parliamentary legislation became a specialist skill. The Gold and Silver Wire Drawers' Company in 1698, for example, employed an agent to draw up a clause for the Lace Importation Bill designed to ban imports of gold and silver thread, to meet the MPs who sponsored the bill to organize a petition in its favour, to draw up a summary of the bill, to solicit MPs to attend select committee meetings and to attend the House of Lords to help the bill to get through.

The Lords and the Commons

The re-establishment of the Lords in 1660 meant that the art of managing a bicameral parliament had to be relearnt. Over the next few years there were numerous small disputes between the two Houses, over the acknowledgement of the privileges of the Lords in general legislation, such as tax grants and laws requiring searches of individual property, in which the Lords were often determined to assert special treatment for themselves. From the late 1660s, however, a series of disputes centred on the powers of either House. Partly this was because a group of senior politicians, many of them important figures in the regimes of the 1640s and 1650s, began to use inter-cameral confrontations as a way of persuading the king to abandon the 'Cavalier' Parliament and call fresh elections. The Lords' decision in April 1667 to hear the dispute between Thomas Skinner and the East India Company involved the acceptance of a case of first instance, rather than an appeal, to which they had previously restricted themselves: it became a dispute when the company claimed that as several of its directors were members of the Commons, the Lords' action amounted to a breach of the privilege of the lower House. The row continued into the following session, when the Commons sent up a bill which attempted to define the Lords judicial powers, and dragged on until the king finally succeeded in engineering a compromise, though one that failed to settle the underlying issue, in 1670. The following year, though, the Lords provoked a further row when they sought to amend a supply bill to alter the rates of duty on sugar, with the result that the much-needed bill was lost altogether. In 1675 an appeal in the Lords against a decision in chancery in favour of a member of the House of Commons revived the dispute over jurisdiction: *Shirley* v. *Fagg* only became as bitter a dispute as it did because it was deliberately used to create a deadlock between the two Houses in order to prevent the progress of the earl of Danby's Test Bill, limiting office to Anglicans.

After the revolution, if anything, relations between the two Houses became worse. Some of this continued to be down to politics: a number of confrontations after 1700 reflected the opposition of a whig majority in the Lords to measures passed by a tory-dominated lower House. But though made worse by party-politics, the irritations behind the confrontations were genuine and a measure of different conceptions of the role of each House in the constitution. If the Lords occasionally strained at the traditional restriction on their rights to amend supply bills (as in their attempt to amend the Land Tax Bill of 1693) the Commons would try to restrict their ability to amend other legislation by 'tacking', or incorporating provisions within supply bills which were unwelcome to a majority in the Lords and had nothing to do with supply. The exercise of the judicial role of the House of Lords continued to cause friction, particularly in the

---

Reporting the House

In 1675 the earl of Danby was told of a small business based at the premises of two booksellers, to which were sent every afternoon 'all resolutions of Parliament that are either voted or a preparing for vote in either House, perfect true, or artificially corrupted, or penned by halves on purpose as may make most for the Faction. All speeches of the most eminent members of each House that way affected, upon every business, are also sent them. Addresses also intended and at any time preparing by either House are here to be had in copies.' Danby's informant went on to explain how these documents were copied and sent nationwide, and to drive home the point he enclosed 'a copy of the intended address to his Majesty which the Houses have not yet agreed to'.

Source: H. Love, *Scribal Publication in Seventeenth-Century England* (Oxford, 1993), 21.

Ashby v. *White* case concerning an election petition, which infuriated the lower House in 1704.

Reporting the House

Though formally its proceedings were held in private and not disseminated, news of what went on in the Commons could spread quickly through London. Having agonized over the subject a number of times the House finally resolved in October 1680 to print its *Votes and Proceedings*. The practice was abandoned in the parliament of 1685, but from 1689 the *Votes* were printed on a regular basis.

While it had accepted the inevitability of the *Votes* – purely a formal record of decisions taken – being widely disseminated, the House, in theory at least, tried to stop any more detail of its proceedings being published. Nevertheless, it became increasingly common for political factions and parties to publish without approval accounts of debates, or lists of those who had voted in a particular division. *A Seasonable Argument to Perswade all the Grand Juries in England to Petition for a New Parliament* (1677) was 'a list of the Principal Labourers in the Great Design of POPERY and ARBITRARY POWER'. *A List of One Unanimous Club of Voters* (1679) gave the names of MPs who were regarded as compromised by their support for (and, in many cases, payment by) the earl of Danby, and publicized the details of the investigation that had been carried out by the Commons into the use of secret service money. There were many similar subsequent lists, for example the whig 'black list' of 1701 and a list of those who had supported the tory tactic of 'tacking' a bill against occasional conformity onto a supply bill. The House itself – at the behest of one or other political party temporarily in control of a majority – sometimes ordered the publication of material such as reports of committees, to ensure public circulation for matter of political interest. Publications of this kind included, for example, details of the proceedings on the impeachments of the junto whigs in 1701 and the highly controversial Occasional Conformity Bills.

Constitutional Questions

The underlying assumption of Restoration politics had been that it was possible to recreate the constitutional structures of before the civil war. The unreality of such an ambition was quickly apparent. The logic of international and domestic politics made it ultimately impossible to keep parliament as a minor partner in the constitution. Monarchs aiming at power and influence needed it and felt hemmed in by it: William III complained that the Commons 'used him like a dog', and said he was so weary of it that 'he could not bear them'.[12] But for all the radicalism and energy of some parliamentarians in the 1690s, parliament remained an essentially

---

[12] Quoted in Stephen R. Baxter, *William III* (1955), 255.

rather conservative and reactive body, supportive or critical, but reluctant to be drawn into a close embrace with government.

And yet parliament had also been drawn, albeit reluctantly, into a new relationship with the people. As the lively politics of party had brought with it a new level of engagement with the electorate, as parties began to appeal beyond parliament to the wider interests they represented, politicians started to recognize some of the warning signs and to worry about the stability of the system as a whole.

Chronology

1660
March	Dissolution of the Rump Parliament
April	Convention Parliament assembles
May	Convention agrees to invite Charles II to return from exile
December	Dissolution of the Convention Parliament

1661
May	'Cavalier' Parliament assembles
November	Restoration of bishops to the House of Lords

1663
Unsuccessful attempt to impeach earl of Clarendon

1664
Triennial Act repealed; requirement for elections every three years removed

1667
Impeachment of earl of Clarendon; establishment of statutory commission of accounts

1670
Lords and Commons dispute over *Skinner* v. *East India Company* brought to an end

1673
Declaration of indulgence cancelled following opposition of Commons

1675
Lords and Commons dispute over *Shirley* v. *Fagg* begins

1679
January	Dissolution of 'Cavalier' Parliament
March	Parliament of 1679 assembles; impeachment of earl of Danby; Commons begin work on bill to exclude James, duke of York from the throne
October	New elections held, but parliament does not meet until late 1680

1680
November	House of Lords reject Commons' Exclusion Bill

1681
March — Parliament of 1681 meets in Oxford; dissolved after first reading of Exclusion Bill

1685
February — Death of Charles II; accession of James II
May — Parliament meets; prorogued in November

1687
Parliament dissolved

1688
November — Landing of William of Orange
December — Departure of James II for France

1689
January — Convention Parliament assembles
February — Declaration of Rights tendered to William of Orange and Princess Mary, with offer of the throne

1690
February — Convention Parliament dissolved
March — Parliament assembles

1691
Statutory commission of accounts established

1694
Death of Mary II; Triennial Act

1695
March — Speaker Sir John Trevor expelled from the House

1701
February — First parliament of 1701 assembles
April — Impeachment proceedings begin against junto whigs
November — First parliament of 1701 dissolved
December — Second parliament of 1701 assembles

1702
March — Death of William III; accession of Anne
October — Parliament assembles

1704
Ashby v. White judgment in the Lords

1705
October — Parliament assembles

1706
Regency Act requires all members taking office to resign their seats

1707
April — Parliament prorogued, and continued by proclamation as first parliament of Great Britain

Further Reading

D. Hirst, *The Representative of the People? Voters and Voting in England under the Early Stuarts* (Cambridge, 1975)

The History of Parliament: The House of Commons, 1690–1715, ed. E. Cruickshanks, S. Handley and D. W. Hayton (5 vols, Cambridge, 2002), i (Introductory Survey)

G. Holmes, *British Politics in the Reign of Anne* (rev. edn, 1987)

—— 'The Electorate and the National Will in the First Age of Party', in his *Politics, Religion and Society in England, 1679–1742* (1986), 1–34

H. Horwitz, *Parliament, Policy and Politics in the Reign of William III* (Manchester, 1977)

M. A. Kishlansky, *Parliamentary Selection: Social and Political Choice in Early Modern England* (Cambridge, 1986)

M. Knights, *Politics and Opinion in Crisis, 1678–1681* (Cambridge, 1994)

—— *Representation and Misrepresentation in Later Stuart Britain: Partisanship and Political Culture* (Oxford, 2005)

P. Seaward, *The Cavalier Parliament and the Reconstruction of the Old Regime, 1661–1667* (Cambridge 1989)

W. A. Speck, *Tory and Whig: The Struggle in the Constituencies* (1970)

Parliament of Great Britain, 1707–1800

13 The House of Lords, 1707–1800
Clyve Jones and Stephen Farrell

The second parliament of Queen Anne, elected in 1705, ended its second session on 24 April 1707. On 1 May 1707 the Anglo-Scottish parliamentary union, negotiated in 1706, came into effect, creating a united kingdom of Great Britain. Two days earlier, by a royal proclamation, dated 29 April, the parliament of England was declared to be the first parliament of Great Britain. And its first session (the third of Anne's second parliament) started on 23 October 1707.

Anne (1702–14) was the fourth female to occupy the English throne (if one excludes Matilda and Lady Jane Grey) and was important in two respects in the history of the institution of parliament. First, as one-third of the parliamentary triumvirate of monarch, Lords and Commons, she, like her predecessors, had the right of veto over legislation by refusing the royal assent, and Anne was the last monarch to use this right, when on 11 March 1708 she rejected the Scottish Militia Bill. Second, monarchs had often used in the later 17th century the right to attend the proceedings of the House of Lords incognito (that is, not wearing robes and not carrying the regalia which were worn on formal occasions such as the opening of parliament), when custom dictated that the House formally took no notice of the monarch's presence. Anne attended incognita on many occasions, often at the behest of the ministry to put pressure on the members of the House to support its position. Here she was following the practise of her immediate predecessors, particularly Charles II, who revived the practice when he first attended incognito on 21 March 1670, telling the House that he had 'come to renew a Custom of His Predecessors, long discontinued, to be present at Debates, but not to interrupt the Freedom thereof'.[1] On such occasions, Charles was sometimes to be seen standing by the fireplace talking to individuals or to small groups of peers, and once was forced to intervene in the proceedings calling their lordships to order.[2] Both James II and William III followed his initiative. Anne was the last monarch to do so; the practice stopped with the succession of the Hanoverians.

---

[1] *LJ*, xii, 318.
[2] *LJ*, xii, 412–13 (26 January 1671): he told the House, 'That He observed very great Disorders among their Lordships in this House, both at the Hearing of Causes, and in Debates among themselves; and did make it His earnest Desire to their Lordships, that they would henceforward observe better Order, and not prophane such a Presence as this is with the like Disorder; but to keep their Places, and proceed in Businesses according to their Orders prescribed in the House.'

The Royal Veto

On 11 March 1708 Queen Anne gave the royal assent to seven bills with the words 'La Raine le veult', before she vetoed the Scottish Militia Bill with the words 'La Raine se avisera.' She went on to assent to a further three private bills with the words 'Soit fait come il est desiré'. Bishop Nicolson of Carlisle recorded the event in his diary: the House of Lords 'prepared several Bills for the Queen; who came to them about Four and (having given Royal Assent to Several, and Rejected that for Modelling the Militia in Scotland) acquainted both Houses that the Pretender was on the Suffolk coast; that Sir George Bing was near him, and 10 Squadrons on Board at Ostend ready to follow him'. This was the first time Queen Anne had used her veto over proposed legislation, and it turned out that this was the last time any British monarch would use this part of the royal prerogative. A modern historian, Geoffrey Holmes, has commented that this event 'produced not even a ripple of political excitement at the time, let alone a sense of constitutional "occasion"'. This comment was made from the advantage of hindsight. First, as the extract from Bishop Nicolson's diary shows, the queen after the veto announced a prospective invasion of Britain by the pro-French, Jacobite claimant to the British throne in the midst of a war with France. This news would undoubtedly have dwarfed the use of the royal veto in the Lords that day, even though it was the first veto for 12 years. Second, no one at the time could have been aware that this would be the last use of the veto. Also, third, while Henry VIII is known to have withheld assent from one bill in 1540, Elizabeth I did so in each of her ten parliaments, James I and Charles I had used the veto only once each (though James I did throw out six bills at one go), and Charles II and James II had only use the veto six times between them, Anne's immediate predecessor, William III, used it on five occasions between 1692 and 1696, including once against the Triennial Bill in 1693, and twice on bills which would have imposed restrictions on MPs in 1694 and 1696. The veto of the Triennial Bill did cause an outcry. According to Bishop Gilbert Burnet, '[t]he rejecting of a bill, though an unquestionable right of the crown, has been so seldom practised, that the two houses are apt to think it a hardship when there is a bill denied.' Various protests over William III's subsequent vetoes were tried by the Commons, and the king did not use the veto after 1696. The Harley ministry threatened to use the veto in 1714 over the resumption of Scottish ecclesiastical revenues but it was never used. Whether or to what extent the monarch's theoretical power of veto has ever in modern times influenced a government's legislative programme is a matter of conjecture.

CJ

Sources: LJ, xviii, 506; *The London Diaries of William Nicolson, Bishop of Carlisle, 1702–1718*, ed. C. Jones and G. Holmes (Oxford, 1985), 461; G. Holmes, *British Politics in the Age of Anne* (rev. edn, 1987), 186; G. R. Elton, *Reform* and *Renewal: Thomas Cromwell and the Common Weal* (Cambridge, 1973), 96; J. E. Neale, *The Elizabethan House of Commons* (1949), 427; C. Russell, *Parliaments and English Politics, 1621–1629* (Oxford, 1979), 45; *The History of Parliament: The House of Commons, 1690–1715*, ed. E. Cruickshanks, S. Handley and D. W. Hayton (5 vols, Cambridge, 2002), i, 382–3; *Gilbert Burnet's History of His Own Time* (6 vols, Oxford, 1833), v, 192.

Membership

The size of the membership of the House of Lords was not the same as the number of peers, as minors, women, lunatics and Roman Catholics were excluded from the House. But the number of the excluded varied from session to session. Thus the potential size of the membership can only be gauged by looking at the number of peers at any one time. The rate of those who were raised to a peerage through the 18th century fluctuated from reign to reign: Queen Anne, George I and George II raised roughly the same number to the peerage (about 30 each), though the length of their reigns differed (12, 13 and 33 years respectively), while George III from 1761 to 1800 created 128 (excluding promotions, re-creations and peerages awarded to women). But a substantial number of extinctions had cut into the number of creations. Thus the number of English and British[3] peers had risen from 162 at the end of the reign of William III to about 270 by 1800. To these potential members of the Lords, must be added the 26 English and Welsh bishops and the 16 Scottish representative peers, giving a potential membership of the upper House of 301 by 1799.

Not all peers and bishops attended, of course, and the size of the attendance varied enormously from day to day. In the early 18th century the average daily attendance was around 80, rising to 120 plus for the great political occasions and sinking to below 20 for days on which the bulk of the business was legal cases. By comparison, the average daily attendance was about 45 for the years 1762–83.

Scottish Members

The most obvious impact of the union on the upper House was the expansion of its membership to include the 16 Scottish representative peers, elected by the whole of the Scottish peerage eligible to vote at general and

---

[3] At the union, both the English and Scottish peerages were 'frozen' and no new titles were created in these peerages (unlike the Irish peerage after the 1801 Anglo-Irish union when Irish titles continued to be conferred, though in much smaller numbers. The last was created in 1898. Technically Irish peerages could still be created today.) New titles after 1707 were created in the new British peerage. English peers with a Scottish title (e.g. the duke of Marlborough) could, however, continue to vote for the 16 representative peers.

The Election of the 16 Scottish Representative Peers

The election from 1707 of the 16 Scottish representative peers (which was governed by articles 22 and 23 of the Treaty of Union and by the act 6 Anne, c. 8) took place at every general election usually at the palace of Holyroodhouse in Edinburgh. (The 1707 election – as did that of 1955 – took place in the Parliament House.) Those Scottish peers (or English peers with Scottish titles) who had taken the oaths of allegiance, security and supremacy, and who had subscribed to the declaration against popery, and who were not minors, either gathered at Holyroodhouse and voted in person by voice or entrusted their proxies to a fellow Scottish peer, also having been certified as having taken the oaths, who voted on their behalf. The proxy (no more than two of which could be held by a peer) simply gave the proxy-holder the power to vote for whom he wished on behalf of the proxy-giver, though many would have received instructions for whom to vote. A second method of absentee voting was the 'list', whereby the absent voter supplied the officials in Edinburgh with a signed and dated list of up to 16 peers for whom he wished to vote. The government from 1708 drew up an official list, later known as 'the king's list', of the 16 it wanted elected and much pressure was put on electors to return the government's preferred peers, which is what normally happened, much to the opposition's anger. Although all the qualified peers of Scotland were summoned, the complete body of the peerage never attended, the record attendance of 60 being at the contentious election of 1734. (The lowest attendances were at by-elections, which were caused by the death of a sitting peer or, after a new practice was adopted in 1787, by the granting of a British title to a sitting peer.) There were never fewer than 11 peers present at any 18th-century election. In 1806 the prime minister, Lord Grenville, proposed that the Scottish representative peers be placed 'precisely in the situation of the Irish peerage, both as to sitting in the House of Commons and for life in the House of Lords'.* This plan came to nothing, even receiving opposition from some Scottish peers. The last general election was in 1959, for this system ended in 1963 when the Peerages Act granted all Scottish peers and peeresses in their own right seats in the upper House.

CJ

* PRONI, T3472/2/7: Aberdeen to Abercorn, 28 November 1806 (also British Library, Add. MS 43225).

by-elections. Those excluded from taking the oaths and thus from voting were minors, women, lunatics and Catholics.[4] The 16 peers elected in 1707 and 1708 included supporters and opponents of the English (now British) ministry in London. This was to be the last time for about 60

[4] These categories were also excluded in the English peerage. But because of the more extensive use in Scotland of patents in heirs general rather than heirs male of the body, many more women succeeded to peerages in Scotland than in England.

years that opponents of the current ministry were elected. From the general election of 1710 onwards the government's list of 16 was almost invariably elected,[5] providing what the ministry in the House of Lords hoped would be a reliable bloc of supporters. (Sometimes peers elected on the government's list later turned into opponents during the course of the parliament. Such individuals usually found themselves excluded from the list at the next general election, and so were not returned. Examples are the duke of Argyll's younger brother, the earl of Ilay, in 1713,[6] the *Squadrone Volante* peers in 1734, and the 3rd earl of Bute and the 2nd duke of Buccleuch in 1741.) In the years immediately after the union, the support of the Scots for the ministry was not always forthcoming, particularly over Scottish matters which were before parliament. The pro-Scotland opposition culminated in 1713 in an unsuccessful attempt by some Scottish representative peers (together with some of the 45 Scottish MPs in the Commons) to repeal the union. As far as the representative peers were concerned the early years of the union had seen a display of anti-Scottish resentment on behalf of the English peers in the upper House, a resentment which had become embroiled in whig and tory party differences, the results of which the Scots regarded as breaches of the spirit, if not the letter, of the union treaty. First, in 1709 there was a ruling of the House (largely directed against the unpopular duke of Queensberry) that Scottish peers who sat in the Lords by the right of their newly created British peerages (Queensberry had been created and sat as duke of Dover) could neither stand nor vote in the election for the 16 representative peers.[7] Second, in 1711 the duke of Hamilton was refused the right to sit by reason of his new British peerage as duke of Brandon.[8] Xenophobia, social anxieties and party politics all played a part in both these decisions: the English feared being swamped by waves of new British titles being given to the Scots peerage, which the English largely regarded as a second class order. There was, however, a loophole in the 1711 Lords' ruling, which had only stated that Scottish peers given British titles could not sit in the

---

[5] The first exception to this 'rule' came in the by-election of 1721 when the tory earl of Aberdeen was elected against the wishes of the whig government. This breach was reinforced when at the succeeding general election in 1722 he was re-elected. There was also an unsuccessful attempt in 1734 to break this ministerial hold over the return of co-operative peers.

[6] Argyll was not a representative peer; he sat by virtue of his *English* earldom of Greenwich, conferred in 1705, and thus could not be removed from the Lords by an administration.

[7] The only breach of this resolution was in 1734 when the dukes of Hamilton and Queensberry both voted, tendering a formal protest of their right to do so because they were not allowed to sit in the Lords by virtue of their British titles. The clerks accepted their votes, but the House of Lords chose to ignore this incident and the 1709 resolution remained in force until 1793.

[8] Thus Hamilton and later Scottish peers granted British titles were doubly disenfranchised: they could not stand (or vote) for the 16 representative peers, and could not sit in the Lords.

> ### The Creation of the 12 New Peers by the Earl of Oxford, 1711–12
>
> Between 28 December 1711 and 1 January 1712, the 'prime minister', the earl of Oxford, persuaded Queen Anne to create ten new peers and to call up to the Lords two heirs of peers in their fathers' baronies. This bold stroke, which saw the largest creation of new peers in such a short time, was part of a package, which also included the dismissal of the duke of Marlborough from his post as commander-in-chief, and which was designed to wrench the political initiative back from the whigs to the tory ministry and to take control of the upper House in order to ensure the acceptance of the peace proposals to end the War of the Spanish Succession negotiated at Utrecht. The creations were considered, even by some of Oxford's supporters, as an excessive use of the royal prerogative and possibly unconstitutional. The adverse reaction to these creations was to resurface at various times of political crisis, such as the Great Reform Act of 1832 and the Parliament Act of 1911.
>
> CJ

Lords.[9] Scottish commoners, who included the heirs of Scottish peers, even though they usually bore their father's courtesy title, could still be created British peers. The first such creation was Lord Dupplin, who was raised to a British peerage, as Lord Hay, as one of the 12 creations in late 1711/early 1712, designed to give the ministry of Lord Oxford a majority in favour of the peace at the end of the War of the Spanish Succession.

Hay was Oxford's son-in-law and, as Lord Dupplin, was heir to the earl of Kinnoull. On Hay's succession to his father's earldom in 1719, he continued, as Lord Hay, to sit unchallenged in the Lords. This loophole was, however, used very sparingly as the various ministries did not wish to provoke further anti-Scottish measures from the House.[10] The situation was

---

[9] The 1711 ruling did not affect Hamilton's seat in the Lords; he continued to sit as a representative peer until his death in a duel in 1712, as he had been elected a representative peer before the 1709 ruling. Scottish peers with English titles, however, continued to sit in the Lords after the 1711 ruling (e.g. Argyll, see n. 6 above), presumably because there was no fear on behalf of the English peerage of being swamped by Scots with English titles as no more English peerages could be created.

[10] In 1722 the heirs of the dukes of Montrose and Roxburghe, as minors, were created British earls and sat when they came of age, and continued to sit when they succeeded to their respective dukedoms. (The 1st Earl Graham, Montrose's heir, died before his father, so the younger brother, the 2nd earl, succeeded Montrose.) In 1766 Argyll's heir was created Lord Sundridge (the family's English earldom had become extinct on the death of the 2nd duke of Argyll in 1743), and in 1776 the earls of Marchmont and Bute were created Lord Hume of Berwick and Lord Cardiff respectively. Hume died before his father and the title of Marchmont died out in 1794; while Cardiff did not succeed his father until 1794 after the 1711 ruling had been reversed in 1782.

not settled to the satisfaction of the Scots until the 1711 ruling was lifted in 1782, when the then duke of Hamilton was allowed to sit as duke of Brandon.

An earlier solution to the 'Scottish peerage problem' had been attempted in 1719 with the unsuccessful Peerage Bill. Amongst its proposals had been one to replace the 16 elected peers by 25 hereditary Scottish members. This idea was attractive to some peers from the higher echelons of the Scottish peerage (who expected to be granted an hereditary seat), but was generally opposed by the body of the Scottish peerage. The unsuccessful attempts in 1720 by the 3rd duke of Queensbury to take his father's seat in the Lords and to reintroduce the Scottish provisions alone of the failed Peerage Bill left the problem unresolved.

The Peerage Bill of 1719

In March 1719 the ministry of the 3rd earl of Sunderland and the 1st Earl Stanhope introduced into parliament the Peerage Bill as part of their 'reform' programme (which included the successful repeal of the Occasional Conformity and the Schism Acts and the unsuccessful attempt to repeal the Septennial Act). The Peerage Bill was designed to curb the crown's prerogative in the creation of peerages by, after an initial creation of six new titles, limiting the numbers of further creations to the replacement of extinct titles. Princes of the blood royal were to be exempt from this limitation. The 16 elected Scottish representative peers were to be replaced by 25 hereditary seats in the Lords, to be replenished from the Scottish peerage only on the extinction of a title carrying such a seat. The long-term effect of the bill would have been the creation of a closed caste of 209 peers at the apex of society, and the inability of any ministry to create titles in order to control the upper House, as Lord Oxford had done in 1711–12. This latter was the main immediate reason for the bringing in of the bill by the ministry, which feared losing power and possible retaliation against it upon the accession of the prince of Wales, with whom the ministry was at odds. It must be remembered that Oxford had been impeached, albeit unsuccessfully, but had been imprisoned for two years by the whigs following the succession of George I, only being released from the Tower in July 1717. In April 1719, the ministry, fearing opposition in the Commons to the bill, postponed proceedings on it so that it lapsed at the prorogation. It was reintroduced into the Lords in November 1719 and passed with virtually no opposition, but was rejected by the Commons, led by Robert Walpole, then in opposition to the ministry, on 8 December by 269 votes to 117. Moves to reintroduce the Scottish clauses of the bill in 1720–2 came to nothing, and the problems of the election of Scottish representatives in the Lords remained until the 1960s.

CJ

Bishops

The two archbishops and the 20 bishops of the Church of England from England and the four bishops from Wales continued to sit after the union as lords of parliament (not as spiritual 'peers'). During the reign of Anne the whig majority on the episcopal bench were largely controlled by Archbishop Tennison of Canterbury and supported the whig junto whether in or out of government. During the early years of George I's reign the whig majority grew and the bishops were increasingly seen as a safe pro-government bloc of votes in the House. In 1721 the 3rd earl of Sunderland claimed the government had 19 whig bishops out of 26. By 1742 19 bishops had received their initial promotion during Walpole's ministry and of the remaining seven all but one had been translated to richer sees. The bishops' support for the ministry was not always reliable, and on some social and religious matters some of the bench could and did revolt against the administration. Good examples were the defeats of the bill to prevent stockjobbing in 1734 and the Quaker Tithes Bill in 1736. In the latter case, the bench to a man voted against the bill. By the end of Walpole's ministry a small group of bishops were in more or less permanent opposition.

Developments in the Management of the House

Unlike the House of Commons, where the Speaker controlled the proceedings in the chamber, the proceedings in the Lords (which had a 'Speaker', but with much reduced powers, in the person of the lord chancellor, who was a peer, or the lord keeper,[11] who was not) were under the control of the members themselves following procedures and customs which were more formal than in the lower House. However, two factors in the 1690s and the early years of Anne's reign combined to change matters.

First, administrations, having realized much earlier that a cohort of supporters was an advantage in controlling, and even dominating business, began to build a 'party of the crown' in the Lords. Briefly, such a party was first developed in any systematic way by the tory 'prime minister' Robert Harley (created earl of Oxford in 1711), and continued with further refinements by the whigs Lords Sunderland and Stanhope, and Robert Walpole under George I, and consisted of office-holders and pensioners of the crown ('servants of the crown' in the Lords rose from 69 in 1714 to around 100 in 1739), the bishops and the Scottish representative peers. Except sometimes in unexpected crises, this party of the crown was a reliable bulwark for the ministry in the Lords.

Second, in the 1690s several members of the whig junto, who as MPs had played a prominent role in the lower House, succeeded to peerages or

---

[11] The last lord keeper ceased to hold office in 1761, when Sir Robert Henley, who had been created Baron Henley the previous year and was then occupying that position, became lord chancellor.

were created peers, and moved from the Commons to the upper House and brought with them the much more informal and aggressive style of conducting business they had developed in the lower chamber.

Succeeding ministries in the early years of the 18th century sought to cope with these developments by seeking a more 'institutionalized' control of the Lords. To begin with, this took two forms: the development of the positions of chairman of committees and the 'leader' of the House. The first emerged at the end of Anne's reign when the 3rd earl of Clarendon gradually came to dominate the chairmanship of both the select committees and the committee of the whole House (by his death in 1723 he was virtually the only lord performing these functions). After Clarendon, the chairmanship was assumed by successive peers, who each held the post for many years (the 8th earl of Warwick was chairman 1734-59).

Important as it was for the ministry to have a loyal supporter in the position of chairman of committees, his role in the overall management of the Lords was limited. Much more important was the emergence of the office of 'leader', which also began to develop in the second half of Queen Anne's reign, and was given a boost by the whig schism of 1717-20, when the ruling faction of the whigs under Sunderland and Stanhope, facing both the opposition of the tories, the followers of the prince of Wales (who had quarrelled with his father, George I), and the schismatic whigs under Walpole and Townshend, needed to develop a tighter form of control. The leader's initial function was the organizing of the pre-sessional meetings of government supporters amongst the peers and bishops in order to acquaint them with the contents of the monarch's speech which opened parliament. This function arose out of a need to co-ordinate an address in reply to the speech from the throne. Thus the meeting also chose the mover and seconder for the address. It was not until around 1717 that *regular* pre-sessional meetings appear to have become a feature of the ministry's management of the Lords. The person who emerged as responsible for co-ordinating these meetings was the senior (usually, the northern) secretary of state; after the administrative reorganization of 1782, it was normally the home rather than the foreign secretary who led the House. This major cabinet officer thereafter provided the focal point of the government's strategy of management, and, though the evidence is scanty, the senior secretary appears to have also co-ordinated management once the House was in session. However, if other cabinet offices were occupied by important political figures from the House of Lords, such as the 1st earl of Hardwicke as lord chancellor, or the duke of Newcastle, then they almost inevitably were involved in management of the upper House. If the 'prime minister' was in the Commons and was a dominant and forceful character, then he might well be involved directly in the management of the Lords, as was Robert Walpole in the 1730s.

The First Age of Party and its Decline

Factions in parliament were probably as old as the institution itself, but political parties (coalitions of the willing held together by an ideology and an organization, though not yet the near monolithic and highly professional parties of the modern era) began in the reign of Charles II. By Anne's reign, which saw the 'rage of party', whig versus tory had come to dominate political life at the centre and in the localities. Parties became the mechanism through which a ministry controlled parliament and an opposition was organized. During the long period of whig hegemony from 1714 to the 1750s, when the tories were reduced to a rump, party enabled the remaining tory leaders to develop the strategy of leading a war of attrition against the seemingly all-powerful whig ministry, together with improved tactics of opposition. These included the sporadic adoption of the ministerial pre-sessional meeting, and of the meetings of supporters during the parliamentary session, particularly in a time of crisis.

But the most important of these tactics in the House of Lords was the appeal to the politically literate public through the use and publication of protests against lost divisions in the House. Peers and bishops in the upper chamber had the right to enter a dissent in the journals of the House, which could be accompanied by a protest listing in detail the reasons. Such protests had on occasions been used effectively in the past, but the 'new opposition' of 1721–3, led by the disgruntled former whig lord chancellor, Lord Cowper, but consisting mainly of tories, broke new ground in the frequency with which protests were made and in the publication of these protests as propaganda. This stream of protests (together with much other printed material from the ministry and the opposition) gave a wide audience access to parliamentary news, which was read everywhere from coffee houses to foreign chancelleries. The use of printed protests for public consumption continued throughout the 18th century, though at varying rates, and the 1760s–70s saw a revival of mass protesting.

By the time Walpole left office in 1742 (and the decline in his majority in the Lords in 1741–2 did contribute to his fall), not only were the fortunes of the opposition in the Lords at a low ebb, but the status of the Lords as the dominant House also seemed to have declined compared to the Commons. Walpole's retirement peerage (the earldom of Orford) was a consolation, and the one given in the same year to William Pulteney, a leading whig in opposition to Walpole (he became the earl of Bath), was less a sign that his powers were in the ascendant than that his career had been eclipsed. Bath's failure to form an administration in 1746, like the short-lived appointments as first lord of the treasury of Lord Wilmington (1742–3) and the duke of Devonshire (1756–7), testified to the preeminence of the talented Commons leaders Henry Pelham and Pitt the Elder. On the death of Pelham in 1754, his brother Newcastle succeeded as prime minister, and once Newcastle formed a government with Pitt in

Dissenting and Protesting

Members of the House of Lords had the right, which members of the Commons did not, to enter a dissent or protest into the journals of the House against a decision or vote taken by the House. The first dissent where lords signed their names under the word *'dissentientibus'* next to the record of a decision was recorded in 1549. The earliest protest with reasons and signatures originated in 1641. The procedure was officially defined by a standing order of 1642. Such protests continued to be used sparingly until the 'new opposition' led by Lord Cowper in 1721–3, when protests in considerable numbers were recorded with many of them printed for sale to an increasingly interested and politically literate public as propaganda (publication had also previously been used only sparingly). This led to retaliation by the ministry of Lord Sunderland which expunged the most contentious protests (a practice first used in 1690) and persuaded the House to amend its standing order so that the time allowed for the entering of a protest was reduced and the ability of lords only represented at a vote by their proxies to protest was terminated in theory, though the practise continued occasionally to the end of the 18th century at least. After the death of Cowper in 1723 the practice of printing protests fell away as did the number of protests entered into the journals, only to be revived (but not to the same extent) in the period 1760–82. With the publication of Hansard (the debates of the Lords and Commons) from the early 19th century, the use of protests declined; and more so from the mid-19th century, after the printed journal began to publish division lists showing on which side a lord had voted. In the late 19th and early 20th centuries the protest had largely become the preserve of the loner who wished to make his mark on the Lords' proceedings. The last 'mass' protest, of 14 signatures, was against the passing of the Parliament Act of 1911. Less than a dozen have been entered since then, with the last one (so far) being made by Lord Tebbit on 16 July 1998.

CJ

Source: Clyve Jones, 'Dissent and Protest in the House of Lords, 1641–1998: An Attempt to Reconstruct the Procedures Involved in Entering a Protest into the Journals of the House of Lords', *Parliamentary History*, xxvii (2008), 309–29.

1757, it was the latter who effectively dominated their wartime coalition, even if Newcastle was still first lord of the treasury. Newcastle, who dealt with the Lords in his habitual frenzied style, was a shrewd and experienced operator, particularly in the arts of patronage, but the middle years of the 18th century were relatively calm politically. Opposition, when it arose, only produced an average of just under five divisions per session from 1739 to 1769, and the number of protests fell to an average of under two per session.

The Judicial Function of the Lords

As in the case of *Ashby* v. *White* in 1704, in which the upper chamber resisted the Commons' claim to be the sole arbiter over disputed elections of members to the lower House, the Lords attempted to assert its superior judicial position within the constitution. The case was never finally settled, but it left a legacy of concern whenever a dispute occurred between the two Houses, as it did in 1734 over the Lords' attempt to deprive Scottish burghs of certain rights.

In 1698–9 two Irish legal cases were appealed from the Irish to the English House of Lords. In both cases the English Lords decided that the Irish House had no appellate right. These decisions encouraged further appeals, culminating in *Annesley* v. *Sherlock* in 1718. The legal position was finally regularized by the Irish Declaratory Act of 1720, which denied any right of appeal to the Irish House of Lords. This arrangement was effectively reversed from 1783, after the granting of Irish legislative independence the previous year, but was reinstated at the time of the union in 1801.

The Anglo-Scottish union articles of 1707 had not provided for an appellate jurisdiction to replace that of the Scottish parliament. The new British House of Lords soon filled this vacuum in 1708 when it heard the case of *Rosebery* v. *Inglis*. By the 1720s much of the Lords' judicial activity was concerned with Scottish and Irish matters, and this contributed to the slow increase in casework throughout the 18th century.

Apart from the high profile and prolonged political trial of Lord Oxford in 1715–17 and the corruption charges brought against Lord Chancellor Macclesfield in 1725, impeachment proceedings were brought against seven of the Jacobite rebel lords in 1716. Lord Lovat was impeached following the '45, when three other Scots were tried, and convicted, by their peers in the Lords. The impeachment of Warren Hastings, who was accused of abusing his powers as governor general in India, lasted off and on from 1788 to 1795. He was eventually acquitted, but the interminable proceedings brought the impeachment procedure into disrepute; the last such case was that of Lord Melville (Henry Dundas) in 1805.

As in impeachment cases (in which the Lords collectively acted as the jury, deciding on a prosecution brought by the Commons), lords of parliament were theoretically entitled to speak and vote on any case brought into the Lords, even if they had no legal expertise. However, the convention that judicial work should be confined to the lawyers in the chamber (peers holding or having held high judicial office) gradually hardened across the century. The interference of non-specialists, especially for partisan reasons, was increasingly frowned upon by the senior judges, and the favourable outcome obtained in the case of the *Bishop of London* v. *Ffytche* in 1783, when 13 bishops voted in the majority of 19 to 18, against the advice of all but one of the judges, was considered reprehensible.

The specialization of the judicial function of the Lords was related to another development. Whereas it had continued to be the case that senior

A Public Spectacle

On the 'great commoner' Pitt the Elder becoming earl of Chatham in 1766, Lord Hardwicke wryly inquired of Lord Rockingham, 'as we are to have the great *actor* in our House next Session, what do you think of moving to put up the gallery?'* Apart from brief periods in the early 18th century, there was no physical gallery in the chamber, although the theatricality of some of the Lords' more unusual proceedings – most of its sittings were excruciatingly dreary – encouraged growing public attention. Proceedings on divorce bills, with their quasi-judicial proceedings, were always something of a draw both for members and non-members. Under George III, who was assiduous in attending the House on formal occasions, the reading of the king's speech at the opening of each session provided the opportunity for brightly attired aristocratic women to occupy the benches. As was the case with impeachments, Westminster Hall was transformed into an arena for the well-attended murder trials, by their peers, of Lord Ferrers in 1760 and of Lord Byron in 1765. When the duchess of Kingston was prosecuted for bigamy in 1776, London high society exhibited the most frantic anxiety to obtain tickets of admission. Great debating occasions were witnessed by merchants, colonial agents, foreigners, distinguished guests and celebrities, such as Omai the Tahitian, while during the Gordon Riots in June 1780 the mêlée almost reached the floor of the House. Like the hospital for lunatics which was always known as Bedlam, the Lords was a place to visit and be seen visiting. Appropriately enough, given that his occasional histrionic displays were a star attraction, it was Chatham's seizure, while speaking against granting American independence on 7 April 1778, that led to the creation of one of the most popular, if in some way misleading, representations of the Lords. This was John Singleton Copley's grand historical painting known as 'The Death of Chatham' (in the National Portrait Gallery), which sold enormously as an engraving; its title is inaccurate for Chatham did not die until 11 May. Yet, in the exploding print culture of the period, the awesome spectacle of the patriotic statesman apparently expiring in the heat of parliamentary battle helped create a visual image of indomitable Britishness.

SF

* George Thomas [Keppel], Earl of Albemarle, *Memoirs of the Marquis of Rockingham and his Contemporaries* (2 vols, 1852), ii, 11.

judges (who were still requested to attend the Lords to give their opinion on technical matters, though this practice was in decline), were commoners, from the mid-century it became the practice for the chief justice of king's bench to be ennobled on appointment (although this convention applied only sporadically to chief justices of common pleas). In this way, not just exceptionally astute and authoritative lord chancellors – such as Hardwicke (1737–56; first created a peer in 1733) and Thurlow (1778–92) – but such figures as Lord Mansfield (chief justice of king's bench, with a peerage, 1756–88) and Lord Ellenborough (chief justice of common pleas, with a peerage, from 1780 to 1793, when he became lord chancellor) came to dominate the proceedings in the Lords generally. The lord chancellor, a cabinet minister, and his legal colleagues were among the most frequent speakers in debate, in which only about 20–30 peers regularly participated, and they almost always supported the government of the day.

Legislation, Committees and Records of Proceedings

The Lords began its sittings later in the day as the century progressed, but also sat for longer each day and for more days in its annual sessions. This was largely caused by the dramatic expansion of the workload of the Lords in the field of legislation. During the period from 1760 to 1800 8,351 public and private Acts were passed, more than twice as many as in the period 1714–60. All these required at least some degree of consideration by the House, as did many of the unsuccessful bills, whose number also increased across the century. While the proportion of those originating in the Lords seems to have dropped, it became rare for the Commons to throw out bills brought down from the Lords, although the reverse was not so unusual, demonstrating that the upper House continued occasionally to operate as a legislative backstop. The rising success rate of bills was partly due to a refinement of legislative procedures, most notably in the exacting standards imposed by the 2nd Baron Walsingham as chairman of committees (a position at last given official recognition by resolutions passed on 23 July 1800).

By the time of Walsingham's appointment in 1794 there were 280 committees a session, which was the average for the 1790s. (This compares to an average of 104 for the first decade of the century, a figure which declined to a low of 74 committees in the 1730s, after which the trend was invariably and increasingly steeply upwards, except for the comparatively low average of 158 for the 1780s.) In any one decade about two-thirds of them were second reading committees on local (e.g. enclosure) bills or private (e.g. estate) bills, on both of which the Lords made a significant contribution in terms of drafting and revising, with the committee effectively providing a forum for mediation between particular or individual interests, notably over conflicting property rights. It was in this way that some of the new manufacturing pressures found an outlet for parliamentary attention. Sometimes it was to what would later be called 'select' committees that specific issues were investigated, as in the lengthy proceedings on the dearness of provisions in 1765. More normally, as on public bills, consideration was taken in the committee of the whole House. Committees of this type, some of which had greater significance as being inquiries into the 'state of the nation', occurred during wars (1711, 1742, 1766, 1778) or over major constitutional questions (for instance, the Middlesex election in 1770 and the union with Ireland in 1800).

It was the journals committee that was instructed in 1767 to oversee the printing of the manuscript journal, the official record of the decisions made in the House, following the precedent that had already been adopted for the Commons journal. Some publication of accounts of debates had been tolerated in the early 18th century, but prosecutions in 1747 effectively stifled this practice. With the *de facto* lifting of reporting restrictions in 1774, when strangers were again allowed into the chamber after a four-year period of exclusion (which had also applied, controversially, to MPs), knowledge of Lords' debates became more widespread, a trend accelerated by the printing of parliamentary papers and statutes. Both Houses remained jealous guardians of their privileges, but the growing number of London newspapers increasingly included parliamentary coverage in their columns during the late 18th century. This provided the main source for the published compilations of debates which began to appear by the end of this period.

The Revival of Opposition and Party Tactics

Such opposition as had existed in the Lords in the mid-18th century was usually centred on personal connections, such as the group of peers who backed the reversionary interest of Frederick, prince of Wales, until his untimely death in 1751. Frederick's heir, who succeeded his grandfather George II as George III in 1760, had the same views on party as his father. Ironically, the young king's desire to end the stranglehold of the court whig party in office contributed both to the political instability of the 1760s (with high rates of peers voting against government on at least one occasion) and the rise of a new kind of party opposition. The appointment of his Scottish favourite, the 3rd earl of Bute, and his dismissal of Newcastle's followers (the 'Pelhamite innocents') in 1762, produced a decade of conflict, in both Houses, between the 'ins' and the 'outs'. But even more unsettling than his choice of unpopular ministers was his conduct in undermining governments of which he disapproved, including by intervening directly in proceedings in the Lords. Most blatantly, by airing his personal views in favour of modification rather than repeal of the American Stamp Act, he encouraged some of the household and ministerialist peers to vote against the marquess of Rockingham's first administration, producing two defeats in the committee on the Repeal Bill in February 1766. This was a precursor of his role in provoking the fall of the Fox–North coalition over the India Bill crisis in 1783.

The Rockinghams, as the remnant of Newcastle's displaced court whigs became known, at times co-operated with the Bedfordite and Grenvillite peers, notably in their concerted opposition attacks over colonial issues in April 1767. But the reabsorption of such separate elements back into the administration in the 1770s, with the exception of the maverick earl of Chatham (as the elder Pitt had become) and his sidekick Lord Shelburne, left the Rockinghams isolated. Led half-heartedly by Lord Rockingham,

Fox's India Bill

If ever there was an occasion when the Lords acted as a counterpoise in the tripartite constitutional balance of king, Lords and Commons, it was in defeating Fox's India Bill in December 1783. At least, so it would appear, for the upper chamber threw out a bill to reform the management of the East India Company – by creating a board of commissioners appointed by, and answerable to, the lower House – in order to protect the recognized prerogative powers of the crown. In fact, it was widely accepted that the demands of administering large parts of the subcontinent required the creation of a political board of control in London (and this is more or less what was introduced by the younger Pitt the following year). Where Charles James Fox, in unholy alliance with the former prime minister Lord North, conspicuously failed, was in his barefaced attempt to pack the proposed board with his cronies. Given that George III detested the Fox–North coalition and was only biding his time to dismiss it until a viable alternative could be arranged, the India Bill offered the king the perfect opportunity to precipitate its demise. Cocking a snook at constitutional niceties, the king let it be known that those who 'voted for the India Bill were not only not his friends, but he should consider them as his enemies'.* In crucial divisions on 15 and 17 December, ministers were defeated by 87 (including 18 proxies) to 79 (including 22 proxies) and by 95 (including 20 proxies) to 57 (including 19 proxies). As more than half the bishops, and about half the household and Scottish representative peers present on those days voted against the government, its fate was sealed. Once the king had withdrawn his confidence, the division had little to do with the merits of the bill, and much to do with individual lords altering course in the direction of the prevailing wind. The defeat of Fox's India Bill was not an example of the peerage acting collectively, as an 'order', to bring the constitution back into equipoise, it was simply the endgame of a desperate power struggle within the executive (the members of which sat in both Commons and Lords), a struggle which, for reasons of short-term political tactics, happened to take place in the upper House.

SF

* John Cannon, *The Fox–North Coalition: Crisis of the Constitution, 1782–4* (Cambridge, 1969), 133.

---

who was never an accomplished speaker, they nevertheless maintained a distinct identity, challenging North's government, if not consistently, then at least with conviction and courage on occasion. Pressing for inquiries into the running of the war against revolutionary America proved a better long-term strategy than the attempted secessions (as in 1776–7) from parliament, but it was not until the end of that decade, when several peers – and even the odd bishop or Scottish representative peer – abandoned the government, that the Rockinghams started to make an impact in the Lords, for example in their attacks on Lord Sandwich's handling of the Admiralty in 1779.

Apart from its development of a new credo of party, the Rockinghamite opposition survived this lean period in two main ways. First by carrying over into opposition some of the managerial tactics used by government, notably in the context of encouraging attendance, securing proxies and confronting major items of ministerial business. The issuing of an invitation 'card' summoning supporters over the New Shoreham Bill in 1771 by the 3rd duke of Richmond, who was then deputizing for Rockingham, is probably the first extant example of an opposition 'whip' in the Lords.[12] From 1774 the address of thanks on the king's speech opening the session was routinely opposed, and usually divided (and protested) against. The number of divisions rose in the 1770s and early 1780s, with proxies being deployed at almost every opportunity, and it was at this time that a regular opposition teller emerged in the person of Lord Effingham. The number of divisions in the 1777–8 and 1778–9 sessions (35 and 36) were the highest in any one session since 1721–2 (36), and, at about 20 divisions per session, it was only in the 1770s that the average returned to the rate prevailing during the period 1690–1719. Among new, though informal, procedural features were the first known instance of pairing (between Lords Audley and Burlington in 1767), evidence of co-operation in the organization of business between the government and opposition leaders, for instance in 1775, and the emergence by the 1780s of the sporadic and unregulated practice of asking questions of ministers.

Second, and this very much marked a reinvention of early 18th-century practice, the Rockinghamite peers at times used the entering of protests both as a means of supplementing and unifying the strength of their forces in the Lords, and as a way of appealing to an audience beyond parliament. The numbers of protests rose to nearly four a session during the last three decades of the century, and the carefully worded written dissents in effect provided a kind of widely circulated public manifesto. Significantly, an increasing number of minority division lists survive from this period in printed form (rather than in private manuscripts), presumably because they were intended to influence extra-parliamentary opinion. Though wary of being seen to ally too closely with the Association Movement's demand for parliamentary reform, the Rockingham whig party was at the forefront of the popular campaign to reduce government expenditure and the corruption that went with it.

---

[12] Sheffield Archives, Wentworth Woodhouse Muniments, R1-1376: Rockingham to 'the whig lords' [6 May 1771] (copy).

Pitt's Peers and the Aristocracy in the 1790s

The reduction in places and pensions, brought about by the brief second Rockingham ministry's economical reform programme, reduced the scope that governments traditionally had to reward or secure adherents. This was one of the reasons that Pitt the Younger gave for so dramatically increasing the size of the peerage during his long first administration. Hitherto George III had been as sparing as his immediate predecessors in creating titles, only allowing about two per year (excluding promotions, re-creations and peerages awarded to women) for the first 23 years of his reign, although this included the nine that, for reasons of shoring up support for Lord North's ministry in the chamber after a four-year moratorium on peerage creations, were all made on 20 May 1776.[13] This reflected his concern to safeguard the dignity of the peerage as an order, although in some cases his refusal to grant peerages was a way of withholding confidence from his ministers. From 1784 to 1800, 79 new British peerages were created (including those given to seven Scottish peers and 22 Irish peers), and there were 30 promotions within the British peerage and 11 re-creations (usually, in the absence of a son, for the purpose of specifying who should inherit the title), plus the award of two peerages to women. Some of these were rewards for political service in the Commons (including as boroughmongers), but many were in recognition of military and naval achievements during the wars against revolutionary France. Like the bishops, office-holders and the Scottish representative peers, these new recruits were an element in the strengthened party of the crown. Moreover, the overturning of the Hamilton judgment (of 1711) in 1782 meant that Scottish peers holding British titles could now sit by virtue of the latter qualification. Indeed, the number of British (and soon to be United Kingdom) peerages given to Scottish and Irish peers began the formation of an effectively much more unified nobility for the three kingdoms.

Since most of the newly created or promoted peers came from families connected to the existing aristocracy – the exception usually cited was the Nottingham and London banker Robert Smith, who became Baron Carrington in the Irish peerage in 1796 and Baron Carrington in the British peerage in 1797 – the Lords remained as socially exclusive and politically conservative as it had ever been. Sectional interests found ready support for their resistance to change, whether they were the west country peers who objected to the cider tax in 1763, the bishops who opposed granting relief to dissenters from subscribing to the 39 Articles in the 1770s, or the West Indian proprietors who impeded regulation of the African slave trade in 1788. Not surprisingly, the House gave short shrift to Lord Stanhope's proposals for parliamentary reform, even before the escalation of the French revolution had rendered such proposals hopelessly

---

[13] A tenth peerage was given to a woman; that same month the marquess of Carmarthen, as heir to the duke of Leeds, was called up in his father's barony as Baron Osborne.

> ### 'The thanes, high priests and household cavalry'
> The 'party of the crown' is the phrase that has been used by historians to describe the natural supporters of the government of the day in the House of Lords. In many ways the concept is a straightforward one, describing the mutually beneficial relationship which must have existed between a monarch, whose government had to have a majority in parliament, and the king's supporters, who were ambitious for office and its spoils. In that sense, the idea is exactly analogous to the government 'payroll vote' of modern times. As this chapter has shown, 'the party of the crown' came first into acknowledged existence as an entity to be managed in the opening decades of the 18th century, a period of instability during which not just the parliamentary, but also the dynastic, survival of the regime was sometimes at stake. The 'court and administration party', as it has also been called (in relation to the Commons), was thereafter a standard feature of 18th-century parliaments. In a seminal article,* David Large argued that the party of the crown took on a new solidity in the 1780s. It was from that point that almost all the members of each component of the party displayed a strict adherence to the ministry: the slate of 16 Scottish representative peers, ably corralled by Henry Dundas (later Viscount Melville); the 26 bishops, many of them George III's creatures; the roughly two dozen officials of the royal household, who were subject to dismissal for disobedience; and the many newly honoured or promoted peers, who were considered duty bound to repay the younger Pitt for his generosity. It was only when the tory party in opposition, under Wellington in the 1830s, could apparently offer more than could the whig governments of Lords Grey and Melbourne, that the 'party of the crown' (by then including the Irish representative peers as well) dissolved into the emerging two-party system. Of course, it is a moot point whether it is not the promise of an appointment or reward which is a greater security for loyalty on the floor of the House than the actual fulfilment of such a promise. Many who had received little must have supported government in hopes of gaining something, while even those who had received much needed the additional bait of having more of the fruits of royal largesse held out to them if they were to remain loyal.
>
> SF
>
> * David Large, 'The Decline of "the Party of the Crown" and the Rise of Parties in the House of Lords, 1783–1837', *English Historical Review*, lxxviii (1963), 669–95.

visionary. In the Lords, where Pitt's cousin Lord Grenville provided a new level of parliamentary expertise as leader during the last decade of the century, the entry of the Portland whigs into government in 1794 reduced the Foxite opposition to an ineffective rump. From outside the chamber, radical opponents of hereditary 'aristocrats' (a term of abuse recently imported from France) depicted them not, as earlier critics had done, as parasites luxuriating ineffectually in corruption and depravity, but as a class deliberately usurping authority from the people: 'assuming and asserting indefeasible, irrevocable rights and authority, wholly independent of the Nation', as Tom Paine put it.[14]

The peerage, as members of the House of Lords and as electoral patrons controlling the return of many MPs, undoubtedly dominated the oligarchy that formed the governing elite in Britain for most of the 18th century. The younger Pitt sat in the Commons, but, as for many of his successful predecessors as prime minister, almost all his cabinet colleagues were in the Lords. In the central government more widely, peers continued to monopolize the leading offices, just as they did in the localities, which gave them valuable weight as authorities when speaking in parliament. The distribution of their country estates, and the breadth of their legislative concerns, meant that peers, as 'virtual' representatives, in a sense compensated for some the defects of the unreformed electoral system. By the end of the century, prefiguring trends which would become ever more evident in the following decades, they were beginning to allow themselves to be harnessed as figureheads to projects which reflected predominantly middle-class aspirations. This was seen in the Lords' chamber itself, where they were increasingly subjected to effective interest group lobbying. The development of likeminded sets of peers, dedicated to such causes as the reformation of manners on the one hand or the promotion of emerging types of industrial activity on the other, demonstrated an increased willingness to push forward the moral imperatives of the dawning commercial and imperial ruling class in the upper House.

[14] A. Goodrich, *Debating England's Aristocracy in the 1790s: Pamphlets, Polemics and Political Ideas* (Woodbridge, 2005), 60.

Chronology

1707
Union with Scotland forming Great Britain

1711
Hamilton case

1711–12
Creation of the 12 peers by Queen Anne

1714
Death of Queen Anne; accession of George I

1717
Regular pre-sessional meetings of ministerialist peers date from about this year

1718
Annesley v. Sherlock

1719
Peerage Bill

1720
Irish Declaratory Act

1727
Death of George I; accession of George II

1736
Quaker Tithes Bill

1742
Fall of Sir Robert Walpole

1751
Death of Frederick, prince of Wales

1760
Death of George II; accession of George III

1767
Beginning of the printing of *The Journal of the House of Lords*

1774
Reporting restrictions on debates effectively lifted

1776
Trial of the duchess of Kingston for bigamy

1782
Hamilton judgment overturned

1783
India Bill crisis

1788
Bishop of London v. *Ffytche*

1788
Impeachment of Warren Hastings (to 1795)

1800
Formal recognition of the office of chairman of committees

1801
Union with Ireland forming the United Kingdom of Great Britain and Ireland

Further Reading

British Parliamentary Lists, 1660–1800: A Register, ed. G. M. Ditchfield, D. Hayton and C. Jones (1995)

J. Cannon, *Aristocratic Century: The Peerage of Eighteenth-Century England* (Cambridge, 1984)

G. M. Ditchfield, 'The House of Lords in the Age of the American Revolution', in *A Pillar of the Constitution: The House of Lords in British Politics, 1640–1784*, ed. C. Jones (1989), 199–239

—— 'The House of Lords and Parliamentary Reform in the Seventeen-Eighties', *Bulletin of the Institute of Historical Research*, liv (1981), 207–25

Failed Legislation, 1660–1800: Extracts from the Commons and Lords Journals, ed. J. Hoppit (1997)

S. Farrell, 'The Practices and Purposes of Party Leadership: Rockingham and the Lords, 1765–82', in *Leaders in the Lords: Government Management and Party Organization in the Upper Chamber, 1765–1902*, ed. R. W. Davis (Edinburgh, 2003) [special issue of *Parliamentary History*, xxii/1], 13–28

A. Goodrich, *Debating England's Aristocracy in the 1790s: Pamphlets, Polemics and Political Ideas* (Woodbridge, 2005)

C. Jones, 'The House of Lords and the Fall of Walpole', in *Hanoverian Britain and Empire: Essays in Memory of Philip Lawson*, ed. S. Taylor, R. Connors and C. Jones (Woodbridge, 1998), 102–36

―― 'Lord Oxford's Jury: The Political and Social Context of the Creation of the Twelve Peers, 1711–12', in *Partisan Politics, Principle and Reform in Parliament and the Constituencies, 1689–1880: Essays in Memory of John A. Phillips*, ed. C. Jones, P. Salmon and R. W. Davis (Edinburgh, 2005), 9–42

―― 'The New Opposition in the House of Lords, 1720–3', *Historical Journal* xxxvi (1993), 309–29

―― '"Venice Preserv'd; or A Plot Discovered": The Political and Social Context of the Peerage Bill of 1719', in *A Pillar of the Constitution: The House of Lords in British Politics, 1640–1784*, ed. C. Jones (1989), 79–112

D. Large, 'The Decline of "the Party of the Crown" and the Rise of Parties in the House of Lords, 1783–1837', *English Historical Review*, lxxviii (1963), 669–95

Lords of Parliament: Studies, 1714–1914, ed. R. W. Davis (Stanford, CA, 1995)

W. C. Lowe, 'George III, Peerage Creations and Politics, 1760–1784', *Historical Journal*, xxv (1992), 587–609

―― 'Peers and Printers: The Beginnings of Sustained Press Coverage in the House of Lords in the 1770s', *Parliamentary History*, vii (1988), 241–56

M. McCahill, *The House of Lords in the Age of George III, 1760–1811* (Parliamentary History Text and Studies 3, Oxford, 2009)

―― *Order and Equipoise: The Peerage and the House of Lords, 1783–1806* (Royal Historical Society Studies in History Series no. 11, 1978)

―― 'Peerage Creations and the Changing Character of the British Nobility, 1750–1830', *English Historical Review*, xcvi (1981), 259–84

M. McCahill and E. A. Wasson, 'The New Peerage: Recruitment to the House of Lords, 1704–1847', *Historical Journal*, xlvi (2003), 1–38

Peerage Creations: Chronological Lists of Creations in the Peerages of England and Great Britain, 1649–188, and of Ireland, 1603–1898, comp. J. C. Sainty (Parliamentary History Text and Studies 1, Oxford, 2008)

A. J. Rees, 'The Practice and Procedure of the House of Lords, 1714–1784' (PhD thesis, University of Wales, Aberystwyth, 1987)

J. C. Sainty, 'The Origins of the Leadership of the House of Lords', *Bulletin of the Institute of Historical Research*, xlvii (1974), 53–73

—— *The Origins of the Office of Chairman of Committees in the House of Lords* (House of Lords Record Office Memorandum No. 52, 1974)

S. Taylor, 'The Bishops at Westminster in the Mid-Eighteenth Century', in *A Pillar of the Constitution: The House of Lords in British Politics, 1640–1784*, ed. C. Jones (1989), 137–63

A. S. Turberville, *The House of Lords in the Age of Reform, 1784–1837* (1958)

—— *The House of Lords in the XVIIIth Century* (Oxford, 1927)

14 The House of Commons, 1707–1800
Bob Harris

'That the united Kingdom of Great-Britain be represented by one and the same Parliament, to be stiled the Parliament of Great Britain': so stated Article III of the Treaty of Union of 1707, which created the new state of the United Kingdom of Great Britain. In practice, union made relatively little difference to the nature and role of the Commons, besides bringing some additional support to the ministry in the House. Symptomatic of this was the survival of the current membership of the English parliament until a general election was due in 1708 under the terms of the Triennial Act (1694). The first Scottish representatives at Westminster were chosen by the existing members of the now defunct Scottish parliament, not the Scottish electorate, a decision dictated by the very reasonable fear that elections would produce an anti-Union or even Jacobite majority among the new Scottish MPs. The issue of how many MPs the Scots should be allocated in the new parliament might have proved a serious obstacle to the successful completion of the negotiations preceding the Union, with the Scots demanding a greater number than was initially offered by the English commissioners. The Scots sought representation based on population, while the English proposed monetary wealth as the key. The English commissioners made clear their expectation that the Scots should accommodate themselves to the 'ancient constitution' of England's parliament, further evidence that union was not envisaged, at least by the English, as a constitutional rupture. In the event, the way out was to split the difference between the initial offer by the English of 38 MPs and the 60 which the Scots appear to have been seeking. The addition of 45 Scottish MPs brought the total number of MPs at Westminster to 558.

The Commons which the Scots joined in 1707 had seen its importance enhanced considerably by the events of the Glorious Revolution. The court remained in the 18th century a crucial arena in the search for political power, and the political importance of the House of Lords continued to be considerable, especially before the final years of Queen Anne's reign. It was, however, the Commons which had the ultimate power to decide the fate of ministers and the passage of key business. If one political career demonstrates the trajectory of influence above all others, it is that of Sir Robert Walpole, first lord of the treasury and chancellor of the exchequer between 1721 and 1742. Unlike his immediate predecessors as first minister, Walpole chose to remain in the Commons. It was also the Commons which brought about his political end when a crumbling majority produced his resignation in early February 1742. All the successful leading ministers of this period – Walpole, Lord North, and William Pitt the Younger – led their ministries from the Commons, were extremely able and effective debaters, a consequence in North's and Pitt's cases in part of prodigious memories; were masters of lucid explication of, to many MPs at least, the perplexing business of public finance; and were widely recognized to be committed parliamentarians. Lord North protested in 1776, following a reproach from a fellow MP for a brief absence of 10 minutes from a debate of 14 hours: 'I may, Sir, be deficient in many respects, but I never imagined that a want of respect, diligence as a member, or attention to this House, would have swelled the long catalogue.'[1] As Peter Thomas notes, this was no empty protest from a man who probably spoke around 2,000 times in the House during the 12 years of his administration.[2]

The importance, however, of the Commons in this period should not simply be seen in terms of the fates of ministers and of government measures. After 1689 parliamentary sessions were annual; parliament had, as Bill Speck has put it, finally been 'transformed from an event into an institution'.[3] One result of this was that the amount of legislation passed grew very significantly. So too did the authority of parliament and statute law. In the case of the latter, this was partly for pragmatic reasons, in so far as there was an obvious need for a final arbitrator in disputes and conflicts of interest; in the previous century this role was sometimes played by the privy council. Whatever the causes, the trend was clear. By the 1760s few doubted the 'omnipotence' of parliament, apart from a small minority of radicals, and even here it was only the credentials of the Commons as currently constituted which were questioned. As Peter Marshall has emphasized in the context of the government of empire, what stands out is the boldness of the later 18th century Commons in relation to the regulation of property rights.[4] Access to parliament and the Commons became consequently increasingly important to a great range of interests, groups and indeed colonies. Lobby groups became more sophisticated and, in some case, ambitious in their scope and aspirations. And while ministers certainly came to control ever more tightly and effectively the passage of fiscal legislation, they did not seek to control the deliberation and fate of many other areas subject to legislative intervention. Indeed, it was only in 1835 that any formal and procedural distinction was made between government and other business. To this extent, the 18th-century Commons was accessible to the influence of a great many different groups, a fact which has led one group of modern historians to describe the 18th-century British state,

[1] Quoted in P. D. G. Thomas, Lord North (1976), 41.
[2] Thomas, Lord North, 41.
[3] W. A. Speck, Reluctant Revolutionaries: Englishmen and the Revolution of 1688 (Oxford, 1988), 246.
[4] P. J. Marshall, 'Parliament and Property Rights in the Late Eighteenth Century British Empire', in Early Modern Conceptions of Property, ed. J. Brewer and S. Staves (1995), 530–44 esp. 542.

with parliament at its centre, as a 'reactive' state.[5] There is an important caveat to be made here – legislation, to be successful, usually had to be particular or local in effect. This could be a source of frustration to activist MPs seeking national answers to social problems, for example, Poor Law reformers such as the MP for Seaford in Sussex, William Hay, in the 1730s and 40s and later in the century, Thomas Gilbert, MP for successively Newcastle-under-Lyme and Lichfield. This legislative pattern was to change significantly only from around the 1820s.

Government in Britain after 1689, therefore, was increasingly through and not just limited by parliament. This had crucial implications for the role of MPs. Thanks to the efforts of several parliamentary diarists before 1774 and the press thereafter, we know a considerable amount about the identity of speakers in major debates. However, because of the destruction of the records of the House of Commons in the 1834 fire, information about attendance and activity on committees is very patchy. A commonly expressed view is that attendance, beyond major parliamentary occasions, was poor, and certainly Houses were often reportedly thin. Does this mean that many MPs were indifferent towards their constituents' interests and the 'national interest' (however this was defined)? The salient issue may rather be in any case what or who did MPs represent; we will examine this briefly below.

The business of the Commons in the 18th century also took place subject to increasingly close public scrutiny. From the early 1770s, a lively, rapidly developing newspaper press was able to inform its readers on the proceedings of the Commons and the substance of Commons debates. Linked to this change were several broader shifts in the nature of political culture outside parliament – deepening consciousness of national political events and popular political articulacy, and, in certain types of constituency, growing independence on the part of electorates. The later 18th century also saw the slow rebirth of party. Uneven in incidence, in the course of the 19th century these changes, together with major electoral reform, technological and cultural change, and the inexorable rise of party as a central feature of political life locally and nationally, were to transform notions and modes of accountability in political life.

Membership

Who became an MP in this period and what implications did this have for the culture and codes, implicit as much as explicit, of the body they joined? The Landed Qualifications Act of 1711, passed by an assertive tory-dominated parliament in a period of acute concern about the influence of the 'monied interest', required MPs to swear to the possession of an unencumbered freehold estate worth £600 a year in the case of a county

---

[5] The idea of a 'reactive' state is advanced in the introduction to *Stilling the Grumbling Hive: The Response to Social and Economic Problems in England, 1689–1750*, ed. L. Davison et al. (Stroud, 1992).

member, and £300 for a borough member. Despite various efforts to prevent this – including an amending act in 1760 – it was a measure readily and frequently circumvented by the creation of fictitious legal qualifications. Edmund Burke, whose only property at this stage was in Ireland, and therefore did not qualify, was probably provided with such a qualification by Earl Verney – through collusive transfer of property for long enough to satisfy the House of Commons – on his election to the House in 1765 and 1768 as MP for the borough of Wendover in Buckinghamshire. Notwithstanding such practices, 18th-century MPs remained overwhelmingly drawn from the ranks of landowners and the established ruling elites. If anything, this predominance only increased after 1715. On its own, however, this bald statement can mislead. Members whose wealth derived principally from non-landed sources – trade, office, professions – were always able to gain a significant presence in the House. In the 1790s every general election was producing around 60 businessmen, 70 army officers, and 50 practising lawyers, figures roughly in line with those for the 1754 parliament. More importantly perhaps, the interconnections between land and business were many and profound in this period, whether in respect of the person and activities of MPs themselves or through their family connections. Merchant MPs usually had landed estates, while many gentry MPs had, for example, interests in coal mining. Investment in stocks was widespread among MPs by the middle of the century.

The social composition of the Commons attracted relatively little adverse comment, although the reformer and pamphleteer, James Burgh, urged that 'there can hardly be too many merchants in Parliament'.[6] Burgh, however, was not a merchant, and was hardly representative of merchant opinion. What stands out is, despite the spectacular growth in overseas trade in the 18th century, how little demand there was for an increase in the number of merchant MPs, although this is perhaps not so surprising given the incompatibility of Commons membership with a successful mercantile career, the existence of other ways of influencing the House, and the strength of the political consensus in the 18th century that trade was the national interest. Much more apparent was concern about non-landed MPs or candidates for membership, those whom Sir Roger Newdigate, the MP for Warwickshire, was to call on one occasion 'birds of prey from the East and the West'.[7] In the 1760s and 70s, much ink was spilt decrying the efforts of 'nabobs', wealthy returnees from India, to buy their way into parliament. To a significant degree, this vein of commentary reflected the tenacity of the assumption that the country gentleman was the ideal, indeed only proper, guardian of the people's liberties and independence of the Commons. Trading boroughs in England and Scotland were not slow to elect landed MPs, something

---

[6] James Burgh, *Political Disquisitions* (3 vols, 1774–5), i, 54.
[7] Quoted in *The History of Parliament: The House of Commons, 1754–1790*, ed. L. Namier and J. Brooke (3 vols, 1964), iii, 198.

which partly explains the declining number of businessmen MPs after 1715. Simple designations can again, however, hide as much as they illuminate. George Dempster of Dunnichen was the MP for Perth Burghs between 1768 and 1790. 'Honest George' may have owned the Dunnichen estate in Angus and, on leaving parliament, devoted the rest of his life to improving an estate in Sutherland at Skibo; but he had been born in Dundee, the son of a merchant. Paul Langford, meanwhile, has suggested that authentic country gentlemen – those whose wealth was solely derived from land – were, in fact, in a minority in the 18th-century House of Commons.[8]

Where MPs were subject to criticism, at times hysterical in tone, was in terms of their independence. We will return to this issue below when examining the role of the Commons in holding government to account. Most of the time what this meant was independence from government influence in the form of pensions or offices, either for themselves or their kin and connections. Between the 1690s and 1716, attempts to exclude office holders from the Commons were a near continuous feature of parliamentary life. The legislative results of all this effort were quite limited, certainly when viewed alongside the ambitions of some promoters of the attack on 'influence' – no less than a blanket exclusion of office holders – but included several acts (1694, 1700, 1701) excluding specific categories of official from the Commons, while under a clause in the Regency Act (1706), MPs who took office during a session were obliged to seek re-election. With Walpole's rise to political dominance, criticism of government influence reached a new pitch of intensity. Throughout the 1720s and 30s, measures designed to 'restore' the independence of the Commons and, increasingly, the electorate were periodically advocated in parliament and more regularly in the opposition press. The end of 'whig' one-party rule in the early 1760s saw no diminution in the denunciation of corruption. Indeed, criticism intensified with the Middlesex election crisis (1769) and failure in the War of American Independence. One of the main aims of the campaign for 'economical reform' launched in the later 1770s was further to reduce government influence over MPs. However, the corruption of the Commons was regularly exaggerated. The number of placemen in any one parliament was around 100, and these MPs were never sufficient on their own to control the Commons.

Before 1760, MPs were also identifiable as either whigs or tories, although it was certainly not the only political division evident in the chamber. Running alongside it was a court-country split, the relationship between these two shifting over time and according to context. As David Hayton has emphasized, country principles migrated from whig to tory during the first two decades of the century.[9] Moreover, from the 1720s,

---

[8] P. Langford, *Public Life and the Propertied Englishman, 1689–1789* (Oxford, 1991), 294

[9] D. Hayton, 'The "Country" Interest and the Party System, 1689–c. 1720', in *Party and Management in Parliament, 1660–1784*, ed. C. Jones (Leicester, 1984), 37–85.

party allegiance did not dominate the pattern of politics in the same way or to the extent that it had done since 1689. The whigs in Scotland were divided between those in the Argyll interest and the so-called *Squadrone*, an opposition grouping which had its origins in the immediate pre-Union period and which vied for political supremacy with the Argathelians after 1714. By the later 1740s, the tories had little or nothing to distinguish them from the 'country interest', excepting tradition and distinctive patterns of sociability and education. What finally brought about the end of the tory party was the tories' readmission to the court on the accession of George III (1760). Thereafter, MPs were identifiable as so-called 'king's friends' – i.e. regular supporters of the ministry – independents or members of a shifting constellation of political factions. In 1788 one analysis of the House reported the following: party of the crown 186; Pitt the Younger 52; detached parties supporting the administration 43; independents 108; Charles James Fox 138; Lord North 17; absentees and neutrals 14.[10] During North's administration, the Rockingham whigs, called themselves whigs and their opponents tories, but they were joined in opposition by other, smaller groups. In 1784 the Whig Club was founded, and it became an important instrument of Charles James Fox's influence. There was no opposing tory club established, however, and Pitt and his supporters did not call themselves tories.

The majority of 18th-century MPs came, therefore, from a relatively small group of landowners, and a narrowing one over the course of the century. Most were members of the Church of England and many shared common educational experiences. Around half went to university. In London, they probably visited the same places, the same coffee houses and clubs, although we know relatively little about the social life and activities of MPs when in London. In what ways this contributed to the distinctive character of the Commons is hard to say, although it can only have reinforced the intensely intimate, club-like atmosphere of the Commons. This was a consequence also of exiguous space. With seating for only around 300, the Commons chamber was small – around 58' long by 33' wide; it also had a low ceiling. It was frequently hot, especially on occasions when it was crowded, and also noisy. The Commons in this period was no place for faint hearts. Prejudice was easily stirred in such an environment, and reputations, private as well as public, stuck. The modern authority on the debates of the Commons is generally dismissive of the learned credentials of members.[11] The leading debaters persuaded through command of detail, clarity, command of legal and constitutional precedents, and often sheer force of personality. With his histrionic and dramatic debating style, William Pitt the Elder's remarkable command of the chamber in a Commons career which spanned 1735 to 1766 may well have been

---

[10] *The History of Parliament: The House of Commons, 1790–1820*, ed. R. G.Thorne (5 vols, 1986), i, 346.

[11] P. D. G. Thomas, *The House of Commons in the Eighteenth Century* (Oxford, 1971), esp. 7–8.

as much physical as a consequence of the substance of his contributions. Most members had a strong adherence, however, to the forms and privileges of the House, a readiness to protect these from the encroachment of the executive and people outside alike; and it was this, probably as much as social background, that shaped the culture of the Commons.

Functions

The 18th-century Commons had two main functions: holding ministers to account; and redressing the people's grievances. The former was achieved by various means, although between the 1720s and 80s this was mainly done through debate and calls for information and papers. In the years which immediately followed the revolution, many MPs regarded the expansion of the executive with a great deal of suspicion. Government departments struggled with the growth in business. Much energy in parliament was devoted to examining the activities of executive government and its servants through the appointment of House of Commons commissions, bodies whose members were elected from the House by ballot but who were paid a salary out of public funds. From the 1710s, this effort lessened. Partly this reflected the determination of ministers to prevent such scrutiny and the growing competence and control of the bureaucracy, especially the treasury. Enquiries had also been regularly been subverted by or subordinated to partisan purposes, which may also have served to discredit them.

The rise of whig oligarchy after 1714, together with the passage of the Septennial Act (1716), which lengthened maximum parliamentary terms from three to seven years, was accompanied by less intrusive Commons inspection of the activities of government, hence, in part, John Kenyon's judgement that government after 1689 was less a parliamentary monarchy than an aristocratic one.[12] This development was particularly apparent in the area of fiscal policy. With ending of commissions, the job of scrutiny fell on two committees – the committee of supply and the committee of ways and means. Both were always committees of the whole House, which almost certainly impeded their effectiveness, and under Walpole opposition members on three occasions made unsuccessful attempts to return to small committees. Defeat of government proposals for supply in committee in the 18th century was almost unheard of, and a convention grew that supply bills should not be opposed. Growing treasury and government control in fiscal policy was symbolized by the advent of votes of credit. First introduced in 1717, against the background of fears of a Swedish invasion, these were granted without estimates, and were also for unspecified amounts. Under whig oligarchy, they became routine in times of war and emergency. Although initially arousing some opposition, by the mid-century their use was largely uncontroversial. Periodic attempts

---

[12] J. P. Kenyon, *Stuart England* (Harmondsworth, 1978), 356.

to revive parliamentary commissions of accounts were unsuccessful or easily deflected, until North's establishment of a statutory commission of accounts in 1780.

If the Commons after 1714 became more compliant, therefore, to the executive, certainly in the business of raising supply, it still had to be managed carefully. Procedural conventions provided plenty of opportunities for individual MPs to raise questions about ministerial policies, while from the 1760s the practice of asking questions of individual ministers grew. Ministers could be taken by surprise by opposition attacks, as happened to Walpole in 1730 in relation to French refortification of Dunkirk contrary to the terms of the Peace of Utrecht. In the final decades of the century, opposition members resisted strongly government demands for automatic prior notice of parliamentary attacks.

Nor was parliamentary debate unimportant, even if ministers almost never lost divisions where their political survival was at stake. As Horace Walpole, youngest son of Robert, himself an MP and long-term observer and chronicler of Commons debates, declared: 'Every topic is treated in Parliament as if the liberty and fate of the country depended upon it: and even this solemnity, often vested in trifles, has its use. The certainty of discussion keeps Administration in awe, and preserves awake the attention of the representatives of the people.'[13] Writing in 1962, and summarizing a great deal of scholarship on 18th-century politics, Graham Gibbs declared: 'no administration which wished to last for long could afford to dispense with able parliamentary leadership, capable of defending on the floor of each house all aspects of government policy'.[14]

Securing Commons support for the conduct of diplomacy and war – the main activity of government in the 18th century – was particularly important even though key powers such as declaring war and peace remained part of the royal prerogative. William III had been forced to concede the necessity of doing this in 1701, and thereafter ministers worked hard to nurture Commons support for their policies. The speech from the throne which commenced parliamentary sessions regularly contained a statement about foreign affairs designed to give a lead to discussion. While parliament had the right to see certain papers – declarations of war and some treaties – ministers regularly presented other material to encourage support for a particular line of conduct or policy. Government retained a very significant degree of control over information about its activities, but what to reveal and when were problematic questions. On the one hand, outright refusal would invariably invite criticism; on the other, most MPs seem to have accepted the argument that on occasion revelation of information could be contrary to the national interest and unhelpful to the conduct of diplomacy. In the closing days of the Walpole

---

[13] Quoted in Thomas, *House of Commons*, 16.
[14] G. C. Gibbs, 'Parliament and Foreign Policy in the Age of Stanhope and Walpole', *English Historical Review*, lxxvii (1962), 18–37 at 18.

administration, and pushed hard by the opposition, Walpole was able to get the Commons to leave out the expression 'all letters' from a series of resolutions calling for correspondence between the British court and Vienna, Paris, and the United Provinces. He was also able to get a call for correspondence with Berlin delayed. A number of MPs had diplomatic experience and an expanding domestic and European press provided MPs with an independent source of information on foreign affairs, not that this necessarily led to well-informed debates. 'Very low' is one historian's judgement of the standard of parliamentary discussion about foreign affairs in the 1760s and 70s.[15] Foreign diplomats regularly attended the Commons, reporting back on debates to their governments. In the 1780s French officials appear to have compiled a regular journal of parliamentary proceedings, one which, according to William Eden, 'had the appearance of being executed with some ability and accuracy'.[16] Diplomats were not slow either to provide information to opposition politicians when it suited their interests, such as Benjamin Reichenbach, Prussian envoy between 1726 and 1730, or the Russian envoy Simon Vorontsov in 1791 who had close links to the Foxite opposition. Strong Commons support was an important lever in diplomatic negotiation, which provided a further reason for careful presentation of policy and management of the Commons.

Ministers could not afford, therefore, to ignore actual or presumed parliamentary opinion in their formulation of foreign and other policies. This was not a constant influence on foreign policy; nor was it necessarily decisive in determining policy; it was also more apparent in some areas than others, notably, Anglo-French relations and commercial and colonial matters. It was, however, a recurrent feature. Subsidies to foreign powers in peace time were unpopular with MPs, one reason why George Grenville did not pursue a Russian alliance in 1763. In the early 1770s discussion over a rapprochement in relations with France led nowhere, partly because of presumed parliamentary hostility. Not the least important constraint on successive ministries in their policies towards the North American colonies in the 1760s and 70s was the strength of Commons opinion in favour of a strong line towards colonial recalcitrance and against conciliation. In 1791, in the face of Commons opposition, Pitt the Younger was forced to back down from armed confrontation with Russia over Catherine the Great's plans to retain the Black Sea port of Ochakow. 'Pitt knew when to bow to the feelings of the House', as Michael Duffy observes.[17] Concession became an important tool in his parliamentary and political armoury, a tactic he regularly deployed to steer his way through periods of trouble in the Commons.

---

[15] H. M. Scott, *British Foreign Policy in the Age of the American Revolution* (Oxford, 1990), 21.

[16] J. Black, *A System of Ambition? British Foreign Policy, 1660–1793* (Harlow, 1991), 55.

[17] M. Duffy, *The Younger Pitt* (Harlow, 2000), 124.

Legislation, Lobbying and Representation

One of the most striking features of the Commons in this period was the growth in the range of business before it. Most obviously, the number of bills before the House grew very significantly, especially in the final third of the 18th century. Most were local, or very particular or personal in their scope and concerns. A high proportion concerned communications, especially turnpikes and enclosures, and such measures could have a huge impact on communities and individuals. The Commons was ready too to investigate all sorts of grievances. During Walpole's supremacy, especially notable were enquiries into gaols (1729-30), the sale of the forfeited Derwentwater estates (1732) and the Charitable Corporation (1731-2). This was the tip of a veritable iceberg. There were repeated committees on the poor laws. In 1763 a committee was established to inspect and redress what Horace Walpole called 'the grievous abuse of madhouses', the effectiveness of which, according to Walpole – admittedly not always the most reliable witness – was undermined by the lawyers.[18] The role of the East India Company was examined by a succession of Commons committees from 1767. The select committee on India of 1781-3, dominated by Burke, produced a series of reports, several of them very detailed and lengthy.

Very little modern work has been done on committees of enquiry, their modes of operation and evolution, partly because of paucity of evidence. Membership of select committees was increasingly decided by ballot, which provided ministers with an opportunity to pack committees if they saw the need. Many were a preliminary to legislation, although equally they could be used to deflect demands for action. Committees of enquiry grew in number during the century, and in scope and ambition. One reason was their flexibility as a legislative and political tool; another was the growing trend towards the systematic collection of data and information as a tool of government. Much, however, depended on the issue under consideration and the immediate political context. In 1782 the select committee on India, originally convened to investigate petitions against the operation of the supreme court in Bengal set up under the Regulating Act of 1773, was instructed to consider 'the British possessions' in India as a whole and to report on how 'the greatest Security and Advantage to this Country, and ... the Happiness of the Native Inhabitants may be best promoted'. This was at Burke's request, but the latitude afforded the committee and Burke undoubtedly reflected the political instability which followed the fall of North. Burke considered that parliamentary enquiry represented the best way to control government in India and to punish wrongdoers, a view that led him into the quagmire of the impeachment of Warren Hastings in the later 1780s. There was a trend in the later 18th century towards increased use of select committees, as opposed to committees

---

[18] Horace Walpole, *Memoirs of the Reign of King George III*, ed. D. Jarrett (4 vols, 2000), i, 160-1.

> ### Hastings Impeachment
>
> On 10 May 1787 the House of Commons formally impeached Warren Hastings, governor-general of Bengal (1772–85). His trial, held in Westminster Hall, which opened in February 1788 and lasted until Hastings' acquittal in 1795, provided one of the great parliamentary spectacles of the later 18th century. The process of impeachment, which involved prosecution by the House of Commons before the House of Lords, was rare in the 18th century. It had last been used in the trial of the Jacobite, Lord Lovat following the Jacobite rebellion of 1745–6; there also seem to have been plans to impeach Walpole in 1742, although they came to nothing. The driving force behind the campaign in the case of Hastings was Edmund Burke, who saw the former as the epitome of British misrule in India, a view which he had reached in the course of his investigations on the Commons select committee on India of 1781–3, and which was expressed very clearly in the 11th report of that committee, published in 1783. The renewed attack on Hastings represented for Burke a vindication of his view, but also of his role in Charles James Fox's East India Bill, the measure which had provided the opportunity for George III to bring down the Fox–North coalition of 1783 through defeat in the Lords and which had consigned the Foxites to a popular defeat at the 1784 general election, although Fox and Burke escaped the electoral cull. The failure to convict Hastings was due in part to the insistence of the lord chancellor and the judges on applying strict rulings on the conduct of the trial derived from current practice in the lower courts, but also the failure of Burke and his fellow managers to present their case against Hastings in a reasonable span of time. By May 1791, when the prosecution closed its case, only four articles of the charge had been heard.

of the whole House, perhaps because these tended to be more efficient and focused. On occasion, secret committees were established, where proceedings were held in camera and remained confidential. During Pitt the Younger's administration, select committees became a crucial device in parliamentary management.

All the above meant that access to parliament became much more important after 1689. For individuals, business and commercial groups, and communities, it could make a crucial difference to their fortunes and prospects. New, faster roads, to take one example, had the potential to revitalize the prosperity of towns and villages, but equally they could stifle the prospects of others removed from their routes. Well might 'a river or turnpike' have brought MPs crowding into the House, as one MP noted in 1771.[19] The impact of legislation of different kinds on industries, businesses, and trades is difficult to miss, although it does not always

[19] General Henry Seymour Conway, quoted in Thomas, *House of Commons*, 126.

feature in economic histories of this period. In 1779 the introduction into parliament of a bill to remove duties on imports of French cambric led to a major demonstration against the proposed measure on the streets of Glasgow by the weavers of the city and surrounding villages, although, in the event, the bill did not proceed.

Religious groups, quakers and dissenters, were among the first to adjust to the new political conditions after 1689; but they were far from alone. Textile manufacturers, merchants and weavers were persistent lobbyists after 1689. Some, but by no means all, groups of overseas merchants developed a permanent institutional infrastructure for parliamentary lobbying. A West India interest emerged in the 1680s, although it was informal and loosely organized before the 1760s. During the 1760s, however, a Society of West India Merchants was established, while in the 1770s, against the background of war in America, this body began to have regular meetings with the planters. Unity among American merchants was more elusive, and probably not sought before the mid-century owing to the diversity of their interests. For a decade or so after 1763 a central body of American merchants did emerge in London, while after the end of the war a new central body seems to have operated, one which had links to the outports. In other trades – the Levant, Russia, African, and Indian trades – chartered companies were the vehicles for lobbying activity. Beyond London, corporations or long-standing mercantile bodies assumed a lobbying role. In Bristol, the Society of Merchant Venturers remained the main voice of merchant opinion and vehicle for lobbying in that city throughout this period. Of 56 Bristol petitions submitted to the Commons between 1763 and 1783, 28 were from the Society of Merchant Venturers. Links between outports were regularly formed for lobbying purposes, for example, Bristol and Liverpool and indeed other ports. In Scotland, before the 1770s mercantile interests largely worked through the Convention of Royal Burghs, a body which met annually, but which had a permanent standing committee, and which had performed a similar role in relation to the Scottish parliament before 1707. Like many other bodies, including the colonies, the convention often had an agent (or agents) in London to expedite its lobbying activities, employing the well-connected Cromarty agricultural improver, lawyer, and military contractor George Ross for this purpose in the 1750s. Other sectors of the economy seem to have readily improvised *ad hoc* petitioning campaigns when and if these were required.

It is tempting to see major changes in the nature of lobbying towards the end of the 18th century, in particular an evolutionary shift towards greater publicity and exploitation of the press, as well as towards national organization. It is certainly true that the Reverend Christopher Wyvill's association movement established a new way of channelling public pressure on parliament, and several major lobbying campaigns of the later 18th century show clear signs of emulating this model, notably the abolitionist campaigns from 1788 and the dissenting campaigns to repeal the Test and Corporation Acts of 1787–90. The formation of the General

Chamber of Manufacturers in 1785 – which purported to represent manufacturers from throughout Britain – seemed to signal a new departure in the lobbying of manufacturers, although this body was short-lived, collapsing in the following year. By the final third of the century, the press was full of notices regarding lobbying campaigns from a huge variety of bodies and interests, local and national, although the cost of placing such notices could act as a strong deterrent to this. Lobbying had always required tactical flexibility, however, and much depended again on the issue in question, the immediate political context, and the nature of the opposing interests (if such existed) and their tactics. The formation of the General Chamber was a product in large part of Pitt's peremptory response to lobbying from manufacturers in 1785. It was an error he quickly learnt from, and his administration was probably one of the most open to manufacturing and commercial lobbies of any in the 18th century. Print had been fully exploited by lobbying interests much earlier in the century, although less so newspapers. For many groups, the route to success throughout the 18th century was through the politics of the closet, and lobbying parliament was one aspect of a broader relationship to the state. Mercantile lobbies tended to eschew a confrontational or indeed too overtly political a posture. Rather they sought to establish influence through the provision of information and dialogue with ministers and agencies of government, a method more likely to bring success. The same was true in other areas. In 1790 the Church of Scotland sought to follow just this route to remove the supposed burden of the Test Act from Scotsmen. On this occasion a 'modest and decent' approach, involving prior consultation with ministers, was unsuccessful, although this had nothing to do with how the campaign was organized; Pitt and his ministers could not grant to the Scots what they were determined not to grant to the English dissenters.[20]

Access did not always, of course, or necessarily equate to influence. Indeed, as the abolitionists, for example, discovered between 1788 and 1792, the best-supported petitioning campaigns could fail. What mattered was gaining the support and aid of ministers and MPs; and here some bodies and communities had distinct advantages. The West India interest was strongly supported in the Commons, as was the East India Company. So too was the woollen industry. In the latter case this reflected the sense that the woollen industry was England's 'national' industry, but perhaps equally importantly the relatively high number of MPs in the Commons from the west and south west of England. Scottish MPs were regularly castigated in the 18th century as corrupt ministerial lackeys, but from the later 1730s they formed a reasonably effective, active interest group in the Commons, especially on economic issues. In the later 18th century, there

---

[20] This campaign is fully reported in correspondence between the Church of Scotland minister, James Wodrow and the Bewdley dissenter Samuel Kenrick (Dr Williams Library, London, MS 24, esp. fols. 154, 156, 157, 159, 161, 164). See also G. Ditchfield, 'The Parliamentary Struggle over the Repeal of the Test and Corporation Acts, 1787–1790', *English Historical Review*, lxxxix (1974), 569–70.

were also a growing number of Scots representing English constituencies. In 1790 Gilbert Elliot of Minto, for example, was MP for Helston in Cornwall. Previously he had sat for Roxburghshire and Berwick-upon-Tweed. There were obvious limitations to the influence of the Scots at Westminster, especially when faced with a determined ministry, or the opposition of the powerful woollen interest, and they usually needed to gain the support of other groups, but then this was true of nearly all interest groups and lobbies. Irish interests could call on significant parliamentary support, reflecting the presence of Anglo-Irish landowners in the Commons.

If some groups and communities were assured of a hearing in the Commons, the representative credentials of the Commons were of course hardly unimpeachable. One problem was the vagaries of the franchise. The right to vote in parliamentary elections in this period was restricted to adult males possessed of certain property qualifications. In the English and Welsh counties, only freeholders who owned land valued for taxation purposes at 40s. per annum were eligible to vote. In the boroughs the franchise could, at one end of the spectrum, reside purely in members of the town council or owners of certain types of property (burgages), while at the more open end in all householders paying certain specific local rates or taxes. The Scottish electorate was much smaller – in 1774 it totalled no more than 428 – and had distinctive features which rendered it unusually susceptible to management.

The unreformed electorate was, therefore, notably diverse in size and nature. The salient point, apart from under what or whose influence votes were cast, may be less this, however, than who even had the opportunity to vote. In the early 18th century, under the operation of the Triennial Act, the total electorate in England and Wales may have been as high as around 300,000, representing around 23% of the adult male population. By the late 18th century the former figure stood at between 300,000 and 350,000. Because of population increase, this amounted, however, to only between 14 and 17% of the adult male population. At the same time, the number of 'nomination' boroughs – i.e. those controlled by patrons – rose from around 20% in 1715 to 30% in 1800. Moreover, the number of counties and smaller boroughs which regularly went to the polls fell significantly from the middle of the century. In other words, under the conditions created by the Septennial Act (1716) and in the absence of clear party divisions, in many constituencies electoral life descended into a coma. Parliament played only a limited role in this process, apart from passing the Septennial Act, although it did display a marked disinclination to take significant measures to eliminate electoral corruption. Two boroughs, New Shoreham (1771) and Cricklade (1782), were disfranchised and the vote placed in neighbouring hundreds. During the first half of the century, when the Commons was called upon to adjudicate on disputes about voting in boroughs, its decisions, while ostensibly governed by 'last determination' clauses of 1696 and 1729 – which stated that the last determination of a right of election by the Commons was final – tended to reflect party advantage according to local circumstance rather than consistently seeking to impose a narrow franchise.

Equally vulnerable to criticism was the distribution of constituencies. There is not space here to discuss this in any depth, but merely to point out several of the most glaring anomalies. Borough representation was a product of historical accident, and bore little or no relation to the contemporary distribution of wealth or population. Some of the most rapidly growing towns of the period were unrepresented – Birmingham, Leeds, Manchester, Sheffield. Several counties (Cornwall, Wiltshire) were hugely over-represented, while others (Cambridgeshire, Cheshire, Derbyshire, Leicestershire) stood in the opposite condition.

Did any of this really matter, except in so far as it helped to stimulate a growing body of dissident, reforming opinion in the later 18th century? Defenders of the unreformed parliament, and there were many, argued that the existing system of representation produced a Commons which properly reflected the interests of specific types of community and property. It was a narrowly pragmatic defence, and one which asked that the Commons be judged according to what it did rather than any speculative principles or grand constitutional theories. As Paul Langford has argued, on this basis the unreformed parliament had perhaps unsuspected strengths.[21] These partly derived from the residential patterns of MPs, which did not correspond to parliamentary representation. On this basis, Middlesex and London, among other places in the south east, had ready access to MPs. In 1784 five MPs owned property in the parish of Manchester, including Thomas Coke of Norfolk. Opposing Alderman James Sawbridge's motion for parliamentary reform in 1783, Lord North urged:

> Did any gentleman imagine that a petition from Manchester, or Halifax, or Leeds, or Birmingham would be less attended to in that House than a petition from Helleston, which did send members ... But experience proved that petitions from Manchester, from Halifax, from Leeds, and from Birmingham, always received as much attention as petitions from boroughs that were represented; and undoubtedly the same attention petitions from Manchester, Halifax, Leeds, and Birmingham, always would receive, whether these towns were represented or not.[22]

Towns, whether directly represented or not, regularly looked to their county MPs to support their interests, along with others who shared a stake in their fortunes, whether through residence or simply common interests. Birmingham, led by the town's commercial committee from

---

[21] Langford, *Public Life*, ch. 3.

[22] William Cobbett, *The Parliamentary History of England, from the Earliest Period Down to the Year 1803* (36 vols, 1806–20), xxiv, 938.

1783, had 'successfully integrated into the established structure of Warwickshire politics' by the later 18th century. By 1785, John Money notes, 'the town ... was presuming to proprietary rights over both the county's representatives'.[23] In the decade before 1783 Birmingham had no fewer than five bills before parliament.

It was argued too that indirect representation had significant benefits for manufacturing towns such as Manchester. What they got was influence without the disruptive effects of elections on local communities. It was a plausible line of argument, and one which may well have been persuasive to many people of property, if not to the majority of the population. Much of the debate about political reform in the later 18th century focused precisely on its likely moral effects; proponents saw reform as a means of moral as well as political purification, while opponents argued that more frequent elections would only bring greater electoral corruption. Even earlier in the century, opponents of more frequent elections had urged that 'frequent Elections debauch the Lives and corrupt the Morals of the People: habituate the lower Sort to Idleness; ruin their Families; and are very prejudicial to the business and trade and the Nation'.[24] A surprising number of proposals for reform sought not a wider but a narrower franchise, precisely to curtail the populism associated with elections, while in parliament in the 1780s Lord Mahon, supported by Pitt the Younger and others, campaigned for measures to eliminate the 'madness and tumult which had rendered elections in this country, for the most part, a farce'.[25]

The Commons and the Public

How did the public gain knowledge of the activities of the Commons and MPs? A further notable feature of the 18th-century Commons was its accessibility to members of the public. Admission to the galleries of the House, and the lobby seems to have been relatively easy, so easy in fact that one early Hanoverian MP was to complain that the Commons had become a 'Common House', a 'Coffee House' and a 'Play House', from which 'ignorant or Malicious People' carried away 'false or partial representations of Debates'.[26] The House could be cleared of strangers under the request of any MP, and in the 1770s this occurred fairly regularly. No doubt representatives of important constituencies and groups attended debates relevant to them. MPs frequently wrote to constituents. Sir James

[23] J. Money, *Experience and Identity: Birmingham and the West Midlands, 1760–1800* (Manchester, 1977), 212.

[24] *Tory and Whig: The Parliamentary Papers of Edward Harley, Third Earl of Oxford, and William Hay, MP for Seaford, 1716–1753*, ed. S. Taylor and C. Jones (Woodbridge, 1998), 100.

[25] J. Mori, *William Pitt and the French Revolution, 1785–1795* (Edinburgh, 1997), 22–30. The words were Pitt's speaking in support on one of Mahon's proposals. The only major outcome, the County Elections Act (1786), was repealed within two years.

[26] *Tory and Whig*, ed. Taylor and Jones, p. lxv.

Lowther wrote a letter every post day during a session to Whitehaven. These letters were again on occasion copied and circulated. During the 1740s John Tucker, MP for Weymouth, wrote regular, very full accounts of Commons debates to his brother, Richard. On one occasion Richard wrote back that he had 'had the opportunity to entertain our friends at the club, with your accounts of debates on the Hanover troops'.[27] The club was a group of local allies and friends.

Such communication depended on propinquity to the Commons or on contact with an MP. For those who lacked this in the first half of the 18th century, alternatives were relatively sparse, especially once one moved far beyond the metropolis. It is true that the *Votes*, a printed record of parliamentary business issued as separates, had been published since 1680, and were widely circulated throughout Britain, although these contained only a bare outline of proceedings. Manuscript and printed newsletters which provided parliamentary news did circulate, and written accounts of parliamentary proceedings were passed around in London coffee houses. Printed division lists appeared on occasion, usually being linked to electioneering. A list of MPs who supported and opposed the Peerage Bill in 1719 was actually given the title *A Guide to the Electors of Great Britain*. From the beginning of the century it was quite common for accounts of sessions to be published in pamphlet form at their end, albeit from a partisan standpoint. MPs' speeches occasionally made it into print as pamphlets, while accounts of some debates were printed in the 1690s and early 18th century. However, all sides of the Commons carefully guarded its privilege of reporting on its own proceedings, reaffirming this with new resolutions in 1729, 1738 and 1762, ensuring that before the later 1760s newspapers were forced to adopt various subterfuges to comment on parliamentary proceedings; they contained little direct reportage or information, apart from what was present in the *Votes*. Several publishers of monthly magazines, starting with the Huguenot Abel Boyer, were more intrepid, although they usually took steps to deflect the potential ire of MPs and the Commons. Debates did not appear until during the recess following the relevant session, and in the case of the *Gentlemen's Magazine* and *London Magazine* these resorted after 1738 to the device of printing the proceedings of imaginary assemblies. The reports of debates which did appear were highly selective, normally only covering high politics, and often bore limited relation to the actual debates.

From the 1760s relations between the press and parliament began to change rapidly. The Commons itself was partly responsible for this. The *Journals of the Commons* had been published since the 1740s. A growing body of other material was also printed, including, as referred to above, reports of committees of enquiry and parliamentary bills. Burke's *Ninth Report of the Select Committee on India* (1783) was no less than a survey of all aspects of Britain's connection to India, and was written in a deliberately

---

[27] Bodleian Library, Tucker Papers, MS Don. c. 106, fol. 161.

clear and comprehensible manner for a public without specialized knowledge of India. Publication and circulation of the Commons secret committee reports on treasonable activities (1794) was partly designed to prepare public opinion for suspension of *habeas corpus*. Excerpts from the report were widely reprinted in the newspapers. Private bills had to be printed from 1705, while by the end of the century the House was ordering the printing of almost all public bills. The only bills not printed were finance bills, a further symptom of the extent of treasury and administration control of fiscal matters. One historian has written of a 'deluge of information' pouring from the Commons by the 1790s.[28] Groups came to recognize the utility that parliamentary proceedings had for causes, independent of whether a petition led to a successful outcome. It was an argument radicals frequently used in relation to petitions for reform in the 1790s. Parliamentary procedure relative to local bills was a factor promoting public discussion of legislation at the local level, while public measures were increasingly subject to intense, widespread discussion in print and at public meetings.

While these things were important in transforming relations between the public and the Commons, more significant in both the short and longer term was the role of the press in reporting on parliamentary debates and proceedings from the early 1770s. In 1771 John Wilkes and his supporters in the City of London engineered a confrontation with the Commons over its will to defend parliamentary privilege in relation to reporting of its activities, with the result that attempts by the Commons to prevent this ended.

The consequences for the press and public, but also for the Commons, were far reaching. William Windham complained in 1798 that daily reporting on parliament was no less than 'changing the present form of government, and of making it democratical'; while from a very different perspective, the deist educationalist and radical David Williams portrayed press coverage of parliament as 'one of the strongest lodgements of liberty in the fortress of power'.[29] Such comments partly reflected the rapid expansion in circulation of the press in the final third of the 18th century – this had reached around 15 million by 1784. The reporting of debates continued to pose considerable difficulties, especially before 1783 when note-taking was finally allowed in the public galleries, and press reports of debates were frequently quite inaccurate, as well as partisan. It was partly for this reason that a growing number of MPs published their major speeches in pamphlet form. Burke did so on repeated occasions, while copies of speeches by Pitt and other ministers formed crucial elements of the propaganda campaign in favour of union with Ireland in 1799–1800. Burke and others also on occasion corrected copy of their speeches for

[28] Duffy, *The Younger Pitt*, 139.
[29] Quoted in J. Dybikowski, *On Burning Ground: An Examination of the Ideas, Projects and Life of David Williams* (Oxford, 1993), 229.

> ### Middlesex Elections Crisis
>
> The origins of the Middlesex election crisis lay in John Wilkes's decision to return from French exile in February 1768 to face the legal charges against him dating from 1764 and to stand for parliament in the general election of that year. Defeated in an attempt to be elected as one of the City MPs, he was elected for the county of Middlesex. Wilkes also surrendered to the courts given his outlawry resulting from his convictions for seditious and obscene libel from five years previously. The ministry, led by the duke of Grafton at this point, determined to expel him from the House on the grounds of his conviction and imprisonment, although it would be ten months before this occurred, reflecting divisions of opinion within the ministry and the time it took for Wilkes to be sentenced to a term of imprisonment for two years. On 3 February 1769 the Commons duly passed a motion to expel him, also declaring his election invalid, which led to a new poll, in which Wilkes again emerged victorious. This process occurred on three further occasions, but following the third time, the administration decided to propose that Colonel Luttrell, the defeated candidate in the latest poll, should take his seat in Wilkes's place. Luttrell had obtained only 296 votes against the 1,143 gained by Wilkes. This decision provoked a major constitutional crisis and campaign of protest around the country calling for the dissolution of parliament and dismissal of the administration. The crisis also led to the resignations of Grafton and the lord chancellor, Lord Camden. The ramifications of the crisis did not end there. In 1770 George Grenville successfully introduced his Election Act, transferring the decision of disputed election cases from the House to a small committee of MPs chosen by lot. Meanwhile, for the growing body of radicals and reformers who looked to Wilkes for political leadership and as a figurehead for a reform politics, some of whom had formed the Society of the Supporters of the Bill of Rights in February 1769, the Commons decision was seen as the latest and most direct threat to date to English liberty, raising the spectre of the Commons reflecting not the 'sense of the people' but firmly subordinate to the influence and purposes of an executive supposedly bound on establishing tyranny in Britain and its empire. It was this crisis as much as the unfolding conflict with the American colonies, which provoked growing support 'without doors' for parliamentary reform as the way to secure the true independence of the Commons and, with this, the revival of liberty.

newspaper printers. Division lists remained rare in newspapers, although the *Morning Chronicle* regularly printed lists of the opposition minority in the 1790s. Whatever their deficiencies, however, reports of debates rapidly assumed a central place within most types of newspaper, especially dailies and tri-weeklies. Readers expected full and timely reports of major debates. On 4 February 1792, the Edinburgh paper, the *Caledonian Mercury* promised readers a 'distinct and impartial statement of every subject which comes before Parliament'. There was a revival from the 1760s of printing accounts of important debates in pamphlet form. A growing number of periodicals were devoted to printing accounts of debates. John Almon, a bookseller and ally of Wilkes who played a central role in early press reporting of the Commons, was responsible for one of the first of these, his *Parliamentary Register* being continued by John Debrett before William Cobbett's *Parliamentary Debates* became the standard source in 1803; other compilers followed suit, including William 'Memory' Woodfall, the most famous parliamentary reporter of the period. Not all debates were reported, and it was high politics which continued to predominate. On the other hand, newspapers also contained a growing volume of information about other aspects of Commons business, including legislation, although detailed work is needed on this aspect of the changing relations between press and parliament. Provincial papers followed closely the course and fortunes in parliament of relevant local legislation, while such legislation was also increasingly frequently the subject of press controversy in these papers.

Press reporting of the Commons in the later 18th century was one aspect of a broader liberalization of political life in Britain in this period, as has been alluded to at various points above. The importance of petitioning on public issues and legislation grew after 1760, although by no means all major waves of petitioning were to the Commons. A key moment in this context was Wyvill's association movement, which was as much an organizational as a political achievement, and which, as noted earlier, seemed to present new possibilities for mobilizing opinion behind a common political platform. The new importance of petitioning is crudely measured by the substantial increase in the number of petitions submitted to the Commons in any given session in the final decades of the 18th century, but also by changes to the style and origin of many petitions. There was a renewal of electoral vitality in a growing number of open borough and some county constituencies in the same period. (This was the counterside to the electoral somnolence in more closed constituencies and some counties noted earlier.) According to one historian, this development transformed the 'political complexion' of a 'large portion' of England's borough electorate, creating new modes of political behaviour and producing elections 'dominated by parties (both local and national), issues and principles'.[30] This was linked to a revival of ideological and party divisions under the impact of dissenting campaigns against restraints on them, the American war and even more so responses to the French revolution and French revolutionary wars. Public awareness of and interest in parliament, MPs and their actions was unprecedented in the later 18th century. Ministers and MPs were much more conscious of operating in a political world in which the public was a continuous, often vocal presence. They,

[30] J. A. Phillips, *Electoral Behaviour in Unreformed England: Plumpers, Splitters, and Straights* (Princeton, NJ, 1982), 8.

and indeed a growing range of extra-parliamentary groups, were also ever more acutely conscious of the role of the Commons as a vehicle for publicizing causes and issues across the nation.

Chronology

1707
Treaty of Union with Scotland

1711
Parliamentary Qualifications Act

1714
Death of Queen Anne; accession of George I

1716
Septennial Act

1717
First parliamentary vote of credit

1719
Peerage Bill

1727
Death of George I; accession of George II

1729–30
Commons enquiry into state of gaols

1731–2
Commons enquiries in sale of Derwentwater estates and Charitable Corporation

1742
Fall of Sir Robert Walpole

1760
Death of George II; accession of George III

1767
First major Commons committee examining affairs of East India Company

1769
Middlesex election crisis

1770
George Grenville's Election Act

1771
Disfranchisement of New Shoreham; Printers' case

1773
East India Company Regulating Act

1781–3
Burke's select committee on India

1782
Disfranchisement of Cricklade

1785
Formation of General Chamber of Manufactures

1790
Campaign to remove burden of Test Act from Scotsmen

1801
Anglo-Irish union

Further Reading

J. Black, *Walpole in Power* (2001)

—— *Parliament and Foreign Policy in the Eighteenth Century* (Cambridge, 2004)

J. E. Bradley, 'The Public, Parliament and the Protestant Dissenting Deputies, 1732–1740', in *Parliament and Dissent*, ed. S. Taylor and D. L. Wykes (Edinburgh, 2005) [special issue of *Parliamentary History*, xxiv/1], 71–90

J. Brewer, *The Sinews of Power: War, Money and the English State, 1688–1783* (1989)

M. Duffy, *The Younger Pitt* (Harlow, 2000)

B. Harris, 'Parliamentary Legislation, Lobbying and the Press in Eighteenth Century Scotland', in *The Print Culture of Parliament, 1600–1800*, ed. J. Peacey (Edinburgh, 2007) [special issue of *Parliamentary History*, xxvi/1], 76–95

The History of Parliament: The House of Commons, 1690–1715, ed. E. Cruickshanks, D. W. Hayton and S. Handley (5 vols, Cambridge, 2002)

The History of Parliament: The House of Commons, 1754–1790, ed. L. Namier and J. Brooke (2 vols, 1964)

The History of Parliament: The House of Commons, 1790–1820, ed. R. G. Thorne (5 vols, 1986)

J. Hoppit, 'Patterns of Parliamentary Legislation, 1660–1800', *Historical Journal*, xxxix (1996), 109–31

N. C. Hunt, *Two Early Political Associations: The Quakers and the Dissenting Deputies in the Age of Sir Robert Walpole* (Oxford, 1961)

J. Innes, 'Legislation and Public Participation, 1760–1830', in *The British and their Laws*, ed. D. Lemmings (Woodbridge, 2005), 102–32

—— 'Parliament and the Shaping of Eighteenth-Century English Social Policy', *Transactions of the Royal Historical Society*, 5th ser., xxxix (1990), 62–92

P. Jupp, *The Governing of Britain, 1688–1848: The Executive, Parliament and the People* (2006)

P. Langford, *Public Life and the Propertied Englishman, 1689–1798* (Oxford, 1991)

J. Money, *Experience and Identity: Birmingham and the West Midlands, 1760–1800* (Manchester, 1977)

F. O'Gorman, *Voters, Patrons and Parties: The Unreformed Electorate of Hanoverian England, 1734–1832* (Oxford, 1989)

A. J. O'Shaughnessy, 'The Formation of a Commercial Lobby: The West India Interest, British Colonial Policy and the American Revolution', *Historical Journal*, xl (1997), 71–95

A. G. Olson, 'The London Mercantile Lobby and the Coming of the American Revolution', *Journal of American History*, lxix (1982), 21–41

—— 'The Virginia Merchants of London: A Study in Eighteenth-Century Interest Group Politics', *William and Mary Quarterly*, 3rd ser., xl (1983), 363–88

Parliaments, Nations and Identities in Britain and Ireland, 1660–1850, ed. J. Hoppit (Manchester, 2003)

P. D. G. Thomas, 'The Beginning of Parliamentary Reporting in Newspapers, 1768–1774', *English Historical Review*, lxxiv (1959), 623–36

—— *The House of Commons in the Eighteenth Century* (Oxford, 1971)

—— *Lord North* (1976)

15 House of Lords, 1801–1911
Richard W. Davis

The 1801 session of parliament, the first after the Act of Union of Great Britain and Ireland the previous year, found the House of Lords in a new chamber. The addition of 28 Irish representative peers and four Irish bishops necessitated a move from the small and stuffy Parliament Chamber where the Lords had previously sat, to the former Court of Requests in the Palace of Westminster. The new chamber solved previous problems, being 80' long, 40' wide, and 30' high. Three semicircular windows of 6' in height just under the ceiling provided ample light in the daytime, and four magnificent chandeliers illuminated the darkness. These comfortable accommodations would house the Lords until the 1834 fire that destroyed most of the old houses of parliament and forced them to squeeze into the Painted Chamber (until 1847 when the present houses of parliament were completed). The Painted Chamber was about 82' long by 28' wide, with three rows of seats against the walls on either side. According to Lord Duncannon, there was hardly space to pass from the bar to the woolsack.[1] Nevertheless, on a crucial vote on the Irish Corporations Bill of 1836, the Painted Chamber was able to accommodate 343 lords, well in excess of the previous high of 254 on the second reading of the Reform Bill in the old chamber. It cannot have been comfortable, but it was the issue that determined attendance. Without a significant issue, it was difficult to get lords to attend at all.

However, the expanded body never had the chance to undertake what was to have been the major business of the 1801 session. The point of the union was to strengthen the bond between Britain and Ireland in part by merging their institutions, and that had been accomplished, but it would never have been achieved without the tacit acquiescence of the huge Catholic majority in Ireland. Now they expected their reward – removal of laws which prevented Catholics from sitting in parliament and holding public office. William Pitt's government prepared a Catholic Emancipation Bill to remove these grievances, but George III would not allow him to lay it before parliament.

Not surprisingly the Irish Catholics were furious. Pragmatists, such as Pitt, argued that the only way to pacify them was to give them what they wanted. George III contended that only Anglicans had proved themselves loyal to 'church and king', and they alone should serve the state, thus excluding Protestant dissenters as well as Catholics. Such a system had

---

[1] E. A. Smith, *The House of Lords in British Politics and Society, 1815–1911* (1992), 14.

been enshrined in law, becoming a principle of the constitution after 1688. The whigs had yet another position. They fully embraced the pragmatic argument, but also believed in the principle of religious liberty: the right to worship as one chose without any civil penalty or deprivation.

In 1807 George III's whig ministers proposed a measure that would have opened military commissions to all the king's subjects, without regard to religious belief. The king not only insisted that the bill be withdrawn, but demanded a promise that nothing similar would be proposed again. His ministers refused, and the king dismissed them. It was a bitter parting and neither side ever forgave the other.

When did the Spiritual Side of the House become the Government Side?

There is little evidence to determine when the right-hand benches of the House looking from the throne, occupied by the bishops since medieval times, became formally accepted as the government side of the House, and conversely the left-hand or temporal benches became the opposition side. The design of the present chamber of the Lords, which was first occupied in April 1847, provided an equality of seating on both sides of the House so that it was physically possible for government and opposition to occupy opposite sides. Before then the inequality of seating made a formal acceptance of this position difficult. However, by 1832 the two sides of the chamber, then in the old Court of Requests, seem to have been divided into government and opposition as shown by several illustrations on the royal assent being given by commission to the Great Reform Bill. The benches on the left-hand side of the House, then occupied by the tory opposition, are empty as the tory peers absented themselves in protest against the passing of the bill. (The illustrations have the empty benches on the right-hand side as the viewer is looking at the throne.)

The Lords had moved into the Court of Requests in 1801 when the Anglo-Irish Union of the previous year increased the membership of the Lords by adding 28 Irish representative peers and four Irish representative bishops. Compared with the previous House of Lords occupied since the 16th century, the seating in the Court of Requests on the spiritual side was increased, but not enough so that it equalled the seating on the temporal side. This inequality may not have been as critical in the Lords as such an inequality would have been in the Commons as the government side in the upper House could be a minority of the Lords.

In the later 18th century there is evidence of some members of the Commons who supported the administration gathering on the right-hand side as viewed from the Speaker's chair (the east end), and indeed a convention eventually became established of the division of the chamber into government and opposition benches. A similar 'tradition' seems to have existed by the 16th century of the right-hand side of the Lords being regarded as the more prestigious part of the House after the throne, for an illustration of the elevation of the dukes of Norfolk and Suffolk in 1514 shows the queen sat on the right hand of Henry VIII. This was the side nearest to the steps used by the monarch whenever he arrived by river at the House of Lords, and the presence of the queen on that side would have made it the more prestigious of the two sides.

There is evidence in the later 18th century of some peers sitting on the spiritual benches, particularly when the temporal benches were full for the old House was unable to seat all the members who were entitled to attend. In 1779 the duke of Manchester, having risen to speak in the House, 'some disorder having taken place, the opposition benches compelled order.' In the same year, Lord Stormont clarified a previous statement in the Lords by stating 'that if the present Ministry should be removed, they would be succeeded by the noble Lords on the opposite benches and their friends'.* It is with the move in 1801 to the Court of Requests, with its extra seating, that the informal acceptance of the spiritual side as the government side may have slowly developed. In a debate in 1811 on the Regency Bill, a peer referred to 'The noble lord on the opposite side' and to 'the noble lord opposite'.† In 1809 the secretary to the lord great chamberlain witnessed the introduction into the Lords of Lord Byron, the poet, upon his succession to the peerage. According to his account, after being received by the lord chancellor but refusing to shake his hand, as was normal on such an occasion,

> Lord Byron carelessly seated himself for a few moments on one of the empty benches to the left of the throne [the temporal side of the House], *usually* occupied by the Lords in opposition – when on joining me, I expressed what I had felt [about not shaking the lord chancellor's hand], he said 'If I had shaken hands heartily, he would have set me down for one of his party [i.e. on the government benches on the right of the throne], but I will have nothing to do with any of them on either side. I have taken my seat, and will go abroad.'‡

CJ

* *Parliamentary Register, 1775–80*, xiv, 391 (1 June 1779); xv, 49 (25 November 1779).
† *Cobbett's Parliamentary History*, viii, cols. 743, 745.
‡ PA, LGC/9/2/3 (unfoliated): account of the introduction of Lord Byron, 13 March 1809, by W. Dorset Fellowes, emphasis added.

Procedure: Reading and Voting

Catholic emancipation and other legislation was dealt with in a manner still familiar today. Each bill was given three readings. The first was usually a formality and unopposed. Little if anything would be known about the bill at this stage. A lord could make a motion or introduce a bill any time he chose and did not require a seconder. On the second reading the principle of the bill was either accepted or rejected. To reject a bill on its second reading before it had been thoroughly discussed was considered provocative. It mostly depended on how important the measure was and calculations of whether it was likely to be made better or worse in the committee stage that followed. Important public bills were generally dealt with in a committee of the whole House. The third reading was where the bill was either finally passed or thrown out.

Yet within these procedures were further complications. One grew out of every lord's right to name a proxy when he was absent. In order to do this he had formally to take his seat in every new parliament to take the oath. That done, he could provide a proxy empowering another lord to vote for him when he was not present, but if he did appear, his proxy was voided and another had to be arranged when he left. Proxies were no use if not utilized, and the lords who held them had to be present when they were counted, which took place after the counting of lords actually in the House for the division. A lord was allowed to hold two proxies, but a peer's proxy could be held only by another peer and a bishop's by a bishop. When the House was sitting a proxy vote was as good as any other, but in committee it was not allowed.

Another way of dealing with absences, usually for a short time, was by pairing. This took place when two lords with opposing views agreed that each would be absent from the House for a specified period, thus canceling each other out. The practice of pairing was not a right, but grew out of informal agreements. By the beginning of the 19th century, however, lists of pairs were often included in reports of divisions.

Handling proxies and keeping track of pairings were matters too important to be left to the initiative of individual lords. Proxies often made the difference between success or failure, and the absence of a lord holding them could mean the loss of three votes. The lack of enough lords present could allow an undesirable bill to get through committee, or a desirable one to be revised beyond recognition. Lords had also to be summoned at the beginning of a session, and later when an important bill or other business came up.

Governments had salaried officials to do the job. The designation 'whip' appears not to have been much used before 1832. The first to have full responsibility on the government side was the sixth earl of Shaftesbury. When he first assumed the duties of whip is uncertain. He performed them throughout Wellington's 1828–30 government, and there is a hint that he may have served Liverpool before.[2] The first single whig whip, who assisted Lord Lansdowne and the bulk of the party (a small group led by Grey was in opposition) in the Lords in early 1828, was the 2nd Lord Auckland.[3] However, the whigs had done very well before with multiple whips.

---

[2] Huntington Library, ST 98: diary of 1st duke of Buckingham, 12 June 1827.

[3] British Library, Lansdowne MS, 3/9 (E): Auckland to Lansdowne, 1 January 1828.

Parties I

After 1807, the whigs constituted a new party, an amalgamation of two previous parties. The old whig party had split in the 1790s over the French revolution. The Foxite whigs had sympathized with the revolution, and deplored war. The main body joined Pitt determined to defeat the Jacobins. Many of these whigs followed Lord Grenville, who resigned with Pitt in 1801 in protest against the king's banning of Catholic emancipation. Unlike Pitt, who later accepted the king's terms to take office, Grenville never recanted. It was Grenville, as prime minister, and Fox's successor, the future Earl Grey, who were responsible for the 1807 measure that caused the ministry's dismissal by the king. If anything was lacking to amalgamate the two parties, this rebuff supplied it. Thus was born the 'new' whig party.

The new party was confronted with a daunting challenge, for the king could go a long way toward supplying ministers he trusted with an automatic majority in the Lords. He did so by providing the support of lords whose loyalty was to him, not to a party leader. Such individuals were known collectively as 'the party of the crown'.

> ### Irish Representative Peers
>
> The Act of Union of 1800 provided for 28 Irish representative peers and four Irish bishops to sit in the United Kingdom House of Lords. The peers were elected for life. The first election took place in the Irish House of Lords in 1800. Thereafter, by-elections were held as sitting peers died. Unless they happened to be in Dublin, peers sent in by post their choice of candidate to the clerk of the crown in Ireland. On the basis of such reports the clerk made a return of the peer elected to the House of Lords. The most evident difference in the elections of the 16 Scottish representative peers was that they coincided with parliamentary elections and that the peers elected sat for the same term as MPs, having to be re-elected for every new parliament. Also, though proxies were allowed, Scottish peers gathered in Edinburgh for the election. Each peer submitted a list of 16 names. On of the basis of these lists the return was made.
>
> The Irish bishops sitting in the Lords were made up of an archbishop and three bishops, and they attended single sessions in rotation. The primate of all Ireland, the archbishopic of Armagh, sat in the first session. The archbishop of Dublin followed, then the archbishop of Cashel, and finally the archbishop of Tuam, when it all started again. Similarly the 18 bishops went through their rotation three by three.

Election of Peers

Though elected, the Irish representative peers were the last recruits to that party. At their first election when they met as a body a list of candidates was conveniently provided by the British government. Those on it won handily. The by-elections that followed were managed carefully by the government, and at the highest level. Lord Liverpool, or Hawkesbury as he then was, took charge of them in 1804 and continued in charge, with one brief interlude, until his death in 1827. His successor as tory prime minister, the duke of Wellington, followed his example. A measure of their success was that in the 1830s there were only three whigs among the 28 representative peers. One had been elected during the interlude when Grenville was prime minister in 1806–7, another in 1828 when Wellington and his lord lieutenant in Ireland were bitterly divided, and the latter supported a whig. The third was elected in 1812 and later defected. Not much got by the government. It was patronage, or the promise of it, that won the day – not least a promise of support at some future election.

Elections of Scottish representative peers were as closely managed, and lists of the government's candidates were widely distributed beforehand. Two elections in December 1806 and June 1807 are illustrative. In 1806 Grenville's government managed to elect 14 of their candidates, two sitting peers retaining their seats. Just six months later, the 14 Grenville supporters lost their seats. The two who survived in December were reunited with their friends, giving the duke of Portland's government a clean sweep of the 16 Scottish representative peers.[4]

The 44 representative peers were the largest single group in the party of the crown, supporting the king's government whatever it might be. There were others of whom there was the same expectation – members of the king's household, ambassadors, bishops, the commander-in-chief of the army. All told, these and other individuals would have supplied about 100 votes. In a House of 300 lords in 1801, this would have given a government a considerable advantage.

Opposition whigs did not have the resources their adversaries had, but they had a powerful belief in their cause and a fervid determination to realize their objects. Motivated by these sentiments they put together a highly efficient system to deal with the duties that would later be borne by party whips. The two party leaders, Grenville and Grey, bore some of the burden themselves, but for important measures *ad hoc* committees of several peers were set up to manage them. It was a system relying on unpaid volunteers, but very effective.

Grenville himself described the results in 1809: 'In the House of Lords there exists a powerful, respectable, and well compacted body, cemented by mutual confidence, and acting together on the most honourable public

---

[4] A. S. Turberville, *The House of Lords in the Age of Reform, 1784–1837* (1958), 473.

principles.'[5] Until then, unusual for an opposition party, they maintained their numbers (around 80 to 90) from 1807 to 1812, managing to harass and sometimes to defeat the government despite its large majority. A measure of the whig lords' success is that on four occasions, beginning in 1809, the government tried to persuade Grenville and Grey to join it. These offers were firmly rejected. The two lords flatly refused to have anything to do with a ministry not pledged to Catholic emancipation. It became so difficult to form a government that in June 1812 emancipation was declared an open question with ministers and their followers free to support either side. Yet this did not induce whigs to join cabinets in which they would be in a minority. Nevertheless the following month an emancipation bill failed by only two votes.

Obviously the whigs did not deserve the reputation for division and disorganization depicted by historians. The whigs in the Commons – and it was they alone that historians have studied – richly deserved their reputation. The two leaders, of course, were peers, but that was not the only reason that party policy was shaped and enunciated in the upper House. In the Lords, whigs had no difficulty agreeing to amendments to addresses of thanks for previews of government policy, delivered in the speech from the throne at the beginning of the session, or to dissenting resolutions later. In the lower House it was impossible to get agreement on such questions. Thus it was speeches in the Lords where whig positions were laid down. Grey was, and is, generally regarded as the greatest orator of his time. Grenville, who had held a number of key cabinet offices and later became leader of the House of Lords in Pitt's first government, was possessed of a formidable expertise which he displayed in speeches as clearly argued as they were powerful.

Reporting of Proceedings

The speeches of the two leaders were relayed far beyond the lords who heard them in the chamber. Reporters were there, at first probably outside the bar marking the legal limit of the chamber. It was a period of rapid expansion in newspaper publishing. Between 1783 and 1830 the number of London newspapers rose from 19 to 55; for the rest of the United Kingdom the numbers were 61 to 259. There is every reason to believe that readership was very wide, ranging from royalty to artisans and ordinary workingmen. For those who could not afford to buy newspapers, they were available in coffee houses or pubs or by several people clubbing together to buy them. When party leaders spoke, and other lords for that matter, they were speaking to the nation.

This accounts for what might otherwise seem a strange phenomenon. In 1812 the war with Napoleon began to take a positive turn. The popularity of the government waxed, while that of the whig opposition which had

[5] British Library, Add. MS 58951: Grenville to Lord Holland, 6 June 1809.

been a steady critic of the war effort, waned. Under these circumstances any early attainment of whig objectives seemed unlikely and the number of active whig lords in parliament dropped substantially.

Yet in June 1815 Liverpool wrote to Lord Castlereagh of 'the struggle on the Corn bill',[6] the notorious Corn Law of 1815 that had recently passed. The government had carried the second reading by 144 votes to 17, and the third by 128 to 21. The bill would hardly seem to have been in danger.

The problem was that it proposed a high protective tariff, certain to raise the price of bread, and extremely unpopular. There was unrest throughout the country. Meanwhile in the Lords, Grey and Grenville, champions of the popular cause, dominated the debate, with Liverpool, accorded little or no support from his cabinet colleagues, having to carry the government side almost alone. It had been a worrying situation, with the public in an ugly mood and the ministers hardly a model of strength and decisiveness. Under these circumstances, it had been as Liverpool said, 'a struggle' and not one that could be repeated too often. Brute voting strength by itself was not enough.

Catholic Emancipation

In the years that followed, whig attendance remained small, with one important exception – emancipation motions. The motion in 1815 was lost 86 to 60. Whigs accounted for 53 of the minority, and three more proxy votes were lost because the lords who held them were absent. The 1817 vote was 73 to 69. Sixty-seven of these were whig votes. In 1819 the figures were 147 to 101. Eighty-six of the minority votes were whig. The remaining 20 were so-called Catholic tories, expressing themselves on the now open question.

In 1820 the whigs began to rally again, 77 espousing the popular cause of Queen Caroline. Her highly unpopular husband, who had just become King George IV on his father's death, wanted to rid himself of his wife. Liverpool's government unwisely agreed to accommodate him with a bill of pains and penalties – in effect a trial by parliament. When the majority against the queen's cause sank to nine on its third reading in the Lords, the bill was abandoned. The king was livid, threatening to dismiss the government and bring in the whigs. Relations between George and his ministers remained frosty when the next emancipation bill came up to the Lords in April 1821.

The two Houses had been at odds on the question for some time. The Commons elected in 1807, 1812, and now 1820, passed an emancipation measure. However, this was the first time that the actions of the two Houses were synchronized, raising the threat of a direct confrontation. One occurred. The Lords rejected the bill by a vote of 159 to 120. The

---

[6] C. D. Yonge, *The Life and Administration of Robert Banks, Second Earl of Liverpool* (3 vols, 1868), ii, 180.

> ### George IV
>
> In 1829 the king's former mistress, Lady Hertford, told the duke of Newcastle 'a great deal about the king – she Said that he was not to be relied upon – Generally swayed by the last conversation; clever & well informed & very agreeable in society, but wanting on all trying occasions of firmness and common Sense'.* Unfortunately, trying occasions, firmness, and common sense are in the first case frequent and the latter two necessary in a reigning monarch. Raving and hysterics were more in George's line. He could make the lives of his ministers miserable, but he could not control them. Most importantly, he allowed the patronage of the crown to fall into their hands. The most graphic example was the duke of Wellington, taking with him when he left office in 1830 the power to control the return of the representative peers, to be used thereafter for the benefit of the Conservative party.
>
> In 1832 Wellington asked several lords who usually managed the election of Scottish peers to put up a slate of Conservative candidates to challenge the government slate. They put up 15 and won 15. In the next election they got all 16. At the same time, Wellington was regularly returning his candidates for Irish representative peerages. For all intents and purposes the representative peerages of both countries had been merged into the Conservative party.
>
> * *Unrepentant Tory: Political Selections from the Diaries of the Fourth Duke of Newcastle-Under-Lyne, 1827–38*, ed. R. A. Gaunt (Parliamentary History Record Series 3, Woodbridge, 2006), 84.

composition of the majority of 39 caused added concern. It consisted of 25 bishops and only 14 peers. Before the division the future Viscount Dudley wrote to the bishop of Llandaff that though the bill would likely be defeated: 'Some reckon upon a small majority of *lay* peers in its favour, so that the bishops would have all the glory.'[7] Though this did not happen, it was too close for comfort. For the defeat of Catholic emancipation to have rested on the votes of Protestant bishops would have been disastrous.

The government wasted no time. The king's coronation took place in July, accompanied by the usual special creation of peers. Seventeen new peers were created, 12 opponents of Catholic emancipation and five supporters. Three more opponents were ennobled in 1824 and 1825, but creations did not necessarily mean new votes. One of the opponents was already voting as an Irish representative peer, making their net gain 14 votes. Of the five supporters of emancipation three were Irish representative peers, giving them a net gain of two votes.

The vote on the 1825 bill was 178 to 130, a majority of 48, which many found remarkable. Clearly it was not. The increase in the majority was

[7] *Letters of the Earl of Dudley to the Bishop of Llandaff*, ed. S. H. Romilly (1841), 283.

only nine. It did help the ratio of bishops to peers, which despite the addition of two more bishops now stood at 27 to 21. In the next vote in 1828, the penultimate one, the majority fell to 44. The ratio of bishops to peers worsened, 27 to 17. The position of the opponents of Catholic emancipation was just about where it had been in 1821, after an artificial boost in 1825.

Partly through the agency of the prime minister, now Wellington, the principle of civil and religious liberty had already enjoyed a triumph earlier in 1828, when a measure to remove dissenting disabilities comfortably passed the House of Commons. This was backed by a petitioning campaign producing well over 2,000 (a method of expressing public opinion that grew with the growth of the press that informed it). Wellington decided that the government must give way, though he expressed his sentiments as those of the bishops: 'As public men they felt for the consequences of a difference of opinion between the two houses on a question on which the House of Commons would have been supported by public opinion.'[8] It was a highly significant statement, one that would be reflected in the Lords' position for the rest of the century: the Lords must bow to the Commons, *if* the Commons was supported by public opinion. The qualification was crucial.

Reform and Lords v. Commons

Catholic emancipation came the next year, in the storm and fury of Irish discontent, with Wellington informing an hysterical monarch that he must acquiesce. The next important piece of legislation was the Reform Act of 1832. This act is usually portrayed as a severe blow to the stature of the Lords *vis-à-vis* the Commons, achieved in two main ways. One was a drastic reduction of the electoral power of the peerage brought about by the act itself. The other was the manner in which the bill was carried in May 1832. When the Lords amended it in a form unacceptable to Grey's government, a steadfast Commons (and a vocal public opinion) allowed the ministers to demand of King William IV a promise to create enough peers to carry the bill. Faced with being swamped by a massive creation, the Lords gave way.

It is true that the bill greatly reduced the power of individual peers to return members of the Commons. The argument that this reduced the power of the institution by removing an important means of keeping the Commons in line with the Lords, seems untenable given the history of the Catholic question. The contention that the Lords were rendered timid and lastingly submissive by their humiliation will not bear scrutiny.

The first session of the reformed parliament in 1833 disproves it, for the Conservative (or tory) lords would have thrown out the whig government's vital Irish Church Bill had Wellington not prevented them. Just before the voting on the second reading, he rose and walked out of the House followed by loyal supporters. Those who were left went down to defeat by

---

[8] *Lords of Parliament: Studies, 1714–1914*, ed. R. W. Davis (Stanford, CA, 1995), 98.

the whigs. The duke believed that the whig bill would help stem sectarian feuding in Ireland. In the 1834 session the Conservatives threw out three major bills. Irish Tithe Bills and bills to establish elected municipal government in Ireland were held to ransom. The Lords blocked education reforms. Such behaviour went on until the last year of whig governments in 1840.

How could this have happened? The Lords' legislative powers remained precisely the same after 1832 as before. In order for a bill to become an act, it had first to be passed by *both* Houses of parliament. The Lords had the power of veto, which they used to kill bills they did not like and force the amendment of others. How were they able to do these things for eight years? The simple answers are because they had the power, and because the whig governments did not dare to appeal to the people in a general election. In effect, they did not have the support of public opinion. Though there were general elections in 1835 and 1837, they were not called by the whig government as a means of appealing to public opinion.

Some have argued that these eight years were a fluke, when the whigs were insecure in their majorities in the Commons. Yet this is surely to ignore the obvious constitutional remedy of an election. Nor, though these years saw the most concentrated exercise of the Lords' power, were they the last.

In 1841 the whigs finally called a general election and were soundly beaten by the Conservatives, led by Sir Robert Peel. Backed by the Conservative lords, his government passed a number of useful reforms. One that was hard to swallow, however, was the repeal of the Corn Laws. According to the timidity argument, this constituted one of the retreats of the Lords.[9] The year 1832 was a retreat, but the repeal of the Corn Laws in 1846 was not: it was the passage of a bill introduced by a Conservative government and passed in the Lords by a majority made up about half each of Conservatives and whigs (or Liberals). The 40% of Conservatives led by Wellington accepted his argument that it was the only responsible course. The Liberals followed what indeed proved be the best road to office. It was no retreat.

Parties II

The result, however, was to break up the Conservative party in the Lords. For a while after 1846 there were three parties. The protectionists followed Lord Derby. Next in size were the Liberals, but neither of the larger parties could command a majority by themselves. The balance was held by about 40 Peelites, drawn from those lords who had followed Wellington. The Peelites, naturally alienated from the protectionists, usually supported the Liberal and coalitionist ministries that governed for most of

---

[9] L. G. Mitchell, review of *Lords of Parliament, English Historical Review*, cxii (1997), 787.

the period from 1846 to 1858. Lord Aberdeen, himself a Peelite and prime minister from 1852 to 1855, testified that though there were difficulties with the Commons, the Lords always gave him reliable support.[10] A short protectionist government in 1852 tested public enthusiasm for protection and found it sadly wanting. The result was to remove the main impediment that divided them from the Peelites who gradually drifted back to a reunited Conservative party. The process was largely completed by 1858, restoring the Conservative majority in the Lords. In the following year, however, the duke of Argyll joined other prominent Peelites in the Commons in what, with their accession, became a new Liberal party.

Judicial Work

The 1850s also saw the first attempt to establish life peerages prompted by problems on the judicial side of the Lords' business, for the Lords was also the supreme court of appeal in both civil and criminal law. The union with Ireland, among other things, caused a large increase in its caseload early in the century. The lord chancellor, who presided when the Lords sat as a court, also had his own court of chancery, not to mention presiding over the House in its legislative capacity. A number of expedients were tried to ease his burden and unclog the system; establishing the offices of vice-chancellor and deputy Speaker, for example. There were also problems for the jury, the other lords. Those who were not lawyers – most of them – were only frustrated by the technicalities of the law and angered at being dragooned in to make a quorum. As a consequence, by the 1840s appeals had come to be dealt with exclusively by the law lords, the judges who were peers.

This, however, caused another problem. Judges were often made peers, but as their heirs would have to maintain the dignity of the peerage, they had to be very rich. This meant old men at the end of long and lucrative careers at the bar. Not necessarily at the top of their form, their mortality rate was also high. In 1855 it was decided that life peerages would provide the answer to the problem. Lord Wensleydale was ennobled on these terms in 1856. The Lords, however, would have none of it. The committee of privileges, appointed at the beginning of every session, argued that though the crown had the right to create life peerages, only the House could decide who could sit and vote. This dilemma was finally solved in the 1876 Appellate Jurisdiction Act. The House of Lords remained the supreme court of appeal, but there were to be life peerages for at least three salaried lords, professionally qualified and experienced in the law courts.

Another semi-judicial function of the Lords took place in the handling of private bills, meant to serve the needs of individuals and entities such as corporations, both municipal governments and commercial enterprises.

[10] John Hogan, 'Party Management in the House of Lords, 1846–1865', *Parliamentary History*, x (1991), 124–50.

The Wensleydale Life Peerage of 1856

8 January 1856: 'There has been a new peerage created; but only for his [Sir James Parke's] life the peerage lasts. This is an innovation, but why should it not be? Some cry out that if that is done, the old families will become extinct. I should rather say, my lord may be a clever man and his son may be a stick; and is it any reason because the father is a clever man that the sons should be rewarded for it? Not at all. But still I should not like to see the grandson of the duke of Wellington starving, only on account of his grandfather. Or, in the case of a great man dying, without being rewarded for his service to his country, I should then say that his representatives should know the nation is grateful, and they should have something to show that his services were not forgotten. I think this shows that we are getting more enlightened, and if this goes on (which I doubt it will) there will be some chance of the poor deserving man getting to be a great man.'

16 February 1856: 'There have been some sharp debates on the subject of the Wensleydale life peerage (for Baron Parke)* in the Houses, especially the Lords. All the young vagabonds of peers are trembling in their shoes, now they see something like peerages for merit *only* beginning. So the cry among them is that it is unconstitutional. What absurdity! However, the peerage being given is supported by the highest law officer in the Kingdom; I mean the Lord Chancellor, who declares that it is constitutional. The asses who say it is not, for the most part do not know the meaning of the word. It is referred to a select committee [in July 1856 following these complaints the barony was made hereditary].'

CJ

* He was not a baron in the peerage. This was his legal title as a baron of the exchequer court.

Source: *The Apprenticeship of a Mountaineer: Edward Whympers' Diary, 1855–1859*, ed. I. Smith (London Record Society, xliii, 2008). At the time of this entry, the author was a boy of 15.

Their main business in the commercial sphere began early in the century with canals and continued with railways from the 1830s to its end. They were also asked to assist towns that wished to take on improvements not covered by existing legislation. In the last quarter of the century these included such projects as providing gas, water, and tramways promoted by Joseph Chamberlain in Birmingham and the London County Council, among others, and known collectively as 'gas and water socialism'. Select committees were sometimes used for public bills in instances involving great complexity or extensive investigation, the new Poor Law of 1834 and the Municipal Corporations Act of 1835 being perhaps the best examples. But in private legislation they were always employed. In them bills were scrutinized and put into shape. This required judgments of difficult questions of law and property rights, which the committees made and the House rarely questioned. The committees and the lord chairman who oversaw them were a powerful combination.

Parties III

After 1859 there was once more a Conservative majority against a Liberal minority. It is frequently pointed out that the Lords prevailed when the Liberals were weak in the Commons. Though often the case, it is hardly surprising and happened fairly frequently. In 1866 the Liberals, bitterly at odds over parliamentary reform, resigned office. Lord Derby became prime minister and the Lords supported him in carrying a Conservative Reform Bill in 1867. This established a very low householder franchise in the boroughs, which was widely taken as heralding democracy. In 1869 Gladstone carried a bill to disestablish and disendow the (Anglican) Church of Ireland, against the strong opposition of the Lords. However, as he had won a general election on this issue the year before, the Lords were in no position to block it.

Also in 1869 a Scottish Education Bill, dropped after amendment in the Lords, alerted Gladstone to trouble ahead for his English Education Bill the following year. The problem was that he intended to base his state system of education on a previous one in which denominational societies provided the education with some state support. Trying to bring them together in a state system was bound to be controversial and it certainly was. In these circumstances, as Colin Matthew has said, Gladstone settled on 'the only plan likely to survive the Lords'; that is, the one most favourable to the Anglicans.[11]

Gladstone, having been out of office from 1874, returned in 1880. In 1884, as a showpiece of his administration he proposed a third Parliamentary Reform Bill that would make universal the low household franchise adopted for the boroughs in 1867. This step towards democracy was very popular. Lord Salisbury, who had been leader of the Conservative lords since 1881, was, however, not prepared to accept it as it stood. He took the position, similar to Wellington's in the 1830s, that if the Liberal MPs wished to claim to be the genuine representatives of the people, they must be prepared to prove it. Gladstone had proposed a broad franchise, but thinking he would profit more from retaining the existing electoral system, he did not couple his franchise proposal with its natural partner, equal electoral districts. When the bill came up to the Lords it was met with an amendment that it would not be passed until it was accompanied with a redistribution scheme. Gladstone gave way. In 1893 Salisbury struck again. In that year the Lords threw out Gladstone's second and last Irish Home Rule Bill. There was no doubt that that was in accord with public opinion in Britain.

[11] H. C. G. Matthew, *Gladstone, 1809–1898* (1997), 204–5.

> ### The 3rd Marquess of Salisbury and the Referendal Theory
>
> Robert Arthur Talbot Gascoyne-Cecil, the 3rd marquess of Salisbury, who was prime minister (1886–92, 1895–1902), as well as foreign secretary (1887–92, 1895–1900) and leader of the House of Lords, was the last peer to hold the office of prime minister while sitting in the upper House (with the exception of the 14th earl of Home, who was prime minister for five days – 19–23 October 1963 – before he renounced his peerage and metamorphosed into Sir Alex Douglas-Home).
>
> In an increasing democratic age, with the House of Lords seeming to be an institution which was becoming a less significant player as compared with the popularly elected Commons, Salisbury developed, during the 1870s and 80s his 'referendal theory' which he hoped would furnish a justification of the continuation of the hereditary upper House by emphasizing that the Lords had the obligation to act as the 'conscience of the nation'. This would be achieved by referring contentious bills to the electorate via a general election. In other words, the Lords would not oppose such bills if the government of the day had a mandate from the electorate for such legislation. Salisbury's intent was not to provoke a frequent recourse to the voters, but to occupy the moral high ground to dissuade the Liberals from their attacks on privilege. The theory was thus invoked by Salisbury only during Liberal administrations, such as over the Lords' rejection of Gladstone's Second Irish Home Rule Bill in 1893, and was consequently sometimes seen to be partisan. At first, however, the doctrine appeared to receive confirmation at the elections of 1886 and 1895 when the Conservatives under Salisbury defeated the Liberals under Gladstone and Rosebery. However, after Salisbury's death some in his party, particularly Salisbury's son-in-law, Lord Selborne, pushed the doctrine to extremes over the Parliament Bill of 1911 and the Third Irish Home Rule Bill of 1912. Selborne only succeeded in further splitting a divided Conservative Party and it was not until 1922 that the party accepted the Parliament Act of 1911, which had in fact ended the validity of the referendal theory
>
> CJ

Prelude to Reform of the Lords

In 1911 the membership of the Lords was about 600 peers and 26 bishops (after the disestablishment of the Irish Church in 1869 had removed the four Irish bishops). This was about 330 more than membership in 1801. But in 1882 membership was only about 430. The rapid growth thereafter is likely to be explained in part at any rate by the surge of Liberal creations after their electoral victory in 1906, which by 1916 had added 102 peers. After being in a minority in the Lords from their inception Liberals were making up for lost time. The one great change in the Lords' procedure during the century was the suspension of the use of proxies in 1868, on the grounds that they allowed lords to vote on bills they had never heard discussed. By the end of the century the social composition of the Lords did not appear to have changed greatly. Though there were new recruits from business and finance, not all of whom owned large landed estates, their lifestyle and attitude were much the same as those who did.

One last important element in the functioning of the House was present at the beginning and end of the century. Historians have been much concerned about the low attendance in the Lords, 50 being a good turnout for normal business, and many lower than that. Lord Adonis, however, admits that however small the number of auditors, 'At its best the Lords was an important deliberative chamber.' He goes on to say that when the Liberals lost most of their noble followers after Gladstone's espousal of home rule in 1886, 'they kept most of their debaters; and the House owed much of the institutional vitality it possessed to the fact that though a one-party voting assembly, it remained a two-party deliberative assembly'.[12]

The situation described has a strong similarity to the Corn Law debates in 1815. The immediate question, of course, was whether or not the bill would pass. As its participants were all keenly aware, however, the other purpose was to inform the nation. Liverpool's 144 mute supporters would not have added much to that effort. Yet dull and uninspiring as we are told the atmosphere of the House was apt to be, when such as Grenville, Grey, Beaconsfield, Rosebery and Salisbury debated, the nation paid attention.

A change in the new century, unfortunately for the Lords, was in the quality of its leadership. Wellington, Derby, and Salisbury's had been of the highest order. They were not squeamish about wielding power, but they also knew when to draw back. Lord Lansdowne, who followed Salisbury as leader of the Conservative lords, proved to be void of judgment and without backbone. He lost control of a rank and file that, following several years of bitter dispute with the Liberal governments after 1905, finally cast prudence to the winds. The Conservatives, who had always had a soft spot for industrial workers, had since the widening of the franchise began with their own 1867 measure, been especially careful to avoid clashes. That did not change, but in their fury at Lloyd George's budget in 1909, which included taxing the capital value of undeveloped land, and a 20% tax on unearned increment in land values, they failed to appreciate the attraction of the social reforms it was designed to fund, most notably old age pensions. Thereupon, arguing that Lloyd George's was not really a budget but a blueprint for social revolution, they threw it out. That was a flat rejection of a convention on the sanctity of budgets their predecessors had always honoured, and it put in motion a process that ended in the Parliament Act of 1911, which trimmed the powers of the House of Lords and ended an era in its history.

---

[12] A. Adonis, *Making Aristocracy Work: The Peerage and the Political System in Britain, 1884–1914* (Oxford, 1993), 77.

Chronology

1801
Union with Ireland; Catholic emancipation rejected by George III

1807
Lord Grenville's government dismissed on issue of limited emancipation

1809
Grenville and Grey refuse overtures to join a government not pledged on the issue

1812
Catholic emancipation declared an open question

1815
New Corn Law

1820
Death of George III; accession of George IV; Queen Caroline affair

1821
Catholic emancipation bill fails to pass

1825
Second Catholic emancipation bill fails to pass

1828
Test and Corporations Acts repealed; Catholic Emancipation Bill fails

1829
Catholic Emancipation carried

1830
Death of George IV; accession of William IV

1832
Great Reform Act

1837
Death of William IV; accession of Queen Victoria

1846
Corn Law repealed

1867
Second Reform Act

1868
Suspension of proxies

1869
Disestablishment and disendowment of the Irish Church

1870
Gladstone's Education Act

1876
Appellate Jurisdiction Act

1884
Gladstone's Reform Bill passes with pledge of redistribution

1885
Redistribution Act

1893
House of Lords throws out Gladstone's Irish Home Rule Bill

1901
Death of Queen Victoria; accession of Edward VII

1909
Lloyd George's Peoples' Budget

1910
Death of Edward VII; accession of George V

1911
Parliament Act

Further Reading

A. Adonis, *Making Aristocracy Work: The Peerage and the Political System in Britain, 1884–1914* (Oxford, 1993)

J. Hogan, 'Party Management in the House of Lords, 1846–1865' *Parliamentary History*, x (1991), 124–50

D. Large, '"The Decline of "the Party of the Crown" and the Rise of Parties in the House of Lords, 1783–1837', *English Historical Review*, lxxviii (1963)

Leaders in the Lords: Government Management and Party Organization in the Upper Chamber, 1765–1902, ed. R. W. Davis (Edinburgh, 2003) [special issue of *Parliamentary History*, xxii/1]

Lords of Parliament: Studies, 1714–1914, ed. R. W. Davis (Stanford, CA, 1995)

M. W. McCahill, *Order and Equipoise: The Peerage and the House of Lords, 1783–1806* (Royal Historical Society Studies in History Series no. 11, 1978)

H. C. G. Matthew, *Gladstone, 1809–1898* (Oxford, 1997)

E. A. Smith, *The House of Lords in British Politics and Society, 1815–1911* (1992)

16 The House of Lords, 1911–49
William Frame

The 1911 Parliament Act was intended as a temporary measure to resolve the urgent problem of the powers of the House of Lords. The preamble to the act stated that the limits placed on the Lords' veto would remain in place only until the chamber was 'constituted on a popular instead of hereditary basis'.[1] There was thus a widespread expectation in political circles after its passing that a full plan of reform would soon be enacted. In fact political agreement on such a reform proved impossible to reach and the situation established by the 1911 act remained unchanged until the passing of the Parliament Act 1949 by the Attlee government. The latter act also confined itself solely to the powers of the Lords, and the composition of the second chamber was not subject to systematic reform during the period.

Despite this, the first half of the 20th century witnessed substantial incremental changes in the membership and role of the upper House. These were prompted by external factors, including the establishment of universal suffrage, through the Representation of the People Act (1918) and the Equal Franchise Act (1928). The rise of organized labour as a political force was a central feature of the period, from the arrival in power of the first Labour government in 1924 through to Attlee's landslide majority of 1945. Also significant was the decline of the role of the aristocracy in British government and its increasing replacement by a middle class political leadership. All this inevitably impacted on the role of the Lords, both in terms of public perceptions of the institution and in how peers came to view their role. This chapter considers these questions in more detail. It begins with the passing of the 1911 act.

Reform

The Liberal Party's victory in the second general election of 1910 provided it with a mandate to end the House of Lords' power to veto legislation passed by the Commons. A Parliament Bill was introduced in the Commons in February 1911 and passed its second reading by a comfortable majority. George V had agreed that should the Lords reject the bill he would create enough new Liberal peers to ensure the passage of the act. The Conservatives in the Lords were split into two main factions, known colloquially as 'hedgers' and 'ditchers'. These terms denote the distinction

---

[1] Preamble to Parliament Act (1911).

between those willing to compromise (the 'hedgers') and those determined to 'die in the last ditch'. The final act was played out on 10 August 1911, when the Parliament Act was passed by the Lords by 131 votes to 114. The act was a watershed in British politics, clearly establishing that the Lords was no longer even in theory equal in terms of legislative powers to the Commons. However, the *ad hoc* nature of the legislation left open the question of the future role of the second chamber and controversy over the timing and nature of a permanent reform scheme was to be a recurring feature of the following decades.

The Parliament Act included three main provisions. Bills certified by the Speaker as money bills would in future receive royal assent without the consent of the Lords if they were not passed by the Lords without amendment within one month of being sent up from the Commons and at least one month before the end of the session. All other public bills, except those extending the life of a parliament, would become law without the consent of the Lords if passed by the Commons in three successive sessions, with two years between the initial second reading and final passing in the Commons, and provided they were sent to the Lords at least one month before the end of each of the three sessions. Finally, the maximum duration of a parliament was reduced from seven years to five. Although the passing of the Parliament Act resolved the immediate problem of the powers of the Lords, conflict between the two Houses remained and both the Government of Ireland Act (1914) and the Established Church (Wales) Act (1914) were passed using the Parliament Act procedure.

The First World War ended this period of political controversy, and in 1917 the Lloyd George coalition set up an inter-party commission headed by Lord Bryce to examine the question of reform of the House of Lords. The majority of the Bryce commission favoured a reformed House with roughly three-quarters of the members elected on a regional basis by MPs, and one-quarter chosen by a joint committee of both Houses so as to ensure that some hereditary peers remained. Disagreements between the two Houses would be resolved by a joint committee, comprised of members of both Houses. Perhaps more significantly for the future, the Bryce Commission identified four main functions of the second chamber. These were: the examination and revision of bills passed by the Commons; the initiation of comparatively non-controversial bills; the imposition of delay in the passing of a bill into law so as to allow the opinion of the nation to be adequately expressed upon it; and, the full and free discussion of large and important questions in a non-partisan manner.[2]

These functions are worth examining in more detail, both because the Bryce definitions were often referred back to by subsequent reformers and because they identify key areas in which the role of the House was

[2] *Conference on the Reform of the Second Chamber: Letter from Viscount Bryce to the Prime Minister* (Cmd. 9038, 1918).

gradually redefined over coming decades. Three of the four functions were regarded as largely non-controversial and were cited by many as evidence of the value of the Lords. The examination and revision of bills passed by the Commons became increasingly important during this period, due both to the increasing amount of legislation being passed, which meant that the Commons often lacked sufficient time to review bills in detail, and the increasing complexity of many laws, for which the wide-ranging experience and expertise of members of the Lords provided a useful source of scrutiny. Likewise, the initiation of comparatively non-controversial bills helped to reduce the workload of the Commons by ensuring that such bills had been examined and amended in detail before their arrival in the lower House. It was also widely agreed that the Lords provided a useful venue for the discussion of major issues where party politics might act as an obstacle to free debate in the Commons.

Each of these three functions therefore provided an important justification for the retention of the House of Lords in an age of universal suffrage. The Lords, its supporters argued, was not merely a historical survival but instead provided important ongoing support to the political system, showing its ability to evolve and adapt its role to new circumstances. However, the fourth function identified by the Bryce Commission, that of the 'interposition of so much delay (and no more) in the passing of a bill into law as may be needed to enable the opinion of the nation to be adequately expressed upon it', was to be a subject of recurring controversy throughout the period.[3] It was most keenly supported by the right of the Conservative Party, which viewed it as an essential antidote to universal suffrage. It was most keenly opposed by the Labour Party, which saw it as a thinly veiled attempt to ensure a permanent Conservative power of veto over the actions of an incoming Labour government. The question was not finally resolved until the passing of the Parliament Act 1949.

Membership

An important outcome of wartime politics was the radicalization of political opinion in Ireland, with the result that the post-war coalition's attempts to enact home rule were largely boycotted by nationalist politicians. The 1921 Anglo-Irish Treaty led to the establishment of the Irish Free State, and this brought a significant change in the composition of the Lords. Since the Act of Union of 1800, 28 members of the Irish peerage had been elected by their fellows to sit for life in the Lords. Although the Irish peers were not specifically mentioned in the legislation setting up the Free State, it did abolish offices such as the lord chancellor of Ireland and the clerk of the crown in Ireland, which had responsibility for arranging the election of Irish peers as vacancies arose. In 1925 the Conservative government reached a formal decision to discontinue the election of Irish peers,

---

[3] *Conference on the Reform of the Second Chamber* (1810).

although the existing peers would remain for their lifetimes. The last survivor, the earl of Kilmorey, died in 1961.

This was the most significant formal change in composition between 1911 and 1949. However, the first half of the 20th century saw a major acceleration in the number of new creations, with the overall number of peers increasing from 591 in 1901 to 847 in 1950. Around half were former MPs, many from middle-class backgrounds, illustrating the importance of the peerage as a tool for party management. Those from a commercial or industrial background formed the second largest category, and the civil service and the law were also well represented. The periods after the First and Second World Wars saw an increase in the number of former service personnel ennobled. Overall, these changes in composition signalled the decline of the aristocracy as a governing class. If universal suffrage provided the political backdrop to this decline, the increasingly difficult economic position of many aristocratic families was also significant. Death duties were introduced in 1894, and by the 1930s had risen to 60% on the largest estates. The periods before and after the First World War saw the selling off of land from many great estates and a decline in the number of families that could afford to maintain great houses in London. This process continued throughout the period with income tax and austerity leading to a further flood of property sales after the Second World War. The loss of so many young men in the Great War also had a substantial negative impact on the next generation of aristocratic leaders.

Although a small number of hereditary peerages included provision for women to succeed to the title, hereditary peeresses remained ineligible to sit in the Lords up until the 1960s. The passing of the Sex Disqualification (Removal) Act (1919) by Lloyd George's government was intended to remove obstacles to women taking up public and professional roles, and suggested that in future women would be eligible for admission to the Lords. When Margaret Mackworth, 2nd Viscountess Rhondda (a former suffragette and one of the few hereditary peeresses), asked to receive a writ of summons to the Lords her claim was initially upheld by the committee of privileges. However, opposition among the Lords was orchestrated by the Conservative lord chancellor, Lord Birkenhead, and this resulted in her claim being reconsidered and turned down. She then persuaded Viscount Astor to introduce a bill to allow peeresses to sit in the Lords but this failed to win sufficient support, despite being reintroduced on several further occasions in the 1920s. After the Second World War she organized a public petition, which was successful in persuading the Lords to pass a resolution in favour of admitting women peers, but the Labour government declined to bring forward legislation.

The creation of new peerages became a matter of controversy during Lloyd George's post-war premiership. The conferral of peerages on prominent supporters had done much over preceding decades to provide financial support for both the Conservative and Liberal Parties. However, Lloyd George's predicament as a prime minister without an effective party

> ### Maundy Gregory and the Sale of Honours
>
> Although his family originally planned that he would train as a priest, (Arthur John) Maundy Gregory led a varied career, including work as an actor and theatrical manager, journalist, detective agency owner, hotelier, fraudster and blackmailer. Towards the end of the First World War he was introduced to Frederick Guest, the coalition Liberal chief whip, who began to use his services as an intermediary for the sale of honours. Gregory, operating from plush offices in Westminster, offered wealthy individuals honours in return for donations to Lloyd George's political fund. A knighthood could be obtained for £10,000 and a baronetcy for £40,000. By this means it is estimated that £1–2 million was raised up to 1922. The exposure of this practice in summer 1922 created a political scandal and contributed to the fall of the post-war coalition. Following the honours scandal Gregory continued to operate on his own account offering both British and foreign honours in return for cash, although purchasers often found to their cost that the honours promised never materialized. In 1933 he was arrested after offering a knighthood to Commander E. W. Billyard-Leake in return for £10,000. Billyard-Leake reported the offer to the authorities and Gregory became the only person to be convicted under the Honours (Prevention of Abuses) Act 1925. His sentence of two months imprisonment and a fine of £50 was surprisingly lenient, probably due to concerns among the political establishment about what might be revealed should he decide to tell all in court. On release Gregory went to live in France, where he died in 1941.

machine encouraged him to take this practice to extremes by openly offering peerages and other honours in return for donations to his political fund. This practice was publicly revealed following the announcement of the birthday honours list in summer 1922. Lloyd George had included in the list a peerage for the businessman Sir Joseph Robinson, a man whose rather murky reputation was known to have included trading with the enemy during the First World War. During a heated debate in the Lords letters from government agents negotiating the sale of individual awards were read out, causing a storm of controversy in the press.[4] Lloyd George's reputation was severely damaged and the sense of corruption surrounding the coalition played a significant role in its fall from power in 1922. The controversy led to the Honours (Prevention of Abuses) Act of 1925, although Lloyd George's chief fundraiser, Maundy Gregory, was the only person to be convicted under its terms, and then only in 1933, when he was discovered to be continuing to operate on a freelance basis.

In May 1923 the retirement of the Conservative leader, Andrew Bonar Law, created a controversy over the succession to the role of prime

---

4 Hansard, *Lords Debates*, 5th ser., li, cols. 475–512: 17 July 1922.

minister. The most obvious candidate was Lord Curzon, a former viceroy of India and a tory grandee. This raised the question of whether, in an age of universal suffrage, it was appropriate for the prime minister to be a member of the Lords, particularly when the Labour Party, now the official opposition, lacked a front bench in the Lords. Curzon was also unpopular with his colleagues and viewed by many as temperamentally unsuitable for leadership. George V also disliked him, and gratefully received advice from Arthur Balfour and others that it was inappropriate for the prime minister to be a member of the upper House. On receiving the news that Stanley Baldwin was to be appointed it is said that Curzon burst into tears.

Interwar Politics and the Lords

The arrival of the first Labour government in 1924 created new challenges for the British political system, particularly in terms of the role of the House of Lords as the second chamber. The Labour Party had long been committed to the abolition of the Lords, viewing it as a partisan institution which supported the interests of the wealthy against those of the people. However, in 1924 the party was faced with the reality that it could not take office without sufficient peers to form a front bench in the Lords. Philip Williamson estimates that the problem of the Lords was the 'largest single influence' on the composition of the first Labour government.[5] Ramsay MacDonald was helped by the agreement of George V that most of the royal household offices, which were normally filled by government peers, could be treated as non-political appointments. However, the need to find peers able and willing to represent Labour remained a difficult task and MacDonald was obliged to look beyond the party for several appointments. Soon after the election he offered the former Liberal minister Lord Haldane his choice of important offices in order to secure his membership of the government. Haldane became lord chancellor as the price of his agreement, although the weakness of Labour in the Lords allowed him to function as a semi-independent figure, subject to only limited party control, up until his death in 1928. The creation of the front bench involved much negotiation and resulted in a disparate group of peers, of whom none were of working class origin and few had previously been known as Labour supporters. MacDonald was forced to abandon the party's long-held conviction that it should not create new peerages, although with the caveat that those created by Labour should not have sons so that they would in effect be life peers.

Since 1918 there had been considerable tension among Conservatives over the implications of a Labour victory at the polls. Overall the result of MacDonald's government was an assuaging of some of the more

[5] Philip Williamson, 'The Labour Party and the House of Lords, 1918–1931', *Parliamentary History*, x (1991), 317–41 at 321–2.

far-fetched fears regarding a socialist government. This was not just because Labour lacked a parliamentary majority, but also due to a concern on the part of MacDonald and his colleagues that it was essential to the future of the party that it be seen to be working within the established constitutional system, so as to reassure the middle ground of British politics where many of its votes potentially lay. By appointing senior peers such as Haldane and Lord Chelmsford (a former viceroy of India who became First Lord of the Admiralty) MacDonald sent a clear signal that he did not intend radical upheaval in the political system. This went some way to reassuring Conservatives that Labour would govern responsibly.

The Conservative victory of October 1924 provided the party with a large parliamentary majority and this gave hope to those who wished to see second-chamber reform carried through. In June 1925 a cabinet committee was formed under the chairmanship of the lord chancellor, Lord Cave, to consider the issue. A backbench second chamber committee had also been formed and, despite the lack of agreement among its members on the exact nature of any reform, was active in lobbying the government to bring forward legislation. This campaign was boosted by the General Strike of May 1926, which added weight to the proposal that the Lords, once its composition had been reformed, should have the power to delay fundamental changes until such time as an election had been called and the opinion of the people established. This proposal had originated with the 3rd marquess of Salisbury in the late 19th century, had been implicitly endorsed by a majority of the Bryce Commission, and was to be a common refrain of Conservative reformers throughout the interwar years.

Stanley Baldwin was wary of initiating reform proposals, fearing that they would be seen as partisan and would undermine the Conservatives' national appeal. It was therefore not until June 1927 that the Cave proposals were made public. Cave's decision to grant the power to appoint the members of the reformed chamber jointly to the government and the existing hereditary peers was successful in bringing him a large scale of approval among Conservative peers. However, it also brought outright condemnation from the Labour Party and the Trades Union Congress, which saw it as simply an attempt to create a permanent Conservative majority. The proposal was also condemned by a significant number of Conservative MPs, who wished to see reform on democratic lines and feared that pressing ahead with Cave's scheme would alienate non-Conservative voters and thereby allow the Liberals to regain the centre ground of British politics. When Labour introduced a motion condemning the proposals in the Commons Baldwin stated that they had been published purely in order to test political opinion. Speeches by young moderates such as John Buchan and Duff Cooper were effective in outlining the strength of the Conservative opposition and thereby allowing Baldwin to rule out reform.

The second Labour government took office in 1929, albeit again without an outright majority. The front bench in the Lords took on a more settled and less *ad hoc* look, helped by the increased willingness of Labour MPs and supporters to accept peerages. Those who had previously opposed the Lords but now accepted the offer of a peerage included Sidney Webb (Lord Passfield) and Noel Buxton (Lord Buxton). The rule that only those without sons should be ennobled lapsed when the lawyer William Mackenzie (Lord Amulree) effectively became the first hereditary Labour peer. Overall, 18 new peers were created during the second Labour government, as compared to only four created in 1924.

Effective management of government business in the Lords remained difficult. Matters were helped by the Conservative leadership's wish to avoid overt partisan conflict, which generally dissuaded Conservative peers from outright opposition. However, Conservatives in the Lords became effective at altering Labour bills through amendment, forcing the government to compromise on several important items of legislation in order to secure a majority. In the latter part of the parliament there was also controversy over the Commons privilege in regard to financial legislation. The Conservatives argued that since the war there had been a great increase in social and economic legislation, much of which included financial provisions, and that it was not appropriate for these measures to be passed under Commons privilege. This matter came to a head in 1930 over the passing of the Unemployment Insurance Bill, which Conservative peers sought to water down by amendments. Such clashes prompted the leaders of both parties, against their own natural inclinations, to prepare plans for Lords reform. It was only the unexpected fall of the Labour government in August 1931 that prevented reform again becoming a major political issue.

Several Labour peers followed MacDonald and Snowden into the National Government. These included Amulree, De La Warr, Rochester and Sankey, with the latter remaining lord chancellor. The events of 1931 led to the Labour Party moving sharply to the left, with many party members viewing the financial crisis as the result of a plot by the establishment to oust the government. Sir Stafford Cripps, the leader of the Socialist League, a left-wing policy group, was particularly outspoken, calling for the abolition of the House of Lords and the passing of an emergency powers bill as the first steps towards the creation of a fully socialist economy within the space of a single parliament. This in turn reawakened Conservative fears about the actions of a future Labour government and led to three new bills for the reform of the Lords being brought forward. The most important of these was Lord Salisbury's Parliament (Reform) Bill, which had been prepared by a backbench committee of MPs and envisaged reform of both composition and powers so as to prevent a socialist government from gaining a free hand. This was considered by ministers in 1934 but the opposition of National Labour and Liberal National ministers, combined with Baldwin's long-held opposition to inflaming this issue, prevented the government from bringing its own proposals forward.

> ### The House of Lords and the Approach of War
> In the late 1930s the approach of war left little room for debate about the future of the House of Lords. However, the deteriorating European situation did lead to one notable innovation. On 28 September 1938 Neville Chamberlain's speech to the Commons on his meeting with Hitler was relayed via speakers to allow peers assembled in the library of the House of Lords to listen. This was made more dramatic by the arrival of Hitler's invitation to the Munich conference during the speech. The period was also notable because during a great international crisis the foreign secretary, Lord Halifax, was a member of the Lords, which seemed to suggest that membership of the upper chamber was not an absolute bar to the higher cabinet offices. However, there was later a backlash against key posts being held by peers and in January 1940 Chamberlain was forced by political opinion to ask his minister of information, Lord Macmillan, to resign in favour of a member of the Commons.

Judicial Proceedings

The Administration of Justice (Appeals) Act of 1934 was a landmark in the history of the House of Lords as a judicial body. The act was the result of a report in 1933 by the business of the courts committee chaired by Lord Hanworth, and it qualified the right of appeal to the Lords by making this dependent upon the permission of either the court of appeal or of the House of Lords itself. This was prompted by both the increasing number of cases being referred to the Lords and also an increase in the average length of time each case took to decide. In 1920 hearings by the law lords ran for a total of 296 days and covered 206 cases. In 1935 the figures were 327 days to hear 142 cases. This trend had earlier led to the Appellate Jurisdiction Act 1913, which allowed the appointment of two extra lords of appeal in ordinary, specifically to support hearings of the privy council following an increase in appeals from the self-governing dominions. The Appellate Jurisdiction Act 1929 also allowed the appointment of one further lord of appeal.

The year 1935 saw the last trial of a peer in the House of Lords. The right of peers to be tried by the Lords if accused of treason or felony could be traced to the medieval period. Although this was described as a right it was in fact compulsory, meaning that peers accused of these crimes had to tried by the Lords. In 1948 the Criminal Justice Act abolished the right to trial by the Lords, with the relevant clause being inserted as a Lords amendment.

During the inter-war years the nature of appointees as lords of appeal began to change. In the 19th century, political prominence had often been a key feature of appointees and this perpetuated itself in the early 20th century, with figures such as Edward Carson, Thomas Shaw and John

> ### The Trial of Lord de Clifford
>
> Edward Southwell Russell, 26th Lord de Clifford (1907–82), was the last peer to be tried by the House of Lords for felony. In 1935 de Clifford, a prominent motor racing driver, was involved in a head-on car crash on the Kingston by-pass in the early hours of the morning. The driver of the other car, Douglas George Hopkins, was killed and de Clifford was arrested and charged with manslaughter. The right of a peer of the realm to be tried by members of his own order in cases of felony and treason had been legally established since the medieval period, and had originally developed as a means of protecting peers from arbitrary action by the monarch. Although described as a right it could not be disclaimed and therefore the charges against de Clifford had to be heard by the House of Lords. The last occasion on which such a trial had taken place had been in 1901, when Earl Russell had been tried for bigamy. De Clifford's trial, which took place in the Royal Gallery on 12 December 1935, was an elaborate ceremonial occasion. Lord Hailsham, the lord chancellor, was temporarily granted the long-lapsed office of lord high steward by the king, and presided from a seat prepared for him on the steps of the vacant throne. The peers attending wore their state robes of red velvet with bars of minever and cocked hats, and processed to the Royal Gallery in reverse order of precedence. De Clifford, denied the privilege of wearing his robes, appeared at the bar in a morning suit. On being asked 'How will your lordship be tried?' he replied, 'By God and my peers.' Later that day he was unanimously acquitted of the charge after advice from the law lords that there was no case for the defence to answer. The trial ended when Lord Hailsham broke the white staff of the lord high steward, signalling the end of his tenure of this office.

Hamilton being political figures in the Lords in their own right. However, from the 1920s onwards there was a clear trend towards the appointment of non-political judges such as James Atkin, Hugh Macmillan and Robert Wright. Such appointments signalled a stepping back from the political process by the law lords and a greater degree of agreement that law-making was the prerogative of the Commons.

The bombing of parliament during the Second World War was the catalyst for a permanent change in the nature of judicial business in the Lords. Up to this time appeals were heard in the chamber of the House before public business began. However, during the post-war rebuilding work the law lords moved to a committee room to escape the noise made by the repairs. This led to the creation of the appellate committee in 1948 and ended the fiction that appeals were heard in front of the whole House. The removal of hearings from the chamber had the practical impact of greatly reducing the amount of time the lord chancellor was able to devote to the appeals process.

Attendance and Political Affiliation

Authoritative figures for attendance during the first half of the 20th century are difficult to come by. In 1938 Harold Laski estimated that average attendance at Lords debates during the interwar years was around 35 and that the number of peers who made on average more than one speech a year was 98. Roughly half of the 700 members of the Lords had never made speeches in the House, and over 100 had not taken part in its proceedings at all.[6] In 1958 P. A. Bromhead estimated that the average number of peers voting in divisions since 1919 had been 'around eighty', with only a handful of debates seeing more than 200 peers voting. Votes with high attendance included those on the Parliament Bill (1911), the prayer book (1927), the Coal Mines Bill (1930), Indian constitutional reform (1934 and 1935), and on the Parliament Bill (1948–9).[7]

Laski also made an estimate of party affiliations. This showed that in 1938 there were 12 Labour peers, 'three or four' National Labour, and 'about eighty' for the two main Liberal groupings. The remainder either had no known party affiliation or were members of the Conservative Party. Through a study of speeches Laski found 400 peers who had identified themselves as Conservatives.[8] In the 1960s Bernard Crick estimated that in 1939 there were 16 Labour peers, 56 Liberal, 31 National Liberal, 517 Conservatives and 126 for whom party affiliation could not be discerned.[9] A major feature of the first half of the century was the decline of the Liberal peers, from a peak of around 130 in the early 1920s to fewer than 50 by the early 1950s. As discussed above, the Labour Party never had more than a handful of peers in the inter-war years, although the number did rise significantly from 1945 onwards as the Labour leadership proved more willing to create new peerages.

War and Towards Further Reform

The most dramatic effect of the Second World War on parliament came on the night of 10 May 1941 when the Commons chamber was destroyed by a German incendiary bomb. After a brief period in temporary accommodation, the Commons was moved to the chamber of the House of Lords, where it continued to sit until the rebuilding of its original chamber was completed in October 1950. During this period the Lords was relocated to the Royal Robing Room.

The Labour landslide at the 1945 general election meant that for the first time the party was able to take office with a large Commons majority. At the election Labour had not proposed the abolition of the House

---

[6] H. Laski, *Parliamentary Government in England* (1938), 113.
[7] P. A. Bromhead, *The House of Lords and Contemporary Politics, 1911–1957* (1958), 32.
[8] Laski, *Parliamentary Government*, 113.
[9] B. Crick, *The Reform of Parliament* (1964), 103.

of Lords but had stated that it would not permit the Lords to block the will of the people. Attlee's view was pragmatic and his policy in office was to create only those peers necessary to ensure the passage of government legislation. The government's programme was focused on reform of the economy and the creation of a welfare state and it regarded Lords reform as an unnecessary diversion from these tasks. However, one practical change was soon made. This was the agreement in 1946 that peers regularly attending the House should be entitled to travelling expenses. This was applied in practice to refer to those peers who attended at least one-third of all sittings of the House.

The period of the Labour government saw the development of what has become known as the Salisbury convention. This was formulated as a means of dealing with the new situation of a large Labour majority in the Commons supported by only a small group of peers in the Lords. In the debate on the king's speech in 1945 Lord Cranborne, the Conservative leader in the Lords and future 5th marquess of Salisbury, stated that 'it would be constitutionally wrong, when the country has so recently expressed its view, for this House to oppose proposals which have been definitely put before the electorate'.[10] The Conservatives committed themselves not to oppose Labour's manifesto commitments and to allow the passing into law of bills nationalizing key industries and establishing the welfare state. The Salisbury convention again showed the pragmatic ability of the Conservative leadership to avoid damaging conflict over the Lords. It was to become an integral part of post-war British political practice and eventually developed to cover not only manifesto commitments but also a more general reluctance on the part of the opposition in the Lords to vote down government legislation on the second reading.

The Conservative agreement to respect manifesto commitments was observed. However, the introduction of a bill to nationalize the iron and steel industry, which had not been included in the manifesto, led to the breakdown of agreement. In 1947 the government introduced a Parliament Bill, which was intended to reduce the Lords' delaying power for public bills (excluding money bills) from three sessions to two, and from two years to one. This would allow Labour to pass the Iron and Steel Bill in the fourth year of the parliament against the opposition of the Lords. The Parliament Bill received its third reading in the Commons in December 1947. The second reading in the Lords began in January 1948, where it became clear that strong opposition from the Conservative majority could be expected. The debate was suspended and a conference of the party leaders was established to review the whole question of Lords reform.

This conference reached agreement in principle on several aspects of the powers and composition of a reformed House of Lords. These included that it 'should be complementary to and not a rival to' the Commons, that there should not be a permanent majority for one party,

[10] Hansard, *Lords Debates*, 5th ser., cxxxvi, col. 47: 16 August 1945.

that heredity was not in itself a qualification for membership, and that women should be able to sit in the House.[11] However, the conference broke up in April 1948 without agreement on the vexed question of the length of delay that the Lords should be allowed to impose on a bill passed by the Commons. The government pressed ahead with the Parliament Bill, which the Lords rejected on second reading in June 1948 and again in September 1948, with 258 and 238 peers voting in the respective debates. The bill was passed using the procedure established by the Parliament Act 1911, and it received royal assent in December 1949. The long-term effect was to end the Lords' ability to oppose the Commons seriously on matters of major importance. The delay it established of one year after the second reading in the Commons was in reality only a few months longer than the time a bill would normally take to pass through parliament after the second reading.

The years from 1911 to 1949 thus began and ended with a Parliament Act designed to reduce the power of the Lords in relation to the Commons. If the 1911 act was the culmination of a very real battle for power between the two Houses, the 1949 act is perhaps best seen as the final confirmation that the House of Commons had won this battle. The intervening period saw the House of Lords expand its role in scrutinizing legislation, providing valuable support to a House of Commons that was struggling to deal with an increasing amount of ever more detailed and complex legislation. Incremental changes in the composition of the Lords helped to fit it for this task, by providing a growing number of peers with specialized knowledge in varied walks of life. However, more fundamental changes, such as the creation of life peers and the admission of women, not to mention the root and branch reform implied in the preamble to the 1911 Parliament Act, were not implemented during the period.

[11] *Agreed Statement on Conclusion of Conference of Party Leaders* (Cmd. 7380, 1948).

Chronology

1911
Parliament Act

1913
Appellate Jurisdiction Act

1918
Bryce Commission reports

1922
Honours scandal; creation of Irish Free State ends election of Irish peers

1923
Baldwin appointed prime minister instead of Curzon

1924
First Labour government takes office

1927
Cave proposals for reform of the Lords published

1929
Appellate Jurisdiction Act

1933
Salisbury's Parliament (Reform) Bill published

1934
Administration of Justice (Appeals) Act

1935
Lord de Clifford last peer to be tried by Lords

1938
Chamberlain's speech in Commons relayed to Lords

1941
Commons relocated to Lords chamber after bombing; Lords relocated to King's Robing Room

1945
Salisbury convention announced in Lords

1946
Travelling expenses for peers introduced

1947
Parliament Bill introduced

1948
Conference of party leaders on Lords reform; Criminal Justice Act ends trial of peers by Lords; Appellate Committee created

1949
Parliament Act

Further Reading

L. J. Blom-Cooper and G. Drewry, *Final Appeal: A Study of the House of Lords in its Judicial Capacity* (Oxford, 1972)

P. A. Bromhead, *The House of Lords and Contemporary Politics, 1911–1957* (1958)

D. Cannadine, 'The Fall of the British Nobility: 1789–1994', in *The House of Lords: A Thousand Years of British Tradition*, ed. R. Smith (1994), 109–22

B. Crick, *The Reform of Parliament* (1964)

W. Frame, '"Sir Stafford Cripps and His Friends": The Socialist League, the National Government and Reform of the House of Lords, 1931–1935', *Parliamentary History*, xxiv (2005), 316–31

R. V. F. Heuston, *Lives of the Lord Chancellors, 1885–1940* (2nd edn, Oxford, 1987)

—— *Lives of the Lord Chancellors, 1940–1970* (Oxford, 1987)

I. Jennings, *Parliament* (2nd edn, Cambridge, 1957)

H. J. Laski, *Parliamentary Government in England: A Commentary* (1938)

N. McCrillis, 'Taming Democracy? The Conservative Party and House of Lords' Reform, 1916–1929', *Parliamentary History*, xii (1993), 259–80

The Oxford Companion to Twentieth-Century British Politics, ed. J. Ramsden (Oxford, 2002)

I. Richard and D. Welfare, *Unfinished Business: Reforming the House of Lords* (1999)

D. Shell, *The House of Lords* (Oxford, 1988)

R. Stevens, *Law and Politics: The House of Lords as a Judicial Body, 1800–1976* (Chapel Hill, NC, 1978)

Twentieth-Century British Political Facts, 1900–2000, ed. D. and G. Butler (Basingstoke, 2000)

P. Williamson, 'The Labour Party and the House of Lords, 1918–1931', *Parliamentary History*, x (1991), 317–41

17 The House of Lords since 1949
Peter Dorey

As the second half of the 20th century progressed, so the House of Lords appeared ever more anachronistic. With Britain's mature political democracy being accompanied by – and, to a considerable extent, fostering – a mode of social democracy, which (until the end of the 1970s) entailed increased government regulation of the economy, a comprehensive welfare state and the active promotion of various forms of equality and citizenship (and an apparent trend towards meritocracy), so did the continued existence of an unelected second chamber seem increasingly untenable. Moreover, as is noted in the chapter on the House of Commons, wider political trends appeared to be leading to a similarly inexorable decline in the role and viability of the Lords, most notably the trend towards centralization accruing from a state-centric, executive-dominated, approach to decision-taking, as public policy was increasingly formulated inside government departments and in cabinet committees, or between key organized interests and senior civil servants in neo-corporatist policy communities, before being 'rubber-stamped' both by the full cabinet and then parliament. If such trends were leading to a marginalization of the Commons (as many commentators contended), the detrimental impact on the Lords was invariably assumed to be even greater. Certainly, writing in 1963, Richard Crossman – explicitly echoing Walter Bagehot – deemed that the House of Lords had, like the monarchy itself, become a 'dignified part of the Constitution', as opposed to one of the efficient parts, although he acknowledged that its decline might be reversed somewhat if it was willing 'to end the dominance in it of the landed interest by the appointment of a large number of life peers',[1] something which Crossman himself subsequently attempted (unsuccessfully) to do in 1968–9.

Yet also as with the Commons, the Lords was to benefit from a number of developments, both exogenous and endogenous, which facilitated something of a renaissance and revival. Consequently, even as some writers continued to allude to the decline of the Lords, other commentators were able to cite evidence of renewal, and thereby proclaim that the death of the second-chamber parliament had been greatly exaggerated; they thus came, not to bury the Lords, but to praise it. It is notable, for example, that a 1964 study entitled *What's Wrong with Parliament?* focused almost entirely on the apparent deficiencies of the Commons, because although

---

[1] R. Crossman, 'Introduction' to Walter Bagehot, *The English Constitution* (1963; originally published in 1867), 18, 19.

the authors acknowledged that there was a strong case for reform to make the House of Lords more socially and politically representative, 'no such case can, in our view, be made out against the *procedure* of the Lords. For when we turn to consider the quality of the work done by the Lords since the war, there is little cause for complaint.'[2]

In seeking to explicate these developments and ensuing debates, this chapter will combine both a thematic and chronological approach to understanding the Lords since 1949. This will entail discussion of several discrete themes, starting with a brief account of the Lords' relationship with the Commons, paying particular attention to the former's largely subordinate or secondary role *vis-à-vis* the latter, in the context of the Westminster model, as delineated in the following chapter. We will then examine *how* the Lords has become more active and assertive since 1949, and more especially since the late 1960s, thereby imbuing the second chamber with renewed importance in British parliamentary politics. This of course, raises the question of *why* the House of Lords has become more active and assertive since 1949, a question which we will address in the third section of this chapter. Finally, we will briefly consider the issue of House of Lords reform, outlining the main reforms which have been enacted since 1949, and explaining why other reforms have either stalled or been abandoned altogether. In so doing, we will draw attention to the fact that although it has traditionally been the Labour Party which has been most critical of the Lords, Labour MPs and ministers have never been able to agree on what, if anything, should replace the existing second chamber. Moreover, we will note the apparent paradox whereby the Conservative Party, although ostensibly much more favourably disposed to defending the Lords, actually enacted two laws (in 1958 and 1963) which served to modernize the membership (or eligibility thereof) of the second chamber, but with the overall intention of preventing even more radical reform – or even abolition – by a future Labour government; change in order to conserve. The House of Lords has therefore been subject to four substantive (i.e. pertaining to membership or powers) acts of parliament since 1949, two of these passed by the Labour Party, and the other two passed by the Conservatives.

What will become apparent is that although the Lords' constitutional role has not changed (with the exception of the removal of the law lords on the establishment of the supreme court in 2009), the manner in which it performs its functions and responsibilities certainly has. These functions are similar to those of the Commons, namely debating and scrutinizing governmental legislation and other modes of public policy, and generally holding the executive to account. The Lords can, however, introduce legislation itself, either public bills or private members' bills, and some government bills are first introduced in the upper House (rather than the

---

[2] A. Hill and A. Whichelow, *What's Wrong with Parliament?* (Harmondsworth, 1964), 13, emphasis in original.

Table 1 Allocation of House of Lords' time (main activities), 2006–7

Activity	Time spent (hours: minutes)	Proportion of time overall (in annual session)
Public bills	506:45	51.7%
General debates	201:36	20.6%
Starred (oral) questions	65:48	6.7%
Other questions	60:08	6.1%
Statutory instruments	44:23	4.5%
Statements	41:50	4.3%
Debates on European Union committee reports	20:43	2.1%

Source: House of Lords, *Annual Report 2006/07* (2007), 47.

House of Commons) in order to help balance the legislative workload of the two Houses. For example, in the 2006–7 parliamentary session, 21 government bills were introduced in the Commons and nine were introduced in the Lords (legislation in both Houses passes through exactly the same sequential stages, although standing committees in the Lords are conducted 'on the Floor' of the House, enabling all peers to participate, and thus potentially offering scope for much greater detailed scrutiny and amendments). As Table 1 shows, over half of the Lords' time is devoted to debating and scrutinizing legislation – 'By far the most important work of the Lords is the examination and revision of Government Bills coming from the Commons'[3] – while a fifth of its time is devoted to more general debates, and nearly 13% of the Lords' time is devoted to questions (themselves often an important means of scrutinizing governmental activity, and holding ministers to account).

None the less, the Lords remains an institution which is clearly subordinate to the Commons (which is itself largely dominated by the executive), and whose ultimate sanction of vetoing government legislation was further weakened by the 1949 Parliament Act, which reduced the power of delay from two years to just one. Its subordination to the Commons was reiterated by a 2001 white paper on House of Lords reform, which asserted that:

> The House of Commons has ... long since been established as the pre-eminent constitutional authority within the UK. ... This constitutional framework, founded on the pre-eminence of the House of Commons, has provided Britain with effective democratic Government and accountability for more than a century, and few would wish to change it. ... It is vital that reform of the Lords does not upset this balance ... Reform of the House of Lords must there-

[3] B. Crick, *The Reform of Parliament* (1964), 107.

fore satisfy one key condition: it must not alter the respective roles and authority of the two chambers.[4]

Consequently, Britain's parliamentary system has been characterized as one of 'asymmetric bicameralism'.[5]

How the House of Lords has Become More Active and Assertive since 1949

Outlining the main functions of the Lords, and its relationship to the Commons, paints only a partial picture of the second chamber. What is also needed in order to provide a fuller picture is an examination, albeit brief, of the manner in which the Lords has performed its roles with greater energy and enthusiasm in recent decades. To assert, for example, that a key function of the House of Lords is to scrutinize governmental legislation does not in itself inform us about the ways in which it has performed this function with greater assiduousness and effectiveness since 1949.

The increased activism and assertiveness of the Lords can be illustrated in several discrete spheres, most notably the increasing number of sittings, higher attendance, greater number of debates and more questioning of ministers and other government front-bench spokespersons. We will then note how three other developments have both reflected and reinforced the increased importance of the Lords' deliberative and scrutiny functions, namely the expansion of its committee system, the increased linkages with extra-parliamentary organized interest and the slightly looser (compared to the Commons) ties of partisanship and party cohesion in the Lords, which means that peers generally tend to be a little more 'independent' than MPs. This last phenomenon has increased the Lords' propensity to challenge the government, for slightly weaker partisanship means that peers are somewhat less likely to vote strictly or routinely on political party lines; the governing party can be less confident of support from its peers than its MPs.

With regard to the number of days on which the Lords sat, Table 2 shows that these have increased from 100 in the 1950–1 parliamentary session to 146 in 2006–7. This has been accompanied by an increase in the number of peers attending the Lords, for whereas only 86 peers attended in 1950–1, 411 did so in 2006–7.

In short, the Lords has sat with steadily increasing frequency since 1949, and with more peers also attending these sittings. Moreover, this

---

[4] Stationery Office, *The House of Lords. Completing the Reform*, Cm 5291 (2001), paras. 9–10, 13–18. See also J. Straw, *The Governance of Britain*, Cm 7170 (2007), 42, para. 135.

[5] S. C. Patterson and A. Mughan, 'Fundamentals of Institutional Design: The Functions and Powers of Parliamentary Second Chambers', *Journal of Legislative Studies*, vii (2001), 39–60 at 41.

Table 2 Increased activity in the House of Lords, 1950–1 to 2006–7

	1950–1	2006–7
Average daily attendance	86	411
Sitting days	100	146
Sitting hours	295	980
Average length of sitting (hours)	2.57	6.42

Source: Figures for 1950–1 from N. Baldwin, 'The House of Lords', in *Parliament and Pressure Politics*, ed. M. Rush (Oxford, 1990), 158; figures for 2006–7 from House of Lords, *Annual Report 2006/7*, 46

increased attendance has also resulted in a corresponding increase in the average length of daily sittings in the upper House, for whereas the average duration of sittings in 1950–1 was just under three hours, they had increased to well over six hours by 2006–7. Put another way, whereas the House of Lords sat for a total of 295 hours in the 1950–1 session, its sittings totalled 980 hours in 2006–7.

These trends have simultaneously facilitated both more debates in the Lords since 1949, and much greater questioning of ministers and other government front-bench spokespersons. Whereas the upper House held 56 debates in the 1955–6 session, for example, it held 80 general debates in 2006–7. However, this quantitative change has been accompanied by a vitally important qualitative change, for as we note in the next section of this chapter, a parallel change in the composition of the Lords (since 1958) has imbued its debates with greater expertise, thus often rendering them rather more intelligent and better informed than some of the more partisan or polemical verbal exchanges heard in the lower House.

Meanwhile, with regard to the questioning of ministers and government spokespersons, Donald Shell's study revealed that the number of oral questions had increased from 275 in 1961–2 to 742 in 1987–8. Even more notable has been the increase in the number of questions submitted for a written answer, these rising from 72 in 1961–2 (an average of 0.6 a day) to 1,405 in 1987–8 (averaging 7.3 a day).[6] Alongside debates, questions by peers to ministers and other front-bench government spokespersons in the upper House have thus proved another important means by which the Lords has increasingly scrutinized governmental legislation and other forms of public policy, thereby holding it to account for its actions (or, on occasions, inaction), and in so doing, both complementing and supplementing the work of the Commons.

Following on from these key changes, three further institutional and behavioural developments since 1949 have also enhanced the role and effectiveness of the Lords. First, there has been a reconfiguration of its committee system, particularly with regard to select committees, which – like their counterparts in the Commons – routinely conduct detailed

[6] D. Shell, 'Questions in the House of Lords', in *Parliamentary Questions*, ed. M. Franklin and P. Norton (Oxford, 1993).

investigations and inquiries into aspects of public policy and legislation, and thus play a crucial role in scrutinizing the executive and holding ministers to account). However, unlike most of the key select committees in the lower House, those in the Lords do not directly 'shadow' government departments. Instead, the select committees in the Lords are more thematic, focusing on somewhat broader spheres of public policy. For example, whereas in the Commons, fiscal or monetary policy would normally be a suitable subject for the treasury select committee, in the House of Lords, these topics would be investigated by the economic affairs (select) committee, which was established in 2001 (and which has since created its own finance sub-committee). As Table 3 shows, its topics of inquiry have included the economic impact of immigration, and the economics of climate change. Another relatively recently established thematic select committee in the Lords is the constitution committee, which not only investigates constitutional reform *per se*, but also regularly inquires into the constitutional implications of various other aspects of public policy, as indicated by Table 3.

However, the two most renowned Lords select committees are the science and technology committee, and the European Union committee. The former was established in 1979 (prompted in large part by the abolition of such a select committee in the Commons when the departmental select committees were inaugurated, although this was later restored). The House of Lords science and technology committee (which subsequently established two sub-committees) rapidly acquired a justified reputation as a formidable and prestigious investigative body, due both to the expertise of its members – many of them former scientists and engineers – and the importance of the topics investigated, a few of the most recent being listed in Table 3.

Meanwhile, the European Union committee (titled the European Communities committee before 1999) comprises 18 peers, its main role being to examine draft EU legislative proposals before they are formally ratified and thereupon become official European Union law. Given the broad-ranging and ever-increasing jurisdiction of EU policies and directives affecting the United Kingdom, the European Union committee has established seven sub-committees, each focusing on a discrete aspect of EU policies, namely: economic and financial affairs; trade and international relations; the internal market; foreign affairs, defence and development policy; environment and agriculture; law and institutions; home affairs; social policy and consumer affairs. A small sample of the eclectic range of topics examined is provided in Table 3. Each member of the European Union committee (except for the chair) also serves on one of these sub-committees, which also co-opts other peers in the Lords to provide expertise relevant to a particular inquiry. As such, a total of about 70 peers are involved in the European Union committee and its seven sub-committees, this number representing about 10% of the total (post-1999) membership of the Lords.

Table 3 Examples of inquiries conducted by the key
House of Lords select committees since 1997

House of Lords select committee	Topics of inquiry
Economic affairs	Economic impact of immigration
	Apprenticeships and skills acquisition
	Government management of risk
	Monetary policy
	Economics of climate change
Science and technology	Personal internet security
	Radioactive waste management
	Allergies
	Renewable energy
	Therapeutic uses of cannabis
Constitution	The Governance of Britain (green paper)
	Parliament and the waging of war
	Police and Justice Bill (2006)
	Parliament and the legislative process
	The regulatory state and accountability
European Union (including inquiries conducted by its seven sub-committees)	The European Union and Russia
	Developments in European foreign policy
	Future of the Common Agricultural Policy
	EU Strategy on biofuels
	The EU and Africa
	Economic migration to the EU
	European Union fisheries legislation
	European Defence Agency
	The EU and climate change
	Gas: liberalized markets and security of supply
	Combating racism and xenophobia
	A Community immigration policy
	A European Food Authority
	Organic farming and the EU
	Airline competition
	Sustainable landfill
	The EC chocolate directive

Second, there have been increasing linkages between the Lords and extra-parliamentary organized interests (partly as a consequence of the increased role and activity of select committees just noted). In 1990 the published findings of a major survey (conducted under the auspices of the 'Study of Parliament Group') into the changing relationship between parliament and pressure groups confirmed that the Lords – along with the Commons – had increasingly become an important focus for organized interests (or those formally lobbying on their behalf), a phenomenon which itself reflects a wider recognition of the enhanced role of the Lords in contemporary British politics.

The increased contacts between pressure groups and peers have taken a number of forms, including the urging of amendments to bills during (standing) committee stage, proposing private members' bills, providing peers with information or briefing material (to facilitate questions to ministers, or utilize in debates) and submitting evidence to select committee inquiries. No less than 70% of organized interests surveyed had sought to influence public policy through the House of Lords, and nearly 82% of these groups adjudged their contacts with the Lords to be 'useful' or 'very useful'. Moreover, almost 48% of these organized interests considered the Lords to be equal to the Commons in terms of usefulness, while 24% actually deemed the Lords to be *more* useful than the Commons, partly, no doubt, because of the greater expertise often found in the Lords and partly because of the slightly looser – and still loosening – party cohesion and degree of partisanship. A peer with a professional background or political interest in agriculture might sometimes prove rather more receptive or responsive to the advice or suggestions of a body such as the National Farmers Union (which can also help to maintain or reinforce the peer's expertise, and ensure that s/he does not lose touch with developments in their former profession or career), than an MP who might be concerned, first and foremost, with supporting (or opposing) a bill primarily on grounds of ideological conviction, party loyalty or career considerations.

Third, the Lords (like the Commons, although the extent should not be exaggerated) has witnessed something of a decline in party cohesion and loyalty, a development which has increased the incidence or likelihood of governmental defeats and/or the securing of concessions from ministers often desperate to reverse or pre-empt such defeats. Certainly, the upper House has increasingly inflicted defeats on governments since the 1970s, as Table 4 illustrates.

A number of trends are discernible in these figures. First, it is clear that Labour governments have suffered much more frequent defeats in the Lords than Conservative administrations. For example, the 1964–70 Labour government suffered more than ten times as many defeats in the Lords than the preceding Conservative government, while the 1974–9 Labour administration was defeated more than 13 times as often as the Conservative administration which preceded it. It should be noted, though,

Table 4 Government defeats in the House of Lords since 1959

Government	No. of defeats
Conservative 1959–64	11
Labour 1964–70	116
Conservative 1970–4	26
Labour 1974–9	355
Conservative 1979–83	45
Conservative 1983–7	62
Conservative 1987–92	72
Conservative 1992–7	63
Labour 1997–2001	108
Labour 2001–5	245
Labour 2005–7	107

Source: Figures up to 1983 from D. Shell, 'The House of Lords and the Thatcher Government', Parliamentary Affairs, xxxviii (1985), 16–32 at 17; figures from 1983 to 2000/1, P. Strickland and R. Cracknell, House of Lords Reform: Developments since 1997 (House of Commons Research Paper 01/77, October 2001), 14; figures from 2001–2 to 2005–7, House of Lords Annual Reports.

that the 1974–9 Labour government was, for most of its term of office, lacking an overall majority in the Commons (where it also experienced a number of defeats, often as a consequence of cross-voting or abstentions by its own MPs), which may indirectly have encouraged the Lords to challenge more readily the legitimacy of some of the cabinet's legislative measures.

Another trend evident in Table 4 is the extent to which the four Conservative governments from 1979 to 1997 suffered more defeats in the Lords than previous Conservative administrations. While these post-1979 Conservative governments did not experience such frequent defeats as the preceding Labour administration, the first three terms of office did witness successive increases in the number of Conservative defeats inflicted by the Lords, to the extent that the 1983–7 Thatcher government suffered more than twice as many defeats there than Heath's 1970–4 Conservative administration. Part of the explanation might be that, having imposed numerous defeats on the previous Labour government, many peers were not willing to return to a state of relative passivity when faced with a Conservative government, in spite of the preponderance of Conservative peers in the upper House during this period. Having roused themselves and flexed their muscles to considerable effect, they were not inclined to slink back to slumbering; their adrenaline was now flowing.

However, what also doubtless prompted the Lords to inflict an unprecedented number of defeats on Conservative ministers was the latter's often controversial, and sometimes deeply unpopular, policies. Certainly, the manner in which the three Thatcher administrations suffered a successively increasing number of defeats in the Lords seems to correspond closely to the increasing radicalism of these governments, each one becoming politically bolder – or more extreme and reckless – than the previous one. Moreover, for most of the 1980s, the Labour Party proved a pathetically ineffective opposition in the House of Commons – due largely to its own internecine in-fighting and left-right ideological power struggles – which effectively encouraged the Lords to adopt the *de facto* mantle of Her Majesty's opposition.

The other main trend apparent in Table 4 concerns the defeats suffered by the New Labour governments since 1997, particularly the 245 defeat inflicted by the Lords on the 2001–5 administration. While this is obviously rather less than the 355 defeats endured by the 1974–9 Labour government, the 2001–5 defeats are more notable in one particularly important respect, namely that in 1999, the (first) Blair government abolished all but 92 of the hereditary peers membership of the Lords, most of whom had been Conservatives. Furthermore, the manner in which Blair then created a tranche of life peers also served to create a much more politically balanced Lords, in which no single party enjoys a majority. However, this seems to have made the (partly) reformed House of Lords even more willing to inflict defeats on the Labour government, as illustrated by the fact that the upper House imposed twice as many defeats on the second Blair government than it had on the first. With the membership of a majority of hereditary peers now abolished, and somewhat greater parity of numbers between Conservative, Labour and cross-bench peers, the Lords naturally considers itself to enjoy much greater legitimacy than hitherto, and consequently feels even less reticent about defeating controversial or unpopular measures from a government with a large majority in the lower House.

The increased confidence and assertiveness of the post-hereditary Lords looks likely to be maintained, for when New Labour won a third successive general election victory in 2005, it subsequently suffered virtually as many Lords defeats during its first two years as the initial Blair government had suffered in four years.

Very often such defeats will result in the government revising or watering-down one of its original clauses, or tabling a compromise amendment to that opposed by peers, in order to secure the subsequent consent of the Lords, and thereby avoid undue delay. Indeed, if the government or relevant minister does not offer concessions to appease opposition from the Lords, then it is not only the disputed bill which risks being delayed (or subject to being shuttled back and forth between the two Houses), but other measures in the government's remaining legislative programme. A government would need to feel especially committed to retaining, in its original form or wording, a clause which was the subject of strong opposition from the upper House, for ministers would be risking a potential log-jam or backlog affecting other forthcoming measures requiring parliamentary approval. It might also make the government look dogmatic or unreasonable, while allowing the Lords to occupy the moral high-ground, or present itself as a bulwark of liberty or common sense against hasty or dangerous legislation.

All these changes and developments have enhanced the capacity and willingness of the Lords to scrutinize the government of the day, and hold the executive to account. They all exemplify the trend, especially since the late 1960s, whereby the Lords has become more active, assiduous and assertive in performing its constitutional roles. Indeed, it has variously been suggested that during much of the 1980s, when Conservative governments with large majorities were faced by a weak, divided and thus ineffective Labour opposition in the Commons, the Lords provided the main, and most effective, source of parliamentary opposition to Thatcherite authoritarianism, and much the same could be said of the late 1990s and early 2000s, when Labour governments with huge majorities in the Commons were unimpeded by a decimated and demoralized Conservative opposition.

Why the House of Lords has Become More Active and Assertive since 1949

Having examined *how* the Lords has become more active, assertive and assiduous, we now turn our attention to explaining *why* this change has occurred in the post-1949 period. This will involve consideration of two key factors, namely the infusion of 'new blood' into the Lords as a consequence, since 1958, of the creation of life peers, and the weakening of partisanship and party cohesion in the upper House.

The main change in composition derived from the steady increase in the number life peers from 1958 onwards, for this heralded the infusion of new blood into the Lords, whose membership had previously been based almost entirely on the hereditary principle. (Before 1958, the only peers whose membership of the House of Lords was not derived from their inheritance of a title derived from family lineage were those who sat on an *ex officio* basis, namely archbishops and bishops (the lords spiritual), and law lords.) Life peers constituted a new category of members of the House of Lords, for they tended to be people who were awarded such a peerage on the bass of a valuable contribution to public life in the United Kingdom, such as academics, authors, broadcasters, industrialists, scientists, and so forth, as well as sundry former MPs and ministers elevated from the House of Commons. Needless to say, their title lapsed upon their death; it was not passed on to their offspring or descendents. As Table 5 illustrates, the number (and proportion *vis-à-vis* hereditary peers) of life peers has increased markedly from 1958 until 1999. Then, from 1999 onwards, when all but 92 hereditary peers were removed, the number of life peers increased much more quickly, as a large number were consequently created to replace many of the erstwhile hereditary peers.

Table 5 Hereditary and life peers in the House of Lords, 1949–2007
(excluding *ex officio* peers)

Year	Hereditary peers	Life peers	Life peers as a percentage of all peers
1959–60	810	31	3.4%
1983–4	775	178	16.5%
2006–7	92	606	86.8%

Source: Figures for 1959–60 and 1983–4 from N. Baldwin, 'The House of Lords: Behavioural Changes', in *Parliament in the 1980s*, ed. P. Norton (Oxford, 1985), 96–113 at 104; figures for 2006–7 from House of Lords, *Annual Report 2006/0*, 45.

Three other inter-linked changes flowed naturally from the introduction of life peers, and the eventual removal of most hereditary peers. First, the House of Lords has now become more politically balanced, for the hereditary peers had been overwhelmingly Conservative in their party allegiance. This did not actually mean – as was commonly, but erroneously, assumed – that the Conservatives previously enjoyed an overall in-built majority in the upper House, but that they were by far the single largest party bloc, and only needed to be joined by a few 'cross-benchers' (politically independent or non-aligned) peers to prevail on any particular issue or vote. As Table 6 clearly shows, the removal of all but 92 hereditary peers has also eradicated the Conservatives' previous political prevalence in the Lords.

Table 6 Party membership in the House of Lords, 1970–2007
(excluding *ex officio* peers)

Year	Conservative	Labour	Liberal/Lib Dem*	Cross-bencher
1970	468	120	38	110
2006–7	204	211	77	208

* The Liberal Party became the Liberal Democrats in 1988, when it merged with the Social Democratic Party.

Source: Figures for 1970 taken from Baldwin, 'The House of Lords: Behavioural Changes', 109; figures for 2006–7 taken from House of Lords, *Annual Report 2006/7*, 19.

The second change which has flowed naturally from the creation of life peers, and subsequent removal of most hereditary peers, is that the House of Lords has also become somewhat more socially (as well as politically) representative, in terms of the occupational backgrounds of those awarded life peerages. Table 7 illustrates that of the 1,174 life peers created since 1958 (up until the end of Tony Blair's premiership in June 2007), many have emanated from careers in academia, the civil service, the 'two sides' of industry, the legal profession and the voluntary sector.

Of course, it could be objected that such backgrounds do not really render the current House of Lords (more) representative, because those

Table 7 Occupational background of life peers, 1958–2007

Occupation/Profession	Number	As percentage of all life peers
Academia	88	7%
Arts (inc. actors and musicians)	13	1%
Civil service	58	5%
Engineering (inc. architect, surveyor)	10	1%
Finance (banking, insurance)	34	3%
Industry	131	11%
Journalism	16	1%
Land (landowner, farmer)	7	1%
Law (judge, solicitor, barrister)	55	5%
Local government	50	4%
Medical	31	3%
Media	43	4%
Military	18	2%
Politics (former MP, minister)	470	40%
Public sector (inc. quangos)	31	3%
Teaching	8	1%
Trade union	45	4%
Voluntary	40	3%
Other	36	3%

Source: Extrapolated from A. Brocklehurst, *Peerage Creations, 1958–2007: Lords Library Note* (October 2007), 20–1.

emanating from such occupations are overwhelmingly middle-aged, middle-class and male, and as such, do not reflect the occupational and demographic profile of British society (similar criticisms have variously been levelled against the House of Commons too). However, it is true to say that compared to the composition of the Lords when it was dominated almost entirely by hereditary peers, the current second chamber is most definitely more socially representative of British society than it has ever been previously.

As such, the influx of life peers has imbued the reformed and reconstituted Lords with slightly greater legitimacy and moral authority, even thought it remains un-elected. This, in turn, as we noted above, has heralded a more 'activist' role by many peers, and thereby provided the second chamber with a new lease of life, and a more meaningful role in parliamentary politics.

The third change wrought by the creation of life peers, and the consequent development of a more socially representative membership, has been a propensity for better-informed, higher quality debates in the Lords (aided by somewhat looser party loyalty, as discussed next), as almost any topic or bill will attract contributions from peers who have direct knowledge or experience of the issue or policy being discussed. Indeed, such expertise will often take precedence over the political or partisan point-scoring and adversarial mode of debates which are relatively commonplace in the lower House. As such, one author has suggested that 'The capacity of the Lords to stage impressive debates across the range of public policy issues is undoubted – and probably equalled by few other assemblies', for the background of its membership 'equips it for insightful deliberation on virtually any matter'.[7] To give one example, as illustrated by Table 8, when, in April 2004, the Lords held its second reading debate concerning the Blair government's Higher Education Bill, to introduce top-up fees for university students, over half of the 45 peers who participated were, or had been, directly involved with universities, mostly in a (vice-)chancellor or professorial role.

In addition to more intelligent or informed debates in the second chamber, the expertise and professional knowledge possessed by many life peers has also, as briefly alluded to earlier, manifested itself in the operation, effectiveness and prestige of the Lords' select committees. For example, in 2008 the membership of the highly respected science and technology committee included a former civil engineer, a former electrical engineer, two academic zoologists, a consultant obstetrician and an honorary president of the Environmental Industries Commission. Meanwhile, the economic affairs committee was graced by the membership of two former chancellors of the exchequer, a former vice-chair of the Royal Bank of Scotland, a vice-chair of Goldman Sachs merchant bank (who was also previously a professor of banking and finance), a former governor of the Bank of England, an erstwhile director-general of the Confederation of British Industry and a professor of economics.

The second substantive factor which has facilitated a more active and effective Lords since 1949 has been the weakening of partisanship and party cohesion among some peers, a phenomenon which, to some extent, has mirrored a similar trend in the Commons. Although the decline in partisanship (in either House) should not be exaggerated, it is apparent that a growing number of peers – like MPs – have felt less obligation than yesteryear to vote routinely and obediently in accordance with their party's official stance on a particular bill or policy. On various issues, the support of peers for their party's leadership has generally become more qualified or circumspect; they have increasingly acted as 'critical friends' rather than loyal and subservient subordinates herded hither and thither by their party whips through the Lords' division lobbies. As such, 'members of the House of Lords are rather more unpredictable in their allegiance and voting than MPs ... with marked consequences for legislation'.[8]

Consequently, recent governments have variously encountered strong criticism of, and even opposition to, some of their more contentious legislative measures from 'their' peers in the upper House. For example, in

---

[7] A. Adonis, *Parliament Today* (Manchester, 1990), 144.

[8] R. Rogers and R. Walters, *How Parliament Works* (5th edn, 2004), 121.

Table 8 Peers with professional or occupational backgrounds in higher education who spoke in the House of Lords' second reading debate on the Higher Education Bill, April 2004

Peer	Higher education role or position
Baroness Blackstone	former professor at London University and chancellor-designate of Greenwich University
Lord Butler of Brockwell	master of University College, Oxford University
Lord Desai	professor at the London School of Economics
Lord Eatwell	professor at Cambridge University
Lord Holme of Cheltenham	chancellor of Greenwich University
Baroness Howe of Idicote	former vice-chair of Open University council
Lord Layard	professor at the London School of Economics
Baroness Lockwood	chancellor of Bradford University
Baroness O'Neill of Bengarve	principal of Newnham College, Cambridge University
Lord Parekh	professor at the London School of Economics
Baroness Perry of Southwark	pro-chancellor at Surrey University
Lord Phillips of Sudbury	chancellor of Essex University
Lord Puttnam	chancellor of Sunderland University
Lord Quirk	fellow of University College London and former vice-chancellor of University of London
Baroness Rawlings	chair of council at King's College, London
Lord Renfrew of Kaimsthorn	professor at Oxford University
Lord Rix	chancellor of East London University
Baroness Sharp of Guildford	former lecturer at the London School of Economics and former research fellow at Sussex University
Lord Taylor of Warwick	chancellor of Bournemouth University
Lord Tomlinson	chair of the Association of Independent Higher Education Providers
Lord Wallace of Saltaire	professor at the London School of Economics
Baroness Warnock	former senior research fellow at St John's College, Oxford University and former mistress of Girton College, Cambridge University.
Baroness Warwick	chair of 'Universities UK'
Lord Wilson of Dinton	master of Emmanuel College, Cambridge University
Lord Winston	chancellor of Sheffield Hallam University and professor at Imperial College, London

pushing through the 2003 Criminal Justice Act (which sought to restrict trial by jury in certain cases), the 2005 Prevention of Terrorism Act and the 2006 Race and Religious Hatred Act, several of the strongest critics of the Blair government were Labour peers, some of whom voted against specific clauses when these bills reached the committee stage in the Lords.

One other development which has made the Lords a somewhat less partisan institution in recent decades has been the increase in cross-bench peers, a trend inextricably linked to the steady expansion in post-1958 – and subsequently post-1999 – life peers. While many life peers do 'adopt' a party label upon entering the Lords, there are also a considerable number who eschew such affiliation, and sit on the cross-benches. Table 9 illustrates the party allegiance or political independence of life peers created by each prime minister since 1958. It is clear that cross-benchers or independents were the single largest 'category' of life peers created by both Harold Macmillan and Edward Heath, while for Harold Wilson (during his first premiership in the 1960s), James Callaghan and Tony Blair, they constituted the second largest category after the creation of Labour life peers.

Table 9 Party affiliation of life peers created 1958–2007

Prime minister	Dates	Conservative	Labour	Liberal/SDP/ Lib Dem	Cross-bench/ Independent
Macmillan	1958–63	29	20	0	35
Douglas-Home	1963–4	11	9	0	6
Wilson	1964–70	20	62	6	53
Heath	1970–4	8	9	2	26
Wilson	1974–6	22	39	6	13
Callaghan	1976–9	5	29	1	23
Thatcher	1979–90	98	56	10	41
Major	1990–7	75	40	17	28
Blair	1997–2007	62	163	53	97*
Total	1958–2007	330	427	95	322

* Includes 42 peers nominated by the newly created Appointments Commission.

Source: Extrapolated from Brocklehurst, *Peerage Creations*, 15–19.

Ultimately, cross-benchers/independents constituted 27.4% of all life peers created between 1958 and 2007, and only eight fewer were appointed than Conservative life peers during this period. By June 2007 the 322 cross-bench or independent life peers in the House of Lords constituted a remarkable increase in comparison to the 35 cross-benchers or independents (excluding *ex officio* peers) who had sat in there at the end of Macmillan's premiership in 1963. Their exponential increase has itself been an important factor with regard to the increased propensity of the

Lords to scrutinize more rigorously, and oppose more frequently, the governing party in the Commons.

One final factor worth mentioning with regard to the Lords' increased willingness to challenge the government or Commons in recent decades is the failure of Labour's attempt in 1969 to reform the House of Lords, for the party's evident lack of agreement about *how* the upper House should be reformed, coupled with a view among some Labour MPs and ministers that there were rather more important matters for a Labour government to address, actually made peers feel more confident about their medium-term future, and as such, they felt less reticent about asserting themselves when faced with ministerial measures with which they strongly disagreed or considered to be ill judged.

House of Lords Reform

The House of Lords has experienced what some political scientists and policy analysts term 'punctuated equilibrium', which refers to periods of relative stability which are sporadically disrupted by new activity or reform, but which are themselves then followed by another period of overall continuity. When change does occur, it is often *ad hoc* and pragmatic or piecemeal. This would certainly seem to be a reasonable characterization of the sporadic reforms and proposals for reform which the Lords has been subject to since 1949.

One such reform actually occurred in 1949, when Clement Attlee's Labour government introduced the second Parliament Act (the first having been enacted in 1911). This reduced the House of Lords veto – the power to delay government legislation – from two years to one. However, this legislation was widely considered to be a means of appeasing left-wing Labour MPs who were frustrated by the cabinet's delay in nationalizing the iron and steel industries – attacking the Lords was a way of reassuring the left that ministers had not lost their radical zeal or abandoned their socialist principles. However, the 1949 Parliament Act also reflected the difficulties which the Labour leadership faced – both within their party, and with the Conservative opposition – in securing agreement for a more comprehensive package of reforms concerning the membership of the Lords. Indeed, one cabinet minister in the 1945–51 Labour governments subsequently admitted that: 'The Labour Government was not anxious for the rational reform or democratization of the Second Chamber. For this would have added to its authority ... against that of the House of Commons ... would have tended make the Lords the equals of the Commons.'[9] Many, if not most, Labour MPs and ministers have shared such sentiments subsequently, and still do so today: they do not really want a (more) democratic or powerful second chamber.

---

[9] Lord (Herbert) Morrison, *Government and Parliament: A Survey from the Inside* (3rd edn, Oxford, 1964), 205.

It was actually a Conservative government which eventually introduced legislation to modify the membership of the House of Lords, in the guise of the 1958 Life Peerages Act. As we have noted at various junctures in this chapter, this key reform created a new category of peer, one whose title and seat in the Lords was not derived from inheritance, but had been 'earned' through a record of achievement in a professional capacity, or possibly through a major contribution to voluntary or charitable work. The most obvious consequence of this measure was to infuse the Lords with new blood, and imbue much of its deliberative and scrutiny work with much greater expertise derived from experience of the 'real world' outside the second chamber. A more subtle consequence, however, was to provide the Lords with at least a little more legitimacy, by ensuring that 'ordinary' people could be appointed to sit alongside the hereditary peers, for it was the latter who were the primary target of criticism, particularly by the Labour Party. The Conservative ministers who devised the Life Peerages Act naturally hoped that this reform might weaken some of Labour's attacks on the House of Lords, and thereby secure its long-term future. Indeed, the Conservatives were subtly protecting the hereditary peers by reforming an institution precisely in order to conserve it (the alternatives possibly being atrophy or abolition), for the new life peers were to sit alongside, not in place of, the hereditaries. This is one of the reasons why the Labour Party opposed the Life Peerages Bill by tabling a 'reasoned amendment' which condemned the failure to address the issue of hereditary peers. The Life Peerages Act also allowed women to sit for the first time in the Lords. The first life peeress to be created was Baroness Wootton of Abinger, created on 8 August 1958, who took her seat on 21 October 1958. The first to sit, however, was Baroness Swanborough, who also took her seat, but ahead of Baroness Wootton, on 21 October 1958.

The issue of hereditary peers was the subject of the 1963 Peerages Act, but only in so far as it permitted those who inherited a peerage to renounce it if they so wished, thereby enabling them to stand for election to the House of Commons instead. This reform, also enacted by a Conservative government, was primarily prompted by the high profile case whereby, in 1961, the Labour MP, Tony Benn, became Viscount Stansgate following the death of his father. However, Benn was reluctant to resign as an MP, and fought a by-election in his Bristol constituency. Although Benn doubled his majority from the 1959 election, his Conservative opponent was nevertheless declared to be the constituency's new MP, on the grounds that Benn was ineligible to sit in the Commons on account of his inherited title. The furore this provoked prompted the Conservative government to introduce the Peerages Bill. The 1963 Peerages Act also made other changes to the membership of the Lords. First, women who held hereditary titles were allowed to take their seat in the upper House, thus ending an anomaly created by the 1958 Life Peerage Act which had allowed female life peers to sit. Second, the 16 Scottish representative peers elected at each general election since the Anglo-Scottish Union of

1707 were abolished and all Scottish hereditary peers (and peeresses) were allowed to sit.

Six years later, a Labour government abandoned its efforts (or, rather, those of Richard Crossman) at reforming the House of Lords, largely due to lack of agreement in the party, right up to ministerial level, over precisely how the second chamber should be reformed. The Parliament (No. 2) Bill had proposed a two-tier system of membership, whereby only life peers who attended on a regular basis, would be permitted to vote in divisions (and also be paid a salary), while hereditary peers would be entitled to speak in debates, but debarred from voting; if they wished to continue voting, they would be required to renounce their inherited titles, and accept instead, a life peerage. The bill also proposed reducing the power of delay from one year to just six months.

However, these proposals actually proved highly contentious in the Labour Party, and revealed the range of opinions and divisions which the issue of Lords reform invariably prompted. While virtually all Labour MPs despised the (predominantly Conservative) hereditary peers, many of them were concerned that creating salaried life peers would strengthen prime ministerial patronage, while a shorter power of delay was, some feared, likely to be invoked much more frequently than the rarely utilized one year delay. Furthermore, while some left-wing MPs opposed the bill because they wanted noting less than total abolition (any reform which fell short of this might well enhance the legitimacy of the Lords, making future abolition less likely or popular, while also making the second chamber more confident about challenging a Labour government), some ministers were annoyed that the cabinet seemed to be spending so much time on a constitutional issue which was of little interest to the electorate, least of all Labour voters primary concerned with bread-and-butter issues concerning employment, health and pensions, for example. For all these reasons, the cabinet was eventually – and humiliatingly – obliged to announce that the Parliament (No. 2) Bill was being abandoned (ostensibly to free parliamentary time for other government legislation).

The most recent attempt at reforming the Lords has been the post-1997 Labour government's protracted efforts. In 1999 all but 92 of the hereditary peers were finally removed from the upper House, as part of a professed two-stage programme of reform, although Labour was not sure what the 'second stage' should entail. Even the royal commission appointed in 1999 to propose options for reform, was unable to reach clear agreement, although it did incline towards a second chamber in which the vast majority of peers would be appointed (by an independent appointments commission) as life peers, but with a minority of peers elected. Subsequent votes in the Commons – most notably in 2003 and 2007 – again revealed wide-ranging disagreement among Labour MPs and ministers, with some wanting a fully elected upper House, some wanting a predominantly or even wholly appointed second chamber (partly due to concern that an elected second chamber would have much more legitimacy and thus a greater propensity to challenge the government on the grounds that it now reflected or represented the views of 'the people'), and the remainder supporting a part-elected, part-nominated second chamber, but unable to agree on the precise balance (80:20, 60:40, 50:50, 40:60, 20:80). As such, 12 years after 'New Labour' was first elected, 'stage two' of Lords reform had still not been completed.

Conclusion

Like the Commons, the Lords appears to have experienced something of a dialectical trend, whereby the ostensible impression of inexorable decline and marginalization due to wider political trends has been accompanied by often subtle internal developments which have actually imbued the upper House with greater expertise and effectiveness. Indeed, in many instances, the post-1949 Lords has itself sought to respond positively and actively to these wider trends, and thereby contribute towards its own relevance and survival. Moreover, in the 1950s especially, it was Conservative peers who were often most cognizant and candid about the need for the Lords to accept changes in it composition in order to remain credible and legitimate, and the thereby protect itself from atrophy or abolition.

The post-1958 influx of life peers was therefore of signal importance in imbuing the Lords with much greater breadth and depth of expertise, and of making it somewhat less detached or cut-off from the world beyond the second chamber. This also meant that, in due course, debates in the Lords were increasingly notable for the knowledge and experience with which they were imbued, and which ensured that many debates and contributions were less partisan or polemical than speeches in the Commons. This development has been further enhanced both by the gradual weakening of party cohesion in the Lords (although this should not be exaggerated), and to the marked increase in the number of cross-bench or politically independent peers which has accrued from the creation of life peers.

In turn, the expansion of life peers was also instrumental in facilitating a reconfiguration of the Lords' select committee system, whereby the expertise and authority of many peers has significantly enhanced the scrutiny function of the second chamber, and enabled it to conduct often more in-depth inquiries into aspects of public policy than those undertaken by MPs, particularly with regard to (proposed or draft) European Union legislation.

Consequently, since 1949 the Lords has become a much more active, assertive and assiduous institution. It sits more frequently and for longer hours, conducts more debates, asks more questions, undertakes more select committee inquiries, tables more legislative amendments and challenges more government legislation, to the extent of inflicting more defeats on (and extracting more concessions and amendments from) governments than hitherto.

In spite of remaining a largely unelected institution – even ten years after the removal of most hereditary peers – the Lords has survived into the 21st century for three particular reasons. First, the wealth of experience which accompanied the infusion of life peers has enabled the House of Lords to conduct its core deliberative and scrutiny functions with greater expertise and informed knowledge, thereby enhancing its moral authority and attracting increased respect. Second, but following directly on from this point, peers themselves have pursued various internal reforms in the way that the Lords conducts its business (most notably through the committee system), in such a way as to render it more efficient and effective.

Third, without the upper House, MPs and ministers would almost certainly become overwhelmed, for much of the work undertaken by the Lords complements that of the Commons. In this regard, the Lords shares some of the workload of the government or House of Commons, in spite of the conflicts or disagreement which periodically occur between the two Houses. Indeed, much of the time, the Lords could be characterized as a 'critical friend' to MPs and ministers.

If the Lords did not exist, then a second chamber of some kind would almost certainly have been created. There are certainly differing views about what sort of second House is desirable or necessary, particularly in terms of membership and powers, but the crucial point is that there is little support for abolishing the Lords entirely. Even in the Labour Party, which has traditionally been much more critical of the Lords, only a minority of left-wing MPs are in favour of unicameralism. Most Labour MPs and ministers, along with Conservative and Liberal Democrat MPs, have always accepted bicameralism in Britain, even though they hold divergent views – due to the range of potential options – about what the second chamber should actually be. Indeed, apart from the removal of most hereditary peers in 1999, the lack of agreement (even within the governing Labour Party) over precisely how – or even whether – the Lords should be reformed or replaced has itself been a major reason for its survival into the 21st century.

Chronology

1949
Parliament Act reducing the Lords' power of delay (over legislation) from two years to one year

1958
Life Peerages Act enabling a new category of peer to be created, not based on hereditary principle, but in recognition of outstanding success in, or major contribution to, public or professional life

1963
Peerages Act permits hereditary peers to renounce their titles, in order to seek election to (or continue sitting in) the Commons

1969
Parliament (No. 2) Bill abandoned by Labour government over disagreement within the parliamentary party and cabinet about how the Lords should be reformed

1974
The Lords establishes its European Communities select committee (in 1999 renamed the European Union committee)

1974-9
The Lords inflicts 355 legislative defeats on the Labour government, mainly in the form of rejecting clauses in bills, or insisting on amendments

1979
Labour prime minister, James Callaghan, infuriates the party's left-wing by refusing to include a pledge to abolish the Lords in Labour's election manifesto; the Lords science and technology select committee established

1999
The 'New Labour' government removes most of the hereditary peers, although 92 are given a reprieve until completion of the second stage of Lords reform; a royal commission is established to consider options for reform, although its report in 2000 is inconclusive

2001
The Lords established two new key select committees, the economic affairs committee, and the constitution committee

2003
The Commons vote on various combinations of elected and appointed peers fails to resolve the issue, because no particular option attracts the support of a majority of MPs

2007
The Commons vote reveals majority support for both a fully elected Lords, and one in which 80% of members are elected, and the remainder are appointed, although many ministers had only favoured a 50:50 balance

June   Green paper, *The Governance of Britain*, pledges to pursue 'stage two' of Lords reform by creating an elected or predominantly elected second chamber, but ministers then acknowledge this is unlikely to be achieved before the next (2010) election

2009
Law lords scheduled to be replaced by a new supreme court

Further Reading

N. Baldwin, 'The House of Lords', in *Parliament and Pressure Politics*, ed. M. Rush (Oxford, 1990)

—— 'The House of Lords: Behavioural Changes', in *Parliament in the 1980s*, ed. P. Norton (Oxford, 1985)

R. Blackburn and A. Kenyon, with M. Wheeler-Booth, *Parliament: Functions, Practice and Procedures* (2nd edn, 2003), ch. 12

Peter Dorey, 'Change in Order to Conserve: Explaining the Conservatives' Decision to Introduce the 1958 Life Peerages Act', *Parliamentary History*, xxviii (2009)

—— 'Stumbling through "Stage Two": New Labour and House of Lords Reform', *British Politics*, iii (2008), 22–44

—— '1949, 1969, 1999: The Labour Party and House of Lords Reform', *Parliamentary Affairs*, lix (2006), 599–620

D. Judge, *Political Institutions in the United Kingdom* (Oxford, 2005)

The New Select Committees: A Study of the 1979 Reforms, ed. G. Drewry (Oxford, 1989)

I. Richard and D. Welfare, *Unfinished Business: Reforming the House of Lords* (1999)

D. Shell, 'The House of Lords', in *The Politics of Parliamentary Reform*, ed. D. Judge (1983)

—— *The House of Lords* (2nd edn, 1992)

18 The House of Commons, 1801–1911
Philip Salmon

> When in that House M.P.s divide,
> If they've a brain and cerebellum too,
> They have to leave that brain outside,
> And vote as their leaders tell 'em too.
>
> W. S. Gilbert, *Iolanthe* (1883), Act II

To state that there was scarcely a feature of the 1801 Commons that could still be found in existence in 1911, *pace* Norman Gash, sounds like hyperbole, but it is not far off the mark.[1] During this period virtually every aspect of the Commons, from its procedures to its relationship with the nation at large, underwent fundamental change. Most historians see a broad link between the internal and external developments taking place, and in particular between the procedural reforms and electoral reforms of the 19th century. But beyond this there remains plenty of argument and debate, about which changes were the most significant, why and when they occurred, and with what consequences. This chapter reassesses the most prevalent ideas currently on offer and introduces some new ones, particularly regarding electoral reform and its connection with the kind of behaviour lampooned in the opening quotation. Before doing this, however, it is worth examining the chamber itself, since this also, appropriately enough, underwent fundamental, though not necessarily radical, change.

The Setting

The cramped and unhealthy conditions of the accommodation in St Stephen's chapel, famously likened to the 'black hole of Calcutta' by James Grant, had long been a source of complaint.[2] Most sittings occurred at night, when the poor air quality caused by inadequate ventilation was exacerbated by the burning of hundreds of candles and later by primitive gas lighting. Measuring just 57' 6" × 32' 10" (most images make it appear larger), numerous improvements and plans for new premises had been proposed during the 18th century, only to be rejected on the grounds of cost or taste. The addition of an extra 100 Irish MPs in 1801, as a result of the union with Ireland, took the total membership to 658 and forced

---

[1] N. Gash, *Politics in the Age of Peel: A Study in the Technique of Parliamentary Representation, 1830–1850* (1953), p. x.
[2] [J. Grant], *Random Recollections of the House of Commons* (1836), 2.

> ### Murder in the Commons' Lobby
>
> The Lobby of the old House of Commons was 32' wide by 28' long, giving an area of about 900 'superficial', or square feet. In the early 19th century it was reckoned that 'from 300 to 400 Members are on divisions occasionally contained in the present Lobby'. Also 'in the greater part of the session the Lobby is filled with persons obliged to be there to meet Members on business'. Consequently it seems more than unlucky that on 11 May 1812, the prime minister, Spencer Perceval, was shot while passing through a relatively empty lobby (if contemporary prints are to be believed) on his way out of the House. The shot was fired by one John Bellingham, a deranged merchant, who, it was said by some, mistook Perceval for Robert Stewart, Viscount Castlereagh, the foreign secretary, with whom Bellingham had a grievance after being refused government compensation for debts he had accrued in Russia. Perceval died of his wounds almost immediately. The lord chancellor, lamenting 'a most melancholy and a most atrocious circumstance having taken place in the Lobby of the other House', ordered '[a]ll Officers and attendants of this House to prevent all persons quitting the two Houses of Parliament'. However, there were witnesses to the assassination, including Richard Tayler, a doorkeeper of the Commons, who 'saw the person fire, [and] heard the pistol go off'. Bellingham, however, remained in the lobby and was immediately arrested. He was found guilty at his trial and, refusing to plead insanity, was executed.
>
> CJ
>
> Sources: *House of Commons Reports from Committees*, xii (1833), report no. 17 (17 August – 22 September 1831), 13, 17–18 20; *LJ*, xlviii, 827–8.

the issue. By comparison with the Lords, however, the Commons' solution was makeshift. While the Lords moved to a larger chamber (78' × 38') to accommodate just 28 new Irish peers and four bishops, the Commons crammed in an extra row of benches on each side by removing the wooden panelling, destroying the medieval wall-paintings and dismantling sections of the medieval walls, which added about an extra 3' on each side of the chamber. Even so, barely two-thirds of the MPs could be accommodated, whether seated or standing. Further modifications included an enlargement of the members' lobby, where the prime minister, Spencer Perceval, was assassinated in 1812, and the refitting of a refreshment room (*Bellamy's*) at the end of the new corridor leading away from the lobby, supplied by kitchens underneath.

In the adjacent areas, a smoking room, committee rooms and a purpose-built library were also added. By the time of the accidental fire of 1834, which completely gutted all these facilities, MPs had been assembling in the midst of what amounted to a perpetual building site for well over 30 years. Almost another 20 years' disruption then followed before they were

> ### Bellamy's Kitchen
>
> The kitchen and dining room opened in 1773 by John Bellamy, the deputy house keeper of the Commons, was the first attempt to provide catering arrangements for MPs inside the palace of Westminster. It was made famous by one version of the supposed dying words of the prime minister, William Pitt the Younger, in 1806: 'I think I could just eat one of Bellamy's veal pies.' Originally Bellamy's was one of a series of places of refreshment built on the west wall of the old Court of Requests facing into Old Palace Yard, including *Alice's* and *Wagham's* coffee houses. It probably moved to the south-west corner of the new Stone Building built by James Wyatt on the west side of Westminster Hall around 1800, at the time that he was reconstructing and converting the old Court of Requests into the new House of Lords. It is likely that *Bellamy's* kitchen occupied the first floor with the dining room above. The ground floor was one of a series of new committee rooms built at that time.
>
> The name Bellamy's has been revived for eating-places associated both with the parliament at Westminster and with certain Commonwealth parliaments.
>
> CJ
>
> *Source*: PA, Book/61: O. C. Williams, 'The Topography of the Old House of Commons' (one of only three copies of an unpublished typescript, 1953), 20–1, plate 19.

able to move to the Commons in the new Palace of Westminster, designed by Charles Barry and Augustus Pugin, during which time they occupied the House of Lords.

Two features, in particular, stand out in all of this. The first is the physical chaos in which an institution traditionally associated with the orderly expansion of the Victorian state and administration of the British empire actually operated. It was not until the 1870s that the site as a whole was finally completed. Structural problems and poor ventilation, however, continued to plague the occupants, and as late as 1905 the treasury still considered that 'the result cannot be said to be satisfactory'.[3] The second feature is the inherent conservatism of the Commons and its reluctance to leave the historic setting of Westminster, even temporarily. A number of factors were at work here. Striking an anti-democratic note in 1834, for instance, the prime minister, Lord Melbourne, explained to William IV that by remaining on a site where space was so restricted, they could 'avoid providing much larger accommodation for spectators as well as members' and escape the 'fatal effects which large galleries filled with the multitude have had upon the deliberation of public

---

[3] V. Cromwell, 'The Losing of the Initiative by the House of Commons, 1780–1914', *Transactions of the Royal Historical Society*, 4th ser., xviii (1968), 1–24 at 15.

Bellamy's and the 'Rage for Speaking'

'I was under the gallery of the House of Commons during the debate on the Catholic question in the year 1825. The house was exceedingly full. Mr. [John Leslie] Foster rose to speak, and the effect of his appearance on his legs was truly wonderful. In an instant the House was cleared. The rush to the door leading to the tavern upstairs, where the Members find a refuge from the soporific powers of their brother legislators, was tremendous ... The single phrase "Mr. Speaker" was indeed uttered with such a tone as indicated the extent of the impending evil; and finding already the influence of drowsiness upon me, I followed the example which was given by the representatives of the people, who, whatever differences may have existed amongst them upon the mode of settling Ireland, appeared to coincide in their estimate of Mr. Foster's elocution ... I proceeded upstairs with some hundreds of honourable gentlemen. The scene which Bellamy's presents to a stranger is striking enough. Two smart girls, whose briskness and neat attire made up for their want of beauty, and for the invasions of time, of which their cheeks showed the traces, helped out tea in a room in the corridor. It was pleasant to observe the sons of dukes and marquesses, and the possessors of twenties and thirties of thousands a year, gathered round these damsels, and soliciting a cup of that beverage which it was their office to administer. These Bellamy barmaids seemed so familiarized with their occupation, that they went through it with perfect nonchalance, and would occasionally turn with petulance, in which they asserted the superiority of their sex to rank and opulence, from the noble or wealthy suitors for a draught of tea, by whom they were surrounded. The unfortunate Irish Members were treated with a peculiar disdain and were reminded of their provinciality by the look of these Parliamentary Hebes, who treated them as mere colonial deputies should be received in the purlieus of the state.

I passed from these ante-chambers to the tavern, where I found a number of Members assembled at dinner. Half an hour had passed away, toothpicks and claret were now beginning to appear, and the business of mastication being concluded, that of digestion had commenced ... At the end of a long corridor, which opened from the room where the diners were assembled, there stood a waiter whose office it was to inform any interrogator what gentleman was speaking below stairs. Nearly opposite the door sat two English county Members. They had just disposed of a bottle each, and just as the last glass was emptied, one of them called out to the annunciator at the end of the passage for intelligence; 'Mr. Foster on his legs' was the formidable answer. 'Waiter, bring another bottle', was the immediate effect of this information, which was followed by a similar injunction from every table in the room. I perceived that Mr. Bellamy owed great obligations to Mr. Foster. But the latter did not limit himself to a second bottle; again and again the same question was asked, and again the same announcement returned, 'Mr. Foster on his legs!' The

> answer seemed to fasten men in inseparable adhesiveness to their seats. Thus two hours went by, when at length, 'Mr. Plunket on his legs' was heard from the end of the passage, and the whole convocation of compotators rose together and returned to the House.'
>
> Source: an 1829 article for the *New Monthly Magazine* lampooning John Leslie Foster, reprinted in R. L. Sheil, *Sketches, Legal and Political*, ed. M. W. Savage (1855), 183–6.

assemblies'.[4] Significantly, one of the major complaints about the new Commons chamber, which was first used in 1850, was that, although it had been enlarged to 68' × 45½', it could still seat only two-thirds of the members. And whilst it now had a dedicated press gallery (see below), public accommodation remained limited. Another factor which has been singled out by architectural historians and those interested in the 'politics of place' has been the symbolic importance of projecting an image of stability and continuity at a time of unprecedented socio-economic and political change. This was not only manifest in the decision to construct the new palace in a historic Gothic style, with a Commons chamber laid out along very traditional lines, but in the accompanying revival of old ceremonies and the fashioning of new ones. It was in the middle decades of the 19th century that the speakership, for instance, acquired much of its modern-day constitutional mystique, mainly under Charles Shaw Lefevre (1839–57), but also his successor John Evelyn Denison (1857–72), who oversaw the completion of the grandiose new Speaker's House with its unused official state bed. These essentially conservative qualities of the new palace of Westminster, both in terms of its architectural appearance and the revival of pageantry, have in recent years begun to attract much needed scholarly attention.[5] But they can only be fully contextualized when viewed against the backdrop of the rapid political changes taking place, particularly those concerning how the Commons worked and how it was elected. It is these changes that are the remaining subjects of this chapter.

The Growth of Ministerial Control

One of the most widely noted developments in the Commons during the 19th century was the government's increasing control of day-to-day business. More than any other factor, this transformed the routines and functions of the House. From a situation in which it was mainly individual or 'private' MPs who determined the policy agenda and initiated legislation, ministers started to take the lead, especially on public bills and other matters of national interest. By the second half of the century the cabinet,

---

[4] *Lord Melbourne's Papers*, ed. L. Sanders (1890), 214.

[5] See especially D. Cannadine, 'The Palace of Westminster as a Palace of Varieties', in *The Houses of Parliament: History, Art, Architecture*, ed. C. and J. Riding (2000), 11–29.

according to some observers, had begun to acquire so much power over proceedings that it threatened to undermine the constitutional balance of power. Table 1 lists the main procedural changes associated with this march of ministerial control, which began with two weekdays effectively being earmarked for government business in 1811. Mainly implemented as standing (permanent) orders, these reforms restricted the occasions when individual MPs could speak and vote and tipped the balance of control in favour of the government of the day.

It would be misleading, however, to place too much emphasis on the rules themselves as the actual mechanism of ministerial control. Many of them merely formalized what had already become accepted procedure, amounting to little more than a codification of convention. The suppression of debates on petitions, for example, was in place long before it became a standing order in 1843. More significantly, new ways of side-stepping regulations and fresh tactical ruses were always available to intrepid troublemakers and those determined to act independently, as the activities of the Irish amply demonstrate. The rules assisted control, but they never guaranteed it. Despite many attempts at regulation, for instance, the committee of supply developed into what has been termed a 'paradise of the

Table 1 Procedural reforms associated with the growth of ministerial control

Date	Reform
1811	Order days: precedence given to public bills on Mondays and Fridays
1835	Wednesdays added as order days
1835	End of debates on petitions (confirmed by standing orders in 1843 and 1853)
1837	Ban on moving amendments to orders of the day
1848	Ban on moving amendments on going into committee (on certain bills)
1854	Number of stages at which bills could be debated dramatically cut
1872	Restrictions on amendments on going into committee of supply (Mondays)
1881	Introduction of motions to close debates (ordinary closure); mover must have support of 100 MPs; made standing order in 1882
1882	Restrictions on amendments on going into committee on supply (Thursdays)
1882	First standing committees (miniature houses) established, confirmed by standing orders in 1888 and expanded in number and importance in 1907
1887	'The Guillotine': introduction of cut-off points for debating separate parts of urgent or major bills
1896	'The railway timetable': fixed number of days for bills before closure (embodied in standing orders in 1902)
1902	Introduction of written answers to parliamentary questions

private member' by the 1880s.[6] With plenty of scope left for independent activity, ministers clearly assumed control of the Commons much more by consent than coercion. Why, it must be asked, did the much revered 'private member' surrender his liberties so willingly?

The Increase of Public Business

Many accounts have focused attention on the unprecedented growth of parliamentary business in the 19th century as the key reason behind this development. 'The great increase of debates and the annual accumulation of arrears of public business have combined to make it practically impossible for bills introduced by private MPs to become law, unless by the active assistance of the government', observed a commentary of the 1860s.[7] Charles Abbot, Speaker from 1802 to 1817, reckoned that the business of the House had almost doubled between 1801 and 1813 alone.[8] Legislative output not only expanded in terms of its volume and complexity, from an average of 237 pages of public acts per year in 1831–2 to 514 in 1868–74, but was also accompanied by a burgeoning culture of investigation into the social and economic problems of the age. In these circumstances, it has been suggested, some restraint upon the 'complete freedom' enjoyed by private members and a broad acceptance of the necessity for leadership on complex issues became 'inevitable'.[9]

A closer look at how parliament dealt with all this state activity, however, suggests that its impact on the Commons was not as straightforward as many believed. Too much can be made of the supposed link between the expansion of public business and the squeeze on parliamentary time, and hence the private member. During the first three decades of the century, in particular, many traditional functions of the Commons were either delegated to civil servants or transferred to new bodies, in what amounted to a mini revolution in state management. In two areas in particular, changes were implemented that helped to limit the Commons' exposure to external pressures.

The first concerns private bill legislation, which was of immense importance in providing the infrastructure and services associated with industrialization and urbanization. Mainly comprising bills for local projects (enclosures, roads, canals, railways, jails, harbours, bridges, gas, water, and lighting), the number of private acts passed in each session continued to exceed the number of public acts throughout the 19th century, with roughly 2,000 being passed per decade. What has been called a 'landmark' in their administration occurred in 1810, when Speaker Abbot

[6] P. Fraser, 'The Growth of Ministerial Control in the Nineteenth-century House of Commons', *English Historical Review*, lxxv (1960), 444–63 at 461.

[7] A. Todd, *On Parliamentary Government in England* (2 vols, 1869), ii, 64.

[8] P. Jupp, *The Governing of Britain, 1688–1848: The Executive, Parliament and the People* (Abingdon, 2006), 210.

[9] Cromwell, 'The Losing of the Initiative', 16.

established a private bill office to oversee their preparation.[10] With parliamentary agents taking on more and more of the routine work, and with the development of draft templates from the 1840s onwards, select committees on private bills often became little more than a rubber stamp. In a telling rejoinder to the widely held view that parliament was becoming 'overwhelmed with business',[11] a Commons clerk with 16 years' experience told an 1837 inquiry:

> An unopposed bill is generally attended by only one Member ... The agent having previously submitted the bill to the chairman of committees in the other House ... he generally tells the Member that everything is right, that he need not give himself the trouble of looking into the clauses; he need only sign the bill and put his initials to the clauses, and in the course of five minutes a bill of considerable length is disposed of in that way, though the House has entrusted it to a committee to look narrowly into the matter.[12]

The second area in which the Commons experienced limited exposure relates to parliamentary inquiries. From the 1790s onwards the number of select committees appointed to investigate matters of public concern steadily increased. Between 1801 and 1817 the number appointed per year doubled to almost 40. By the 1820s the select committee inquiry and its printed report had become the standard precursor to most public bills and an integral part of the wider perception of parliament as the so-called 'grand inquest of the nation'. The growing use of royal commissions, however, gradually removed much of this work from the Commons, forestalling what might otherwise have become an overpowering task. Appointed directly by ministers and mostly staffed by up-and-coming lawyers, royal commissions had eclipsed committees as the main method of inquiry and basis for legislation by the late 1830s, when the number of select committees appointed per year fell back to its 1801 level.

Even in the area of public acts, where there was a doubling of output between 1832 and 1874, it does not follow that there was a corresponding increase in the demand on parliamentary time. Throughout the century various reforms helped to streamline the whole law-making process. Between 1848 and 1854, for instance, the number of occasions on which a bill could be fully debated on going to a vote was drastically cut, from 18 to just two, and a few years later the variety of amendments permitted at different stages was also whittled down. Another major development involved splitting the House into two or more miniature houses (standing committees), so that a number of different bills could be dealt with simultaneously. This was first implemented in 1882 and later augmented by standing orders in 1888 and 1907. By this latter date the pressure on

---

[10] D. L. Rydz, *The Parliamentary Agents: A History* (1979), 51.

[11] C. Townsend, *History of the House of Commons* (2 vols, 1843), ii, 380.

[12] PP 1837–8 (679) xxiii, 439, minute 431.

Commons' time had also started to be mitigated in an altogether different way, via the increasing use of delegated or secondary laws. Issued directly by government departments and other authorized bodies, the number of statutory instruments (the most common type of delegated law) rose substantially in the first decade of the 20th century, from 995 per year in 1900 to 1,368 by 1910, and continued to grow steadily thereafter.

For a variety of reasons then, the Commons did not become as 'overwhelmed' with business as is often assumed, and the decline of the private member cannot be directly attributed to the pressures of state expansion on parliamentary time. Of far greater importance was the growing tendency for MPs to speak and intervene in proceedings, not just in greater numbers but also more often and at increasing length.

The 'Rage for Speaking'[13]

The culture of speaking in the House remains something of an understudied phenomenon and accurately assessing this (or indeed any other) activity in the Commons is problematic, with no method being free from flaws. But what is abundantly clear from all the available evidence is an upward trend in terms of participation in debate, the asking of parliamentary questions, the moving of amendments, and voting in divisions. Before 1832 it has been estimated that the 'speaking and business of the House' was conducted by a hardcore of about 150 members (23%). This number rose to 231 (35%) in 1841, 300 (46%) in 1861 and 385 (59%) in 1876.[14] The indexes to the debates in Hansard, listing members who spoke, asked questions, moved motions or otherwise intervened, show a similar trend. Whereas only 31% of the House merited inclusion in 1820, 60% were listed in 1833, 68% in 1874 and an impressive 86% in 1896. MPs like Henry Lowther (1812–67) or Sir Graham Montgomery (1852–80), who between them sat for 83 years without uttering a single word, still existed, of course. But by the 1830s they were fast becoming dinosaurs, a quaint reminder of a disappearing age of the lax attender and silent sinecurist. As Sir Robert Inglis, tory MP for Oxford University, noted around this time, 'Formerly very few members were wont to address the House; now the speaking members are probably not less than four hundred.'

This widely noted tendency for more MPs to speak prompted one of the most significant but least studied procedural reforms of the 19th century, which marks a major divide between the Hanoverian Commons and its Victorian successor. The reform in question concerns the practice of petitioning parliament, usually in order to highlight a grievance or demand some form of action. As expressions of opinion, public petitions had become an essential ingredient of the wider perception of parliament as the 'grand inquest of the nation' and an important barometer of popular

[13] R. Heron, *Notes* (1850), 203.
[14] Todd, *Parliamentary Government*, ii, 401.

feeling, and as such they enjoyed a privileged status. Petitions not only took priority over normal business, but could also be presented repeatedly from different places, even if they were on the same topic. Most crucial of all, each petition could be used to initiate a debate, in effect providing an opportunity for a subject to be discussed *ad infinitum*. This was less of a problem while the number of petitions remained modest. Between 1801 and 1805, for instance, roughly 250 were presented per year. By 1811–15, however, the number had more than quadrupled to 1,125 per annum; by 1827–31 it had risen to over 6,000; and by 1837–41 it had reached almost 17,600, a remarkable 70 times higher than at the start of the century.

Coupled with the growing tendency for MPs to speak, the petition and its associated debate became a defining feature of the early 19th-century Commons, and often hijacked the day's planned events. And though ostensibly initiated outdoors, they soon became a standard vehicle through which a campaigning MP (or group of MPs) might repeatedly pester the entire House with their particular obsession, as is amply demonstrated by the 900 or so petitions about Indian missionaries presented by William Wilberforce in 1813 or the incessant petitions for emigration schemes produced by Wilmot Horton during the 1820s. In short, public petitions became something of a fanatic's paradise, providing a determined minority with disproportionate access to the floor of an unprepared House.

Far more work needs to be done on the subtle devices used in the chamber to rein in the over-zealous – from verbal intimidation to complete walkouts – but in this instance the remedy could not have been more bold. In 1833 debates on petitions were sidelined to morning sittings, when there was usually a very thin attendance. Two years later they were scrapped altogether, by an extraordinary informal agreement between the two front benches. How the broader culture of public petitioning was effected by this change remains unclear. Petitions continued to be presented to the Commons in their thousands, and to provide an invaluable means of popular expression. However, it is perhaps telling that the number of petitions presented per annum peaked at almost 34,000 in 1843, the very year in which the debates on them were formally abolished by standing order.

The tendency for more MPs to speak was clearly of central importance in triggering some of the key procedural reforms of the 19th century. But what lay behind this phenomenon? Why, as the Liberal MP Sir Robert Heron noted in 1833, were MPs becoming 'almost all seized with a rage for speaking'?[15]

Parliament and the Public

Two factors in particular have been singled out by historians, both of which helped to reconfigure the relationship between MPs and the public. The first concerns the electoral reforms of the 19th century, starting with

[15] Heron, *Notes*, 203.

the 1832 Reform Act's disfranchisement (complete and partial) of 85 'rotten' boroughs and the creation of new constituencies, especially in the industrial north. The MPs elected for the newly enfranchised boroughs, it has been shown, were over twice as likely to participate in debate than those who had sat for the old 'rotten' boroughs, often as the silent nominee or paying guest of a patron. The role of electoral reform is examined in more detail further on. What it cannot explain, of course, is the rise of speaking that occurred *before* 1832. Between 1820 and 1828, for instance, there was a 20% increase in the number of MPs who warranted inclusion in the indexes of Hansard.

This is where the second factor, that of public interest in parliament, assumes a central significance. Since the 1770s unofficial reporting of Commons' speeches and proceedings had grown steadily, both in the expanding newspaper press and reviews such as the *Parliamentary Register*. The regency crisis and the war with France, in particular, then polarized political thinking and encouraged unprecedented levels of popular engagement with national politics. Press coverage of parliament exploded, and with it came literally hundreds of printed speeches, often issued as corrigenda to erroneous reports. (Some MPs even began to issue speeches before they had been given, or extended accounts of what they had intended to say.)

By 1803 public interest was sufficiently strong for William Cobbett to start publishing his version of the debates commercially – something that would be inconceivable today. Nine years later his *Parliamentary Debates* was taken over by Thomas Curson Hansard, whose family became synonymous with the title.

By then even the most obscure provincial newspapers were carrying verbatim reports of parliamentary debates, often on their front pages. Nationals like *The Times* and the *Morning Chronicle* provided *in extenso* accounts and division lists on an almost daily basis. Amazingly, this virtually continuous press coverage, with an estimated readership of above 2 million, occurred in direct contravention of the 'official' orders of the House of 1711 restricting the entry of strangers and the publication of proceedings, which were not lifted until 1845. Much has been made of the provision of a special 'press gallery' in this respect, in the temporary chamber used after the 1834 fire, an innovation which became a central feature of Barry's new building. But although there was no 'reporters gallery' as such in the old Commons, since 1803 the back seat of the 'strangers' gallery' had been reserved for their exclusive use by the doorkeepers, who received three guineas a session from an estimated 60 to 70 reporters. They also had their own 'rest room' above the division lobby where they could wait their turn. As one historian has recently suggested, in terms of public awareness of parliamentary business, 'something akin to an "information revolution"' had already occurred by the 1830s.[16]

[16] Jupp, *Governing of Britain*, 207.

Hansard and the Printed Parliamentary Debates

Thomas Curson Hansard (1776–1833) was the eldest son of Luke Hansard (1752–1828), whose printing business, the largest in London, was responsible for the printing of parliamentary materials under the authority of the Speaker of the Commons. In 1805 Thomas Hansard purchased his own printing business. From 1809 he took over the printing of William Cobbett's *Political Register*, and in the immediately following years three other major publications by Cobbett: *Parliamentary Debates*, *Parliamentary History* and *State Trials*. In 1812 he purchased all four from the financially embarrassed Cobbett. 'While Cobbett had the foresight to initiate these important publications, Hansard had the determination and industry to continue their production on a regular basis ... the main burden of the work fell on Hansard, whose *Parliamentary Debates* was soon recognized as the standard record.' Thomas Hansard's eldest son, named after his grandfather Thomas Curson (1813–91) continued to publish the debates until 1889.

Hansard's *Parliamentary Debates* was, however, not a first-hand record of what was spoken in parliament, being collated from press reports. Yet it provided a much fuller report of debates than any one paper, and without any suspicion of bias. Thomas Curson Hansard the younger received a public subsidy from 1877 'on condition he included reports of debates on private bills, committee debates on supply and public bills, and post-midnight debates, areas that were largely ignored in the public prints. It therefore became necessary for him to employ his own reporters in the Press Gallery'. After 1889 Hansard was published by a series of printers, for whom, however, it became an increasingly burdensome financial commitment, and the problems of delay and inadequate reporting did not satisfy MPs. Thus in 1909 the Commons set up its own reporting staff and the officially printed 5th series ran to 1981 and the 6th series saw the separation of the Lords' reports into their own volumes.

Soon after 1833 Hansard became a colloquial term for the published record of parliamentary debates. In 1909, with the establishment of the official reports of debates, the name of Hansard disappeared from their titles. However, in 1943 the Commons reinstated the name to the title page, and it is now used in many Commonwealth parliaments.

CJ

Sources: *ODNB*, xxv, 87–8; M. H. Port, 'The Official Record', *Parliamentary History*, ix (1990), 178–82, esp. 179.

This connection between greater publicity and the 'rage for speaking' was clearly recognized by MPs themselves, though not always viewed favourably. As one disgruntled tory noted in 1833:

In consequence of the publication of debates, Members were anxious that their constituents should see that they took part in the discussion, and the consequence was that honourable gentlemen delivered arguments that had been urged by former speakers, not regarding what had been previously stated, provided they had the opportunity of delivering their sentiments.[17]

The perception that the Commons was becoming, in effect, a platform for addressing the entire nation, rather than a *de facto* debating chamber, as this MP implied, clearly had all sorts of implications for parliamentary oratory. The few studies of 'public speech' currently available suggest that the kind of deliberative rhetoric associated with the age of Pitt and Fox, with its penchant for classical allusions, gradually fell out of favour after their deaths in 1806, to be replaced by a more theatrical and declamatory style of oratory which was more akin to preaching and better suited to public consumption.[18] The effect of banning the reporters (or audience) could be dramatic. When the Irish MP Daniel O'Connell had the regulations enforced and made MPs debate behind 'closed doors' in 1833, following a row with the press, it was noted that:

> The absence of strangers and reporters had a most paralysing effect on their eloquence. There was no animation in their manner, scarcely an attempt at that wit and sarcasm at each other's expense so often made on other occasions. Their speeches were dull in the highest degree, and ... had the merit of being short ... The secret of all this was, they knew their eloquence would not grace the newspapers of the following morning.[19]

Public interest in parliament not only helped to reshape the nature of political discourse in the Commons, but also the very notion of the politician himself. It is no exaggeration to say that by mid-century parliamentary debates had become one of the mass entertainments of the Victorian age, assuming a role not unlike a soap-opera, and that many MPs had acquired the equivalent status of modern celebrities. 'We come here', declared Disraeli, 'for fame'.[20] Politicians, of course, had long been fêted and commemorated, most notably by their own class. What was different about the 19th century was the scale of popular engagement with political figures and the growing commercialization that ensued, with spin-off products and publications catering for every taste and pocket. Fuelled by a cult of domesticity bordering on the obsessive, non-elite Victorians crammed their homes with political mementos and trinkets ranging from pottery busts and transferware to medallions and paperweights, all of which tended to glorify the individual politician rather than the political

[17] Hansard, *Parliamentary Debates*, 3rd ser., xv, 1013 (C. W. Wynn).
[18] J. S. Meisel, *Public Speech and the Culture of Public Life in the Age of Gladstone* (New York, 2001), *passim*.
[19] [Grant], *Random Recollections*, 48–9.
[20] Cited in G. H. L. Le May, *The Victorian Constitution: Conventions and Contingencies* (1979), 154.

event. The 'cult' of the politician had arrived. At another level, the diaries, letters, memoirs and biographies of MPs began to be published on a hitherto unprecedented scale, sometimes only a few years after the events they described. Political tracts and treatises also sold well, but the real sensation of the period was the political novel, that fictional blend of hustings satire and state-of-the-nation theorizing most conspicuously associated with Dickens and Disraeli.

This public hunger for politics in the broader sense was essentially a cultural phenomenon, and as such has yet to receive the multi-faceted and inter-disciplinary treatment it deserves. Electoral reform and the development of political parties, however, also played a crucial role in reconfiguring the relationship between the Commons and the public, as the last section makes clear.

Electoral Reform

The three reform acts of the 19th century – 1832, 1867, 1884/5 – dramatically increased the number of (male) voters who could vote in parliamentary elections as well as redistributing seats to new places of importance. In this sense, these reforms amply deserved the status accorded them by earlier generations of historians, as milestones 'on the path to democracy' that helped ensure Britain's peaceful transition to modern representative government.[21] Table 2 presents the basic data associated with these major extensions of the UK franchise, including an estimate of the proportion of adult males who were entitled to vote before and after each reform.

I use the term 'estimate' advisedly, as recent scholarship on the nature and impact of electoral reform has identified a whole raft of problems

[21] J. R. M. Butler, *The Passing of the Great Reform Bill* (1914), p. vii.

Table 2 UK electors and constituencies, 1801–1911

Year	Estimated no. of electors	Percentage of adult male population	No. of constituencies
1801	503,640	16%	380
1831	497,197*	11%	379
1833	811,443	18%	401
1866	1,364,000	20%	401
1868	2,477,713	33%	420
1883	3,152,000	34%	416
1885	5,708,000	62%	643
1911	7,904,000	–	643

* About 175,000 Irish freeholders were disfranchised in 1829, as part of the 'securities' that accompanied the admission of Catholics as MPs (Catholic emancipation). It was not until 1850, with the passage of the Irish Franchise Act, that the extra qualifications placed on Irish electors were effectively lifted.

affecting traditional quantitative approaches to electoral history. Not only do the available figures for the electorate include 'plural voters', meaning individuals with votes in more than one constituency, but they also tend to count individuals with multiple voting qualifications *within* each constituency more than once. The resulting duplicate entries on the post-1832 registers may have inflated the size of the electorate as much as 10–20%, severely compromising studies of electoral turnout, for example. The difference between the number who in theory had 'the right to vote' (the electorate) and the number who actually had the 'opportunity' to vote (the so-called 'voterate') was further complicated throughout this period by the continued existence of uncontested elections, in which there were no rival candidates and hence no poll. It has long been assumed by historians that uncontested elections occurred because of political inactivity, and that plotting the number of contested elections therefore provides some form of barometer of political vibrancy. But as my own work on electioneering has shown, uncontested elections often occurred precisely because the intensity of pre-election political campaigning had made the outcome of a poll inevitable, persuading one side to withdraw and avoid the expense of a pointless contest. At the same time many contested polls, far from being genuine struggles, were simply token or 'vexatious' oppositions whipped up by local troublemakers, sometimes by proposing 'phantom' candidates who never even showed up.[22]

It is for these and similar reasons that this chapter offers none of the commentary usually associated with the data in the first two columns of Table 2, but instead concentrates on the issues raised by the final column, which simply shows the number of UK constituencies.

It often comes as a surprise to those unfamiliar with this period to learn that an extra 263 parliamentary constituencies had been created by 1885, an increase of some 70% on the number that existed in 1801. More surprise follows the discovery that this dramatic increase of constituencies occurred without any significant rise in the number of MPs. Instead, the number of MPs grew by only a dozen (barely 2%), from a norm of 658 from 1801–85 to 670 thereafter. How was such an apparently conflicting alteration possible?

The answer is that before the 1885 Redistribution Act most constituencies elected two MPs (a few even more), and most electors therefore had two votes. The ability of each elector to deploy just one of these votes, by casting a 'plumper', or to cast votes between candidates from different parties, in what was termed a 'splitter' or 'split vote', created a highly complex set of electoral dynamics at the constituency level, where voters faced some six choices if there were three candidates and an astonishing ten options if there were four, and 15 if there were five. The range of subtle and overt campaigning devices that accompanied this system, in which

[22] P. J. Salmon, *Electoral Reform at Work: Local Politics and National Parties, 1832–1841* (Woodbridge, 2002), 6–7, 39–40, 26, 123–4.

Figure 1 Cross-party votes cast in double-member seats, 1818–1910

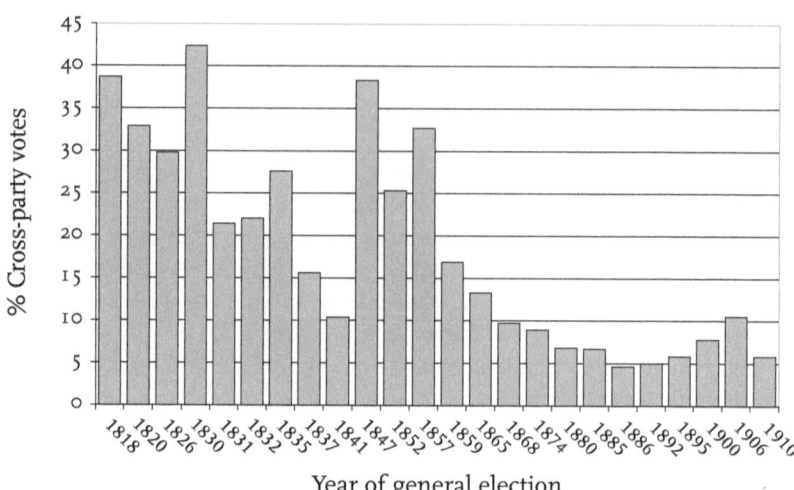

Adapted from G. W. Cox, *The Efficient Secret: The Cabinet and the Development of Political Parties in Victorian England* (Cambridge, 1987), 103, 108.

the withholding of a vote could prove as influential as casting it, made for an entirely different culture of electoral politics to that associated with the modern single-member constituency. By electing both a winner and a runner-up, double-member seats injected an important element of proportional (or minority) representation into Victorian democracy. Most important of all, they offered the opportunity for 'mixed' returns of MPs from different parties, through which non-partisan forms of electoral behaviour and local cultures of political independence might be cultivated and sustained. By contrast, single-member constituencies, as the political economist Nassau Senior noted in 1850, were apt to disfranchise all but the members of a single party.[23]

By assessing the level of cross-party votes cast in these double-member seats (split-votes and non-partisan plumps), historians have charted the growing significance of party-based voting behaviour in British elections during the 19th century. Scholars disagree about the speed of this development, with some opting for 1832 and others for 1867 as a major turning point. They also prioritize different reasons for the rise of voter partisanship, with some arguing that the expansion of the electorate made personal campaigns impossible and the party platform indispensable, and others blaming the activities of local party associations or changes in political culture, such as those mentioned earlier. The overall move towards an electoral system dominated by national parties, however, is beyond dispute. Figure 1, based on a sample involving some 4.5 million voters, shows the percentage of cross-party votes cast in double-member seats at general

[23] *Edinburgh Review*, ix (1850), 508–58.

elections held between 1818 and 1910. The broad trend, though far from linear, is clear. Whereas some 40% of electors cast a cross-party vote in 1818, 1830 and 1847, from 1868 onwards the proportion never exceeded 10.5%. By December 1910 it was barely 6%.

The Development of Parties

These findings are important not only in terms of charting electoral partisanship, but also in terms of helping to explain one of the most dramatic developments within the Commons during the 19th century, namely the rise of party-based voting in the division lobbies. A number of statistical surveys employing 'roll-call analysis' have concluded that 'the more split votes an MP received when elected, the more often he dissented from his party's position in parliament'. In addition, MPs from different parties showed a greater propensity to defy their party whip if they had been elected alongside a party rival. This latter finding, in particular, would seem to indicate that there was a genuine 'local basis to indiscipline' in the lobbies, and that any long-term decline in the level of cross-party voting in elections, such as that revealed in Figure 1, ought to have been accompanied by a corresponding drop in cross-bench voting among MPs.[24]

Figure 2 shows the percentage of 'whipped' divisions in certain years in which more than one out of ten MPs dissented from their party line and cast a cross-bench vote. After reaching very high levels in the 1850s and 1860s, following the split of the Conservative Party and the subsequent confusion of party alignments, indiscipline in the lobbies began to decline as the two main parties regrouped. This drop in cross-bench voting, though again not smooth, became most conspicuous from the late 1880s onwards, when dissidence plummeted to new lows. By 1903 only 14% of the divisions were failing to produce a strict two-party vote. Modern party-cohesion, or at least something approaching it, had arrived.

A broad correlation between the rise of party voting in the electorate and in the legislature seems pretty clear from these two sets of data. Indeed, it has often been suggested that partisanship in the Commons grew out of partisanship in the constituencies. What, of course, is not revealed in this analysis is the declining significance of the double-member seat itself in British electoral politics. As the number of multi-member seats fell, the type of cross-party voting shown in Figure 1 became a form of behaviour restricted to fewer and fewer constituencies. It therefore affected fewer MPs. Before the 1832 Reform Act, for example, 274 (72%) of the UK's 380 constituencies were multi-member. Cross-party voting in these circumstances therefore had the potential to influence 552 MPs (almost 84% of the total). The 1832 and 1867 reforms, however, reduced the number of these constituencies to 224 out of 420 (53%), lowering the

---

[24] G. W. Cox, *The Efficient Secret: The Cabinet and the Development of Political Parties in Victorian England* (Cambridge, 1987), 93, 148–65.

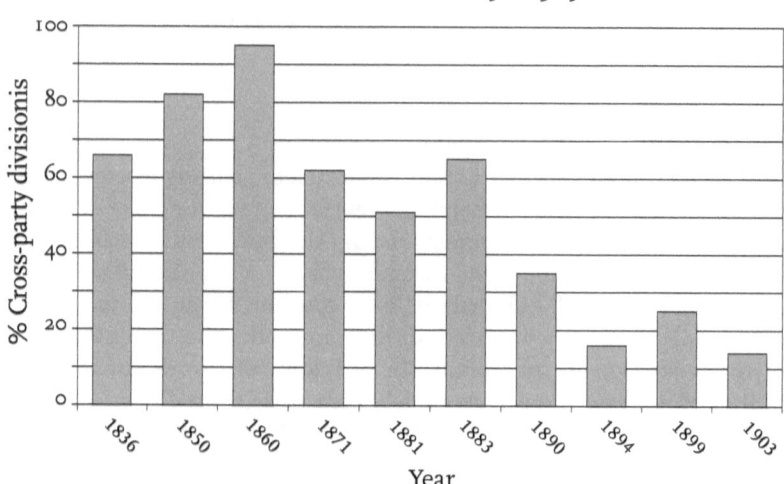

Figure 2 Divisions with cross-party voting in House of Commons, 1836–1903

Adapted from H. Berrington, 'Partisanship and dissidence in the Nineteenth-Century House of Commons', *Parliamentary Affairs*, xxi (1967–8), 338–74.

number of MPs affected to 462 (70%). From a situation in which almost three-quarters of the UK's constituencies were multi-member in 1832, the proportion had fallen to a little over a half 35 years later. This development alone suggests an important dimension to the rise of partisanship, both locally and nationally, which has yet to be fully explored.

It was the 1885 Redistribution Act's almost complete abolition of multi-member seats, however, which most dramatically transformed the UK's political landscape and ushered in a new age of party. Just 27 double-member seats survived this wholesale destruction of the old electoral communities and their replacement by artificial 'winner-takes-all' single-member districts. Cross-party voting was now only feasible in 4% of the United Kingdom's 643 constituencies, and at best could influence a mere 54 MPs (8% of the total). By far the most salient feature of Figure 1, in this context, is not so much the overall decline of cross-party voting across the century, but the continued existence of non-partisan behaviour in the handful of places where it was still possible. In 1906, for instance, the level of cross-party voting in the remaining double-member constituencies was 10.5%, a rate almost identical to that experienced 65 years earlier in the 1841 election. What had mattered numerically in 1841, however, when there were 248 multiple-member seats electing 505 MPs, had by 1906 become an irrelevance, a quaint reminder of a by-gone age of 'splitters' and 'plumps' and 'mixed' returns. Non-partisan voting clearly still clung on, wherever it was possible, but the very small number of double-member seats after 1885 meant that it no longer played any part in national political life.

Other factors, of course, reinforced these trends. The gradual elimination of 'treating' in elections and the introduction of strict spending limits, mainly as a result of the Corrupt Practices Acts of 1854 and 1883, obliged candidates to rely ever more on the army of volunteers that only nationally oriented party associations could muster, intensifying a tendency already apparent after each extension of the franchise. The adoption of the secret ballot in 1872 also helped to undermine the electoral significance of local influences and personal allegiances, although the use of numbered ballot papers (unlike the so-called Australian ballot) did not provide the complete anonymity that many had hoped for and probably mitigated any effect before the enfranchisement of 2.5 million new voters in 1884. More broadly, the increasing reliance on party ties in the constituencies necessitated greater control in the lobbies, since no elector would wish to support a party that was too undisciplined to deliver its policies once elected. The number of whips therefore steadily increased, from a maximum of three per party before 1880 to seven by 1895. Local party associations also began to select candidates themselves, for much the same reasons, and many of the traditional links between MPs and their constituencies started to disappear. Between 1868 and 1900, for instance, it has been estimated that there was a halving in the overall incidence of direct connections, such as an MP owning property or having been born in the constituency. Even the socio-economic composition of the Commons, for so long dominated by the landed aristocracy, began to alter, with a steady rise in the number of MPs having industrial, commercial and financial interests becoming evident after 1868, although most of these were also landowners. Real change in this respect, including a substantial influx of workers' representatives, would have to await the introduction of MPs' salaries in 1911.

Summary

The developments outlined in this chapter provided the United Kingdom with a recognizably modern Commons, dominated by ministers and elected by a representative system where voters polled for candidates of nationally organized parties led by a potential prime minister. The decline of the private MP and the huge rise of popular interest in parliamentary politics were fundamental in bringing this about. Within the House itself, it was not so much the increase of state business as the 'rage for speaking' that forced the pace of change, leading to a growth of ministerial control over proceedings that was for the most part consensual rather than coercive. In the constituencies, meanwhile, an ever-expanding electorate and restrictions on spending undermined older forms of personal campaigning and necessitated an ever greater reliance on the party platform and party association. The dominance of party, however, was far from complete. Traditional idioms of non-partisan politics lingered on, especially in the double-member seats, affecting voters and MPs alike. And it is here that the move to single-member districts, first gradually and then overwhelmingly in 1885, assumes a central significance. By altering the basic unit of Victorian representation and eliminating electoral cross-partisanship, the primary modes of political engagement were transformed and the two-party system became far more permanently entrenched both locally and nationally. With the obvious exception of universal (including female) suffrage, the foundations of the 20th-century representative system were now in place. The extent to which a Commons elected by such a system should have the right to dominate both houses of parliament, however, had yet to be decided.

Chronology

1801
Act of Union with Ireland adds 100 Irish MPs, bringing total membership to 658

1803
Reporters unofficially allotted seats in public gallery; William Cobbett starts *Parliamentary Debates*, later taken over by T. C. Hansard

1810
Private bill office established by Speaker Abbott to oversee private legislation

1829
Catholic emancipation enables Catholics to formally sit as MPs

1832
Great Reform Act (England and Wales) redistributes 143 seats and extends franchise to new groups, including £50 occupiers in counties and £10 householders in boroughs; measures also passed for Ireland and Scotland

1834
Commons chamber and surrounding buildings destroyed by fire; Commons moves into House of Lords (formerly Court of Requests)

1836
Charles Barry wins public competition to rebuild Palace of Westminster

1836
Commons starts to publish official division lists

1841
Fine Arts Commission established to oversee decoration of new palace

1841–2
Acts to prevent bribery in elections and increase powers of election committees

1845
Orders prohibiting entry of strangers and the publication of debates formally repealed

1850
New Commons Chamber used for the first time

1850
Irish Franchise Act enfranchises £12 occupiers in counties and £8 occupiers in boroughs

1854
Bribery Act restricts bribery and 'treating' in elections

1855
Chairman of ways and means (who presides over committees of whole House) assumes role of deputy Speaker

1858
Repeal of Act requiring MPs to own property worth £600 in a county and £300 in a borough

1867
Second Reform Act (England and Wales) redistributes 52 seats and extends franchise to new groups, including borough householders (resident ratepayers and £10 lodgers); measures also passed for Ireland and Scotland

1869
Compound ratepayers (whose rates are included in their rents) formally enfranchised

1872
Ballot Act: secret ballot introduced for municipal and parliamentary elections

1883
Corrupt and Illegal Practices Act restricting election expenditure

1884
Third Reform Act (England and Wales) extends franchise to resident householders and lodgers in counties and £10 occupiers of business premises; measures also passed for Ireland and Scotland

1885
Redistribution Act: single-member constituencies become the norm

1902
Second deputy Speaker appointed

1909
Parliament takes over Hansard, which becomes verbatim and official

1909
House of Lords rejects 'People's Budget'

1911
Payment of MPs: £400 a year plus expenses; Parliament Act: Lords loses control of money bills and its powers reduced to two-year delay

Further Reading

W. Bagehot, *The English Constitution*, ed. M. Taylor (Oxford, 2001)

H. Berrington, 'Partisanship and Dissidence in the Nineteenth-Century House of Commons', *Parliamentary Affairs*, xxi (1967–8), 338–74

N. Chester, *The English Administrative System, 1780–1870* (Oxford, 1981)

G. W. Cox, *The Efficient Secret: The Cabinet and the Development of Political Parties in Victorian England* (Cambridge, 1987)

V. Cromwell, 'The Losing of the Initiative by the House of Commons, 1780–1914', *Transactions of the Royal Historical Society*, 4th ser., xviii (1968), 1–24

—— 'The Victorian Commons, 1832–1884', in *The House of Commons: Seven Hundred Years of British Tradition*, ed. R. Smith and J. Moore (1996), 118–31

P. Fraser, 'The Growth of Ministerial Control in the Nineteenth-Century House of Commons', *English Historical Review*, lxxv (1960), 444–63

The Houses of Parliament: History, Art, Architecture, ed. C. and J. Riding (2000)

J. Innes, 'Central Government "Interference": Changing Conceptions, Practices and Concerns, c. 1700–1850', in *Civil Society in British History*, ed. J. Harris (Oxford, 2003), 39–60

P. Jupp, *The Governing of Britain, 1688–1848: The Executive, Parliament and the People* (2006)

G. H. L. Le May, *The Victorian Constitution: Conventions and Contingencies* (1979)

C. Leys, 'Petitioning in the Nineteenth and Twentieth Centuries', *Political Studies*, iii (1955), 45–64

I. Machin, *The Rise of Democracy in Britain, 1830–1918* (2001)

J. S. Meisel, *Public Speech and the Culture of Public Life in the Age of Gladstone* (New York, 2001)

Parliaments, Nations and Identities in Britain and Ireland, 1660–1850, ed. J. Hoppit (Manchester, 2003)

J. A. Phillips and C. Wetherell, 'The Great Reform Act of 1832 and the Political Modernization of England', *American Historical Review*, c (1995), 411–36

E. Porritt, 'Amendments in the House of Commons Procedure since 1881', *American Political Science Review*, ii (1908), 515–31

A. Ramm, 'The Parliamentary Context of Cabinet Government', *English Historical Review*, xcix (1984), 739–69

J. Redlich, *The Procedure of the House of Commons* (3 vols, 1908)

M. Rush, *The Role of the Member of Parliament since 1868: From Gentlemen to Players* (Oxford, 2001)

P. Salmon, *Electoral Reform at Work: Local Politics and National Parties, 1832–1841* (Woodbridge, 2002)

C. Seymour, *Electoral Reform in England and Wales: The Development and Operation of the Parliamentary Franchise, 1832–85* (New Haven, 1915)

J. A. Thomas, *The House of Commons, 1832–1901: A Study of its Economic and Functional Character* (Cardiff, 1939)

19 The House of Commons, 1911–49
Philip Norton

The period from 1911 to 1922 witnessed major constitutional and political change in the United Kingdom, with important consequences for parliament. However, the most important period for parliament in the years between the two Parliament Acts was that of the Second World War.

The House of Commons and the Electorate

During the inter-war years, the size of the House of Commons declined while the number of electors more than doubled. The size of the House of Commons was 670 before 1918. In 1917 a boundary commission was appointed. In seeking to ensure some equality in numbers between constituencies (the first time the principle had been fully accepted), the commission added a total of 31 constituencies (including six university seats). There were thus 707 seats contested in the general election of 1918. They included 13 two-member boroughs. However, that year proved a high point in the number of members. Events in Ireland resulted in the loss of the Irish seats, other than in Northern Ireland (where 13 were retained), with the result that the number of seats was reduced to 615. This remained the number from 1922 until 1945, when the number increased to 640.

The change in the size of the electorate was more dramatic. The first two decades of the century had seen pressure for the enfranchisement of women. The case was conceded in large measure in 1918. A Speaker's conference had been convened in 1916 and reported early in 1917. It made various recommendations for extending the franchise – universal suffrage for men based on residence, for example, rather than on the payment of rates and compromised on votes for women by recommending those aged 30 and over who were local government electors or were married to local government electors be enfranchised; the compromise was designed to concede the case for women to have the vote but to ensure they were in a minority of the electorate. The Representation of the People Act 1918 gave effect to the recommendations. (Servicemen who had served in the war were also entitled to vote at 19.) The effect of the changes was to more than double the size of the electorate, from 8 million to 21 million. The Representation of the People (Equal Franchise) Act 1928 equalized the voting age for men and women. The electorate increased from less than 22 million to nearly 29 million.

The effect of the 1928 act was also to bring into alignment the age at which women could vote and stand for election to parliament. A separate act in 1918 had allowed women to stand for election on the same basis as men (that is, once they had attained the age of 21). It was thus possible, between 1918 and 1928, for a woman aged between 21 and 29 to contest a parliamentary election even though she was not entitled to vote, and at least one (Irene Ward) did so; she was unsuccessful, though later did become an MP. The 1918 act did result in a few women entering the Commons. The first female MP to be elected, Countess Markievicz, was a Sinn Féin member who had been involved in the Dublin uprising; she did not take her seat. She was the only one of the 17 women candidates in 1918 to be successful. The first three women to be elected and take their seats (Nancy, Lady Astor in 1919, Margaret Wintringham in 1921 and Mabel Philipson in 1923) succeeded their husbands in the seats.

The other principal changes in electoral law in the period came in the years from 1944 to 1948. (There were also various measures making minor adjustments as well as measures to continue the parliament in wartime.) Following a Speaker's conference on electoral reform and redistribution of seats, which reported in 1944, a Redistribution Bill was introduced in 1944, providing for the creation of permanent Boundary Commissions for the different parts of the UK and for the creation, as an interim measure, of 25 new constituencies to deal with excessively large constituencies. The 1945 Representation of the People Act assimilated local government and parliamentary franchises. A 1947 act allowed for some relaxation in the rules to which the Boundary Commissions were required to adhere, in order to preserve existing communities. (The Commissions reported at the end of 1947. Only 80 seats were left with unchanged boundaries.) The more substantial Representation of the People Act 1948 abolished plural voting (whereby voters who owned property of a certain value in another constituency had a second vote in that constituency), which had been retained by the 1918 act, and removed the remaining 12 university seats (where members were elected by the graduates) and double-member seats (where the voters in one borough elected two MPs).

The abolition of the university seats removed some prominent independent members, such as the novelist A. P. Herbert, as well as doing away with the only use of proportional representation in UK parliamentary elections: all but three of the university members were elected in two or three-member constituencies utilizing the single transferable vote.

Otherwise, the period was notable for proposals for reform, none of which was enacted. The Speaker's conference on electoral reform in 1917 had recommended a system of proportional representation (the single transferable vote). A number of private members' bills designed to reform the electoral system failed, but – following a report on electoral reform from a committee under former Speaker Lord Ullswater – the government in 1931 introduced a bill providing for the alternative vote (AV) in parliamentary elections. The bill was passed by the Commons but amended significantly in the Lords; it fell in the August when the government fell.

> ### University and Double-Member Seats
>
> University representation was introduced in the 17th century. Oxford and Cambridge universities each returned one MP (later increased to two) with the electorate comprising MA graduates of the university. By 1911 there were nine university seats: Cambridge (2), Dublin (2), Edinburgh and St Andrews (1), Glasgow and Aberdeen (1), London (1) and Oxford (2). The addition of six seats in 1918 meant that in the general election of that year there were MPs returned from Cambridge (2), Combined English (2), Dublin (2), London (1), National (1), Oxford (2), Queen's Belfast (1), Scotland (3), and Wales (1). The Dublin and National university representation disappeared with the loss of Irish seats. The remaining 12 university seats ceased to exist in 1950.
>
> Though single-member seats became the norm in the 1880s, some double-member seats continued to exist until 1950. In each seat (other than the university seats), two members were elected through the 'first-past-the-post' (or, in this case, the 'first-two-past-the-post') method of election. Each elector had two votes. In 1945 the two-member seats were Antrim, Blackburn, Bolton, Brighton, City of London, Derby, Down, Dundee, Fermanagh and Tyrone, Norwich, Oldham, Preston, Southampton, Stockport, and Sunderland. In the two (or three) member university seats, the single transferable vote (STV) was employed.

The extension of the franchise resulted in more people voting, though in proportional terms turnout did not increase substantially; if anything, there was a slight dip relative to the turnout in the 1906 and two 1910 general elections. The turnout in 1918 was affected by the effects of war, and turnout fell from 81% in December 1910 to 59%. The figures may not be as stark as they appear to be on the face of it. Before 1918 there was no compulsory registration, and the percentage is of those who had registered to vote. After 1918 turnout always exceeded 70%. Fears of how women might vote, or fail to vote, were not realized, and in the elections of 1924, 1929 and 1931 turnout exceeded 76%. Even in 1945, when there was major problems collecting service votes, turnout was estimated at almost 73%. As David Butler has noted, 'the figures for the percentage of the electorate voting show no very marked trend until the elections of 1950 and 1951 when there was a decided increase'.[1] The significant development in the period was not how many people voted, but rather how they were casting their votes. The political landscape, as we shall see, changed remarkably in the inter-war years.

---

[1] D. Butler, *The Electoral System in Britain since 1918* (Oxford, 1963), 171.

> ### Electoral Systems
>
> The **alternative vote** (AV) is used in elections where a single candidate is to be elected. It is not a proportional system, but provides that the winning candidate achieves an absolute majority of the votes cast. Electors mark their preferences on the ballot paper, putting 1 against their first preference, 2 against their second preference and so on (though they are not required to put more than one preference). If a candidate achieves 50% + 1 first-preference votes, that candidate is declared elected. Otherwise, the candidate at the bottom of the poll is eliminated and his or her second-preference votes are then distributed. The process is continued until a candidate achieves an absolute majority of the votes case.
>
> The **single transferable vote** (STV) is a proportional system employed in multi-member constituencies. Electors mark their preferences (1, 2, 3 etc.) on the ballot. To be declared elected, a candidate has to achieve a set quota of votes. The quota comprises the total ballot divided by the total number of seats plus one, with one then being added to the figure. Any candidate who reaches the quota on the count of first-preference votes is declared elected. Any surplus votes received by the candidate are then redistributed according to a formula. If the redistribution of surplus votes fails to produce the requisite number of candidates to meet the quota, the candidate at the bottom of the poll is eliminated and the second-preference votes then distributed. The process continues until the number of seats is filled by candidates reaching the quota.

The Role of the MP

Changes in the nature of parties also had an effect on the type of MP that was elected. The period witnessed the election of Labour MPs drawn from working-class backgrounds. Until 1945 a majority of Labour MPs were classed as workers, most having no more than an elementary education. In 1911 the Liberals – needing Nationalist and Labour support – decided to agree to the payment of MPs. A salary of £400 was introduced in 1912. In moving the motion to make provision for payment, Lloyd George emphasized the change in the nature of the role of the MP as well as the background from which previously they had been drawn. (He also noted that they were reverting to a much earlier tradition, when MPs had been paid by the constituencies.) Parliament, he said, had changed completely in the last year or so. 'The work of Parliament is greater, infinitely greater; it is greater in the quantity and volume of work. Not only that, but it is very much greater in the attention it demands at the hands of each individual Member.'[2]

---

[2] Reproduced in *The Law and Working of the Constitution: Documents 1660–1914*, ii: *1784–1914*, ed. W. C. Costin and J. Steven Watson (2nd edn, 1964), 208–9.

He said that when parliament was not sitting, the MP was off to the constituency and to address all sorts of meetings. Certainly, the work of the MP changed in this period, though constituency service was not on a par with what it was to become in later times. There were some changes in the different constituency roles fulfilled by the MP. The increase in the number of MPs without independent wealth meant that they were not able to serve as local benefactors to the extent that was the case with other MPs. Members, though, were still expected to help with election expenses and contribute to the local party. On the Labour side, the task of carrying the burden of election expenses was taken over by the party and in 1933 a limit placed on what MPs could contribute to local parties; only in 1948 were Conservative MPs limited in what they could donate to their local parties: a maximum of £50 a year (£25 in the case of candidates).

The role of benefactor and local dignitary were to the fore for most of the period, certainly on the Conservative side, and – despite the increase in business in the House – MPs still had time to pursue other careers and be away from the House. Most did not live in or near their constituencies and visits were sometimes infrequent. Demands from constituents in the form of letters and visits were also not numerous.

During this period some MPs were able to build up lengthy political careers, not least as a result of long parliaments resulting from war. Most MPs sat in the House for at least ten years. Nevertheless, electoral volatility resulted in some substantial turnover in membership and the period of service was shorter in the years 1918–44 than it was in the period from 1900 to 1917. Conservative MPs continued to be predominantly public-school educated graduates drawn from the professions (not least the law and the armed services) and businessmen; Liberal MPs tended to be similar, though only a minority were public-school educated.

If the introduction of payment was for the convenience of MPs, there were two measures enacted that were for the benefit of those MPs appointed to ministerial office. Because such office was an office of profit under the crown, an MP appointed as a minister had to fight a by-election. The provision was inconvenient as well as potentially expensive, politically as well as financially. In 1919 a compromise measure was enacted – the Re-election of Ministers Act – providing that ministers need not vacate their seats if appointed within nine months of the start of a new parliament. In 1926 another act was passed applying the provision to all ministers.

Party Development

The most significant political change in the period was that affecting the political parties and their relative position. The early years of the period saw the emergence of the Labour Party – it became the official opposition in 1922 – followed by a period of three-party competition (A. J. P. Taylor

> ### Party Leaders and Leaders of the Opposition
> There have been exceptional periods when the leader of the opposition was not the leader of the second largest party. This has been the case during wartime when coalitions have been formed and the leader of the second largest party has entered government. In 1915, when the Unionists joined a coalition with the Liberals, Unionist MP Henry Chaplin was designated as the nominal leader of the opposition. In 1940, with Labour leader Clement Attlee joining the cabinet, Labour MP H. B. Lees-Smith became the official leader of the opposition (later succeeded by F. W. Pethick-Lawrence and Anthony Greenwood). There have also been occasions when a party leader lost his seat and, until his return to the Commons, another leading figure in the party has served as opposition leader. In 1906 Arthur Balfour lost his seat and Joseph Chamberlain served temporarily as leader of the opposition. In 1918 H. H. Asquith, leader of the (Asquithian) Liberals lost his seat and Sir Donald Maclean fulfilled his functions as opposition leader until Asquith returned to the House two years later. Arthur Henderson became Labour leader when the Labour government collapsed in 1931 and was promptly defeated in the general election. George Lansbury fulfilled the role of opposition leader, before succeeding to the position in his own right the following year when Henderson retired.

referred to the 1929 general election as 'the only fully three-cornered contest in British history')[3] and then what amounted to dominance by a single party. Two world wars also, as we shall see, created an unusual constitutional position with the formation of coalition governments.

The period was unusual in seeing the collapse of three governments – in 1922, 1924 and 1931. The coalition government came to end in 1922 following a vote by Conservative MPs at the Carlton Club, the first Labour administration was brought down by a censure vote on the Campbell case (where the attorney general had withdrawn a prosecution of J. R. Campbell, the editor of *Workers' Weekly*, for publishing a 'Don't shoot' appeal to soldiers) and the second Labour government was brought down by economic crisis. The period was also unusual in that, formally, two governments fell through defeat on a vote of confidence: the Baldwin government faced parliament in January 1924, following electoral defeat in the December 1923 election, and was defeated by 72 votes. The MacDonald government was then defeated in the autumn.

Although the party conflict was complex during this period, there was greater institutionalization in terms of party organization within parliament. The Ministers of the Crown Act 1937 provided a salary for the leader of the opposition and stipulated that the Speaker should determine who

---

[3] A. J. P. Taylor, *English History, 1914–45* (1970), 332.

was leader of the largest out-of-office party. There had been some confusion in the 1918–22 parliament as well as during wartime, when the leader of the opposition was not a party leader; the problem re-emerged in 1940. There were also short periods, as when the party leader lost his seat, when the party leader was not in the Commons and the role of leader of the opposition was filled by another leading figure.

The important point was the recognition that there needed to be a formally designated leader of the opposition. The period also saw the greater organization of a shadow cabinet, especially on the Labour benches. When the Conservatives were in opposition, Stanley Baldwin was reluctant to summon many meetings of the shadow cabinet. The Parliamentary Labour Party (PLP) elected a parliamentary committee, which became a shadow cabinet, and with members sitting from 1926, as of right, on the opposition front bench. When in government, the PLP also established a consultative, or liaison, committee – comprising back-benchers and ministers – to act as links between the party and the government. It was only in the 1945–50 parliament, though, that the committee appeared to have much success in fulfilling a communicative role.

The period was also significant for the growth of back-bench organization on the Conservative benches. The PLP, since its inception, had held regular meetings and elected officers. There was no equivalent on the Conservative benches. A number of Conservative MPs newly elected in 1922 decided to establish a committee 'for the purpose of mutual co-operation and assistance in dealing with political and parliamentary questions, and in order to enable new members to take a more active interest and part in Parliamentary life'.[4] It met for the first time in 1923 but because of the date of the members' election it was titled the Conservative Private Members (1922) Committee. It received some co-operation from the chief whip, and it was soon the practice for a whip to attend each week to announce forthcoming business. The membership expanded and in 1925 was opened to all Conservative private members. By the end of 1925 the parliamentary party had developed an organized body that was to operate as a forum for all Conservative MPs (other than the leader when in opposition and other than ministers in government) and which operated in a manner that was to remain the norm. An executive committee met before the full meeting, the meeting would then be opened by the chairman, a whip would announce business (and respond to questions), reports (if any) would be taken from back-bench committees, and there would be an address by a guest speaker, be it a front-bencher or an invited outside speaker. The committee served as a platform for members to voice concerns as well as respond to current issues. A sudden controversy could help swell attendance. The two largest attendances in the 1930s – each of about 200 members – were at meetings to discuss the white paper

---

4 P. Goodhart, *The 1922: The Story of the Conservative Backbenchers' Parliamentary Committee* (1973), 15.

on Indian constitutional reform and to listen to the dominions secretary, J. H. Thomas. The committee became a central part of Conservative parliamentary life and a body through which back-bench feeling could be made clear to the leadership.

The period also saw the growth of Conservative back-bench party committees. These differed from the 1922 Committee in that they were officially created bodies. (The 1922 Committee initially formed sub-committees. These, however, disappeared when Baldwin decided to create official specialized committees.) The committees elected their own chairmen (usually members of the shadow cabinet when in opposition) and secretaries, and met regularly: sometimes weekly or fortnightly. Committees covering topics of importance to the party, such as agriculture and foreign affairs, and headed by active chairmen attracted substantial participation by members. MPs were free to attend whichever committee meetings they wished, and attendance could be swelled by a major speaker or important topic. Over 150 MPs attended the agriculture committee in March 1927 to consider the minister of health's Poor Law reform proposals. Any dissension expressed in a party committee would be reported by a whip to the chief whip or leadership. The committees became important means of enabling back-benchers to specialize in a particular subject and as means of conveying views to party leaders.

The decline in the number of Liberal MPs and the small size of the PLP meant that there was not the same scope in the inter-war years for other parties in parliament to establish specialized committees. The PLP had various groups, such as the Independent Labour Party (ILP) group and a trade union group – and there were some attempts to create advisory committees – but there was no developed infrastructure comparable to that on the Conservative benches. It lacked the numbers and also the specialized knowledge. The situation changed in 1945, with the emergence of the PLP as the largest parliamentary party and many MPs with expertise in particular policy sectors. In October 1945 eleven subject groups were formed; another nine were subsequently added. Some created sub-committees. Though not meeting as regularly as Conservative committees, some proved active bodies, discussing policy and listening to speakers; some established good links with ministers and some had an input into the development of policy. However, ministers generally kept them at arm's length and felt that – with fixed memberships – they could be unrepresentative. There were some clashes between ministers and subject groups, and members generally came to view the groups in a negative light, a perception that was to persist for some years. Overall, though, the period is notable for the degree to which party in parliament became organized, not least in ensuring a voice for back-bench members.

Institutional Development

However, it was not just the parties that witnessed greater specialization. The House of Commons also witnessed institutional development. This was notably the case with committees. The public accounts committee already existed, but it was joined in 1912 by an estimates committee. The committee went into abeyance from 1914 to 1921 (though a select committee on national expenditure was appointed from 1917 to 1920) and again during the Second World War. Its main functions were to consider the presentation of the estimates and to consider ways in which policies could be carried out more cost-efficiently. It was not meant to address policy, though after 1945 it did not always confine itself to administrative matters. It proved useful in exploring how effectively policy and expenditure programmes were implemented, and it helped make more transparent the work of departments. It was hampered, though, by the financial information presented by government and by the absence of a specialized support staff analogous to that of the comptroller and auditor general. In 1926 it was given an expert adviser (a seconded treasury official). In the opinion of Sir Ivor Jennings, the committee duplicated work done more effectively by the public accounts committee.[5]

The period also saw the consolidation of the role of standing committees. With the expansion of public business, bills needed to be processed expeditiously; standing committees enabled several bills to be dealt with simultaneously. The committees also saw the greater development of whipping, especially after 1945. Previously it had not been unusual for a minister's parliamentary private secretary to ensure government members attended, but after 1945 it became usual for a whip to be appointed to membership.

The reliance on standing committees was but one manifestation of the growth of government business. Another was the length of the session. Until 1929 the ideal session was deemed to be one that ran from February to July, though in practice some sessions ran on to August or even September. In February 1928 the prime minister, Stanley Baldwin, announced that it was intended to start the new session the following year in the autumn. With the outbreak of the Second World War it was decided not to prorogue parliament in July but rather to adjourn for the summer. This practice, enabling the House to meet for a spill-over session after the summer, was maintained in peacetime.

[5] I. Jennings, *Parliament* (Cambridge, 1948), 312.

Effects of War

The two world wars created new situations for parliament. One was in terms of government formation: both saw the creation of coalitions. The other was in terms of the relationship between the executive and parliament: normal partisan conflict was suspended. The need to prosecute the war resulted in great powers being vested in government. The Emergency Powers (Defence) Act of 1940 conferred power to require persons to put themselves and their property at the disposal of the crown. Parliament was seen as having little to do – the number of bills fell to about a third of the pre-war average – other than support the government. Many MPs were, in any event, often away serving in the forces (by early 1941, 116 were serving). Another, an extreme anti-Semitic MP, Sir Archibald Ramsay (Conservative MP for Peebles), was arrested under the emergency legislation and sentenced to four-and-a-half years in gaol. Despite public unity, there were various criticisms – sometimes of a partisan nature – voiced in meetings of the 1922 Committee and PLP, both of which continued to meet.

However, despite apparent marginalization, the House of Commons during the Second World War fulfilled an important role. It remained active – it met for about 120 days a session – and debates could attract a large number of members. Major votes could draw 400 MPs into the division lobbies. However, most importantly of all, the government rested on the confidence of the whole House. It was no longer government versus opposition. The House reflected the unity that was needed in time of war. 'During the war', wrote Ronald Butt, 'the Churchill Government relied on a majority of the whole House which, beside giving it great authority, also obliged it to respond to all sections of the Commons'.[6] The government could not afford to see its broad support jeopardized. Recognizing this, various MPs formed ginger groups to probe government. Various concessions were made in response to pressure from members and ministers were especially sensitive to any criticism of the war effort. Given the reliance on the opposition, the PLP exercised influence disproportionate to its size. Members were able to express their views privately, through the PLP or 1922 Committee, and to leave open the threat of going public on the floor of the House. The government variously reported on the conduct of the war in secret session. There was also scrutiny through committees. A select committee on national expenditure was established, along with six sub-committees, and a select committee on statutory rules and orders (later the select committee on statutory instruments) in 1944. The war years also saw the development of an all-party parliamentary and scientific committee: it addressed such issues as the nutritive value of bread and the use of scientists in the war effort.

The fact that parliament continue to sit during the Second World

---

[6] R. Butt, *The Power of Parliament* (1967), 175.

War was itself noteworthy. London was subject to extensive bombing. Parliament did not always sit in the Palace of Westminster. Both houses variously sat in Church House, in Dean's Yard, Westminster, known as the Annexe. The Chamber of the Commons was destroyed by enemy bombing on 10 May 1941. The Chamber of the House of Lords was thereafter utilized for the Commons – the Speaker's chair placed at the opposite end of the Chamber to the Woolsack – and the Lords met in the Royal Robing Room. The Commons sat in the Lords' Chamber from 1941 until the new Chamber was completed in 1950. At Churchill's insistence, the rebuilt Chamber resembled the old.

One consequence of the Second World War was that parliament emerged with its reputation enhanced. In a celebrated 1946 broadcast, American commentator Ed Murrow declared: 'I am persuaded that the most important thing that happened in Britain was that this nation chose to win or lose this war under the established rules of parliamentary procedure.'[7] A procedure committee established in 1946 concluded that the prestige of parliament had probably never been higher. As a consequence, it saw little need for change. It thus extrapolated from conditions of wartime as to what should apply in peacetime. The result was no significant reform designed to strengthen parliament in its relationship to the executive.

[7] P. Norton, 'Winning the War but Losing the Peace: The British House of Commons during the Second World War', *The Journal of Legislative Studies*, iv (1998), 33–51 at 46.

Chronology

1911
Parliament Act

1912
Payment of MPs; appointment of select committee on estimates

1917
Speaker's conference on electoral reform

1918
Representation of the People Act; Parliament (Qualification of Women) Act; first female MP elected but does not take her seat; conference on reform of the second chamber

1919
Re-Election of Ministers Act

1922
Fall of Lloyd George coalition

1923
Formation of the 1922 Committee

1924
21 January   Government loses confidence vote
8 October   Government loses confidence vote on the Campbell case

1926
Re-Election of Ministers Act

1928
Representation of the People (Equal Franchise) Act

1930
Ullswater committee on electoral reform

1931
Select committee on procedure on public business

1944
Select committee on statutory rules and orders; conference of electoral reform and redistribution of seats

1945
Enunciation of the Salisbury convention

1946
Third report from the select committee on procedure

1948
Conference of party leaders on reform of the House of Lords

1948
Representation of the People Act

1949
Parliament Act

Further Reading

S. Ball, 'The 1922 Committee: The Formative Years, 1922–1945', *Parliamentary History*, ix (1990), 129–57

J. Eaves, *Emergency Powers and the Parliamentary Watchdog: Parliament and the Executive in Britain* (1958)

P. Norton, 'The Growth of the Constituency Role of the MP', *Parliamentary Affairs*, xlvii (1994), 705–20

—— 'The Organisation of Parliamentary Parties', in *The House of Commons in the Twentieth Century*, ed. S. A. Walkland (Oxford, 1979), 7–68

—— 'The Parliamentary Party and Party Committees', in *Conservative Century: The Conservative Party since 1900*, ed. A. Seldon and S. Ball (Oxford, 1994), 97–144

R. M. Punnett, *Front-Bench Opposition: The Role of the Leader of the Opposition, the Shadow Cabinet and Shadow Government in British Politics* (1973)

M. Rush, *The Role of the Member of Parliament since 1868: From Gentlemen to Players* (Oxford, 2001).

20 The House of Commons since 1949
Paul Seaward

Even during the post-war glow of satisfaction with parliament there were some dissenting voices: Christopher Hollis's *Can Parliament Survive?*, published in 1946, expressed a then relatively unusual scepticism. It was more common by the 1960s, and well before the end of the century a narrative about parliament's inexorable decline became firmly embedded in academic, political and popular discussions of the subject. Influential voices, like those of Richard Crossman and Bernard Crick, pointed out how policy was really made elsewhere, in cabinet, or by civil servants; many others assumed that MPs were simply creatures of their party whips; anti-Europeans protested that parliament's sovereignty was being gradually ceded to Europe. Some of this was exaggerated, and some of it repeated old critiques. But it was true that in the late 20th century the formal powers of the executive in the House of Commons continued to grow, while the respect in which parliament and its members were held by the public went into a steep decline, and the constraints under which parliament operated became ever tighter. At the same time, however, there was an alternative, and in some ways contradictory, story: the House of Commons acquired new tools helping it to hold the government to account; its members became more professional and more effective, and also less ready to accept without demur a party line; and parliament and its members began to become more open to public scrutiny than ever before.

The Scope of Westminster Politics

The most significant changes related to external institutional pressures. Underlying the discussion of the future of democracy and democratic control of policy in the west has been the notion of globalization. As it has become more apparent how easily one country's financial, industrial and scientific activities can affect another's, calls to collaborate with other states – and even to subordinate domestic political imperatives to those of the collaboration – have become more insistent. Domestic concerns at the apparent loss of control over various areas of foreign and domestic policy have grown with them. The structures of formal co-operation between nation states established in the second half of the 20th century – the United Nations, the European Union, NATO and the international financial institutions – have been loaded with significance for parliament, although initially they had relatively little impact. A parliamentary aspect to the creation of shared defensive systems was accepted with the creation of the Western European Union in 1955 and the North Atlantic Assembly (subsequently the NATO parliamentary assembly) in the same year, both bringing together parliamentarians from all the member states; in 1991, when the Conference on Security and Cooperation in Europe was developed into a more formal institution (the OSCE), it, too, was given a similar parliamentary assembly.

The most significant step towards interstate collaboration, however, has been the European Union. The United Kingdom's accession to what was then the European Economic Community on 1 January 1973 began a series of fiercely debated shifts in constitutional theory and reality. The European Communities Act 1972 provided for certain legislation agreed through the institutions of the Community to have direct legal effect in the UK. Initially, this only covered a limited field. But it was expanded under the Single European Treaty of 1986 (given effect in the UK by the European Communities (Amendment) Act 1986) and the Maastricht Treaty of 1992 (given effect in the UK by the European Communities (Amendment) Act 1993). The judgements of the European Court of Justice and the House of Lords in the *Factortame* case of 1989–90, according to some, showed that the 1972 act had effectively put an end to the UK's parliamentary sovereignty: the courts recognized that it required them to ignore a subsequent act of parliament which conflicted with European law.

As much new domestic legislation was now being created through negotiations between ministers and civil servants at European level, ensuring the democratic legitimacy of that process became a key concern for parliamentarians and policy makers. The European parliament has provided a measure of democratic accountability for the law-making structures of the Community. It was, at first, very feeble, while it consisted merely of delegations from the parliaments of each member state, like the assemblies for the WEU and NATO. The introduction of a system of direct elections to the parliament in 1978 (under the European Assembly Elections Act 1977) created a more significant body, though many parliamentarians did not think it so.

At Westminster, however, parliamentarians were more concerned to retain their own oversight of European legislation. In order to ensure that the House of Commons was aware of European legislation in draft, and could influence the UK government's position on it, the House set up a new mechanism to examine legislative proposals emanating from the European institutions. A select committee was established in 1974, responsible for sifting all proposals and making recommendations to the House on whether they raised issues of major political or legal importance and required to be debated. The Labour government made an undertaking that it would not agree to any legislative instrument recommended by the committee for debate until after the debate had been held, a commitment which was converted into a resolution of the House in 1980. At the same time, in order to cope with the volume of instruments which the committee were recommending for debate, new standing committees on European legislation (on the analogy of the then structure of standing committees dealing with statutory instruments) were created to provide a forum for debate on these measures. The EU legislation 'scrutiny system' is regarded as a success, and generally seen in the UK as more effective than similar structures operated in other EU countries; European legislation has also become a specialist area in which the skirmishes between the supporters and opponents (of various shades) of the UK's involvement in 'Europe' have been fought out. Nevertheless, across Europe, there is a general feeling that the growth and elaboration of the inter-governmental European institutions has not been sufficiently controlled by parliamentary bodies at either national or European level. Strengthening scrutiny and democratic control within the European Union, and greater co-operation between national parliaments and the European parliament has been one of the themes of debate since the mid-1990s on the 'democratic deficit' and the EU's constitutional future.

A second challenge to the doctrine of parliamentary sovereignty was presented in 1998. The UK was the first country to ratify the European Convention on Human Rights in 1951, and after the convention came into force two years later it became binding on the UK in international law. It was not, however, enforceable by UK courts. While the courts did interpret the law in cases of ambiguity as consonant with the convention, no change in domestic law was made to give the convention direct effect. This position changed in 1998, when the Human Rights Act incorporated the European Convention on Human Rights into UK law. In an attempt to square parliamentary sovereignty with commitment to the convention, the act did not permit the courts to strike down or otherwise affect the validity of a UK statute where it found it incompatible with human rights under the convention. Instead it invented the 'declaration of incompatibility', a statement that a provision of UK legislation was in violation of the convention, which the court would make when necessary: it would then be for parliament to choose whether or not to change the law as required.

A third way in which parliament accepted constraints on its own powers was to devolve them to sub-parliaments. A system of devolution had been created for Northern Ireland under the Government of Ireland Act 1920, although direct rule was restored in Northern Ireland following the first stage of the insurgency there in 1972. Discussions on reviving devolved government continued intermittently for the next three and a half decades, though hampered by the bitterness of hostilities and the strength of Irish republicanism. In Scotland and Wales the devolution question, forced by the rise to electoral strength of the Scottish National Party and Plaid Cymru, pushed the Labour Party, reluctantly, to agree to devolved parliaments there in the late 1970s. However, the persistent hostility of many Labour members (whose opposition focused on the so-called West Lothian Question, persistently put by Tam Dalyell) forced them to make their introduction (under the Scotland Act 1978 and the Wales Act

1978) subject to referenda in both countries. In Wales there proved to be no appetite for a devolved assembly; in Scotland not enough to meet the high threshold that was required.

Twenty years later, however, and following the steady growth of the nationalist parties and the decline of the Conservatives in both countries, another Labour government tried again. After another referendum only six months after their election, in September 1997, the Scotland Act 1998 created the Scottish parliament, with powers to legislate in a set of defined areas, with 73 members elected on a first-past-the-post basis, and an additional 56 members elected from local party lists. Parliament did not quite give up its right to legislate on devolved matters, although there is an undertaking by the UK government (known as the 'Sewel Convention') not to do so without the consent of the Scottish government. In Wales, where devolution never attracted the same level of support as in Scotland, the Government of Wales Act transferred only powers delegated under statute, and no primary law-making powers. The first elections took place in May 1999: the 60-seat assembly is divided between first-past-the-post and additional members on a similar basis to that used on Scotland. Doubts that the system of devolution in Wales would be sustainable in the long term led to the government establishing a commission, chaired by Lord Richard, which in 2004 recommended that primary law-making powers be conferred on the assembly: the government agreed to cautious moves in this direction, though it said that full primary legislation powers would only be conceded on the basis of the support of a two-thirds majority of members and a referendum, as well as approval by both houses of parliament. In Northern Ireland the Good Friday Agreement and a referendum in 1998 paved the way for the restoration of devolved government, with primary law-making powers: over the next few years it made predictably bumpy progress, suspended for over five years from 2002.

Quite apart from parliament's voluntary – and theoretically reversible – surrender of its freedom of legislative manœuvre, a debate has grown concerning the relationship between the courts and parliament and the extent to which the overriding sovereignty of parliament continues to be defensible or operable. Some have argued that besides the Human Rights Act or the European Communities Act domestic law sets limits to what parliament may do, or, as one influential judge has put it, there is a 'bipolar sovereignty of the Crown in Parliament and the Crown in its courts'.[1] Furthermore, the increasing use of referenda over the past 30 years have indicated the importance of the issues at stake; but they have also suggested declining confidence in the full-blown theory of parliamentary sovereignty – something which has fuelled a messy political debate over whether or not a referendum is required for the UK to accept the latest changes to the European treaties under the 2007 Lisbon Treaty.

---

[1] Stephen Sedley, quoted in C. Turpin and A. Tomkins, *British Government and the Constitution* (Cambridge, 2007), 67.

The Electorate and Parliament

The redistribution of 1948 was the last to be done by a specific act of parliament. In 1949 the House of Commons (Redistribution of Seats) Act created a set of boundary commissions which would keep the boundaries, size and number of parliamentary constituencies under review. This has meant regular changes in the number of constituencies and thus members: in 1950 it changed to 625; in 1955 to 630, in 1974 to 635, in 1983 to 650, 1990 to 651 and in 1995 to 659. The statutory requirement for Scotland to have a minimum of 71 constituencies at Westminster was removed by the Scotland Act 1998. Following a recommendation of the boundary commission in 2003, Scottish representation was reduced from 72 to 59. Therefore there were 646 constituencies in the parliament elected in 2005.

Post-war dissatisfaction with British politics initially focused on the way the electoral system created two parties which were ideologically deeply opposed but in terms of actual policy (in the corporatist and 'Butskellite' politics of the 1950s and 1960s) not all that dissimilar. The drawbacks of the UK's 'first-past-the-post' electoral system received regular, but rarely too serious, airings, particularly when it delivered massive majorities as a result of relatively small shifts of opinion (as it did in 1945, 1959, 1966, 1983 and 1997). The most significant discussion of an alteration to the UK's electoral system took place shortly after the Labour win in the election of 1997. In 1997 the Labour Party had committed itself to a referendum on the voting system for the House of Commons, seeking some sort of coalition of social democratic forces. But the scale of Labour's victory in the general election of that year meant that the subsequent report into voting systems, the output of a commission headed by Roy Jenkins, a former Labour cabinet minister, but one of its defectors to the new Social Democratic Party (SDP), was in reality shelved before it was even completed – although the use of proportional voting systems for the devolved assemblies created a laboratory in which proportional representation can be tested in the UK.

Even if the voting system remained the same, the conduct of elections in the UK changed dramatically as they became dominated by national media campaigning. The first – extremely incompetent – televised party election broadcasts were held in 1951; but perhaps of greater significance was the effort poured into national campaigning through advertising and determined efforts to manipulate the media. All this required money, and resulted in what came to be seen by many as an 'arms race' in party funding. The committee on standards in public life calculated in 1998 that Conservative expenditure in an election year had grown from £3.6 million (£6.6m at 1997 prices) in 1983 to £28.3 million in 1997; Labour spending from £2.2 million (£4 million at 1997 prices) to £26 million in 1997. It has been argued that the 'race' has been largely illusory, the result of Labour spending catching up with Conservative spending; but the idea of a race has been enormously influential, and it has coincided with a rapid decline in the membership of political parties – and thus their income from ordinary members. The committee on standards in public life produced a report on the issue which resulted in an attempt to regulate national election expenditure. The existing system of controls on political spending was effectively that of the Corrupt and Illegal Practices Act 1883, which carefully limited the expenditure of each candidate within the constituency, but said nothing about the national expenditure of the parties. The Political Parties, Elections and Referendums Act 2000 (PPERA) established a complex (and much criticized) system of regulation for political parties and their funding, and an electoral commission to oversee it. The act required parties to supply to the commission details of their income and expenditure and to declare details of donations they had received; it also imposed limits on national expenditure by each political party, in addition to the limits on expenditure in individual constituencies. Despite this, the funding of party politics is still seen as a problem after the 2005 election, particularly as it was apparent that loans had been used to circumvent the declaration requirements of PPERA. Meanwhile, other aspects of elections came under scrutiny, as turnouts have fallen steeply, and efforts to encourage people to vote through devices such as postal voting proved susceptible to fraud.

Members of Parliament

The second half of the century saw a transformation in the nature of MPs and their conception of their task. The post-war expansion of the welfare state and the further growth of regulation dramatically increased the way in which the individual came into contact with the state – and so dramatically increased the demands on MPs to help their constituents to negotiate their relationship with it, while also increasing the areas in which MPs could work to achieve reform. There remained for years wide variations in the degree to which individual members accepted an obligation to act as an advice service for individual constituents, but the pressure was clearly felt, most obviously in the size of MPs' postbags, frequently quoted as a measure of the degree to which they were subject to the demands of their constituents. The creation of the parliamentary commissioner for administration (the 'ombudsman') in 1967 provided MPs with an arm of sorts enabling them to refer the complaints of their constituents against maladministration by central government, although the system helped only a very small minority.

It was not just constituents who made new calls on members' time. Interest and pressure groups had been part of the British political landscape since well before the 19th century, but the proliferation of specialized organizations since the war (often related to the activities of the welfare state), each with a cause to promote and MPs to convince, helped to fill up the days of representatives as never before. A lively lobbying industry grew, with clients to impress with their contacts. By 1995, according to the committee on standards in public life, almost 30% of members had consultancy arrangements; 26 MPs had agreements with public relations or lobbying firms. There have been several calls for a mandatory register of lobbyists: committees of the House proposed on a number of occasions that the House itself should adopt such a register, most recently in 1991, although this was rejected by the government. The committee on standards in public life also rejected the idea in 1995 and 2000. Pressure for members themselves to be regulated was inevitable. A 1947 resolution signalled the growing importance of the lobbying industry by making it explicit that it was improper for a member to enter into a contractual agreement with an outside body which limited his freedom of action, or made him a representative of anyone other than his constituents. In 1969 a select committee on members' interests (the Strauss committee) proposed a public register of members' interests, but it was only after the bankruptcy and trial of John Poulson in 1971–4 exposed his corruption of a number of members that the idea was accepted and a register was introduced in 1974. Little more was done until the early 1990s. The John Browne case in 1990, the 'cash for questions' affair of 1994 in which two members agreed to table parliamentary questions in exchange for payment, and subsequent allegations about the conduct of two junior ministers in receipt of financial benefits from Mr Al Fayed, the owner of Harrods, suggested that self-declaration and registration was not quite enough to change a complacent parliamentary culture. The result (by way of the committee on standards in public life, set up by Prime Minister John Major in 1995) was a new structure for handling conflicts of interests: a committee of the House, the standards and privileges committee, together with an independent officer, the parliamentary commissioner for standards, and the prohibition of members from paid advocacy.

With these pressures, it inevitably became more difficult except in the safest constituencies to undertake the role on an amateur basis. Although governments were extremely wary of feeding criticism of the political gravy train, there was pressure to provide adequate compensation for undertaking a role that was becoming less and less compatible with a substantial outside career. The pre-war salary of £600 was increased to £1,000 in 1946 following the work of a select committee; a further select committee review of 1953–4 proposed a further £500 increase, but the government substituted a more voter-friendly allowance of £2 a sitting day. The appointment of an external committee – the Lawrence committee – in 1963 indicated a new approach to a perennial problem: its recommendation of an increase to £3,250 (including an element of £1,250 for expenses) was accepted the same year. In 1971 the issue was referred to the Review Body on Top Salaries, whose recommendations included the principle that members should be paid on the basis that they were undertaking a full-time job. Since then, the body and its successor (the Senior Salaries Review Body, SSRB) have made periodic recommendations on pay, although these have often been resisted by the government of the day. In 1987 the House created a formal link with civil service pay, a system which has survived, with some changes in the uprating formula and three-yearly reports from the SSRB.

The role of an MP was now more than just a full-time job, however. The 1971 Top Salaries Review Body report recommended that members should not themselves be responsible for financing the facilities they needed in order to do their job. An allowance for secretarial assistance was introduced under the Labour government in 1969, originally of £500, and in subsequent years this developed into an overall budget for employing secretarial and research assistance: by April 2005 the maximum staffing allowance had grown to over £84,000, and in the 2004–5 session, there were almost 2,600 staff for 659 members.

With such pressures, and increasing rewards, the profile of the MP changed. Already by the 1970s most members were full-time politicians. The number of MPs with political backgrounds (as researchers and special advisers) grew rapidly in the 1990s, to 14.1% classified as 'politician/political organizer' after the 2005 election. The number of women members remained from the war until 1987 around 3% to 4% of the total. But the elections of that year saw a modest increase to 6.3% – perhaps the result of the example of the first female prime minister – and in 1992 there was a further step to 9.2%. The real change came with the election of 1997 and the Labour party's policy of introducing all-women shortlists to select candidates in some constituencies. In that year 120 women were elected, 18.2% of the total, of which 101 were Labour. With this the gender balance seems to have reached a new plateau, although in the Scottish parliament a third of the members are women, and in the National Assembly for Wales numbers are almost equal. MPs remain almost entirely white: in 1987 the first non-white MPs since the war were elected (four Labour members); by 2005 there were 13.

The change in the membership has had significant effects on the culture of parliament. The demand to allow breastfeeding in committee rooms was only the most startling of new approaches to the way parliament might conduct its affairs, and one that encouraged broader debate about how an ancient institution, still somewhat set in its ways, might change.

Parties and Parliament

If the nature of the membership of the House of Commons and MPs' conception of their role have been transformed over the last half century, party has remained the constant and dominant organizing principle of the House. The government was already well able to control the business of the House, both because the machinery by which it could do so was set out in standing orders, and because a parliamentary majority would enable it to timetable the work of the House largely as it chose within that framework. Nevertheless, business has normally been organized by negotiation through the 'usual channels', the informal meetings of the government's business managers with the opposition. The process is presided over by the private secretary to the government chief whip, a civil servant. The post was held by a handful of individuals since the war, concentrating sufficient knowledge and power to make them seem to many members (including Crossman as leader of the House) as *éminences grises* of the government's operation in the Commons and key links in the relationship between government and opposition. Oppositions themselves became more organized and more formal in the period immediately after the war, with Clement Attlee establishing for the first time a system of shadow ministers before the 1945 election. An allowance for the opposition parties introduced in 1974 – known as 'Short money' after the Labour leader of the House, Ted Short, who brought in the proposals – was intended simply to support them in their activities within parliament, to allow them to confront the civil-service backed government on a rather more equal basis.

The iron grip of the party leaderships and the whips has been seen as parliament's ugliest feature. Yet the whips – although they included formidable disciplinarians such as Michael Cocks, the chief whip in the James Callaghan government of 1976–9 – were less frightening than many would have them believed, the sanctions at their disposal meagre to all but the feeblest or the most avid for foreign travel. Members have voted against the party line in all parliaments since the war, but the number of 'rebels' and the frequency with which they have rebelled has climbed. Up until the Conservative government of 1959 rebellions were rare enough for it to be commonly accepted that a defeat for the government in the House of Commons would make it necessary to resign. But during the 1970s, and as a result especially of the European Communities Bill of 1972, rebellions became much more common; the Conservative government of 1970–4 was defeated on five occasions as a result of the dissenting votes and abstentions of its own backbenchers. Such dissent became regular under the Labour government of 1974–9, partly because of the factionalism of the party in the late seventies and the effectiveness of the Tribune Group: the minority government suffered 42 defeats, 23 of which were attributed to the dissenting votes and abstentions on its own side. That parliament witnessed a post-war high of dissenting votes (28% of all divisions witnessed dissenting votes – compared to 0.5% in the parliament of 1964–6, also under a Labour government). Amid the enthusiasm and the discipline of the first parliament of the Blair premiership, 1997–2001 intra-party dissent dropped back to levels not seen since the 1960s, although dissent continued to be high in comparison with the late 1940s and 1950s. Yet in the second Blair term, 2001–5, it grew to higher levels than ever: the vote on going to war in Iraq in March 2003 resulted in what was claimed to be the highest party rebellion since the revolt against Peel over the corn laws in 1846. Party discipline changes with circumstances:

parties which are hungry for power (such as the Labour Party in 1997) may be more willing to suppress individual views for the sake of party cohesion. But party discipline overall has weakened in an age in which the more professional career politicians who now constitute a larger element of the membership of the House are less content than before to follow a party line, and more concerned to carve out their own political careers, while in the media age MPs are more exposed to condemnation if they seem to say one thing and vote another.

Modernizing the House: Government and Parliament

During the 1960s the doubts about parliament and national efficiency, first heard decades before, were revived. One strand of opinion doubted that parliament was an adequate political structure to deal with the quickening pace of change in the structures of economic life. Was it not simply too cumbersome, too old-fashioned, too amateurish to respond? Another, though, began to worry again about executive dominance. Was parliament strong enough and independent enough to check a powerful executive? Were its members too much dominated by the whips – and did they have the tools at their disposal to undertake their task in a professional way?

Such criticisms reflected other debates about Britain's role in the world and about all of Britain's institutions; they reflected the changes in the membership of the House; and they reflected the return to power in 1964 (for the first time since 1951) of a Labour Party with an ambitious programme of economic and social reform, but a small majority, a change from the big majorities to which post-war governments had been accustomed. But the questions formulated by Labour's leader of the House Richard Crossman when he thought about parliamentary reform in 1966, and the understanding of parliament they implied – that parliament was not, and had not been for some time, a policy-making body, but one whose function was to influence policy and to legitimize government – profoundly influenced subsequent thinking about the modernizing of parliament.

It was not the only strand of thought on reforming parliament: there have long been plaintive calls to temper executive dominance by providing backbenchers with a formal say in the way business is organized, through a business committee such as those which are responsible for setting the parliamentary timetable in other legislatures. But this has rarely been considered seriously by governments, and since the 1960s government-backed reform proposals have usually tried on the one hand to ease the passage of government business while on the other to offer more effective systems of holding the government to account. The greatest change was achieved only at the end of the period, when the new Labour government of 1997, backed by an unusually large number of new members less tolerant of what were seen as outdated parliamentary practices, determined to streamline the House. The committee on the modernization of the House of Commons, particularly under the chairmanship of two reforming leaders of the House, Ann Taylor and Robin Cook, became the agent for major change.

Many regarded the House's long sitting hours as the most obvious emblem of its antiquated practices. The ambitious legislative programmes and the difficult political circumstances of the governments of the 1960s and 1970s helped to push the average length of each day's sitting to well over eight hours (the last time it had regularly reached those levels was in the first decade of the 20th century). The number of sitting days in each session had grown as well, more routinely lasting between 150 and 200 days (in the first half of the century sessions tended to be between 100 and 150 days). Governments had long tinkered with proposals to overcome the problem. Among the proposals pursued when Crossman was leader of the House was an experiment with morning sittings, abandoned when it was found to have had little impact. In the mid-1990s a specifically created committee (the 'Jopling committee') proposed, and the government agreed, to move some non-government business into weekly morning sittings. They also made life a little more comfortable for members by abandoning a number of Fridays on which private members' business was taken.

But the only real means of reducing sitting hours was to use the time in the chamber more effectively. Shifting more legislation into standing committee was one way of doing so. Since 1945–6 standing committees had become the routine method of dealing with the committee stages of almost all bills. Without them, the government legislative programmes of the 1940s, 50s and 60s would have been scarcely possible, although the spread to those committees of all the devices of party and parliamentary discipline – whips and guillotines – would give complaints of a 'legislative sausage machine' much justification. Timetabling proceedings on a bill, however, through the guillotine, or more properly, allocation of time orders, was the most effective way of speeding up progress. There was a major drawback: though effective, guillotines made it possible for oppositions to claim that bills had been railroaded through, with parts of them poorly considered, or not considered at all. Although informal deals to timetable the progress of a bill, through the 'usual channels', were common, formal and enforceable guillotines were rarely used more than once or twice a year before the mid-1970s; their frequency increased a little in the later 1970s, 1980s and early 1990s, with highs of ten bills in 1975–6 and 13 in 1988–9. Governments hoped to make the guillotine more acceptable by inventing a procedure in which a formal timetable for the consideration of a bill would be drawn up in collaboration with the opposition. 'Programming' of this kind was regularly proposed in external reports and internal committees, but was finally achieved through the recommendations of the modernization committee in 1997: after co-operation between the parties had broken down it was introduced by the government without the agreement of the Conservative opposition, at first on an experimental basis, and then was made permanent in 2004.

Programming had now become routine, the most significant change in the legislative process since 1946.

The committee proposed other time-saving devices which were subsequently introduced by the government: deferred divisions – saving time wasted in the division lobbies – were brought in in 2000; a 'parallel chamber', sitting in the old Grand Committee Room off Westminster Hall, began in 1999 and was incorporated into standing orders in 2002. Enabling bills to be 'carried over' from one session to another eased some of the pressure on the legislative timetable. Furthermore, the government brought forward the time at which the House began business each day, providing for an earlier finish to its main business on most days of the week.

While all this made lives a little easier for members condemned to wait on three-line whips or forced to spend long hours hoping to make a speech in the chamber, it did nothing to increase the opportunities for individual members to pursue agendas independent of their party: indeed, the party machines were highly suspicious of any attempt to do so. Private members' time, removed entirely during the war, was grudgingly restored after the 1948–9 session, with after 1950 20 Fridays provided for individual backbenchers to propose bills, or motions. Motions – already seen as a waste of time before the war – were eventually abandoned and swapped for more bill time, and notable private members' bill successes (though often achieved because the government eventually lent the bill concerned some of its own legislative time to ensure its passage) included the Abortion Act 1967 and the Sexual Offences Act 1967. In general, though, most private members' bills were blocked either by governments themselves or those acting on their behalf. Although the amount of time available for private members' bills had not markedly diminished over the century, their success rate did. By the later 20th century most of them achieved no more than to draw attention to the issue concerned and to emphasize the degree to which the government now dominated the House.

Modernizing the House: Holding the Government to Account

Not surprisingly, modernization in general had favoured government. More efficient processes for handling business, especially legislation, during the late 20th century may have made parliament seem more 'modern' but they speeded the passage of government business at the expense of more close scrutiny of the detail of its legislation. Oppositions, as they concentrated on headline policy issues, rather than the nitty-gritty of expenditure and administration, had in some ways helped the government to establish a commanding position. Long before 1949, for example, the government's financial estimates had become pegs on which to hang debates on the key party political issues of the day rather than the opportunity for searching audit of ministers' sums. Indeed, this became recognized as the old formalities of the committee of supply were gradually forgotten, and supply debates became 'opposition days', chances for the opposition parties to select a topic for debates which rehearsed well-established policies rather than seriously tested ministers and their civil servants. Much of the process of agreeing the estimates became purely formal. Question time in the House, too, continued to grow into a forum for ritual, but intensely political exchanges, particularly once Harold Macmillan began in 1961 the fixed twice-weekly slot for questions to the prime minister, replacing the previous practice of taking questions to the prime minister each day after all the questions put down for departmental ministers had been disposed of. (In 1997 the Labour government replaced two 15-minute slots with a single half an hour each Wednesday.) Prime minister's question time quickly developed into the focus of the political week: to much of the media an effective way of gauging the political temperature, to many reformers a boorish display of all that was appalling about party politics.

But while the House of Commons seemed to be engaged in a permanent election campaign, more professional and more assertive individual members – and their growing numbers of staff – were finding other ways of looking at the detail of what the government was up to. During the 1960s they discovered the value of putting down questions for written answer ('unstarred' questions) as a way of obtaining information both for their own political campaigns and to help pursue constituency issues. The result was rapid growth: around 18 questions were put down for written answers each day in the 1950s. By the mid-1990s it was more like 200, despite numerous attempts to control it. The asking and answering of parliamentary questions became an elaborate sort of game played out between governments and MPs, in which it was crucial for government departments not to be found out providing an inaccurate or misleading answer – but in which, on sensitive points at least, they sought to reveal as little as possible. It was a game that was exposed in lurid detail in the exhaustive 1996 enquiry by Sir Richard Scott into the export to Iraq of components for Saddam Hussein's 'super-gun'; but the enquiry also showed how astute use of written questions could leave a government dangerously exposed.

The most outstanding weapon in the emerging new doctrine of 'scrutiny', however, was the government's gradual acceptance of a systematic structure of committees, the creation of what has come to be called the select committee 'system'. Post-war governments, especially the Labour government of 1945–50 with its heavy legislative agenda, were reluctant to strengthen bodies which might divert the resources of departments or, worse still, try to exercise their influence over them. The post-war estimates committee and its six sub-committees did, albeit gently, push at the boundaries of what government regarded as tolerable inquisitiveness concerning the detail of the running of individual departments. Worries about how the nationalized industries could be held accountable to parliament led also to the creation (as a result of Conservative back-bench pressure on the Conservative government) of the nationalized industries select committee from 1951. But although the inquiries of the estimates committee led to more information being placed in the public domain, their achievements were extremely modest, limited by the small number of members engaged in them (49 on the estimates committee), and a lack of access to specialized knowledge of their subject. Pressure built up for something more sophisticated, and the Labour governments of the mid-1960s gingerly made some concessions. The procedure committee in the 1964–5 session proposed expanding the terms of reference of the estimates committee into 'how the departments of state carry out their responsibilities and to consider their Estimates of Expenditure and Reports'. The Labour government broadly accepted the point, but when in 1966 the leader of the House, Richard Crossman, introduced his proposals, they were seen as half-hearted and unsatisfactory: a select committee on science and technology, four 'departmental' committees, and, later, a race relations and immigration committee. In 1971 the Conservatives rationalized it a little, with an expenditure committee and four sub-committees, to look at matters of policy and efficiency and economy in administration. The modern select committee system, though, came through back-bench pressure. In the 1977–8 session a procedure committee report proposed a much more logical, and potentially powerful, structure. A year later it was accepted by the incoming Conservative government, whose leader of the House, Norman St John Stevas, enthusiastically suggested that it would 'redress the balance of power (as between parliament and the executive) to enable the House of Commons to do more effectively the job it has been elected to do',[2] although the lingering doubts of ministers and government departments were perhaps reflected in the lengthy delays before the system actually began to operate, in the carefully drawn 1980 'Osmotherley rules' governing how civil servants could deal with the committees, and in the dissatisfaction that was routinely expressed by committees concerning the co-operativeness of departments. The expenditure committee, the nationalized industries committee, and the other specialized committees were abolished and replaced by 14 'departmentally related' select committees to 'examine the expenditure, administration and policy' of the departments concerned. Over the following 20 years or so, although their performance was variable, they had the effect of making parliamentarians' engagement with the processes and personnel of government much deeper; they contributed to the opening up of government and the civil service; and they dug their way into the major policy issues of the day.

There remained many reasons to be dissatisfied with the system, though. There was never enough time or energy or expertise among members or staff to match the growing professionalism of the bureaucracy. There were justified suspicions about the interference of ministers

---

[2] Hansard, *Commons Debates*, cmlxix, cols. 34–253.

and party whips in the deliberations of individual committees, as well as resentment from backbenchers about the way in which appointments to committees were filtered through party structures. As the 1997 Labour government's modernization programme was criticized for removing many of the remaining obstacles to the easy passage of government legislation, many commentators returned to the ideal of creating a more powerful select committee system. In 1999 the liaison committee, made up of the chairmen of all select committees, pushed for 'shifting the balance' (picking up St John Stevas's phrase of 1979) between parliament and government. Some response was made to such criticisms in the report of the modernization committee in 2002. By providing an enhanced salary for the chairs of select committees it aimed to encourage talented members to pursue a more parliamentary, rather than ministerial, career. But the idea that parties and their whips should lose their control over appointments to committees was extraordinarily rejected in the House itself by what was seen by many as subterfuge on the part of the whips themselves. The proposed new six-monthly sessions at which the liaison committee interrogate the prime minister did bed down as a permanent feature of the constitutional landscape, although the early sessions tended to emphasize the political skills of the prime minister rather than those of the committee.

Organization

The House of Commons returned in 1950 to its own chamber, albeit one completely reconstructed to designs by Giles Gilbert Scott. Since then, the demand for office accommodation for members and their growing staff – as well as the expansion of the permanent staff of parliament – has resulted in further building work and, eventually, the expansion of the parliamentary estate. The Norman Shaw buildings on the Embankment were refurbished for the House in 1973–9; buildings on Parliament Street were occupied from 1991, and others on Millbank have been used since the early 1990s. The construction of a new office block on Bridge Street was first proposed in the early 1960s, but it was not until 2001 that Portcullis House was completed and occupied.

The sprawling growth of the parliamentary estate, and the House's increasing legal responsibilities for the employment of its own staff was the catalyst for the development of the House as an organization in its own right. Before 1978 expenditure on the House was directly under the treasury's control. The House of Commons (Administration) Act of 1978 was the most significant milestone in the way to a more corporate approach to the increased demand from members for a more comprehensive and more professional service. The act established the House of Commons commission, a body composed of the Speaker, the leader of the House, shadow leader, and backbench representatives. It created a unified service for the House of Commons, and gave the House control over its own financial estimates and its own estate. A series of three reviews of the management and services of the House have coaxed it further. Sir Robin Ibbs's review of 1990, followed by the Braithwaite report of 1999 and the Tebbitt report of 2007, encouraged the House's departments to work more closely together and adopt management practices now common in government departments, on the way creating for the House a proper chief executive.

The House moved extremely tentatively into a new media age. Members were anxious to secure full coverage of their parliamentary utterances, but reluctant to expose parliament or themselves to too much vulgar commentary or criticism, of the kind that would increasingly be the normal style of political reporting. Parliament's attempts to hold back the challenge from the media to its assumed right to be the principal forum of political debate were sometimes absurd – as in the resistance during the 1950s to the abandonment of the rule which prevented the BBC broadcasting material on a subject which would be debated within the next 14 days – and were frequently undermined by those members who were less nervous of publicity. It was only in 1975 that the House agreed to let its proceedings be regularly broadcast by radio, and not until 1989 that it finally succumbed to television broadcasting.

Parliament in a Crowded Political World

Bernard Crick – who was the most dominant voice among those calling for reforms to parliament in the 1960s – wrote in 1970 that:

> After all these criticisms, I hold ... to a somewhat old-fashioned but true view of things: that as much as one needs to specialise and distinguish, something has to pull all threads together and look at all things that affect each other as part of one system. And in our national life that is Parliament ... this is the ultimate point and test of select committee procedure and 'opening up' the civil service; that all those who have problems in common should meet, and that meeting place is Parliament. When people of real or believed importance think that Parliament can be by-passed, be they Ministers, industrialists, trade union leaders, it is up to Parliament to prove that they are wrong. The power of Parliament was never great, so cannot be restored; but its authority, influence and prestige was once greater, and should be greater again – but in a very different manner.[3]

Since then, parliament can lay claim to modest advances: its members have become more professional, competent and (despite many laments for the greats of the past) more independent than before; it has found new and effective ways to challenge governments and its civil servants; and it

---

[3] B. Crick, 'Whither Parliamentary Reform?', in *The Commons in Transition*, ed. A. H. Hanson and B. Crick (1970), 275–6.

has, once or twice, provided the sort of focus for national life that Crick talked about – most notably during the 2003 debates on the Iraq war. But paradoxically its authority, influence and prestige seem, if anything, to have diminished. In part this has been due to the unshakeable cynicism of the British media; in part it has reflected the hostility of the public to a salaried political class; in part it is the result of a more open political system in which the things that are remembered are the scandals, rather than the systems that have exposed them. But there are more fundamental changes as well. At the beginning of the 21st century the House of Commons was the legislature of a less powerful state exercising a more tempered power; it operated within a much better informed, more plural, society which no longer automatically assumes that parliament should be the natural meeting place of 'our national life', and may no longer completely understand the concept of a national life anyway. As it talks more about scrutiny and less about sovereignty, the House of Commons has lost the grandeur that once it had; as it has grown up into an institution and not just an event, it risks becoming just another institution, venerable, maybe, but no longer quite the national event that once it was.

Chronology

1949
Parliament Act; Boundary Commission established under the House of Commons (Redistribution of Seats) Act

1951
Creation of national industries committee

1961
Introduction of fixed weekly slot for prime minister's questions

1966
Crossman reforms: introduction of new select committee structure

1967
Creation of the parliamentary commissioner for administration (the ombudsman)

1972
European Communities Act; direct rule restored in Northern Ireland

1973
UK's accession to the European Economic Community

1974
Introduction of first register of members' interests; introduction of 'Short money' for opposition parties

1978
House of Commons Administration Act; devolution bills for Scotland and Wales; direct elections to European parliament introduced under the European Assembly Elections Act

1979
'New' select committee system established

1981
Official launch of Social Democratic Party; common policy programme with Liberal Party later in the year

1986
Single European Treaty and European Communities (Amendment) Act

1989
Television broadcasting of proceedings of the House of Commons begins; *Factortame* case in conflicts between UK domestic and EU law

1997
Creation of select committee on the modernization of the House of Commons

1998
Human Rights Act; devolution acts for Scotland, Wales and Northern Ireland (Scotland Act, Government of Wales Act and Northern Ireland Act)

2000
Political Parties, Elections and Referendums Act

2001
Completion of new parliamentary building, Portcullis House

Further Reading

P. Cowley, *The Rebels: How Blair Mislaid his Majority* (2005)

The House of Commons in the Twentieth Century, ed. S. A. Walkland (Oxford, 1979)

P. Norton, *Dissension in the House of Commons, 1945–1979* (Oxford, 1980)

P. Seaward and P. Silk, 'The House of Commons', in *The British Constitution in the Twentieth Century*, ed. V. Bogdanor (2003), 139–88

Westminster and Europe: The Impact of the European Union on the Westminster Parliament, ed. P. Giddings and G. Drewry (Basingstoke, 1996)

21 The Parliament of Scotland to 1707
Julian Goodare

A Scottish parliament was established in 1999, answerable to the sovereign Westminster parliament by which it was created. This chapter deals with the previous Scottish parliament, which existed up to 1707. In the middle ages that parliament was a typical feudal assembly; in the 16th century it evolved to become a sovereign body. Although it had a number of differences from the English parliament, there were also enough similarities between the two bodies for them to be able to unite in 1707, creating what was officially a new body – the parliament of Great Britain.

Origins and Development

The Scottish parliament originated in the 13th century, with the classical Latin term *'colloquium'* being first recorded in 1235. Its functions then included the dispensing of justice, though evidence is scanty. A parliament was essentially a fuller and more formal meeting of the king's 'court', with multiple functions in decision-making.

Parliaments became more prominent with the succession crisis following the death of Alexander III (1286), which in turn escalated into the wars of independence. During interregnums, groups of 'guardians' were appointed, often by parliaments, and the reign of King John (1292–6) also saw a high level of parliamentary activity. Contentious decisions like the treaty of Birgham with England (1290) or the suspension of the king from authority (1295) tended to be taken by, or with the concurrence of, parliaments. Contact with the more institutionally developed English parliament may have encouraged the idea of the Scottish body as a distinct entity; the term *'parliamentum'* was first recorded at Birgham in 1290.

Membership

A Parliament of Estates

The earliest parliaments consisted of the king, nobles and higher clergy, though there are hardly any attendance lists. Perhaps from 1295, and more regularly from 1326, the royal burghs sent representatives. The 'community of the realm' – a phrase that could sum up the whole political nation – was often understood to mean parliament, as when the Scottish guardians, elected by parliaments, described themselves as 'guardians of the realm of Scotland elected by the community of that realm'.[1] However, phrases such as 'earls, barons and other magnates and the community' (1318) may treat the 'community' as a non-noble additional element.[2] This phrase also introduces the idea of distinct groups within the 'community', and here we encounter the idea of the 'three estates'. For most of its history, the Scottish parliament was a parliament of estates, though there were not always three.

The celebrated phrase 'three estates' was first recorded in 1357.[3] It was evidently already familiar, and soon became a conventional description of Scottish parliaments. There was probably no single moment at which a division into estates was formally adopted; rather it emerged gradually once burgh commissioners started to attend regularly. The threefold division into estates reconciled two existing sets of twofold divisions: clergy and laity on the one hand, and 'lords' and burgesses on the other.

Clergy

The clerical estate consisted of the higher clergy. Descriptions of 13th-century parliaments sometimes mention 'bishops' as a distinct group. From the early 14th century there are regular mentions of 'abbots' (in practice also including priors and other heads of monasteries); these were more numerous than bishops but attended more rarely. There were 13 bishops (14 after 1634); the monastic houses that could be represented numbered 47 to 49, not including nunneries, friaries (which were not feudal property-holders) or Trinitarian canons ('Red Friars'). Small numbers of lesser clergymen occasionally attended. In the 16th century, the monasteries were gradually secularized, coming into the hands of lay 'commendators'; then between 1587 and 1606 the principal monastic lands were 'erected' into secular lordships. Their holders, the 'lords of erection', became secular peers, though still taxed (at a higher rate) with the clergy. Bishops, the remaining part of the clerical estate, were virtually eclipsed in the 1590s, revived gradually after 1600, abolished in 1638, revived in 1661 and abolished for good in 1690.

Nobles

The noble estate originally consisted simply of 'lords' – lay freeholders (feudal tenants in chief). A handful of these held earldoms based on ancient provinces, and there were other great magnates. Lesser freeholders might attend but were less likely to do so. In the late 14th and early 15th centuries, some provincial earldoms became fragmented, while new non-territorial earldoms were created. A distinct group of 'lords of parliament'

---

[1] *Documents Illustrative of the History of Scotland, 1286–1306*, ed. J. Stevenson (2 vols, Edinburgh, 1870), i, no. 27 ('custodes regni Scotiæ per communitatem ejusdem regni electi', 1288).

[2] *Acts of the Parliaments of Scotland*, ed. T. Thomson and C. Innes (12 vols, Edinburgh, 1814–75) (hereafter *APS*), i, 466 ('comitibus baronibus & aliis magnatibus communitateque').

[3] *APS*, i, 491 ('tres communitates').

emerged between 1437 and 1444. These earls and lords became a hereditary peerage with the personal right to attend parliaments.

In 1428 James I tried to remodel the Scottish parliament on English lines, with lesser freeholders sending representatives, but this took no effect. Personal attendance by lesser freeholders remained competent even after the emergence of the parliamentary peerage, but their numbers declined. Handfuls of lesser freeholders sometimes attended parliaments as late as the 1540s. However, in 1560, when lesser freeholders suddenly attended parliament in large numbers, this was regarded as unprecedented and would lead to the establishment of a new estate.

Numbers of peers grew slowly in the 16th century and more rapidly in the 17th. There were 49 peers in 1500, and 136 (some holding more than one peerage) in 1700. To the traditional earls and lords (and occasional dukes), small numbers of marquesses and viscounts were added from the late 16th century onwards. After the union of crowns in 1603, Englishmen were occasionally granted nominal Scottish peerage titles, but rarely if ever attended parliaments. Peers occasionally gave proxies to other peers. Peers' eldest sons occasionally attended, either alongside their fathers or substituting for them.

Burgesses

The burgess estate consisted of commissioners from the royal burghs – those towns liable to pay royal taxation, which also had a monopoly of foreign trade (until 1672). A few important burghs, notably St Andrews and Glasgow, technically had a churchman rather than the crown as their superior, but were treated in practice as royal burghs. All the burghs were real towns, though sometimes small, paying real taxes; there were no English-style 'rotten boroughs'. Charters were occasionally granted for burghs that failed to take root, but the emphasis on payment of taxes meant that these were never considered for parliamentary representation. A handful of small burghs attempted to resign their status (and their tax liability) in the 17th century, though only one, Cromarty, succeeded. Overall, numbers of burghs expanded. By 1488, 33 different burghs had been represented in parliament, though numbers at any one parliament were much smaller. Numbers of burghs on tax rolls were 43 in 1579 and 66 in 1705.

Burgh representatives were chosen by burgh councils. Until 1469, councils were usually elected annually by the burgesses; thereafter the old council chose the new. A few burghs continued to involve the wider burgess community in council elections, in the choice of parliamentary commissioners, or both.

Burghs sometimes sent several commissioners, though only one would normally appear in the official attendance register. There was only one vote per burgh, though Edinburgh (which usually had two commissioners registered) may have had two votes from the late 16th century. Commissioners had plenary powers, though sometimes following a mandate from the burgh in the exercise of these.

The crown sometimes became suspicious of noble influence in burghs and tried to insist that their provosts should be actual trafficking merchants (or, occasionally, craftsmen). This was formalized in 1609, and was taken to apply also to the burghs' parliamentary commissioners. This, plus the fact that the burghs were all real towns, prevented their parliamentary representation from being taken over by the gentry as in England, though the beginnings of such a trend may be discernible in the late 17th century.

The crown sometimes interfered in the representation of particular burghs (especially Edinburgh). James VII nominated burgh councils systematically, which might in due course have given him a large block of parliamentary votes, but this was swept away in 1689. The revolutionary Convention of Estates, uniquely, had its burgh commissioners elected by a poll of the burgesses. Thereafter the franchise remained with unelected burgh councils until 1832.

The burghs' collective identity became more formal in the early 16th century with the emergence of the Convention of Royal Burghs. This institution met more often than parliament (often twice a year), making collective rules, settling inter-burgh disputes, and negotiating with the crown – and parliament. It even sent its own foreign embassies on commercial matters. The Convention of Royal Burghs came to have much the same membership as the burgess estate in parliament. Conventions of Royal Burghs were often held just before parliaments, to prepare legislative proposals and lobbying strategies, and to exercise collective discipline over burghs' parliamentary voting. Parliament in turn found the Convention of Royal Burghs useful in apportioning the burghs' share of taxation among individual burghs.

Shire Commissioners

The process that would lead to the representation of shires began with the 'Reformation' Parliament of 1560. Over 100 Protestant lairds turned up, outnumbering all the other estates put together, and demanded to participate. Their demand was accepted for that occasion, with the promise that the position would be regularized at a future date. There was intermittent debate on this for some years, during which large numbers of lairds sometimes attended conventions of estates (and perhaps parliaments too, though their attendance was not minuted). Eventually, in 1587, an act was passed reviving the previously inoperative act of 1428 for shire representation, adding a definition of the franchise and machinery for holding elections.

The shire electors were freeholders with land valued at 40s. of old extent. Old extent, a traditional valuation, often bore little logical relationship to current land values, but the Scottish 40s. freeholder was usually a substantial landed proprietor – a laird. Each shire had two commissioners except the small Clackmannan and Kinross, with one each. There were 28 shires in 1587, rising to 33 by 1707. Elections were to be held annually at Michaelmas rather than for specific parliaments, though most shires eventually compiled an annual roll of qualified electors rather than holding annual elections. In parliament, the commissioners had one vote per shire until 1640, when the shire representation was effectively doubled by granting them one vote each.

Attendances at some Scottish Parliaments

Parliament of 1290
Bishops	12	
Abbots	34	
Earls	12	
Barons	50	
Overall total		108

Parliament of 1469
Bishops	7	
Abbots	13	
Lesser clergy	3	
Clerical estate total		23
Dukes	1	
Earls	11	
Lords	20	
Lesser freeholders	22	
Noble estate total		54
Burgesses	22	
Burgess estate total		22
Overall total		99

Parliament of 1540
Bishops	10	
Abbots	12	
Lesser clergy	3	
Clerical estate total		25
Earls	10	
Lords	7	
Lesser freeholders	4	
Noble estate total		21
Burgesses (from 7 burghs)	8	
Burgess estate total		8
Officers of state	3	
		3
Overall total		57

Parliament of 1681
Bishops	12	
Clerical estate total		12
Marquess of Atholl president	1	
Dukes	1	
Marquesses	2	
Earls	34	
Lords	19	
Noble estate total		57
Shire commissioners (from 33 shires)	57	
Shires estate total		57
Burgesses (from 59 burghs)	60	
Burgess estate total		60
Officers of state	4	
		4
Overall total		190

The largest number ever in attendance was 232 in 1705. A minimum number cannot be so clearly established, but there were only 13 (from only two estates) in 1526.

In 1661 the franchise was extended to feuars (proprietors with heritable leases), and a qualification of a current rental of £1,000 Scots (£83 sterling) was introduced, reduced in 1681 to £400 (£33 sterling). This allowed the regular representation of Orkney and Shetland, which had an allodial ('udal') tenure without feudal freeholders. The traditional qualification of 40s. of old extent was retained as an alternative, and in 1681 both qualifications were extended by being based 'on property or Superiority' (the latter word meaning feudal overlordship, by then a conveyancing technicality).[4] This franchise remained until 1832, and in the 18th century (aided by the removal of the court of session's electoral jurisdiction in 1707) would allow the large-scale creation of fictitious votes on feudal superiorities.

The shire commissioners were usually termed 'barons'. Strictly speaking, a baron was someone entitled to hold a baron court, roughly equivalent to an English lord of the manor; many shire commissioners did have such courts but there was no requirement for them to do so. The term, however, was more formal and polite than the colloquial 'laird'. Land as such could no longer be considered to be represented in parliament, since some land was held by freeholders whose holdings were too small to qualify them for the franchise.

There were thus four estates – an embarrassingly non-standard number – once the shire commissioners were established. The official phrase 'the three estates' was replaced by the uneasily non-committal 'the estates', which continued even when the abolition of bishops brought the number of estates down to three again.

Others in Parliament

A further group of members of parliament, small but influential, was officers of state. From at least the 15th century the crown's leading ministers, such as chancellor, treasurer, comptroller, clerk register and secretary, attended parliaments; often they were nobles or churchmen, but if not members of another estate they sat *ex officio*. They were all personally members of the lords of the articles, parliament's influential committee. A maximum of eight officers of state was established in 1617.

As a feudal court, the medieval parliament required 'suitors', freeholders obliged by their charters to attend, who in lesser courts constituted the group from which assizes were drawn. They had no substantive function in parliaments, and were certainly not members, but numerous suitors did attend. Shire commissioners, once introduced, were treated as suitors, and suitors as a distinct institution fell into abeyance.

Summons

Parliament, as a feudal court, required 40 days' notice of its summons. The decision to summon it was made by the king. The earliest known

---

[4] *APS*, viii, 353, c. 87.

summonses, in the 1290s, were by individual writs to the magnates, but by 1328 at least, summons was by writs to the sheriff and proclamation. From the late 14th century at least, individual precepts under the signet were also sent to higher clergy, lay magnates and royal burghs – all the members except lesser lay freeholders.

Scottish kings were often personally unavailable. When they were minors, parliaments were held by regents in their name. When David II and James I were in English captivity (1346–57, 1406–24) no parliaments were held, but general councils were held by the king's lieutenants.

Factional disputes occasionally led to rival parliaments, particularly during the civil wars of 1567–73. In May–June 1571 two rival parliaments met almost simultaneously, one in the name of the queen in Edinburgh, the other in the name of the king in nearby Canongate. The covenanters passed a triennial act in 1640 (anticipating the English by a year); this was repealed at the Restoration and not revived even after the Glorious Revolution. Parliament was thereafter required to meet more frequently because it controlled supply, but the parliament of 1689 continued until dissolved by the king's death in 1702, and that elected in 1703 continued until the Union.

Location and Buildings

Medieval parliaments were held in various places, usually monasteries (even the naves of churches). Scone Abbey was the most popular in the 14th century, and the Blackfriars in the town of Perth in the early 15th century, though these never established a monopoly. With the emergence of a more formal capital at Edinburgh in the late 15th century, this became the normal parliamentary venue. The town's tolbooth, the main civic building, was the usual meeting place. Venues of general councils and conventions of estates varied more widely; as late as 1630 a convention of estates was held in the Palace of Holyroodhouse. In 1632–9, with attendances rising, the king persuaded the burgh of Edinburgh to build an imposing Parliament House with a splendid arch-span timber roof.

Ceremonial

The chief ceremony was the 'riding' of parliament, at its opening, by which the members processed on horseback from a royal or fortified venue to a neutral, public one. For parliaments in Edinburgh, the procession was from the Palace of Holyroodhouse to the tolbooth or (from 1639) the Parliament House. Strict precedence and an elaborate, hierarchical dress code were observed. A return procession was conducted at the close. The regalia – crown, sword and sceptre – were borne by leading noblemen. By the time of the last riding of parliament (1703) the numbers in the procession, including servants, exceeded 1000.

The lord lyon and heralds were important in the riding of parliament.

Other officers were the hereditary constable and marischal (both earls), responsible for maintaining order outside and inside the chamber respectively. There were macers, an usher, and a 'dempster' – an ancient inheritance from Celtic law, who announced the 'doom' (verdict) of judicial decisions.

Parliament was formally constituted by being 'fenced', that is by uttering a formula making it a court, by a group of royal commissioners. Parliaments were sometimes fenced and then 'continued' to a later date without the necessity for the members to assemble.

Deliberative Procedure

Until the covenanting revolution, parliament's proceedings were usually short, typically lasting a week or ten days. The chancellor normally presided in plenary session; there was never a 'speaker', though James I tried to introduce one in 1428. Covenanting parliaments, held in defiance of the king, elected their own presidents. After 1603 a royal commissioner was also necessary, and was often the principal manager of government business; representing the king, he was not regarded as a member of the estates.

Early parliaments seem to have deliberated in plenary session. In 1367 the estates appointed a committee of 41 members (about half those present) to conclude business, with the rest receiving licence to depart. This procedure soon became common, but disappeared in the late 1420s. In the 1450s a new type of committee emerged – one that drafted acts to be presented to the full estates for a decision. This committee, which became known as the lords of the articles, was central to the Scottish parliament's deliberations for most of the rest of its history.

The lords of the articles were usually elected at the beginning of a parliament, and consisted of representatives of each estate – eventually eight per estate. This committee met daily (often with the monarch) to discuss legislative proposals, while the remaining members of parliament held informal meetings of individual estates and negotiated with their representatives on the lords of the articles. The parliament reassembled in plenary session on its final day, to receive the lords of the articles' report. Normally this was accepted, since it represented the outcome of a consensus-seeking process.

It was once thought that the lords of the articles reduced the Scottish parliament to a rubber stamp for the crown. In the 17th century the crown did largely control the committee's selection. By then, the bishops and nobles chose *each other's* representatives, with those representatives then choosing those of the shire and burgh commissioners – and bishops, all royal nominees, would choose compliant nobles. But the committee in earlier centuries had sometimes been dominated by opponents of the crown. Even in the 17th century the lords of the articles gave the crown no extra votes in the full parliament – and the full parliament was quite capable of voting down anything it did not like. The lords of the articles' one power was to block proposals that were unwelcome to the government, and for this reason the committee was abolished in 1640, restored in 1661 and abolished again in 1689. Conventions of estates, which never had lords of the articles, seem to have met daily in plenary session and to have held debates in these sessions. Plenary debates were often held in parliaments from 1639 onwards. Claims to freedom of debate were occasionally made in this period, but several members were censured or imprisoned for undutiful speeches. However, freedom from arrest during parliamentary sessions was established.

In the late 16th and early 17th centuries, acts of parliament sometimes appointed executive committees to implement them. From 1640, to replace the lords of the articles and to deal with the revolutionary expansion of parliamentary business, there was a proliferation of committees on all subjects, usually with each estate electing its own representatives. In 1641, each day, the individual estates met separately from 7 am to 9 am, the full parliament from 9 am to 12 noon, and committees from 3 pm to 6 pm. As well as these 'session' committees, there were also 'interval' committees, meeting *between* parliaments – especially the committee of estates, an executive body that could include members who were not members of parliament. During the 1640s, the committee of estates largely eclipsed the privy council as the government's central executive body.

Voting seems to have been rare before the 17th century, with decisions being reached by consensus. Votes were taken by the roll being called, each member standing up in turn to say 'Agree' or 'Disagree'. The clerk register wrote down the votes. Individual estates (particularly the burgesses) occasionally tried to claim that the assent of each estate was essential to the passage of an act, but this was never accepted.

The royal assent was required. At least from the reign of James VI, the king or his commissioner 'touched' acts with the sceptre to ratify them. Covenanting parliaments legislated without the royal assent.

Judicial Business

As a feudal court, the medieval parliament could conduct judicial business, both civil and criminal. From at least 1341, committees were often appointed to hear judicial cases, reporting their recommendations to the full parliament. In the 15th century, two judicial committees emerged: one, for 'causes and complaints', to hear first-instance business, and one, for 'falsing of dooms' (contradicting of verdicts), to hear appeals. The 'lords auditors of causes and complaints' were gradually differentiated from the 'lords of session', the king's council sitting as a civil court, and the latter had eventually more success in attracting cases. Parliament's first-instance business in civil cases ceased after the court of session was established as a college of justice in 1532. Committees for 'falsing of dooms' faded away after 1544. Judicial business was thereafter restricted to forfeitures for treason, conducted before the full parliament; these were rare outside times of political crisis. In a celebrated case in the 1670s an attempt was made to establish a right of appeal from the court of session to parliament; this failed at the time but led to the right to such appeals being established in 1689.

Legislation

The medieval parliament could change the law, but in practice rarely did so. Many of its acts were temporary administrative orders of the kind that would later be made by the privy council. It could also tax, but again rarely did so. It did nevertheless have a monopoly in these fields; kings could not tax or legislate without parliament.

Early acts were rarely more than a short paragraph, though prolixity steadily grew. Brief preambles to acts were sometimes used in the 15th century, and these became lengthier in the 16th century, though statutes without preambles remained quite common. Enacting clauses were varied in early acts, and rarely specified whether crown or estates or both were enacting. By the early 17th century a typical enacting clause was 'Our sovereign lord, with advice and consent of the estates of parliament, statutes and ordains'. The 'consent' was often omitted in the 16th century; by contrast, phrases like 'Our sovereign lord and estates of parliament ordain' were also common. These variations in terminology did not affect an act's legal force.

Private acts, typically ratifying an individual's possession of their property, began gradually in the 16th century, and increased until they sometimes outnumbered public acts. They were never printed. Their enacting clauses tended to say 'ratifies and approves' rather than 'statutes and ordains' (although such a formula could also be used for public acts). In the 17th century, parliaments often enacted that their private acts were to be construed *'salvo jure cuiuslibet'* (excepting whomever's right).

From the late 16th century onwards, a view took shape that a statute that had never taken effect should be in 'desuetude' and thus void. In the 17th century this doctrine was more widely accepted by the courts, and extended to statutes that had fallen out of use.

Taxation

Taxation became important in 1326 and 1328, when parliaments granted direct taxes for warfare and for a peace settlement with England, and in 1357, when customs duties on exports were raised to pay for David II's ransom. The customs continued thereafter, normally being regarded as a prerogative of the crown – though when customs on imports were imposed in 1597, this was done by parliament. Direct taxes were usually small and always temporary; there was conflict over the large taxes voted for James I's ransom in 1424–5. Nevertheless, parliament retained control of the granting of direct taxation. Taxes were apportioned between the three estates of clergy, nobles and burghs in proportions of 2:2:1, changing in the early 16th century to 3:2:1. The burghs assessed themselves; clergy and nobles (the latter including all freeholders) were assessed by fixed valuations of the 1320s, increasingly outdated but remaining in use when taxation became more regular and then heavy in the 1580s and 1590s. The covenanters modernized the assessment system, imposing taxes on current land values.

Records of Proceedings

Records were in Latin until 1424, thereafter in Scots. Rolls of parliament were seized by Edward I during the wars of independence, but the nature of early parliamentary registers is unclear; these registers are missing before 1466 (with later gaps too), though copies of some kind often survive. The earliest registers probably contained only acts, but during the 15th century it became usual to record one or more attendance lists. In the 17th century, supplementary records for committees began. The clerk register was responsible for the records.

Correspondence and chronicles tell us something about proceedings, and for the 17th century there are several diaries outlining debates. Mostly written by government managers, they rarely approach the detail of English parliamentary diaries. Division lists are extremely rare; there are none before 1621, and more than half of all surviving division lists concern the Union debate of 1706–7.

Early acts seem to have been published by sending them, in writ form, to sheriffs and others with an order to make them known. Gradually it became conventional for acts of parliament to be proclaimed in the head burgh of each shire, and for sheriffs to be required to provide copies of them on request. There were experimental printings of the acts of the parliaments of 1540 and 1563. In 1566 appeared a magisterial edition of all the public acts of parliament from 1424 onwards; from then on, the statutes of each parliament were always printed immediately afterwards, and there were further collected editions in 1597 and 1681. Proclamation of the acts declined once printing became normal, though acts were always proclaimed in Edinburgh, and important ones could still be proclaimed in all head burghs or even in individual parishes.

Parliamentary Sovereignty

The power of its parliament meant that Scotland, like England, had a 'political and royal' rather than simply 'royal' government – as Sir John Fortescue recognized when he was in Scotland in the 1460s.[5] Medieval

---

5 J. H. Burns, *The True Law of Kingship: Concepts of Monarchy in Early-Modern Scotland* (Oxford, 1996), 12.

parliaments tended to meet annually, not because the king always needed new laws or taxes, but simply because he needed to consult his estates in order to govern effectively. A great deal of political power was local power, wielded by feudal lords; when assembled in parliament they could exercise decisive influence.

This influence can be seen in many fields. Parliament regulated the succession to the throne. Parliament appointed guardians or regents, particularly in the wars of independence and in the troubled reigns of the early Stewarts. Parliament was important in foreign policy from 1290 until about 1590. It did not have a monopoly of this field; the barons' letter to the pope known as the Declaration of Arbroath (1320), prominent in modern myths of popular sovereignty, was not a parliamentary document. But parliaments were often involved in treaties, and successfully thwarted foreign policy initiatives by David II in the 1360s and James III in the 1470s. Parliament regulated transfers of royal property, restricting royal alienations. Parliament virtually acquitted James II of murder after he angrily killed the earl of Douglas in 1452. Kings routinely governed with the consensus of parliaments.

By the mid-16th century the Scottish state had evolved to become a more integrated body, and the Scottish parliament – conceived, as in England, as the 'crown in parliament' – can begin to be regarded as the sovereign body of the state. Its commands were binding on all other bodies, and no other commands were binding on it. It was parliament that legislated the Reformation in 1560, abolishing the supra-national power of the pope. Within Scotland, even the greatest magnates eventually had to modify their behaviour when the Act anent Feuding (1598) outlawed vengeance killings. Parliament's control of taxation also became more important in this period.

Traditionally, then, parliament was a forum in which the government – formally the king alone – consulted the political nation on major decisions. The king took the advice of his councillors on small everyday matters, and the advice of his parliament on major matters. Parliament's members thus negotiated with the government. However, from the 1580s, a flood of important acts transformed Scots law, while parliamentary taxation became heavy, regular and controversial. Legislative sovereignty opened up the possibility that parliament, instead of negotiating with the government, could *become* the government.

However, it was natural to see the crown as the government; James VI indeed claimed to possess power to legislate alone. There was a trend towards Continental-style absolute monarchy in the early 17th century. The royal prerogative took over numerous areas of parliamentary business, notably the customs and foreign policy; the flood of legislation receded, though taxation remained important. Royal absolutism, nullified at the revolution of 1638, made a partial recovery after 1660, but in 1689 the estates firmly declared James VII to have 'forfaulted' the throne (there was no fiction of abdication) and awarded it to William and Mary.[6] Parliamentary sovereignty had been vindicated.

Parliament and Other Bodies

As well as parliaments, Scotland had other meetings of the estates. In the 14th and 15th centuries these were called 'general councils'; in the early 16th century the term 'convention of estates' came into use. These bodies were so similar to parliaments that Scottish parliamentary history must include them. They were not feudal courts and could not make binding, permanent legislation, but they could make political and administrative decisions, and they could tax. Their procedure was more flexible; conventions of estates were summoned by missive letters from the monarch, usually at shorter notice (usually 20 days in the late 17th century, sometimes less before then). Before the late 17th century they did not require a royal commissioner in the king's absence. They were public meetings, like parliaments but unlike (for instance) the privy council.

In the 14th century the special judicial competence of parliament distinguished it from a general council; by the 16th century, with the emergence of parliamentary sovereignty, the distinction between a parliament and a convention of estates appeared most clearly in parliament's monopoly of permanent legislation. Taxation was temporary, however, and continued to be competent to conventions of estates. The continuity of general councils and conventions of estates was obscured by the 19th-century edition of the *Acts of the Parliaments of Scotland*, which included minutes of conventions of estates but not of general councils (with one exception, 1513). At the time, neither body had its proceedings recorded in the parliamentary registers.

General councils and conventions of estates could take high-level political decisions. In 1571 the regent was killed during a session of parliament; a *convention of estates*, with largely the same membership as the parliament, immediately met to elect a new regent, whereupon the parliament resumed its business. Presumably people thought that a parliament could not validly be held without a regent. In 1689 a convention of estates carried through the revolution; it was later converted into a parliament.

In the late 16th century there were periodic meetings described as 'conventions' which did not contain all three estates (usually burgesses were omitted) and which often approximated to conventions of the nobility alone, or to enlarged meetings of the privy council. Such bodies rarely if ever claimed to be conventions of estates or to exercise the powers of a meeting of the estates, but historians have sometimes treated them as conventions of estates and have drawn inappropriately negative conclusions from them about conventions of estates in general.

The privy council, an executive body established on a permanent

[6] *APS*, ix, 39, c. 28.

basis in 1545, exercised wide administrative powers but never attempted to legislate or tax. Earlier scholars, pessimistic about the Scottish parliament, regarded the privy council as a rival to it, but this view is no longer accepted. Another alleged rival to parliament, the general assembly of the Protestant church, in fact consistently recognized parliamentary authority and frequently lobbied for religious legislation. Not only did parliament maintain its legislative monopoly, but at times it rivalled the privy council in the executive sphere. In the late 16th century, not only did parliaments often appoint privy councils, but they created a number of *ad hoc* executive committees. In the revolutionary period, the covenanters usually bypassed the privy council, governing instead through a committee of estates.

The End of Ane Old Song

The Scottish parliament was a vigorous and effective body. Throughout its history it often made vitally important political decisions. Every century of its history saw it occasionally curbing the power of monarchs, while remaining sufficiently useful to monarchs to ensure its continued existence. It had two main periods of decline. The tradition of roughly annual parliaments was dispensed with by James IV; he summoned only two between 1496 and his death in 1513, largely because he obtained other sources of finance. The early 17th century was another period of at least potential decline, when the 16th-century flood of legislation slackened and kings tried to assert their prerogative. But both declines were reversed – the latter dramatically, in 1638, through revolution. The covenanting parliaments took the decisive step towards the establishment of parliamentary limited monarchy.

Another threat to the Scottish parliament's existence came from England. After the union of crowns in 1603, union of parliaments could always be discussed. In the union schemes of James VI and I, parliamentary union was envisaged but harmonization of laws and churches took priority. Not surprisingly, these schemes failed by 1607. The covenanters sought a federal union in the 1640s, in which national parliaments would continue and foreign policy would be made by a joint Anglo-Scottish commission. Union was actually implemented after Scotland was conquered by Cromwell in 1651; Scotland had 30 seats in the Protectorate parliaments, with members elected under the existing franchise by groups of shires and burghs. In addition, there were four Scottish seats in Cromwell's 'Other House', though one of these was for Monck, the English commander-in-chief, and in the end only one Scot (Sir Archibald Johnstone of Wariston) ever took up a seat in the Other House.

The Cromwellian union was dissolved at the Restoration in 1660, but the kind of union that eventually emerged was discussed intermittently thereafter – particularly in 1669–70, 1689 and 1702. It was recognized that a united Britain could maintain separate laws and churches for Scotland and England, subject to *ad hoc* revision by a united British parliament. Fiscal union, by contrast, became more important with the rise of England's Navigation Acts, creating a colonial trading zone that excluded Scotland. Scottish interest in access to English colonial markets intensified after the failure of the Darien scheme to create a Scottish colony (1698–1700). Meanwhile, the English saw a union as a solution to the post-1700 succession crisis; the Scots pointedly failed to follow the English when the latter adopted the Hanoverian succession in 1701. The road to parliamentary union was a complex one and remains controversial. The initiative certainly came from the English, and once they made clear that the *status quo* was no longer an option, the Scots had little choice. Economic union was attractive to the commercial classes, though the common folk saw that they were going to be taxed more heavily. Anti-unionists failed to offer credible economic proposals or to unite round any obvious alternative to the Hanoverians. Many Scots were Jacobites, but many others were committed supporters of the 1689 revolution settlement, and saw union as the best way of maintaining this.

The parliamentary clauses of the treaty of union provided for Scotland to send 45 members to the British House of Commons, elected (as in the 1650s) by groups of shires and burghs under the existing franchise. The Scottish peers elected 16 of their number to the House of Lords. The result was the 'end of ane old song' – the words of the chancellor, the earl of Seafield, as he signed the engrossed Act of Union.[7] The Scottish parliament was dissolved by proclamation on 28 April 1707. Scotland continued to be governed by a parliament, and in many ways its parliamentary history remained distinctive, but it was now part of a larger state.

---

[7] *'Scotland's Ruine': Lockhart of Carnwath's Memoirs of the Union*, ed. D. Szechi (Aberdeen, 1995), 204.

Chronology

1235
'*Colloquium*' first recorded

1290
'*Parliamentum*' first recorded

1326
Regular attendance by burgesses begins

1357
'Three estates' first recorded

1428
Abortive act for shire representation and Speaker

1466
Earliest surviving parliamentary registers

1469
Burgh councils (controlling burgesses' representation) become self-selecting

1532
College of justice established

1560
'Reformation' Parliament

1566
Acts of parliament printed

1587
Shire commissioners introduced

1638
Bishops abolished

1640
Shire commissioners' representation doubled; lords of the articles abolished

1661
Bishops and lords of the articles restored; shire franchise extended

1681
Shire franchise further extended

1689
Lords of the articles abolished

1690
Bishops abolished

1707
Union with English parliament

Further Reading

The Architecture of Scottish Government: From Kingship to Parliamentary Democracy, ed. M. Glendinning (Dundee, 2004)

E. W. M. Balfour-Melville, 'Burgh Representation in early Scottish Parliaments', *English Historical Review*, lix (1944), 79–87

K. M. Brown, 'Parliament, Crown and Nobility in Late Medieval and Early Modern Scotland, c. 1250–1707', in *Rappresentanze i territori: parlamento Friuliano i istuzioni rappresentative territoriali nell Europa moderna*, ed. L. Casella (Udine, 2003), 119–39

A. Bruce, 'The Parliament of Scotland, 1296–1707', in *The House of Commons: Seven Hundred Years of British Tradition*, ed. R. Smith and J. S. Moore (1996), 173–81

J. H. Burns, 'Institution and Ideology: The Scottish Estates and Resistance Theory', *Institute of Historical Research, E-Seminars in History* (1997; archived 6 September 2005 at http://www.history.ac.uk/eseminars/sem14.html)

J. A. Casada, 'The Scottish Representatives in Richard Cromwell's Parliament', *Scottish Historical Review*, xl (1972), 124–47

A. A. M. Duncan, 'Councils General, 1404–1423', *Scottish Historical Review*, xxxv (1956), 132–43

—— 'The Early Parliaments of Scotland', *Scottish Historical Review*, xlv (1966), 36–58

W. Ferguson, 'The Electoral System in the Scottish Counties before 1832', *Stair Society Miscellany*, ii (1984), 261–94

J. Goodare, 'The Admission of Lairds to the Scottish Parliament', *English Historical Review*, cxvi (2001), 1103–33

—— 'The First Parliament of Mary, Queen of Scots', *Sixteenth Century Journal*, xxxvi (2005), 55–75

—— 'Parliamentary Taxation in Scotland, 1560–1603', *Scottish Historical Review*, lxviii (1989), 23–52

—— 'The Scottish Parliament of 1621', *Historical Journal*, xxxviii (1995), 29–51

—— 'The Scottish Parliamentary Records, 1560–1603', *Historical Research*, lxxii (1999), 244–67

—— 'Who was the Scottish Parliament?', *Parliamentary History*, xiv (1995), 173–8

—— 'Scotland's Parliament in its British Context, 1603–1707', in *The Challenge to Westminster: Sovereignty, Devolution and Independence*, ed. H. T. Dickinson and M. Lynch (East Linton, 2000), 22–32

—— 'The Scottish Political Community and the Parliament of 1563', *Albion*, xxxv (2003), 373–97

—— 'The Scottish Parliament and its Early Modern "Rivals"', *Parliaments, Estates and Representation*, xxiv (2004), 147–72

A. Grant, 'The Development of the Scottish Peerage', *Scottish Historical Review*, lvii (1978), 1–27

W. B. Gray, 'The Judicial Proceedings of the Parliaments of Scotland, 1660–1688', *Juridical Review*, xxxvi (1924), 135–51

P. J. Hamilton-Grierson, 'Appellate Jurisdiction of the Scottish Parliament', *Scottish Historical Review*, xv (1918), 205–22

—— 'The Judicial Committees of the Scottish Parliament, 1369–70 to 1544', *Scottish Historical Review*, xxii (1925), 1–13

R. K. Hannay, 'Observations on the Officers of the Scottish Parliament', *Juridical Review*, xliv (1932), 125–48

R. K. Hannay and G. P. H. Watson, 'The Building of the Parliament House', *Book of the Old Edinburgh Club*, xiii (1924), 1–78

The History of the Scottish Parliament, I: *Parliament and Politics in Scotland, 1235–1560*, ed. K. M. Brown and R. J. Tanner (Edinburgh, 2004)

The History of the Scottish Parliament, II: *Parliament and Politics in Scotland, 1567–1707*, ed. K. M. Brown and A. J. Mann (Edinburgh, 2005)

T. Innes, 'The Scottish Parliament: Its Symbolism and its Ceremonial', *Juridical Review*, xliv (1932), 87–124

R. Lee, 'Retreat from Revolution: The Scottish Parliament and the Restored Monarchy, 1661–1663', in *Celtic Dimensions of the British Civil Wars*, ed. J. R. Young (Edinburgh, 1997), 185–204

B. P. Levack, *The Formation of the British State: England, Scotland and the Union, 1603–1707* (Oxford, 1987)

P. Little, 'Scottish Affairs at Westminster: A Letter from the Union Parliament of 1654–5', *Scottish Historical Review*, lxxxiv (2005), 247–56

A. R. MacDonald, *The Burghs and Parliament in Scotland, c. 1550–1651* (Aldershot, 2007).

—— 'Deliberative Processes in Parliament, c. 1567–1639: Multicameralism and the Lords of the Articles', *Scottish Historical Review*, lxxxi (2002), 23–51

—— 'Ecclesiastical Representation in Parliament in Post-Reformation Scotland: The Two Kingdoms Theory in Practice', *Journal of Ecclesiastical History*, l (1999), 38–61

—— '"Tedious to rehers"? Parliament and Locality in Scotland, c. 1500–1651: The Burghs of North-East Fife', *Parliaments, Estates and Representation*, xx (2000), 31–58

G. H. MacIntosh, *The Scottish Parliament under Charles II, 1600–1685* (Edinburgh, 2006)

A. Mackechnie, 'Housing Scotland's Parliament, 1603–1707', *Parliamentary History*, xxi (2002), 99–130

J. D. Mackie and G. S. Pryde, *The Estate of the Burgesses in the Scots Parliament and its Relation to the Convention of Royal Burghs* (St Andrews, 1923)

A. J. Mann, 'Inglorious Revolution: Administrative Muddle and Constitutional Change in the Scottish Parliament of William and Mary', *Parliamentary History*, xxii (2003), 121–44

—— 'The Scottish Parliaments: The Role of Ritual and Procession in the Pre-1707 Parliament and the New Parliament of 1999', in *Rituals in Parliaments: Political, Anthropological and Historical Perspectives on Europe and the United States*, ed. E. Crewe and M. G. Müller (Bern, 2006), 135–58

T. Pagan, *The Convention of the Royal Burghs of Scotland* (Glasgow, 1926)

The Parliaments of Scotland: Burgh and Shire Commissioners, ed. M. D. Young (2 vols, Edinburgh, 1992–3)

J. Patrick, 'The Origins of the Opposition to Lauderdale in the Scottish Parliament of 1673', *Scottish Historical Review*, liii (1974), 1–21

—— 'The Scottish Constitutional Opposition in 1679', *Scottish Historical Review*, xxxvii (1958), 37–41

P. J. Pinckney, 'The Scottish Representation in the Cromwellian Parliament of 1656', *Scottish Historical Review*, xlvi (1967), 95–114

R. S. Rait, *The Parliaments of Scotland* (Glasgow, 1924)

P. W. J. Riley, 'The Abjuration Vote of 27 June 1702 in the Scottish Parliament', *Parliamentary History*, ii (1983), 175–90

—— *The English Ministers and Scotland, 1707–1727* (1964)

—— *King William and the Scottish Politicians* (Edinburgh, 1979)

—— 'The Scottish Parliament of 1703', *Scottish Historical Review*, xlvii (1968), 29–50

—— *The Union of England and Scotland: A Study in Anglo-Scottish Politics of the Eighteenth Century* (Manchester, 1978)

The Scots and Parliament, ed. C. Jones (Edinburgh, 1996)

K. Stewart, 'The Scottish Parliament, 1690–1702: A Study of Scottish Parliamentary Government', *Juridical Review*, xlix (1927), 10–37, 169–90, 408–33

R. J. Tanner, '"I Arest You, Sir, in the Name of the Three Astattes in Perlement": The Scottish Parliament and Resistance to the Crown in the Fifteenth Century', in *Social Attitudes and Political Structures in the Fifteenth Century*, ed. T. Thornton (Stroud, 2000), 101–17

—— 'The Lords of the Articles before 1540: A Reassessment', *Scottish Historical Review*, lxxix (2000), 189–212

—— 'Outside the Acts: Perceptions of the Scottish Parliament in Literary Sources before 1500', *Scottish Archives*, vi (2000), 57–70

—— *The Late Medieval Scottish Parliament: Politics and the Three Estates, 1424–1488* (East Linton, 2001)

E. E. B. Thomson, *The Parliament of Scotland, 1690–1702* (St Andrews, 1929)

J. M. Thomson, 'A Roll of the Scottish Parliament, 1344', *Scottish Historical Review*, ix (1912), 235–40

J. R. Young, *The Scottish Parliament, 1639–1661: A Political and Constitutional Analysis* (Edinburgh, 1996)

—— 'Scottish Covenanting Radicalism, the Commission of the Kirk and the Establishment of the Parliamentary Radical Regime of 1648–1649', *Records of the Scottish Church History Society*, xxv (1995), 342–75

—— 'The Scottish Parliament and the Covenanting Revolution: The Emergence of a Scottish Commons', in *Celtic Dimensions of the British Civil Wars*, ed. J. R. Young (Edinburgh, 1997), 164–84

—— 'The Scottish Parliament and National Identity from the Union of the Crowns to the Union of Parliaments, 1603–1707', in *Image and Identity: The Making and Re-making of Scotland through the Ages*, ed. D. Broun, R. J. Finlay and M. Lynch (Edinburgh, 1997), 105–42

—— 'The Scottish Parliament and European Diplomacy, 1641–1647: The Palatinate, the Dutch Republic and Sweden', in *Scotland and the Thirty Years' War, 1618–1648*, ed. S. Murdoch (Leiden, 2001), 77–106

—— 'The Scottish Parliament in the Seventeenth Century: European Perspectives', in *Ships, Guns and Bibles in the North Sea and Baltic States, c. 1350–c. 1700*, ed. A. I. Macinnes, T. Riis and F. Pedersen (East Linton, 2000), 139–72

—— 'The Scottish Parliament and the Covenanting Heritage of Constitutional Reform', in *The Stuart Kingdoms in the Seventeenth Century: Awkward Neighbours*, ed. A. I. Macinnes and J. H. Ohlmeyer (Dublin, 2002), 226–50

—— 'The Scottish Parliament and the War for the Three Kingdoms, 1639–1651', *Parliaments, Estates and Representation*, xxi (2001), 103–23

—— 'Seventeenth-Century Scottish Parliament Rolls and Political Factionalism: The Experience of the Covenanting Movement', *Parliamentary History*, xvi (1997), 148–70

22 The Parliament of Ireland to 1800
Charles Ivar McGrath

The Irish parliament originated out of the process by which English government and law was transferred in a piecemeal fashion to Ireland over a lengthy period, commencing with the arrival of the Normans in 1169. The classic history of the early Irish parliament stated that '[s]ince ... the English parliament evolved as a tribunal and council set above the courts and departments of government, so we must expect the Irish parliament to be occupying a similar position'.[1] Accordingly, the Irish assembly contained many of the key trappings of its relative in England and retained a striking structural, institutional and procedural resemblance throughout its existence. Time, geography and particular circumstances, however, ensured that there were crucial differences with regard to certain procedures and constitutional limitations.

As far as can be ascertained, the assembly of the leading notables of the country in parliament first commenced in the later 13th century, shortly after similar gatherings had commenced in England. The first clearly documented parliament took place in 1264 in Castledermot, County Kildare, in the province of Leinster, while Dublin hosted the assembly for the first time in 1279. Elected representatives were recorded for the parliament of 1297, with two knights being summoned from each of ten counties and five liberties. In 1299 a number of towns were represented, and in the following year the first known summons of both knights and burgesses occurred.

These early parliaments met on a regular basis – at times annually and even biannually – alternating on occasion with meetings of great or general councils. Whether a parliament or council, they constituted a pertinent part of the governmental system of the areas populated by descendants of Norman and English settlers, newer arrivals and assimilated Gaelic Irish. Before the Tudor conquest, however, the true extent of parliament's reach was dependent upon the fluctuating power and jurisdiction of the Dublin government. At its largest, that reach extended to 14 counties and liberties and 12 towns – at its smallest, to four counties around Dublin.

Despite the early evidence for elected knights and burgesses, the medieval parliament was not a representative assembly. There were ongoing fluctuations and inconsistencies in the status and number of those who were invited or able to attend. The emphasis upon the importance of the

---

[1] H. G. Richardson and G. O. Sayles, *The Irish Parliament in the Middle Ages* (Philadelphia, 1964), 7.

attendance of elected representatives of the commonalty was a gradual process. Even though from its inception in the 13th century parliament met with great regularity, it was not until the late 14th and early 15th century that it transformed into a body to which the elected representatives of the commons and the diocesan clergy – the proctors – were always summoned. At the same time, those who were summoned by individual writ to attend in their capacity as lords spiritual and temporal became more clearly defined and restricted.

In the 1490s parliament began to be transformed as part of a Tudor reformation in government. Following a substantial reduction in its administrative and judicial functions, on occasions in the 16th and 17th centuries the country was governed for lengthy periods without recourse to parliament. Increasing governmental financial pressures, however, facilitated a further transformation in the late 17th and early 18th centuries which resulted in increased regularity of sittings and the emergence of parliament as the main focus for political life and power for the last 109 years of its existence before its final dissolution in 1800.

Constitutional Limitation, Alteration & Reconfiguration

There were two key limitations for the Irish parliament which differentiated it from its English counterpart. The first was that the English parliament assumed a right to legislate for Ireland. The Irish parliament of 1460 was the first to declare that the country was not bound by laws passed in England unless such laws were first agreed by the Irish assembly. In 1494–5 a compromise was adopted via an Irish act which allowed for all existing English legislation to be binding in Ireland. However, there was no provision for the future, which meant that difficulties could arise again.

The second limitation came from another statute of the 1494–5 parliament, which had convened under the chief governorship of Sir Edward Poynings. The statute, which became known as Poynings's Law, enacted that an Irish parliament could not be convened without prior licence from the English monarch and council. In order to obtain such licence, an Irish chief governor and council had to certify into England the causes and considerations for calling parliament along with all bills to be enacted. If the causes and considerations were deemed valid, the bills were sent back to Ireland along with the necessary licence for holding parliament.

The original intention of Poynings's Law was to prevent independent action by Irish chief governors. However, it also imposed constitutional restrictions upon the English executive and the Irish parliament. In 1557 an amending act was passed aimed at clarifying a number of interpretations that had developed. The power of the English executive to alter or amend bills certified from Ireland was made explicit, as was the restriction of all legislation to be considered by parliament to bills that were returned under the great seal of England. The Irish executive was also explicitly empowered to make further certification of bills into England while parliament was actually sitting in order to address issues that arose during any given session.

There were two temporary suspensions of Poynings's Law in 1536 and 1569. On both occasions the purpose was to circumvent the Irish executive and allow for the presentation of legislation that had been drafted and sent directly from England. A third attempt to suspend the law in 1585 was rejected by the Commons, demonstrating how at that time the act was seen in Ireland as a defence against overly powerful chief governors and English interference.

A change in attitude emerged in the 17th century. The 1613–15 parliament demonstrated some desire to renegotiate how Poynings's Law was interpreted but was ultimately rebuffed by James I. When parliament met again in 1634–5 the new chief governor, Thomas Wentworth, interpreted Poynings's Law so as to deny parliament any legislative initiative. Reacting against that experience, in 1640–1 the Commons tried to clarify the procedural forms for certification of bills and to establish their right to initiate legislation.

Although these endeavours were cut short by rebellion in 1641, parliament picked up where it had left off following the Restoration. In the 1661–6 parliament a new practice commenced which became known as the heads of bills procedure. Heads of bills differed from ordinary bills in the form of address in the title and in the method of enactment. In the late 17th and early 18th centuries a procedure was established whereby a particular House would draft the heads of a bill and send them to the Irish council for transmission to England in the form of a standard bill. The procedure for heads was not an exact science. On occasion, particularly when time was of a premium, heads did not actually go through a reading or committee stage. Instead, the initial resolutions or the first draft might be sent to the council for completion. Once in England the bill could be amended, rejected or returned to Ireland. If returned, it would then be considered in both Houses.

Heads of bills became a central issue in the post-Glorious Revolution contest between the executive and legislature over the interpretation of Poynings's Law. Following a crisis in 1692 when the Commons claimed to have the sole right to initiate heads of supply bills, a compromise was reached whereby the government recognized the right of the Commons to initiate supply legislation by means of heads in return for the acceptance in the first session of a token government supply bill as recognition of the crown prerogative in initiating legislation and of Poynings's Law. It was also accepted that parliamentary provision of money would be based on a two-year duration of taxation thereby dictating that parliament met biennially. The government's increasing financial needs where thereby facilitated through short-term additional excise and customs duties and other taxes, and, after 1716, through the introduction of parliament-sanctioned government borrowing and a national debt.

The question of English legislation binding Ireland was also revisited in the 17th century. The fallout from the collapse of royal authority in the 1640s led to renewed agitation, with arguments taking various forms, such as queries drawn up by parliament in 1641, a speech by the Galway recusant, barrister and MP, Patrick Darcy, which was published as *An Argument* in 1643, a parliamentary 'Declaration' of 1644 and an unpublished 'Disquisition' by Sir William Domville in 1660.[2] In the 1690s it was addressed in print by a Dublin MP, William Molyneux, in *The Case of Ireland's Being Bound by Acts of Parliament in England, Stated*. The issue appeared to be finally resolved in 1720 with the passage at Westminster of the Declaratory Act, which gave statutory force to the claim of the British parliament.

The galvanizing of Irish Protestant political sentiment in the 1760s and 1770s helped to bring to a conclusion the ongoing renegotiation and reinterpretation of the constitutional relationship between the Irish parliament and the Irish and English governments and the Westminster assembly. A series of acts passed in 1782 constituted concessions gained as a result of a series of events: Britain's military set-backs in America and the ensuing disruption within British government; agitation in Ireland for free trade; the expression of public sentiment especially in the guise of armed Volunteers; Protestant agreement on the commencement of repeal of the laws penalizing Catholics; and the long-standing and ongoing political manœuvring in parliament. The key Irish statute was Yelverton's Act, which further regulated Poynings's Law by completely removing the Irish council from the legislative process and restricting all legislation to that which originated in the Irish parliament. However, all acts still had to be sent to England for final royal approval, with the crown retaining its veto. Other statutes secured the independence of the judges, confirmed all relevant acts and decrees made in England up to 1782, and recognized the Irish Lords as the final court of appeal for Ireland. For its part, the Westminster parliament repealed the 1720 Declaratory Act and renounced all rights to legislate for Ireland.

Thereafter the Irish parliament commenced sitting on an annual basis until its final dissolution in 1800. Increasing radicalization within Irish society in the 1780s and 1790s in the wake of the American and French revolutions contributed to the demise of parliament, as did the unresolved confessional divisions within the country. Most immediately, the 1798 rebellion gave the British prime minister, William Pitt, the excuse to push through the union in 1799–1800. However, other factors also had a role to play. By stripping away the last vestiges of the centuries-old limitations,

---

[2] Sir William Domville, 'A Disquisition touching that great Question Whether an Act of Parliament made in England shall binde the Kingdome and people of Ireland without theire Allowance and Acceptance of such Act in the Kingdome of Ireland', ed. P. Kelly, *Analecta Hibernica*, xl (2007), 17–70. There are seven extant 17th-century manuscript versions of the 'Disquisition': one a piece in the Public Library, Armagh, and the National Library of Ireland, Dublin, and five in Trinity College Dublin, of which four are in MS 890 and one is in MS 1746.

legislative independence helped to highlight the unresolved anomalies in the long-standing role of the English in Ireland. The 1798 rebellion highlighted the greatest danger that might thereby arise – total separation.

The only alternative seemed to be union. Having existed in practice in the 1650s, union had been considered on occasion in England and Ireland – though always at different times and in opposition to thinking on the other side of the water – as a possible final solution to the unresolved constitutional, religious, social and economic difficulties that dogged the relationship between the two countries. At the end of the 18th century, however, there was finally sufficient support on all sides. Unfortunately, enacted amid allegations of bribery and corruption and further tainted by the ensuing failure to bring in full Catholic emancipation immediately afterwards, the act that brought into being the United Kingdom of Great Britain and Ireland in January 1801 was 'stillborn'.[3] The unresolved difficulties remained.

Significant Legislation

Parliament's legislative output was significant despite the limitations placed upon it. At various times key acts were passed which had important consequences for both the institution and the country.

One of the most noteworthy acts of the medieval parliament was the Statute of Kilkenny of 1366. Prompted by the increasing Gaelicization of the English in Ireland, the act imposed a wide range of prohibitions and requirements upon those living in English areas of settlement. Much of it was copied from or built upon existing ordinances issued in both Ireland and England. The statute was re-enacted on several occasions in the 15th century before being repealed in the 1613–15 parliament.

In the 15th century the key pieces of legislation were the declaration of 1460 and Poynings's Law. In the 16th century the focus turned towards governmental and religious reform, which was facilitated by the 1534 rebellion and fall of the ambitious and independently minded house of Kildare. The religious reformation commenced in 1536 with the Act of Supremacy establishing Henry VIII as head of the church in Ireland, and was followed by acts of succession, slander and appeals. The opposition of the representatives of the lower clergy in 1536 to the royal supremacy led to the abolition of that grouping in parliament by statute in 1537. Further enactments in 1537 included two clerical taxes – first fruits and 20th parts – and acts of faculties, succession, and against the authority of the pope. Following the short-lived repeal of all of this legislation under Mary I in the 1557–8 parliament, the key provisions were re-enacted and developed in Elizabeth I's first parliament in 1560, most notably in a new Act of Supremacy and an Act of Uniformity.

[3] P. M. Geoghegan, *The Irish Act of Union: A Study in High Politics, 1798–1801* (Dublin, 1999), p. vii.

The keystone to constitutional reform was the 1541 Act of Kingly Title by which all inhabitants of Ireland became subjects of Henry VIII. It was a two-way recognition, however, as the varied support enlisted for the act constituted a practical commitment on the crown's part to parliament as part of the new arrangements. The English monarch was no longer just lord of those areas in which existing subjects lived, but was now king of all Ireland with responsibility for that extended jurisdiction and increase in subjects.

In the 17th century questions of religion, land and finance were central to the key enactments. The crown's increasing need for money under Charles I led to protracted negotiations with leading Irish peers and gentry that resulted in a promise of parliamentary supplies in return for reforms listed in 51 'Instructions and Graces' concerning landownership and other concerns agreed in May 1628. However, the parliament to be convened under article 34 of the 'Graces' in that year was postponed indefinitely owing to the government's failure to adhere to the dictates of Poynings's Law.

The failure to give legislative recognition to the 'Graces' was a central issue for parliament when it finally convened in 1634. However, although supplies were granted, the 'Graces' remained unconfirmed. Supply remained the key concern when parliament was next summoned in 1640, though the greatest success on the part of government in this area did not occur until after the Restoration.

The land and financial settlements voted in the 1661–6 parliament were dramatic in their proportion and impact. The 1662 Act of Settlement and 1665 Act of Explanation were attempts at solving the land question. The Act of Settlement, based upon Charles II's Gracious Declaration of 30 November 1660 and ensuing instructions, was particularly unsatisfactory for Irish Catholics who had been dispossessed in the 1640s and 1650s, but was also a focus of grievance for Protestants. The Act of Explanation was an endeavour to address many of those grievances but, like its predecessor, proved unequal to the task.

On the other hand, the new revenues agreed by parliament proved wholly satisfactory to the crown. In 1662 two acts for new customs and excise duties granted substantial revenues to Charles II and his heirs and successors forever. A perpetual hearth tax was also granted in acts passed in 1662 and 1665. These statutes formed the core of a financial settlement that allowed Ireland to be governed without further recourse to parliament during the remainder of Charles II's reign. They also established the basis for the development of a modern professional revenue collection bureaucracy.

Religion served as the impetus for substantial legislative activity in the 18th century. The all-Protestant membership of parliament from 1692 onwards and the advent of regular meetings paved the way for the imposition between 1695 and 1750 of a comprehensive body of laws penalizing Catholics. The first two acts of 1695 prohibited foreign education and disarmed and dismounted Catholics. In each session thereafter up to 1709 at least one anti-Catholic measure was enacted, with the cornerstone of the Penal Code being passed in 1704. The act to prevent the further growth of popery affected Catholic land ownership, education, guardianship, voting rights and office-holding amongst other matters, and enforced inheritance by gavelkind whereby on the death of any Catholic his estate was divided up equally among all his sons or, if there was no male issue, among his daughters or collateral branches of the family. It also imposed a sacramental test which impacted upon Protestant dissenters as well. A further act in 1709 closed a variety of loopholes and added further penalties. The Catholic Church was targeted in a series of statutes commencing in 1697 with an act for banishing all papists exercising ecclesiastical jurisdiction and all regular clergy. Catholic legal practice also came in for particular attention in a series of acts passed between 1699 and 1734.

Constitutional reform came to the fore once again in the second half of the 18th century. The 1768 Octennial Act (inspired by the English Septennial Act) limited the duration of parliaments to eight years, and was part of the reforms aimed at by a grouping of MPs and peers known as 'Patriots'. This term has been applied to a variety of political viewpoints that encompassed a range of attitudes from civic duty to economic improvement to political reform. More often than not such sentiments were most evident among the parliamentary opposition. By the 1760s a Patriot agenda had emerged that, along with the desire for regular elections, centred around long-standing issues such as the tenure of judges, habeas corpus, and an Irish mutiny act.

The Patriot interest also played a role in the repeal of the penal code. However, the most significant factors in the agitation for repeal were the British government's military needs and the Catholic lobby in Ireland and England. Having legislated in 1774 to enable Catholics to testify their loyalty to the crown without having to subscribe oaths that were anathema to their religious belief, the first major Catholic Relief Act was passed in 1778, allowing for 999-year leases among other provisions. Further measures were enacted in 1782, 1792 and 1793, though complete Catholic emancipation was not completed until 1829.

Speakership

The first reference to a specific individual acting as Speaker on behalf of the commonalty occurred in 1416. As far as can be ascertained, thereafter the position of Speaker evolved on similar lines to that of England. A Speaker was elected by the Commons at the beginning of a new parliament. On most occasions these elections seemed to have passed without difficulty, often with the government's nominee being returned. However, on several occasions contests did arise. The confessional divide led to a short-lived crisis in 1613. When both a Catholic and Protestant candidate were put forward, a physical contest ensued as MPs tried to push their preferred Speaker on to the chair. While the Protestant candidate and government nominee, Solicitor General Sir John Davies, was eventually returned as Speaker, the dispute resulted in the withdrawal of Catholic MPs and the curtailing of the first session. Months of disharmony ensued before parliament could reconvene in 1614.

In the period 1692–1714 the speakership again became the focus for conflict, though on this occasion against a backdrop of party politics. Contests were recorded in 1710 and 1713, with the latter resulting in the tory government's nominee being defeated by the whig opposition candidate 127 to 131. As in 1713, there were other occasions during this period when the Speaker ended up as leader of the opposition as fluctuations in whig and tory party fortunes turned traditional patterns on their head.

In 1715 a new pattern emerged with the rise of the undertaker system. Between 1715 and 1769, in return for patronage, power and position, leading Irish politicians undertook to manage parliament for a government led by chief governors who absented themselves from the country for 18 months out of every two years, only turning up when parliament convened. The speakership became a key position for such undertakers, with the last holder resigning in 1771 after the reimposition of direct government with resident chief governors and a court party in parliament controlled by the executive in Dublin Castle. Between 1771 and 1800 the last two Speakers of the Irish Commons, although both considered independent-minded gentlemen, were also both acceptable to government.

In the Lords from an early stage the lord chancellor became the presiding member of the House. Although the other senior judges of the courts of exchequer, common pleas and king's or queen's bench were *ex officio* associates of the House, unlike the lord chancellor they did not have a vote and were primarily in attendance in order to advise on legal matters.

Committees

It is difficult to establish when and how a committee system emerged in parliament. Certainly committees of sorts were in use in the 15th century, including joint committees of both Houses. By the 17th and 18th centuries a clearly defined use of committees had evolved. At the beginning of a session, both Houses established standing committees to deal with key areas such as privileges, grievances, trade, and – in the Commons only – elections. Thereafter, committees were appointed for a variety of reasons and with a variety of structures. Key committees of the whole House of Commons included those on supply, ways and means, and the state of the nation. Smaller select or *ad hoc* committees were appointed in both Houses for various purposes including drafting heads of bills, preparing addresses and answers thereunto, considering petitions, meeting with the other House in conference, and – in the Commons only – for consideration of the public accounts. After it first emerged in the 1690s, the committee of public accounts quickly became the most important select committee because the whole procedure on supply, and with it the timetable for every session, became dependent upon the report that emanated from that committee.

Location and Topography

For much of its early life parliament was a moveable feast, convening in various towns of the English settlement such as Castledermot, Kildare, Kilkenny, Drogheda, Naas, Trim, Wexford and Dublin in Leinster and Cashel, Ross, Clonmel, Waterford, Limerick and Cork in Munster. However, Dublin was the most common place of assembly and by the beginning of the 17th century had become parliament's permanent residence. Until 1661 meetings took place in Dublin Castle, but in that year parliament moved to Chichester House, which was located outside the medieval city boundaries at College Green, beside Trinity College and opposite the site of the Viking *Thing* or meeting-place.

By the 1690s Chichester House was in a state of irretrievable disrepair, and concern was expressed about personal safety and the damage being done to records held within the building. Eventually in 1729 temporary arrangements were made for parliament to convene at the Bluecoat School in Oxmantown, Dublin, while a new building was constructed on the site of Chichester House, which had been demolished in 1728. Completed during the 1730s to the designs of Edward Lovett Pearce, the new building was the first custom-built parliament house in early modern Europe, having a Palladian south facade with Ionic portico and projecting galleries, a domed octagonal chamber for the Commons, and a more traditional rectangular chamber with apse for the Lords. The first session in the new building commenced in October 1731, long before construction was completed. In the 1780s the parliament house was extended eastward with a Corinthian portico entrance to the Lords' chamber designed by James Gandon, and, despite a fire in 1792, continued as the seat of parliament until the union. Following the union, the building was sold to the Bank of Ireland and was redesigned so that the Commons' chamber was broken up into three separate rooms. The Lords' chamber survives to this day in a slightly altered state.

Records and Reporting

The systematic recording of proceedings in parliament began in 1613. In 1611 William Bradley, who had been appointed clerk of the Commons in 1608, was sent to London to assess the manner in which the English parliament kept its records. The end result was the commencement in 1613 of the hand-written record of the information that in 1752 began to be published in printed form as *The Journals of the House of Commons of the Kingdom of Ireland*. In both the original method of recording information and the later decision to print and publish those accounts, the example was set by the actions of the English parliament. In the interim the printing of the votes of the Commons had begun in 1692. The detailed recording of debates in the Commons commenced in 1781 with the publication of *The Parliamentary Register: or, History of the Proceedings and Debates of the House of Commons of Ireland*. Records of proceedings in the Lords commenced in 1634, while the first printed volume of *The Journals of the House of Lords of the Kingdom of Ireland* appeared in 1780.

In 1762 work began on a comprehensive collection of the statutes. Earlier incomplete versions had been printed in 1572 and 1620, with a reprint of the latter, with additions, in 1678 and without further additions in 1723. In 1765 the statutes from 1310 to 1761 were published in eight volumes as *The Statutes at Large passed in the Parliaments held in Ireland*. Further volumes were published thereafter, with a second edition comprising 18 volumes bringing the record up to 1798. Two final additional volumes covering the last two years of parliament's existence were published in 1801, with a final additional index being published in 1804.

Anomalies

On several occasions during the tumults of the 17th century arrangements were made that do not fit within a traditional history of parliament. The general assembly of the Confederation of Kilkenny, which met from 1642 to 1649 in Kilkenny and once in Waterford, was the representative body for Irish Catholics during the civil wars of the 1640s. It was modelled on the Dublin parliament, replicating the existing electoral system and constituencies in the country though excluding Protestant voters and restricting the assembly to one House, with the elected representatives sitting alongside bishops and peers who had an automatic entitlement to attend meetings. Despite the similarities, however, the Confederates were keen to emphasize that the general assembly was not a parliament and that they had no desire to usurp the power of the crown in relation to that institution. Most of the records for the general assembly were destroyed in two separate fires, in Dublin Castle in 1711 and in the Four Courts in 1922. Since that time, historians have had to rely upon a variety of disparate manuscript sources in various archives including the Bodleian Library, the British Library, the National Archives, Kew, and the National Library of Ireland.

The final defeat of the Confederate Catholics by parliamentarian forces in 1653 led to the first experiment with direct representation in the English parliament. Six Irish members were sent to the 'Barebones' Parliament, while the number was increased to 30 in the Protectorate parliaments with a further five representatives, including Henry Cromwell and Lord Broghill, being summoned in 1658 to attend the short-lived Other House. When the Protectorate collapsed in 1659 and early 1660, Ireland experienced its one and only general convention, which met in Dublin from

February to May 1660. The representatives were elected to the unicameral assembly in accordance with the existing electoral constituencies though with some limitations on numbers and some flexibility regarding eligibility which resulted in three peers and a bishop being among the 138 members.

The last alternative arrangement occurred in 1689, with the convening of the Jacobite parliament at the King's Inns in Dublin in the presence of the exiled James II. Also known as the Patriot Parliament, it was in theory a continuation of the existing parliamentary tradition, though it was rendered unique by a number of circumstances: the presence of James II, which helped to rationalize his government's failure to comply with the dictates of Poynings's Law; the parliament's predominantly Catholic – both Gaelic and Old English – membership; and the legislative programme for constitutional reform and repeal of the Restoration land settlement. However, its authority and jurisdiction were short-lived. From the outset it was referred to by Williamites as the 'pretended parliament', its acts were declared null and void by the Westminster parliament in 1690, and the records of its proceedings were destroyed by order of the Irish parliament in 1695.

Membership, Constituencies and Electorate

It was not until after the completion of the Tudor conquest in 1603 that parliamentary membership and constituencies began to be clearly defined and regulated across the whole country. Previously the number of constituencies, and hence membership, fluctuated according to the geographical extent of the government's jurisdiction. All the constituencies returned two MPs. In 1560 there were 49 constituencies, comprising 20 counties and 29 boroughs, while by 1585 they had increased to 63, with 27 counties and 36 boroughs.

In the early 17th century the number of MPs increased substantially owing to the inclusion of all the counties and through the creation of new boroughs. These latter creations arose in large part because of the Tudor and Stuart plantations. In 1613 there were 116 constituencies, comprising 33 counties and 84 boroughs. By 1634 the overall number had increased to 128, including 95 boroughs, and in 1641 to 127 owing to a reduction to 32 counties. In 1661 the number of boroughs had risen to 105, and during the ensuing years was further expanded to a final total of 117.

These various increases resulted in the membership doubling between 1585 and 1634, from 126 to 256 MPs. While the figure dropped to 240 in 1640 because of the temporary disenfranchisement of a number of seats, it increased by 1641 toward the levels of 1634, though no final figure exists because of the absence of information regarding the results of by-elections. In 1661 the number had increased to 276.

From the 1690s until the final dissolution in 1800 the number of MPs remained settled at 300. Deriving from 150 two-member constituencies, that membership arose from 32 counties returning 64 members, 117 cities and boroughs returning 234 members, and the University of Dublin returning two members.

With regard to the Lords, the early 17th century saw a dramatic increase in the creation of new Irish peerages which resulted in a multiplication of the numbers entitled to sit in the upper House. An almost three-fold increase occurred between 1613 and 1634, from 45 to 123 in total. By the beginning of the 18th century the upper House consisted of 22 spiritual lords and a varying number of peers. The later 18th century saw further dramatic increases through new creations – by 1778 the figure stood at 147; in 1800 it was recorded at 210. However, a significant number of peers were permanent absentees: for example, the division of 75 to 26 in favour of the Act of Union in 1800 was considered a particularly high turnout. Of course, in this as in other divisions, voting in the upper House included the use of proxies, thought an abuse of the system by the government in the early 17th century which prompted the Lords in the 1660s to impose a limit upon themselves of two proxies per attending member. There is evidence, however, that this restriction was at times flouted during the 18th century. In order to utilize a proxy, an absentee had to nominate a colleague to represent and vote for him – peer for peer, bishop for bishop – and had to pay fees of between two and three pounds to register his proxy with the relevant clerk.

Confessional allegiance remained significant until the end of the 17th century. From a position of complete Catholic dominance in the 16th century, the balance began to move slowly in favour of Protestant numbers in the early 17th century. In 1585 Catholics had been in a complete majority in the Commons. After the 1613 elections they were in a minority, with 100 Catholic and 132 Protestant MPs. By 1634 the figure was 112 Catholic and 142 Protestant, while in 1640 the balance had shifted to 75 Catholic and 163 Protestant. During 1640–1, owing to re-enfranchisement of seats and by-elections, Catholic numbers increased though the final figure is not known. However, even though there was still no legal impediment, there were no Catholic MPs in the 1661–6 parliament.

In the Lords the altered balance was initially even more dramatic. There were 45 individuals able to attend in 1613, of whom 20 were Protestant spiritual lords, 17 were Catholic peers, five were Protestant peers and three were minors. In 1634 the balance had shifted to 24 Protestant spiritual lords and 99 peers, of whom the vast majority were newly created and Protestant. Out of 78 new creations since 1616, there were 67 Protestants and only 11 Catholics. The right of every peer to an individual writ of summons ensured that Catholics continued to sit in the Lords in the 1661–6 parliament, when a dozen or so were active among the 30–40 peers who attended on a regular basis.

The short-lived Catholic resurgence under James II resulted in an overwhelming number of Catholics being elected to the Jacobite parliament in 1689. James's Irish government had remodelled the borough corporations by *quo warranto* proceedings so as to ensure Catholic majorities. As a result, of the 230 or so MPs returned only five or six were Protestant. (The failure to fill all 300 seats came about because some constituencies did not make returns.) In the Lords, the majority of the peers were Old English Catholics, though there were also several Gaelic Catholic peers and five Protestant peers. The spiritual lords all came from the Church of Ireland, though only four actually attended.

The Catholic dominance of the Jacobite parliament ultimately served to place an even higher premium upon ensuring their exclusion after the Irish war of 1689–91, an exclusion that was achieved by means of the Westminster act of 1691 for abrogating the oath of supremacy in Ireland and appointing other oaths. From 1692 onwards parliament was a wholly Protestant assembly until its demise in 1800. Even though during the following years Catholic peers continued to be summoned they were unable to take the required oaths. To finally close the door on Catholic representation, in 1704 a clause was included in the act to prevent the further growth of popery which prohibited Catholics from voting unless they took the oaths of allegiance and abjuration, while in 1728 an act for further regulating the election of MPs ensured the complete exclusion of Catholics from the franchise.

The franchise in 17th- and 18th-century Ireland was based upon an act of 1542. The electorate for the county constituencies were the 40s. freeholders. Before 1793, when Catholics were finally re-enfranchised, the largest county electorate was 6,000 in County Down. The remaining county electorates were all under 4,000, with five having electorates of less than 1,000.

The electorate in the cities and boroughs varied through time, location and character. It was not unusual for boroughs to be controlled by various landed interests, resulting in significant groupings of MPs who were identified with a particular patron. The method and purpose behind many of the 17th-century creations also meant that a significant number of boroughs were corrupt, venal or rotten (occasionally all three) and bore little relevance to the geographical place which was nominally represented. The most common and restricted electorate was in the 55 corporation boroughs and constituted the mayor and council. In the 36 freemen boroughs those who were admitted to the freedom of the borough formed the electorate along with the members of the corporation. The Newtown Act of 1748 exemplified the unrepresentative nature of many of these boroughs, by making residence unnecessary for burgesses and freemen, thereby creating corporations of absentees.

There were also eight medieval county boroughs with an electorate comprising the corporation, freemen and freeholders, varying in number from 500 to 4,000. The remaining 18 boroughs were made up of 12 potwalloping boroughs in which the right to vote lay with the resident 'potwallopers' – holders of houses worth £5 per annum who controlled their own front door and cooking facilities – and six manor boroughs in which the 40s. freeholders of the manor voted. The university electorate comprised 22 fellows and 70 scholars.

Elections were not, however, a common occurrence. In the 17th century, aside from some early results from several constituencies in 1628 for the aborted parliament, there were only seven general elections – 1613, 1634, 1640, 1661, 1689, 1692 and 1695. The need for elections in close proximity in 1692 and 1695 arose out of political conflict and emerging whig and tory party politics, which also accounted for two elections during Anne's reign in 1703 and 1713. Thereafter, however, until 1768 the norm was for a parliament to continue sitting biennially for the life of the reigning monarch, with general elections only occurring in 1715, 1727 and 1761. After the passage of the Octennial Act in 1768 there were general elections in 1769, 1776, 1783, 1790 and 1798. There were also numerous by-elections during and between sessions following an MP's death, expulsion, elevation to a peerage or judgeship, or entry into holy orders. It was not possible for an MP to resign until the 1793 Place Act, when the Irish equivalent of the Chiltern Hundreds – the office of escheator of one of the provinces – made it possible for an MP to do so. On those occasions when an election was necessitated, each elector had two votes, since each constituency returned two MPs. On occasion, voters would plump for one candidate by not exercising there right to use their second vote.

With the passage of the Act of Union in 1800, Irish representation at Westminster was fixed at 100 MPs and 32 lords (of whom four were spiritual). The MPs were returned on the basis of two from each of the 32 county constituencies, two each from the two county boroughs of Dublin and Cork, and one from each of 31 other boroughs and one from the University of Dublin.

Chronology

1264
First clearly documented parliament

1279
First parliament in Dublin

1297
First record of knights being summoned

1299
First record of towns being represented

1300
First summons of both knights and burgesses

1366
Statute of Kilkenny

1460
Declaration that the Irish parliament was not bound by laws passed in England unless first accepted in the Irish assembly

The Parliament of Ireland to 1800

1494–5
Enactment of Poynings's Law and a further act for allowing all existing English acts to apply to Ireland

1534
Kildare rebellion

1536
Acts for temporary suspension of Poynings's Law, of Supremacy, Succession, Slander, and Appeals

1537
Acts abolishing the representation of the lower clergy by proctors, of first fruits, 20th parts, and faculties, establishing the succession, and against the authority of the pope

1541
Act declaring the king of England to be king of Ireland

1542
Franchise Act

1557
Act to amend Poynings's Law

1560
Acts of Supremacy and Uniformity

1569
Act for temporary suspension of Poynings's Law

1585
Failed legislation for suspending Poynings's Law

1613
Dispute over the election of the Speaker

1628
The 'Graces' and the aborted parliament

1641
Outbreak of rebellion in Ulster

1642
Confederation of Kilkenny meets for the first time

1643
Publication of Patrick Darcy's *An Argument*

1649
Confederation of Kilkenny ceases to convene

1653
Ireland represented by six members in the 'Barebones' Parliament

1654
Ireland represented by 30 members in the Protectorate parliament

1660
General Convention meets in Dublin

1661
Parliament moves to Chichester House, College Green, Dublin

1662
Acts of Settlement, Customs, Excise, and Hearth Tax

1665
Acts of Explanation and Hearth Tax

1689
Jacobite/Patriot Parliament

1690
Act declaring the acts of the Jacobite Parliament to be null and void (Westminster)

1691
Act to abrogate the oath of supremacy in Ireland and appointing other oaths (Westminster)

1692
Sole Right conflict

1695
Acts to restrain foreign education and for the better securing the government by disarming papists

1697
Act for banishing all papists exercising any ecclesiastical jurisdiction and all regular clergy

1698
Publication of Molyneux's *Case of Ireland*

1699
Woollen Act (Westminster)

1704
Act to prevent the further growth of popery

1709
Act for explaining and amending an act, entitled 'An Act to Prevent the Further Growth of Popery'

1716
Introduction of parliament-sanctioned government borrowing and a national debt

1720
Declaratory Act (Westminster)

1728
Final disfranchisement of Catholics and demolition of Chichester House

1729
Parliament convenes in Bluecoat School, Oxmantown, Dublin

1731
First session in the new Parliament House at College Green, Dublin

1734
Act for the amendment of the law in relation to popish solicitors

1748
Newtown Act

1768
Octennial Act

1774
Act to enable Catholics to testify their loyalty to the crown

1778
Act permitting Catholics to hold 999-year leases

1782
Repeal of the Declaratory Act (Westminster)

1782
Acts allowing Catholics to purchase land and to teach school, to amend Poynings's Law (Yelverton's Act), and for the independence of judges

1783
Renunciation Act (Westminster)

1793
Place Act; re-enfranchisement of Catholics

1798
Rebellion

1800
Passage of the Act of Union in the Irish and Westminster parliaments

1801
Act of Union takes effect on 1 January

Further Reading

B. Bradshaw, *The Irish Constitutional Revolution of the Sixteenth Century* (Cambridge, 1979)

R. E. Burns, *Irish Parliamentary Politics in the Eighteenth Century* (2 vols, Washington, DC, 1989–90)

A. Clarke, *The Old English in Ireland, 1625–42* (2nd edn, Dublin, 2000)

—— *Prelude to Restoration in Ireland: The End of the Commonwealth, 1659–1660* (Cambridge, 1999)

D. Englefield, *The Printed Records of the Parliament of Ireland, 1613–1800* (1978)

P. M. Geoghegan, *The Irish Act of Union: A Study in High Politics, 1798–1801* (Dublin, 1999)

The Irish Parliament in the Eighteenth Century: The Long Apprenticeship, ed. D. W. Hayton (Edinburgh, 2001) [special issue of *Parliamentary History*, xx/1]

The Irish Parliamentary Tradition, ed. B. Farrell (Dublin, 1973)

F. G. James, *Lords of the Ascendancy: The Irish House of Lords and its Members, 1600–1800* (Dublin, 1995)

E. M. Johnston-Liik, *History of the Irish Parliament, 1692–1800: Commons, Constituencies and Statutes* (6 vols, Belfast, 2002)

H. F. Kearney, *Strafford in Ireland, 1633–41: A Study in Absolutism* (2nd edn, Cambridge, 1989)

J. Kelly, *Poynings' Law and the Making of Law in Ireland, 1660–1800* (Dublin, 2007)

J. L. McCracken, *The Irish Parliament in the Eighteenth Century* (Dundalk, 1971)

C. I. McGrath, *The Making of the Eighteenth-Century Irish Constitution: Government, Parliament and the Revenue, 1692–1714* (Dublin, 2000)

A New History of Ireland, II: *Medieval Ireland, 1169–1534*, ed. A. Cosgove (Oxford, 1987)

A New History of Ireland, III: *Early Modern Ireland, 1534–1691*, ed. T. W. Moody, F. X. Martin, and F. J. Byrne (Oxford, 1976)

A New History of Ireland, IV: *Eighteenth-Century Ireland, 1691–1800*, ed. T. W. Moody, and W. E. Vaughan (Oxford, 1986)

A New History of Ireland, VIII: *A Chronology of Irish History to 1976*, ed. T. W. Moody, F. X. Martin and F. J. Byrne (Oxford, 1982)

A New History of Ireland, IX: *Maps, Genealogies, Lists*, ed. T. W. Moody, F. X. Martin, and F. J. Byrne (Oxford, 1984)

M. Ó Siochrú, *Confederate Ireland, 1642–1649: A Constitutional and Political Analysis* (Dublin, 1999)

Parliament and Community: Historical Studies XIV, ed. A. Cosgrove and J. I. Mcguire (Belfast, 1983)

Penal Era and Golden Age: Essays in Irish History, 1690–1800, ed. T. Bartlett and D. W. Hayton (Belfast, 1979)

H. G. Richardson and G. O. Sayles, *The Irish Parliament in the Middle Ages* (Philadelphia, 1952)

J. G. Simms, *The Jacobite Parliament of 1689* (Dundalk, 1974)

23 The Northern Ireland Parliament and Assembly at Stormont

Graham Walker

The parliament of Northern Ireland was brought into being by the Government of Ireland Act of 1920.[1] It should be noted that this act of the Westminster parliament was devised with the intention of producing a very different situation in Ireland from that which actually transpired in its wake. It was, in effect, a fourth legislative attempt on the part of a London government, to grant a limited measure of home rule to Ireland. The first three attempts, in 1886, 1893 and 1912, had all provided only for a parliament to sit in Dublin and had sought to address Irish Nationalist demands. The 1920 act, recognizing the implacable opposition of Ulster Unionists to being governed from Dublin, proposed to set up two devolved administrations, one in Belfast with jurisdiction over the six north-eastern counties of Antrim, Down, Armagh, Londonderry, Fermanagh and Tyrone, and one for the other 26 counties of Ireland. However, the act also provided for a Council of Ireland to function as a mechanism through which both administrations would co-operate on issues of common concern. Indeed, the Council of Ireland proposal indicated that the spirit of the act was to preserve a sense of Irish unity: it looked forward to the two entities joining as one, though still within the orbit of the United Kingdom.

In fact, the Council of Ireland never sat; moreover, the parliament meant for Dublin was boycotted by the great majority of those entitled to take their places in it and rapidly became a dead letter. Political turbulence in the south of the country, against the background of the Anglo-Irish war between 1919 and 1921, necessitated a different course being taken, that of the establishment in 1922 of an Irish Free State with dominion status. By then the Northern Ireland parliament had been established on the basis of the 1920 act. On 7 June 1921, following elections, the parliament assembled for the first time. It met in Belfast's City Hall and accepted full responsibility as a legislative body. Even so, the treaty agreed between the British government and Irish Nationalist and Republican representatives in December 1921 required Northern Ireland to vote herself out of the new Irish Free State within one month of the treaty's ratification. The Northern Ireland parliament duly availed of this option. The 1920 act was then modified to apply only to Northern Ireland. The Irish Free State (Agreement) Act of 1922, which included the stipulation about the north having to opt out, nevertheless also made it a consequence of

---

[1] Research for this chapter was assisted by a Fellowship from the Leverhulme Trust.

such a choice that a commission be set up consisting of representatives of the Northern Ireland, Free State and British governments to determine the boundary between Northern Ireland and the rest of Ireland. This commission's report in 1925, recommending only minor transfers of territory, led the three governments to agree to leave the border as it was and confirm Northern Ireland as a six-county unit. This was given effect in the Northern Ireland (Confirmation of Agreement) Act, 1925.

Northern Ireland thus became the United Kingdom's first example of devolved government. As a constitutional experiment it arguably carried a significant burden from the beginning, and the initial uncertainties surrounding the workability of the arrangements put in place by the 1920 act were exacerbated by the context of political violence and instability throughout Ireland until at least 1923. As a former Northern Ireland civil servant reflected: 'There was turmoil everywhere, uncertainty about the intentions of the British government, doubt even about the responsibility for military and police services.' Moreover, he pointed to the fact that Belfast had never been a capital city and lacked the apparatus of government, and that civil servants had to be hastily transferred from London, Dublin and Edinburgh.[2] The transfer of executive and legislative powers took place haltingly, some not until well into 1922. Indeed, it was not until the end of May 1922 that the Royal Ulster Constabulary police force was authorized.

Structure, Membership and Procedures

The parliament of Northern Ireland consisted of the sovereign and the two Houses, namely the Senate and the House of Commons. It was closely based on the Westminster model, and its practices and procedures largely followed Westminster conventions. The House of Commons consisted of 52 members elected by universal adult franchise,[3] in the early years (the 1921 and 1925 elections) from multi-member constituencies by a process of proportional representation. From the 1929 election the 52 members were elected from single-member constituencies, with the exception of the university constituency, by a simple majority 'first-past-the-post' system.

The Senate consisted of 26 members, 24 of whom were elected by the House of Commons on the principle of proportional representation. Each elected senator held office for eight years before having to seek re-election; however, the periods of membership of the senate were arranged so that half of the seats fell vacant at the end of every fourth year. The two other senators were the lord mayors of Belfast and Londonderry. The

---

[2] John Oliver, 'On the Stormont Administration', in his *Aspects of Ulster* (Antrim, 1994), 105.

[3] Note, however, that there was a measure of plural voting from 1921 until 1968 and a tighter residence qualification than in Britain. See R. J. Lawrence, *The Government of Northern Ireland: Public Finance and Public Services, 1921–1964* (Oxford, 1965), 20–1.

Sir James Craig

Sir James Craig, the first prime minister of Northern Ireland, was the only member of the first devolved executive to have held previous office. He was secretary to ministry of pensions at Westminster in 1919, and secretary to the admiralty in 1920–1. He became leader of the Ulster Unionist Party in February 1921 and combined the roles of premier and party leader until his death in 1940. A senior Orange Order member, he had led – along with Sir Edward Carson – the Ulster Protestant resistance to rule from Dublin. Some of his utterances in the Northern Ireland parliament during the 1920s and 30s were to be endlessly quoted back to him by Nationalist opponents who argued that Craig and his party cared only for the welfare of his own community. However, he also had to exert a restraining influence on many of his followers when passions over the 'national question' ran high, and he was regularly subjected to populist pressure from the right of his own governing party. Craig showed firmness and resolve in establishing the Northern Ireland parliament as a working institution, and steering the province through the political turbulence of its early years.

House of Commons, like its counterpart at Westminster, had a maximum life of five years before fresh elections had to be held, and, again following Westminster, each House of the Northern Ireland parliament elected one of its members as Speaker to preside over business. The Speaker was entrusted to decide on disputed points in the procedure of the House.

The standing orders system in both Houses followed their respective Westminster counterparts, and the powers, privileges and immunities were those of Westminster with very few exceptions. Two differences of procedure with Westminster concerned first, the ability of a government minister to make a statement or answer a question in either House, though he or she could only vote in one House; and second, a procedural device never used namely that if the two Houses failed to reach agreement by the ordinary procedures of passing a bill through its different readings in each House and accepting amendments, then the two Houses were to meet in one assembly and settle their differences by vote. More use was made of joint committees of the two Houses than was found at Westminster, although in general the Westminster committee system was adopted if in a considerably reduced form.

The parliament moved its location following the state opening on 22 June 1921 attended by King George V and Queen Mary. It took up residence in Union Theological College in Belfast, where it remained until the new parliament buildings at Stormont in the east of the city were opened by the prince of Wales in 1932. Subsequent to this it became common to refer to the Northern Ireland parliament as 'Stormont', and the Greek

> ### Sir Norman Stronge
>
> Sir Norman Stronge, who became a member of the Northern Ireland House of Commons for Mid-Armagh in 1938, was appointed Speaker of the House in 1945. He held this post until 1969, making him the longest serving Speaker in the parliament's 51-year history. Stronge met a violent death in retirement when he was shot dead along with his son at the family home, Tynan Abbey, close to the border with the republic in January 1981. The killings were the work of the Provisional Irish Republican Army, who described father and son as 'symbols of hated Unionism'.

classical style of the building ensured that it soon became a well recognized image and symbol of the province.

After receiving devolution, Northern Ireland's representation in the House of Commons at Westminster was set at 12 members, and constituencies and elections in this regard were regulated by United Kingdom law. The Northern Ireland parliament was overseen by the governor, an appointee and permanent representative of the crown. The governor's office was created when the constitution of the Irish Free State came into force in December 1922; previously the representative of the crown had been the lord lieutenant. The governor summoned, prorogued and dissolved the Northern Ireland parliament in the name of the monarch, read the monarch's speech at the beginning of a new session, and gave or withheld the royal assent to bills passed by both Houses.

> ### A Painting of the Battle of the Boyne
>
> A painting hung in the parliament building at Stormont in March 1933 became the subject of a bizarre controversy and court case. The work, by the 17th-century Dutch artist Pieter van der Meulen, depicted the Orange hero King William III apparently being given a papal blessing. The painting had been purchased by the Northern Ireland government. However, when it was displayed certain members of the House of Commons voiced their outrage, and called for the painting to be replaced by a more traditional portrait of 'King Billy' at the Battle of the Boyne in 1690. Matters took a remarkable turn in May 1933, when a party of visitors, members of a group called 'The Scottish Protestant League', were taken on a tour of the parliament. On reaching the painting one member of this party threw paint over it, while another slashed it with a knife. Both were arrested and later convicted of causing malicious damage. The political row rumbled on, and the painting, although restored, was moved to a less exposed site.

Functions and Relations with Westminster

The Government of Ireland Act classified the functions of government as transferred, reserved and excepted, an arrangement which lasted the life of the Northern Ireland institution from 1921 until 1972. The transferred functions essentially covered everything not 'reserved' or 'excepted' and thus conferred a considerable degree of legislative and executive autonomy on the new devolved entity. Such functions included education, law and order, health, social services, industry, agriculture, local government and transport. The reserved functions were largely those which had been designed by the 1920 act to be the remit of the Council of Ireland: matters such as external trade, shipping, radio, posts, coinage and patents. In the event, these remained permanently reserved to London. The excepted functions were those retained by the central government in London as matters of national – United Kingdom – importance such as the crown, the succession, foreign affairs, treaties, the armed forces, passports, visas and immigration. The Westminster parliament, as indicated in section 75 of the 1920 act, retained supreme legislative power and the Northern Ireland parliament was not able to repeal or alter United Kingdom statutes which extended to Northern Ireland. The governor was empowered to withhold the royal assent to Northern Ireland if so directed. As it happened, a convention was soon established whereby the Westminster parliament did not discuss the transferred matters pertaining to Northern Ireland, and the withholding of assent occurred only once, over the issue of the removal of proportional representation for local government elections in 1922, and was later granted. As Ken Bloomfield has pointed out, the power of the United Kingdom government to control events in Northern Ireland in the transferred fields was essentially an indirect power, related to the power of the purse and the 'ultimate deterrent' of recommending parliament to invoke its own truly sovereign authority.[4] In March 1972 the Westminster parliament agreed to this, and the Northern Ireland legislature was prorogued.

The Northern Ireland parliament possessed a wide field of legislative competence. Yet the nature of the 1920 act created a situation which led to frequent challenges to the validity of the parliament's acts. The parliament's legislation was subject to judicial review on grounds of *vires*, and no statute was ever beyond question. As Oliver has observed, day-to-day problems arose in the overlap or dubiety of the different categories of functions, and he cites the example of the difficulties created by Northern Ireland's lack of powers to control immigration or cross-border travel.[5] Calvert notes that a number of legal challenges to Northern Ireland statutes were made,

[4] Ken Bloomfield was a civil servant at Stormont from the early 1950s and head of the Northern Ireland Civil Service from 1984 to 1991. See his memo dated 19 December 1974 in National Archives, CJ4/536; also his article 'Devolution: Lessons from Northern Ireland?', *Political Quarterly*, lxvii (1966), 135–40.

[5] Oliver, 'On the Stormont Administration', n. 3.

although only one was clearly successful. However, another case, that of an Education Act passed in 1930, was later characterized as *ultra vires* by the attorney general and replacement legislation produced.[6] In the 1973 Northern Ireland Act the Westminster government sought to tackle this problem of *vires* by stipulating that the acts of the new Northern Ireland assembly being provided for should have the same status as the acts of the Westminster parliament and be exempt from judicial scrutiny.[7]

Reference has been made to London's financial control over Belfast. This had important consequences for the Northern Ireland parliament. The 1920 act put in place financial arrangements designed for a two-parliament scenario in Ireland, and in the middle of a trading boom. The arrangements soon proved unworkable in Northern Ireland and in 1925 a new agreement was reached with the British treasury following an arbitration process. This amounted to the alteration of the so-called 'Imperial Contribution' Northern Ireland was supposed to make to meet its share in the costs of maintaining the empire, so as to enable the province to pay social security and welfare benefits on a par with the rest of the United Kingdom. Northern Ireland residents also paid taxes at the same rate as in Britain, but the local parliament controlled only a small fraction of them. The larger taxes such as income tax were reserved to Westminster, and it was British treasury officials who decided on Northern Ireland's share of this 'reserved' taxation. After the Second World War, in order to extend to the province the full range of welfare measures then being implemented in London, a reinsurance agreement was reached by which excess costs of social services were recouped to the extent of 80% to the Northern Ireland exchequer from the United Kingdom exchequer. A joint exchequer board oversaw the evolution of such financial arrangements, but in reality the Northern Ireland parliament had little scope to debate or decide on them. Matters such as income tax were simply not within the competence of the parliament. This, coupled with the resolve of successive Northern Ireland Unionist governments to reproduce Westminster legislation or to provide parallel legislation to it in the field of social reform, restricted significantly the scope for debate in parliament. Giving evidence to the royal commission on the constitution in 1970 the Northern Ireland constitutional scholar, R. J. Lawrence, reflected on the way financial relations had operated in a secretive fashion and on how a popular perception had built in Ulster that Whitehall pressure was constantly being brought to bear on Northern Ireland ministers.[8]

Alterations to the powers of the Northern Ireland parliament were made in a number of Westminster statutes, namely in 1928, 1932, 1945, 1947, 1955 and 1962. These all had the effect of delegating further

[6] H. Calvert, *Constitutional Law in Northern Ireland: A Study in Regional Government* (1968), 288–9.

[7] See National Archives, cj4/981: letter by Ian Burns of the Northern Ireland Office dated 23 April 1975.

[8] National Archives, cj4/338: Lawrence memo dated March 1970.

authority to the local parliament to deal with a variety of topics. R. M. McBirney, for example, has highlighted the way the 1947 act removed the territorial restrictions and enabled the Northern Ireland government to enter into agreements with the government of southern Ireland in relation to matters of common interest such as drainage, electricity supply, fisheries and railway traffic.[9] During the Second World War the adaptability of the Northern Ireland constitution was put to the test by a series of defence of the realm regulations, Emergency Powers Acts and acts relating to rationing, employment and other matters passed at short notice by Westminster. The constitution was maintained mainly by virtue of orders in council made both in Belfast and London. In addition, Westminster passed an enabling act in 1942 to give the Northern Ireland parliament the right to prolong itself in the extraordinary circumstances of wartime. Stormont proceeded to pass the Prolongation of Parliament Act in 1943, and then again in 1944.

Another act of the Westminster parliament, that of the Ireland Act 1949, appeared to make a significant change in the constitution of Northern Ireland. The act was the outcome of the southern Irish state's decision, in 1948, to leave the British commonwealth and become a republic. The 1949 act was designed to clarify the position of those from southern Ireland resident in Britain, and also to clarify the position of Northern Ireland. The latter point was addressed in a clause which stated: 'that in no event will Northern Ireland or any part thereof cease to be part of His Majesty's dominions and of the United Kingdom without the consent of the Parliament of Northern Ireland'.[10] For some commentators this had 'practically the effect' of giving Northern Ireland a federal status within the United Kingdom.[11] Certainly, it raised important questions of constitutional law, and became part of the controversy over the suspension of Stormont by the London government in 1972.

Parties and Elections

Each election for the Northern Ireland parliament until its suspension was won emphatically by the Ulster Unionist Party (UUP). The party was a broad cross-class movement dedicated to preserving the position of Northern Ireland within the United Kingdom. Under the pragmatic leadership of Northern Ireland's first premier, Sir James Craig, the Unionists set out to consolidate the British connection; there was little appetite to use the devolved powers innovatively or to go in different policy directions. Above all, the Unionists took care to maintain their ethnic support base,

[9] R. M. McBirney, 'Stormont–Westminster Relations', *Public Administration in Northern Ireland*, ed. E. Rhodes (Londonderry, n.d.), 7–13.

[10] See text of act in *The Statutes Relating to the Constitution of Northern Ireland*, ed. J. L. Montrose and F. H. Newark (1957), 146–7.

[11] See H. Shearman, *How Northern Ireland is Governed: Central and Local Government in Northern Ireland* (1950).

> ### Éamon de Valera
>
> Éamon de Valera, who participated in the Easter Rebellion of 1916, went on to found the Fianna Fáil party and become taoiseach and president of the Southern Irish State, was also elected for the northern parliament. He stood successfully for the constituency of Down (later South Down) in 1921, 1925, and 1933, but never actually took the seat. As taoiseach in 1937 he introduced a new constitution for the 26-county state which claimed Northern Ireland as part of 'the national territory'.

in effect the two-thirds Protestant majority of the six-county unit. The potential threat to this voting block of issues of social class helps explain why successive Unionist governments were firm in their commitment to the principle of social welfare benefits being 'step by step' with across the water, and why so much Westminster social legislation was simply copied. The scrapping of proportional representation for parliamentary elections and its replacement by 'first past the post' in 1929 was essentially a politically motivated manœuvre by the ruling Unionists to weaken the electoral prospects of the Northern Ireland Labour Party (NILP) and other candidates who threatened to split the Unionist vote. The Unionists thrived electorally in a political struggle with the Nationalist Party (grouped loosely together for most of Stormont's history with an appeal confined to the Catholic minority) over the single issue of loyalty to the Northern Ireland state and support for its membership of the United Kingdom. The Nationalists, up until the 1969 election, were always the party with the second highest number of seats in parliament, yet they refused until 1965 to become the official opposition. Indeed, for many years they engaged fitfully in abstentionism, a development which adversely affected the credibility of parliamentary proceedings.

The combination of continuous one-party rule and irresponsible opposition led Lawrence to comment to the royal commission in 1970 that the Stormont parliament had been 'a weak instrument of political education'.[12] Over the course of the parliament's history the NILP attempted with limited success to attract votes across the communal Protestant–Catholic divide in society, and to compel parliament to focus purposefully on issues such as poverty and bad housing. The highest number of seats won by the NILP was only four, in the 1958 and 1962 elections. There were also independent members who occasionally enlivened proceedings, the most colourful being the representative for Belfast Shankill, Tommy Henderson. Henderson was a fixture in the House of Commons for almost 30 years, and entered Stormont folklore on account of a filibustering speech over a government finance bill which lasted nine and a half hours.

---

[12] National Archives, cj4/338: Lawrence memo.

Stormont has been labelled a 'part-time' parliament, and the long recesses between sessions have drawn comment.[13] There was undoubtedly a strong sense of many legislative matters simply being 'rubber-stamped' rather than exhaustively debated. The lack of strong opposition clearly contributed to such an impression being given. Moreover, the fact that so many parliamentary constituencies were uncontested in general elections further devalued the institution. In the 1933 election 27 seats, or 63.5% of the total, were marked by an unopposed return. Apart from the 1921 contest, there was an overall average per election of 16 uncontested seats.

The Troubles and Direct Rule

One-party dominance led to accusations of discriminatory treatment against the Catholic and Nationalist minority, and such grievances fuelled the civil rights movement in the 1960s. The political instability engendered gave way to violence and to the intervention of the British army in Northern Ireland and the eventual imposition of direct rule from Westminster. Stormont has often been held up since as a symbol of misgovernment. Yet it is important to make clear that the controversies over matters such as the gerrymandering of electoral boundaries, the franchise, and the allocation of housing were all matters of local not regional government. Oliver has pointed to the 'clean bill of health' given to the Stormont administration by the Kilbrandon commission report of 1973.[14] Nevertheless, it was within the competencies of successive Stormont governments to reform local government and this was not done until it was too late. Moreover, the issues behind the minority's sense of alienation had been raised regularly in the Northern Ireland parliament by Nationalist and Labour members.

It is interesting to remember that, as the crisis escalated during the late 1960s, the Northern Ireland premier at the time, Terence O'Neill, was making a significant effort to turn the local parliament into a more independently minded institution. Between 1965 and 1970 it has been noted that only 19% of the parliament's legislation could be described as of a 'step by step' with Westminster kind.[15] O'Neill, indeed, also liked to draw attention to distinctive pieces of Northern Ireland legislation that had brought beneficial social consequences, for example the tuberculosis legislation of 1946 and the act establishing the Northern Ireland Housing Trust in 1945. Before the 'troubles' enveloped Northern Ireland at least some informed observers had reached positive conclusions about the workings of devolution, if only from the point of view of the accessibility of the local institutions.

[13] See P. Arthur, 'Devolution as Administrative Convenience: A Case Study of Northern Ireland', *Parliamentary Affairs*, xxx (1979), 97–106.
[14] Oliver, 'On the Stormont Administration', 117.
[15] See W. D. Birrell, 'The Mechanics of Devolution: Northern Ireland Experience and the Scotland and Wales Bills', *Political Quarterly*, xlix (1978), 304–21.

The Stormont parliament was prorogued following the resignation of the Northern Ireland cabinet on 24 March 1972. Unionist prime minister Brian Faulkner, the sixth and final occupant of the office, had refused to carry on in a context in which Westminster was to assume control of law and order. Faulkner's decision to introduce internment without trial in August 1971 had proved to be the undoing of his premiership and the death knell of the Northern Ireland parliament. Instead of checking the rise of terrorist violence, internment had only made it worse. The British government, led by Edward Heath, felt it could not go on suffering the lash of international opinion for a situation over which it did not officially have control. There had been much speculation since the intervention of British troops in 1969 that direct rule from Westminster would be imposed. Nevertheless, the majority Unionist community was outraged when the step was finally taken, and leading Unionist politicians such as William Craig pointed to the 1949 act and claimed that Northern Ireland's constitutional rights had been breached. As a senior civil servant in the Northern Ireland Office was later to point out, the majority in the province came to treat the Stormont parliament as 'something equivalent to sovereign status'; he went on to add: 'For the average citizen Stormont eclipsed Westminster.'[16]

Postscript

From the suspension of the Stormont parliament in 1972 successive British governments sought to resolve the Northern Ireland problem by trying to engineer Unionist-Nationalist agreement around a new form of provincial government. A white paper issued in March 1973 eventually provided the basis for an assembly of 78 members elected by proportional representation from multi-member constituencies. However, the outcome of the Sunningdale Conference of December 1973, the formation of a power-sharing executive involving both Unionists and Nationalists along with a proposed Council of All Ireland, was repudiated by the bulk of Ulster Unionist opinion, as evidenced in the Northern Ireland results of the Westminster election of February 1974. A major industrial action by the Ulster Workers Council in May resulted in the executive's collapse. The Stormont assembly was formally dissolved in March 1975 to allow for elections to a new constitutional convention. The convention was given the task of devising a system of government with the greatest amount of acceptance throughout the community, but insufficient agreement could be reached. The convention was dissolved in March 1976.

The next attempt to create cross-community political co-operation came in 1982 when the then secretary of state, James Prior, devised a scheme which envisaged power being devolved to an assembly in stages, according to the levels of agreement reached. Elections to the 78-seat assembly took

[16] See National Archives, CJ4/ 981: letter by Ian Burns dated 22 September 1975.

place in October and it met the following month; however, no Nationalists attended. The arrangement was in effect superseded by the structures put in place by the Anglo-Irish Agreement of 1985, and the assembly was formally dissolved in May 1986.

The political deadlock was finally broken by the Good Friday Agreement of 1998 which was endorsed by the electorate in Northern Ireland in May. This allowed for the introduction of the Northern Ireland Act (1998) setting up a devolved assembly at Stormont. Elections were held in June and 108 members (known as members of the legislative assembly) were elected by proportional representation from multi-member constituencies. The assembly was given full executive and legislative authority for all matters that had previously been the remit of the six Northern Ireland government departments during the period of direct rule. The assembly was given powers to enact primary legislation for Northern Ireland, and bills were to be approved by the assembly, then accepted by the secretary of state and finally given the royal assent before becoming acts.

An executive composed of the four leading political parties, the Ulster Unionist Party (UUP), the Democratic Unionist Party (DUP), the Social and Democratic Labour Party (SDLP) and Sinn Féin (SF), was formed in November 1999 and devolution restored. A range of smaller parties provided rather ineffective opposition. Difficulties over Republican decommissioning of weapons then led to a suspension of devolution and a return to direct rule in February 2000. Progress on decommissioning resulted in the restoration of devolution in May; however, the issue continued to cause problems for the UUP leader and first minister, David Trimble, who resigned in July 2001. Trimble was re-elected first minister in November of that year and from then until a further suspension in October 2002 over alleged Republican intelligence-gathering, the assembly made significant progress on a range of issues. Assembly elections held in November 2003 strengthened the position of the DUP and SF at the expense of the UUP and the SDLP, but the political stalemate continued until after the elections of May 2007. Since then an executive headed by Ian Paisley of the DUP as first minister and Martin McGuinness of SF as deputy first minister has presided at Stormont over devolved arrangements still largely based on what was agreed in 1998, although modified by an agreement at St Andrews in 2006.

Chronology

1920
Government of Ireland Act provides for two parliaments in Ireland, one for the six-county North and one for the rest of the island

1921
Northern Ireland parliament set up

1925
Boundary Commission Report; subsequent treaty signed by London, Belfast and Dublin governments confirms existing Irish border and area of northern parliament's jurisdiction

1932
New Parliament Buildings at Stormont opened

1937
De Valera introduces new Irish constitution which lays claim to the territory of Northern Ireland

1949
Ireland Act passed at Westminster

1968
Outbreaks of violence in Northern Ireland over civil rights protests

1969
British Army sent to Northern Ireland to try to restore civil order

1971
Internment without trial introduced at Stormont

1972
Stormont parliament prorogued

1973
Sunningdale agreement paves way for power-sharing arrangement at Stormont

1974
Ulster Workers Council Strike; collapse of power-sharing experiment

1975
Constitutional convention set up

1976
Convention dissolved after failure to achieve sufficient agreement

1982
Rolling Devolution' initiative; assembly set up at Stormont

1985
Anglo-Irish Agreement' signed by London and Dublin governments

1986
Stormont assembly dissolved

1998
Good Friday Agreement and its endorsement in referendum paves way for restoration of devolution to Northern Ireland.

Further Reading

P. Buckland, *A History of Northern Ireland* (Dublin, 1981)

Devolution of Government: The Experiment in Northern Ireland, ed. F. H. Newark (1953)

S. Elliott, *Northern Ireland Parliamentary Election Results, 1921–1972* (Chichester, 1973)

W. D. Flackes, *Northern Ireland: A Political Directory, 1968–83* (1983)

D. Harkness, *Northern Ireland since 1920* (Dublin, 1983)

A. Jackson, *Home Rule: An Irish History, 1800–2000* (2003)

J. Kelly, *Bonfires on the Hillside: An Eyewitness Account of Political Upheaval in Northern Ireland* (Belfast, 1995)

N. Mansergh, *The Government of Northern Ireland: A Study in Devolution* (1936)

A. O'Day, *Irish Home Rule, 1867–1921* (Manchester, 1998)

D. Officer, 'In Search of Order, Permanence and Stability: Building Stormont, 1921–32', in *Unionism in Modern Ireland*, ed. R. English and G. Walker (Basingstoke, 1996), 130–47

T. O'Neill, *Ulster at the Crossroads* (1969)

A. S. Quekett, *The Constitution of Northern Ireland* (3 vols, Belfast, 1928–46)

J. Tonge, *The New Northern Irish Politics?* (Basingstoke, 2005)

Ulster under Home Rule: A Study of the Political and Economic Problems of Northern Ireland, ed. T. Wilson (Oxford, 1955)

G. Walker, *A History of the Ulster Unionist Party: Protest, Pragmatism and Pessimism* (Manchester, 2004)

24 Other Legislatures within the British Isles
Clyve Jones

Isle of Man

The Isle of Man is a crown dependency and not part of the United Kingdom, with the head of state being the British monarch, who has held the tile of Lord of Mann since 1765, and is represented on the island by a lieutenant governor. The British government is responsible for external relations, defence and the good-governance of the island. Man is not a part of the European Union, but it has a limited relationship relating to the free movement of goods, nor is it a member of the Commonwealth, though it does take part in several Commonwealth institutions, including the Commonwealth Parliamentary Association and the Commonwealth Games.

High Court of Tynwald

Tynwald (in Manx *Tinvaal*), or more formally the High Court of Tynwald, is the bicameral legislature of the Isle of Man, consisting of the directly elected, by universal suffrage, House of Keys, and the Legislative Council, which consists of *ex officio* and indirectly elected members (there are plans to transform the Council into a directly elected body). These two bodies meet together in joint session as Tynwald. It has been argued that this joint session makes Tynwald a tricameral parliament (i.e. it has three parts), which makes it unique in the world.[1]

Tynwald was nominally founded in 979 (though the earliest law recorded dates from 1417, with a comprehensive statute book dating from 1422 onwards),[2] and claims to be the oldest continuously existing parliament in the world, though this claim is disputed: from the 11th to the 15th centuries, Tynwald was arguably only a judicial court and did not legislate. During the 15th and 16th centuries the process of creating legislation varied on occasions and Tynwald does not appear to have functioned

---

[1] When the parliament for Northern Ireland (Stormont) was established, it was envisaged that if the two Houses – the House of Commons and the Senate – failed to reach agreement over a bill by the 'ordinary procedures of passing a bill through its different readings in each House and accepting amendments, then the two Houses were to meet in one assembly and settle their differences by vote' – making Stormont theoretically into a tricameral legislature. This procedural device was never used (see above, 341).

[2] This compares with the oldest recorded English act being from 1229, the oldest Irish from 1216 and the oldest Scottish from 1424.

as a single legislature during that period either. In 1600 the House of Keys became a permanent body, and by 1610 Tynwald had developed the power to create new laws. Between 1737 and 1765 Tynwald's agreement was required for all taxation, but this was lost when the island was sold to Great Britain by Charlotte, duchess of Atholl, and the crown assumed all powers to impose and collect taxes. The duchess had inherited the lordship of Mann from her father, the 2nd duke of Atholl, who had inherited it from his cousin the 10th earl of Derby in 1736, Henry IV having granted it to his ancestor Sir John Stanley. Before 1866 Tynwald's main function had been the operation of the island's court of appeal. In 1866 the House of Keys Election Act meant that for the first time members would be elected, and that the legislative and judicial functions would be separated, the judicial power was removed to a separate court.

Most Manx politicians stand for election as independents rather than representatives of a political party, though such parties do exist. The largest such party is the recently established Liberal Vannin Party, which promotes great Manx independence and more accountability in government.

Tynwald meets annually in St John's (normally on 5 July, which is midsummer day according to the Julian calendar, which has been retained in Man for certain limited purposes) at an open air ceremony on Tynwald Hill, where the lieutenant governor presides, unless the monarch or another member of the royal family representing him or her is present. Here, all laws are promulgated (a legal requirement upon which the validity of legislation enacted by Tynwald depends) and special petitions received (an ancient right whereby individuals with grievances can petition, and if such are considered justified they are investigated by a select committee of Tynwald).

When Tynwald meets in Douglas, the island's capital, the president of Tynwald, chosen by the other members, presides. Proceedings in the joint session consist of members of each House formally signing bills, notice of royal assent is received, question can be put to minister, special resolutions authorizing taxes are made, delegated legislation made by government department may be approved or annulled, and petitions may be presented and other important public business is conducted.

When the Tynwald votes while meeting jointly, each House votes separately. If a majority of each House approves, the motion is carried. If the Legislative Council's vote ties, then the president of Tynwald casts the deciding vote in line with the majority in the House of Keys. However, if the Keys approve a motion but the Council disapproves, then the question can be put again at a different sitting. In this latter case the vote is determined by a majority of all the members of Tynwald. If this occurs, the Keys, with its larger size, usually prevails.

Normally both Houses must pass a bill before it goes to the sovereign or the lieutenant governor for royal approval. If the Council rejects a bill or amend it against the Keys' wishes, the Keys has the power to pass the same bill again when the Council's approval is not required and the bill is then presented for royal assent. Such assent is granted or refused following consultation with the ministry of justice in the United Kingdom

The Channel Islands

The Channel Islands were originally part of the duchy of Normandy, and when the duchy was lost by the English crown in 1204 the islands remained loyal to the king of England who promised to rule them observing the duchy's laws, customs and liberties. In 1259 Henry III by the treaty of Paris resigned his claim to the duchy of Normandy except for the Channel Islands, which were not absorbed into the kingdom of England, and two officers were appointed for each of the main islands – the warden (now the lieutenant governor) and the bailiff. Thus the islands secured their own judiciary and freedom from the process of English law. The islands are independent, with the British monarch as head of state, in all matters excepting foreign affairs and defence for which the United Kingdom is responsible. The islands are not part of the European Union, but enjoy special terms which grant access for exports free of tariff barriers. Nor are the islands represented in the United Kingdom parliament, and acts of parliament do not apply to the islands unless extended by an order in council.

The States of Delegation of Guernsey

The States is the unicameral parliament for the bailiwick of Guernsey which consists of six islands other than Guernsey: Alderney, Sark, Herm, Jethou, Brecqhou and Lihou. The States is democratically elected, but there are no political parties in Guernsey. The States and the Royal Court are presided over by the bailiff and deputy bailiff of the bailiwick, both appointed by the crown. Other crown appointments are the procureur (attorney general) and the comptroller (solicitor general), the legal advisers to the crown and the States. The States has the power to raise taxation, determine expenditure and to pass legislation.

The government of the bailiwick, the policy council, comprises a chief minister and ten minister who run the ten government departments (each department also having four members). All are members of the States and all are elected to office by the States. The deputy chief minister is elected by the States from among the ministers of the policy council. Each department has a deputy minister chosen from the four States members, and also may appoint up to two non-States members who do not have a vote.

The States has five committees made up of a chairman and four States members elected by the States. Each committee may appoint up to two or up to four non-States members depending upon the committee, who do not have a vote. The five committees are: house, legislation, public accounts, public sector remuneration, and scrutiny.

Until recently the island of Sark continued to be ruled under a feudal system, possibly the last survivor of such a system in western Europe. In

2007 a start was made in dismantling it in accordance with the European Convention on Human Rights, and in 2008 a new law was approved by the British privy council to establish a 30-member chamber, with 28 of its members elected. The first election for members was held in December 2008 and the chamber first convened in January 2009.

Assembly of the States of Jersey

Originally the island's Royal Court had legislative power but in the 16th century a legislative assembly within the Royal Court was convened. In the early 17h century separate minutes of the States were first recorded. Charles II gave Jersey the power to levy customs duties, a power finally taken over by the States in 1921, thereby enabling the States to control the budget independently of the lieutenant governor.

The Assembly of the States is the unicameral legislative parliament of the bailiwick of Jersey, which up to December 2005 also directly exercised executive power. The executive is now a chief minister and a cabinet elected by the States. The presiding officer or president of the assembly is the bailiff (a royal appointment), who may not cast a vote except as a tie-breaker. In the absence of the bailiff, the deputy bailiff or an individual chosen by the assembly presides.

The voting members of the assembly consist of 12 senators chosen by the whole bailiwick for six-year terms (the terms are staggered so that six senators are chosen every three years), 29 deputies elected for a three-year term by single, or multi-member constituencies, and 12 connetables, or heads of the parishes, elected by the parishes, who sit *ex officio* in the assembly. The latter are not directly elected to the assembly and serve a three-year term.

In addition to the elected members, the assembly also includes three members who may speak but not vote: the attorney general and solicitor general, appointed by the monarch as officers of state and sit in the assembly *ex officio* and speak on legal matters, and the dean of Jersey (the senior Church of England clergyman on the island), also sits *ex officio* and may speak on any topic, as well as acting a the chaplain of the assembly, who conducts the opening prayers for every sitting in French.

The passage of a law by the assembly is generally not subject to any veto. The law is submitted to the monarch and has no effect until it receives royal assent. A piece of legislation passed by the assembly is known as a 'law' and not an act. An 'act' of the States is an administrative enactment and may be in the nature of secondary legislation.

In 1856 the States voted to add 14 deputies to the assembly (first elected in January 1857) to counterbalance the mismatch of population and voting power between the urban and rural areas. The first election by secret ballot was held in December 1891. Until the late 1940s, when reforms were brought in to separate the legislature from the judiciary, the jurats were the senior politician and were elected for life by an island-wide suffrage. They were the presidents of committees and sat in the Royal Court to preside over cases. In 1948 the jurats were replaced in the legislature by directly elected senators for terms of nine years (later reduced to six years). Rectors were also removed from the States (with the exception of the dean of Jersey as rector of St Helier) and replaced by an increased number of deputies.

The Speaker of the assembly is the bailiff, who is also president of the Royal Court. In 2005 as part of the reforms of the legislature and the judiciary the bailiff lost his casting vote in the event of a tie.

Until 1887 the States sat in the Royal Court, when a new chamber was constructed adjacent to it. The benches are arranged in a horseshoe-form around the twin seats of the bailiff and lieutenant governor. The senators sit to the left of the bailiff, then the connetables, and then the deputies filling up the benches to the right.

Irish Parliament (*Oireachtas*)

The parliament of the Republic of Ireland consists of the president of Ireland and the two Houses: Dáil Éireann and Seanad Éireann. The Houses reside in Leinster House in Dublin.

The parliament came into existence in 1922 and was the legislature of the Irish Free State until 1937. Earlier in 1919 Irish republicans had set up and extra-legal, unicameral parliament known as Dáil Éireann which claimed to be a legislature for the whole island of Ireland. Parallel to this body, in 1920, the British government created a home rule legislature called the Parliament of Southern Ireland, made up of the king, the House of Commons and the Senate of Southern Ireland. It was boycotted by most Irish politicians and was abolished in 1922 when the Irish Free State came into existence. Then the Oireachtas consisted of the king, Dáil Éireann (or Chamber of Deputies) and Seanad Éireann (or Senate). These were abolished in 1935 and the present parliament came into being in 1937 with the adoption, after a referendum, of the constitution of the newly established Republic of Ireland.

Article 3 of the new constitution asserted the parliament's jurisdiction over the whole of Ireland, but pending the reunion of the whole island the acts of the Irish parliament would not apply to Northern Ireland. There has been no serious attempt to have Northern Ireland represented in the Dáil, even though Éamon de Valera, Ireland first taoiseach (or prime minister) had been elected to represent a northern constituency. However, subsequent taiosigh have appointed people from Northern Ireland to the Seanad. The Irish parliament abolished by the Anglo-Irish treaty of union of 1800 was the last legislature in Ireland to have the power to legislate for the whole island.

The Dáil Éireann is directly elected at least once in every five years under universal suffrage of all Irish and British citizens who are resident and at least 18 years of age. Elections occur under a system of proportional representation by mean of the single transferable vote. The Seanad is not directly elected but consists of a mixture of selected members: 43 senators are elected councillors and parliamentarians, 11 are appointed by the taoiseach, and six are elected by the two university constituencies. The president of Ireland is directly elected once in every seven years for a maximum of two terms. On a number of occasions a consensus has been reached among the larger political parties: only one candidate has been nominated and thus no ballot has occurred.

Bills must first be approved both by the Dáil and the Seanad, though the Dáil can override a Seanad's refusal to pass a bill. The Seanad's powers are limited to delay rather than veto, thus the Dáil is the supreme tier of the Irish legislature. The bill is then signed into law by the president, who is obliged to sign all bills approved by both the Houses, though he or she has the power to refer most bills to the supreme court for a ruling on their constitutionality. Bills to amend the constitution must be approved by the people before being presented to the president.

Other Parliaments and Legislatures of the British Isles

25 Post-Devolution Legislatures
Clyve Jones

A royal commission on the constitution (the Kilbrandon Commission) was established in 1969 by Harold Wilson's Labour government to investigate the possibility of devolution of parliamentary government for Scotland and Wales. This commission was prompted by a sharp rise in nationalism in the late 1960s. However, suggestions for a devolved parliament had been made in Scotland before 1914. The commission's recommendations formed the basis of the 1973 white paper *Democracy and Devolution: Proposals for Scotland and Wales*, which proposed the creation of a Scottish parliament and a Welsh assembly. However, voters rejected the proposals by a majority of four to one in Wales in a referendum held in 1979, whereas, though 52% of the vote in Scotland was in favour, the proposal for a Scottish parliament failed as this figure did not equal the 40% of the total electorate threshold laid down as necessary to pass the measure, as 32.9% of the electorate had abstained from voting.

After the 1997 general election the new Labour government proposed that a parliament in Scotland and an assembly in Wales would be more democratically accountable than the Scottish or Welsh Offices (for example, between 1986 and 1997 Wales had been represented in the United Kingdom cabinet by a secretary of state who did not sit for a Welsh constituency at Westminster). In September 1997 a second set of devolution referenda was held in which voters approved the creation of a Scottish parliament and a Welsh assembly (in the case of Wales by a small majority of 6,712 votes). In 1998 the acts establishing the two devolved legislatures passed the Westminster parliament.

Scottish Parliament
(Parlamaid na h-Alba)

The Scottish parliament is the unicameral legislature for Scotland, consisting of 129 members (MSPs), elected for a four-year term under a mixed member proportional representation system: 73 MSPs represent individual constituencies elected by the plurality ('first-past-the-post') system, with a further 56 returned from eight additional member regions, each electing seven MSPs. This mixed member proportional representation system, one of the first to be used in the United Kingdom, is a form of the additional member method of proportional representation.

The 1998 Scotland Act established the parliament (which opened in

1999) and delineated the areas in which it can make laws by explicitly specifying powers that are 'reserved' to Westminster: that is, all matters that are not explicitly reserved are automatically the responsibility of the Scottish parliament. The United Kingdom parliament retains the power to amend the terms of reference of the Scottish parliament and can reduce or extend the areas in which it can legislate.

By the terms of the Scotland Act of 1998 Westminster, which continues to constitute the supreme legislature of Scotland, devolved most domestic matters to the Edinburgh parliament, including health, education, agriculture and justice. A degree of domestic and all foreign policy, however, remains with Westminster, though the Scottish parliament can debate such issues. The Scottish parliament also has limited tax-varying powers.

Members of the public can take part in parliament in two ways which are not the case at Westminster: a public petitioning system, and crossparty groups on policy topics where the public can attend meeting alongside MSPs.

The party which holds the majority of seats forms the Scottish government, but the first minister is elected by all members of parliament from a number of candidates (any MSP can put their name forward) at the beginning of each parliamentary term. Normally, of course, it is the leader of the largest party who is elected first minister, who in practice appoints the other ministers, though in theory they could also be elected by the parliament.

The first home for the Scottish parliament was the General Assembly Hall of the Church of Scotland on the Royal Mile in Edinburgh. In May 2000 the parliament was temporarily relocated to the Strathclyde Regional Council debating chamber in Glasgow, and in May 2002 to the University of Aberdeen, to allow for the meeting of the Church of Scotland's General Assembly. Since September 2004 the parliament has occupied the new Scottish parliament building opposite Holyrood Palace in Edinburgh.

The debating chamber has seating arranged in a semicircle. There are 131 seats: 129 of these are occupied by the elected MSPs, and two are reserved for the Scottish law officers – the lord advocate and the solicitor general for Scotland – who are not elected members but members of the Scottish government. MSPs can theoretically sit anywhere in the chamber, but actually sit in party groupings. The front row of the middle section of the chamber is occupied by the first minister, cabinet ministers and the law officers. The largest party sit in the middle of the semicircle, with opposing parties on either side. The presiding officer (equivalent of the Speaker) – who chairs proceedings, is elected by secret ballot (the only one in the parliament) at the beginning of each parliamentary session (and he or she accepts voluntary suspension from their party for the duration of their period of office) – along with two MSPs to serve as deputies, sit, together with the parliamentary clerks and officials, opposite the members at the front of the debating chamber.

Speeches are normally delivered in English, but members may use

Scots, Gaelic, or any other language with the agreement of the presiding officer, and the parliament has conducted debates in Gaelic. Votes are first taken orally, but if there is audible dissent the presiding officer calls for a division and MSPs proceed to vote electronic from consoles on their desks. Party coherence in voting is strong, backed up by the threat of deselection or expulsion from the party, so that the independence of members is low and 'backbench rebellions' rare.

Backbenchers are, however, important in the work of the committees, where much of the work of the parliament is done. In fact the role of committees is stronger in the Scottish parliament than in any other parliamentary system in the United Kingdom, and is designed to partly compensate for the lack of a revising chamber. Such committees conduct inquiries, scrutinize legislation and hold the government to account. There are three kinds of committee, each comprising a small number of MSPs with their membership reflecting the balance of the parties within parliament: first, mandatory committees, which are set down under the parliament's standing orders, and cover such important continuing areas as audit, European and external affairs, finance, procedures, public petitions, and subordinate legislation; second, subject committees where one committee corresponds with one or more department or ministries; and third, private bill committees set up to scrutinize bills submitted by an outside party or a promoter who is not a member of the parliament or government.

Elections to the parliament are normally held every four years on the first Thursday in May, though an extraordinary general election can be held under one of the following circumstances: if the parliament itself resolves that it should be dissolved (with at least two-thirds of the MSP voting in favour), or if the parliament fails to nominate a first minister within 28 days of a general election or of the position becoming vacant, the presiding officer proposes a date for an election and the parliament is dissolved by the monarch. Such elections are in addition to ordinary general elections unless held less than six month before the date due for an ordinary general election, in which case they supplant it, and the following ordinary general elections reverts to the first Thursday in May, a multiple of four years later.

Of the 129 MSPs, 73 are elected in the first-past-the-post constituencies and are known as 'constituency MSPs'. These 73 constituencies shared the same boundaries as the United Kingdom parliament constituencies in Scotland before the 2005 reduction in the number of Scottish MPs, with the exception of Orkney and Shetland, which each return their own constituency MSPs.

The remaining 56 MSPs are elected by the additional member system. Electors have a second vote whereby they vote for a party list instead of a constituency representative. These 56 are elected in eight electoral regions, of which constituencies are sub-divisions. Each region returns seven members, known as 'List MSPs'. If such an MSP resigns, he or she is replaced by the next member on the party list.

One procedural consequence of the establishment of the Scottish parliament is the anomaly known as the 'West Lothian Question', whereby Scottish MPs at Westminster are still able to vote on domestic legislation that applies only to England, Wales and Northern Ireland, whilst English, Scottish, Welsh and Northern Irish Westminster MPs are unable to vote on the domestic legislation of the Scottish parliament. This problem to some extend also applies to the members of the Westminster Commons from Northern Ireland and Wales.

National Assembly for Wales
(Cynulliad Cenedlaethol Cymru)

Established by the Government of Wales Act of 1998, the unicameral National Assembly for Wales opened in 1999. In 2002 the Welsh Assembly government set up an independent commission under the chairmanship of Lord Richard (a former leader of the House of Lords) to review the power and electoral functions of the National Assembly. The commission reported in March 2004, recommending that the assembly should have powers to legislate in certain areas, other powers remaining to the Westminster parliament. It also recommended changing to proportional representation in the voting system: to the single transferable vote. The United Kingdom government in response published in 2005 a white paper, *Better Government for Wales*, which put forward a system of greater law-making powers for the assembly.

Unusually for devolved parliaments in the United Kingdom the National Assembly for Wales initially had no legal or constitutional separation of the legislative and executive functions, but in practice there was a separation of functions and the terms 'Assembly Government' and 'Assembly Parliamentary Service' came into use. The separation of powers was regularized by the Government of Wales Act of 2006, which conferred on the assembly legislative powers similar to those of other devolved legislatures, although assembly orders-in-council requests are subject to a veto from the secretary of state for Wales (who retains a vestigial role in the government of Wales), the House of Commons or the House of Lords. Initially the assembly did not have primary legislative or fiscal powers, which were reserved to Westminster, but only powers of secondary legislation in its devolved areas. (These limited legislative power owed much to the fact that Wales has had the same legal system as England since its union with England in 1536.) The 2006 act converted the assembly into a parliamentary-type institution and established the Welsh government as a separate entity from, but accountable to the assembly, enabling the assembly to legislate within its devolved areas. The act also reformed the electoral system, preventing individuals standing in both constituencies and regional seats (see below). These changes were implemented in 2007.

The assembly has 60 elected Assembly Members (AMs), or in Welsh *Aelod y Cynulliad* (ACs). The electoral system is a mixed member proportional representation or additional member system, where 40 of the AMs are elected from single-member constituencies on a plurality voting system (or 'first-past-the-post') basis (where the constituencies are the equivalent to those used for the Westminster House of Commons), and 20 AMs are elected from regional closed list using the alternative party vote. There are five regions, which are the same as the pre-1999 European parliament constituencies for Wales, and each returns four members.

The assembly was first based in Crickhowell House in the Cardiff Bay area of the city until 2006 when the Senedd (built next door) was opened. It houses the debating chamber (*siambr*) and the committee rooms, while Crickhowell House continues to house the offices of member of the assembly.

The seating plan in the Senedd is laid out in a full circle of two tiers with the members sitting by parties occupying three-quarters of the circle. The presiding officer or chair sits at the centre desk in the middle of the inner of the two tiers of the fourth quarter of the circle. The members of the Welsh government occupy an inner semicircle third tier, with the first minister in the centre desk opposite the presiding officer.

After each election, the assembly elects two of its members to serve as presiding officer (*llywydd*) and as deputy presiding officer. Lord Elis-Thomas of Plaid Cymru has been the presiding officer since the assembly opened. The presiding officer chairs the plenary session of the assembly, maintains order and protects the rights of members, as well as being responsible for standing orders, and is the final authority on their interpretation.

The government is led by the first minister, who is nominated by the assembly and appointed by the monarch.

26 Epilogue
Clyve Jones

One of the functions of an historian is to determine whether there are any patterns of development within a particular historical topic. With the story of the British parliaments from their beginnings to the present day the historian has to be particularly careful in searching for patterns not to commit the teleological sin of our Victorian forebears of imposing a whig interpretation; that is, of seeing the development of parliaments as one of the continuous growth of an increasingly democratic institution. While keeping this warning in mind, it is, however, possible to see certain patterns in parliamentary development from the Anglo-Saxons to the 21st century.

The first such pattern is one of the increasing unity of parliamentary institutions within the British Isles. Three major unions of the three kingdoms and one principality led as a by-product to a developing union of parliamentary institution. First, in 1536 was the union of England and Wales into one administrative unit. Though there was no Welsh parliament in existence in the 16th century, the union did have an effect on the English parliament by the introduction of Welsh MPs in to the House of Commons. As there was no native Welsh peerage, there was no influx of new lords into the upper House (unlike the two unions which followed), though the four Welsh bishops had been members of the Lords for some time.

In 1707 there was the Anglo-Scottish union, which was much more a parliamentary union than an administrative one. The Scottish unicameral parliament was abolished and the membership of the new British parliament was increased by an addition of 45 Scottish MPs and 16 Scottish representative peers, both groups elected at each general election.

The Anglo-Irish union of 1801 was also more of a parliamentary than an administrative union, with the abolition of the bicameral Dublin parliament and the addition of 100 MPs to the Commons and 28 representative peers and four representative bishops of the (Anglican) Church of Ireland to the Lords. The MPs were, or course, returned after each general election, while the peers (unlike their Scottish equivalents) were elected for life and by-elections were only held on the death of a sitting representative peer. The bishops sat for single sessions by means of a rotation amongst the whole episcopacy.

Two further patterns emerged in the 19th century and continued into the 20th. First, there was the growth of the British empire, and with the empire the spread of parliamentary government. The old, white dominions of Canada (1867), Australia (1901) and New Zealand (1852) adopted legislatives modelled on that of Westminster. In 1951 New Zealand's parliament was converted into a unicameral one with the abolition of the upper, nominated chamber, the Legislative Council. Many of the post-Second World War independent countries, mainly in Africa and Asia, also adopted a kind of Westminster model even if in the decades since independence some have cast off this colonial inheritance.

The second pattern was the growth of democracy in Britain in the form of the expanding franchise, starting with the Great Reform Act of 1832 (though few of its movers would have regarded it in this light) and continuing with the further Reform Acts of 1867 and 1884 (plus the Redistribution Act of 1885), and in the 20th century the extension of the vote to women over 30 in 1918 and in 1928 to all women over 21. A tidying up process of the franchise continued in the late 20th century with the abolition of the university seats in 1949, which had given the privileged few a second vote, and its extension to 18-year-olds in 1970.

Concurrent with this extension of democracy at home and democracy and parliamentary government in the colonies and their successor states, the 20th century saw the beginning of the disintegration of the unity of the British state covering all of the British Isles, a disintegration largely based on the development of nationalism within the unitary state. Ireland was the first to go in 1922 with the creation of the Irish Free State with a restored bicameral parliament in Dublin. Six of the eight counties of Ulster in the north opted to remain within the United Kingdom and were granted their own unicameral legislature at Stormont. In the late 20th century through this growth of nationalism (while never reaching a majority of the population and despite the failure through referendums of a proposed devolution in 1975) Scotland gained its own unicameral parliament and Wales its unicameral assembly in 1999. Both legislatures have restricted powers with certain areas of taxation and foreign policy reserved to Westminster. The establishment of Scottish and Welsh legislatures with MPs from these two countries still elected to Westminster has left the tricky problem of the Scots (and the Northern Irish and Welsh) members involvement in purely English matters in the union parliament, the so-called 'West Lothian Question'. The rejection so-far by the English of regional assemblies (the English not being driven by nationalism), led by a failed referendum in the north-east, has left the English in a different position in relation to their parliamentary institutions from the denizens of the rest of the United Kingdom.

Added to all this parliamentary disintegration of the unitary British state is the diminution of the power of parliament posed by two 20th-century developments: membership of the European Union since 1975, with its own parliament at Strasbourg and the Commission at Brussels, and with its own legislation which takes priority over legislation in all the member states; and the growth of a presidential style executive in Downing Street which since the 1980s has increasingly been seen to take less notice of parliament.

Index

Numbers in italic indicate references appearing in an insert on that page.

Abbot, Charles, Speaker of the House of Commons 255
Aberdeen, university of 359
Aberdeen, George Gordon, 4th earl [S] of 204
Abergavenny, Henry Neville, 2nd lord 44
Adonis, Andrew, baron 208
Ælfric, ealdorman 4
Æthelred, king 4
    charters of 3
Albemarle, George Monck, 1st duke of 50, 54, 55, 314
Al Fayed, Mr 289
Almon, John 189
    Parliamentary Register 189
America, colonies in 103, 178, 188
Amesbury, Wilts. 4
Amultree, William Mackenzie, baron 218
Andover, Hants. 4
Anglo-Irish Agreement (1985) 349
Anne, queen 147, *148*
    creation of peerages 55, 149, 152
Argyll, John Douglas Edward Henry Campbell, 7th duke [S] of 204
Armagh, archbishop of 197
Arundel, Thomas Fitzalan, 5th earl of 19
    William Fitzalan, 9th earl of 19
Arundel of Wardour, Henry, 3rd baron 44
Ashridge, Herts. 12
Asquith, H. H. *276*
Association Movement 163
Astor, Nancy, lady 272
Athelstan, king of Wessex 3
    charters of 3
Atholl, Charlotte Murray, duchess of 353
    James Murray, 2nd duke [S] of 353
Atkin, James 220
Atkyns, Sir Robert 69
Atlee, Clement 222, 276, 291
attorney general 30, 276, 344
Auckland, George Eden, 2nd baron 196
Audley, James Touchet, 17th lord 163
Australia 363

Bacon, Francis *see* St Alban, viscount
Bagehot, Walter 226
Baker, Sir John, Speaker of the House of Commons 89
Baldwin, Stanley 216–18, 277–9
Balfour, Arthur 216, *276*
Bangor, bishop of 87
Barkstead, Sir John 50

Barlow, Thomas 57
Barry, Charles 251
Bath, Henry Bourchier, 5th earl of 44
Beaconsfield, Benjamin Disraeli, earl of 208, 261, 262
Beauchamp, Richard *see* Warwick, earl of
Beaumont, John, 6th lord 19
Bedford, Francis Russell, 4th earl of 33, *33*, 38
Belasyse, Thomas
    see Fauconberg, viscount
Belfast, Co. Antrim 339, 340
    City Hall 339
    lord mayor of 340
    Stormont 2, 341, 364
    Union Theological College 341
Bellamy, John 251
    dining room of 250, 251, 252
Bellingham, John 250
Benn, Tony 243
Bennet, Sir Henry 134
Bentinck, William Henry Cavendish
    see Portland, duke of
Berkeley, Charles, 2nd earl of 55
    George, 1st earl of 56
    James *see* Dursley, viscount
    James, 3rd earl of 55
Berkshire, Thomas Howard, 1st earl of 44
Berry, James 50
Bertie, James *see* Norris, lord
    Montagu *see* Lindsey, earl of
Berwick-upon-Tweed, Northumb. 11, 12
Better Government for Wales 361
Billyard-Leake, E. W., commander 215
Bing, Sir George *148*
Birkenhead, Frederick Edwin Smith, 1st earl of 214
Birmingham, Warws. 1, 184, 185, 205
Blair, Tony 241
Blomfield, Ken 343
Blount, Mountjoy *see* Newport, earl of
Booth, George *see* Delamer of Dunham Massey, baron
Bourchier, Henry *see* Bath, earl of
Bowes, Paul 86
Bowyer, Robert 102
Boyer, Abel 186
Boyle, Roger *see* Broghill, baron
Boyne, battle of, painting of *342*
Bradley, William 329
Braithwaite report 298
Brampton, Northants. 5

Brandon, Charles *see* Suffolk, duke of
Bridgwater, John Egerton, 1st earl of, diary of 37
    John Egerton, 2nd earl of 63
Bright, John 1
Bristol, Glos. 12, 118, 181
    Society of Merchant Adventurers 181
Bristol, George Digby, 2nd earl of 61, 134, 139
    John Digby, 1st earl of 30, 44
Brodrick, Sir Alan 60
Broghill, Roger Boyle, baron [I] of 49, 50, 330
Bromhead, P. A. 221
Brudenell of Stonton, Thomas, baron 54
Brussels 364
Bryce, James, viscount 212
Bryce Commission 212, 217
Brydges, John
    see Chandos of Sudeley, baron
Buccleuch, Francis Scott, 2nd duke [S] of 152
Buchan, John 217
Buckingham, George Villiers, 1st duke of 33, 34, 38, 105, 108
    George Villiers, 2nd duke of 62
Burgh, Hubert de 12
    James 173
Burghley, Sir William Cecil, baron of 94, 95, 96, 97
Burke, Edmund 173, 179, 180, 188
    Ninth Report of the Select Committee on India 186
Burnet, Gilbert 148
    History of My Own Time 65
Burton, Thomas 114, *115*, 115
Bury St Edmunds, Suff. 18
Bute, John Stuart, 3rd earl [S] of 151, 161
Butler, David 273
    James *see* Ormond, duke of
Butt, Ronald 280
Buxton, Noel, baron 218
Byron, George Gordon, 6th baron 195
    William, 5th baron 159

cabinet 226
    shadow 277
Callaghan, James 241
Calvert, H. 343
Cambridge, university of 11
Campbell, Archibald *see* Ilay, earl of
    J. R. 276
    John Douglas Edward Henry *see* Argyll, duke of
Campden, Baptist Noel, 3rd viscount 44
Canada 363
Canterbury, Kent 11
Canterbury, archbishops of 69
    see also Cranmer, Thomas; Laud, William; Stratford, John; Tenison, Thomas
Capel, Arthur *see* Essex, earl of
Capel of Hadham, Arthur, 1st baron 44
Carey, Henry *see* Dover, earl of
Carlisle, Cumb. 12
Carlisle, bishop of *see* Nicolson, William
Carlisle, James Hay, 3rd earl of 44
Caroline, queen consort of George IV 200
Carrington of Burford, Charles Smyth, 1st viscount [I] of 44
Carson, Edward 219, *341*
Carteret of Hawnes, George, baron 56, 65
Cashel, Co. Longford 329
Cashel, archbishop of *197*
Cassilis, John, Kennedy, 2nd earl [S] of 50
Castledermot, Co. Kildare 321, 329
Castlereagh, Robert Stewart, styled viscount [I] 200
Catherine de Valois, queen consort of Henry V 19
Catherine Howard, queen consort of Henry VIII 93
Catherine of Aragon, queen consort of Henry VIII 89, 195
Catherine of Braganza, queen consort of Charles II 67
Cave, George, viscount 217
Cavendish, William *see* Devonshire, duke of; Devonshire, earl of
Cecil, James *see* Salisbury, earl of
    Robert Arthur James *see* Cranborne of Essendon, baron
    Sir Robert *see* Salisbury, earl of
    William *see* Salisbury, earl of
    Sir William *see* Burleigh, baron of
Chamberlain, Joseph 276
    Neville 219
chancery, clerks of 116
    masters in 30
    senior officials of 11
Chandos of Sudeley, John Brydges, 6th baron 44
Chaplin, Henry 276
Charitable Corporation 179
Charles, prince *see* Charles II
Charles, prince of Wales
    see Charles I, king
Charles I, king, previously prince of Wales 29, 30, 32, 38, 42, 44, 46, 47, 48, 54, 66, 93, 103, 105, 107, 113, 113, 114, 118, 126, 132, 148, 307, 308, 326
    judges of 68

Index 367

Charles II, king, previously prince
  44, 54, 65, 67, 118 (Charles Stuart),
  126, 132, 136, 140, 147, 148, 159, 161
  creation of peers 54, 55
  Gracious Declaration (1660) of 326
charters, royal 3, 4
Chatham, William Pitt the Elder, 1st earl of
  156, 159, 161, 175
Chelmsford, Frederic John Napier
  Thesiger, 2nd baron 217
Cheshire, palatinate of 88
Churchill, John see Marlborough, duke of
  Sir Winston 281
Clare, Gilbert de see Gloucester, earl of
Clarendon, Wilts., constitutions of 5
  council of 5
Clarendon, Edward Hyde, 1st earl of
  60, 61, 66, 67
  Edward Hyde, 3rd earl of 155
  Henry Hyde, 2nd earl of 55, 59, 64, 67
clergy 13, 24, 79, 80, 110
clerk of the crown 95
Cleveland, Thomas Wentworth, earl of 44
Cleypole, John 50
Clifford, Sir Thomas 134
Clipstone, Northants. 12
Clonmel, Co. Cork 329
Cobbett, William 259
  Parliamentary Debates 189, 259, 260
  Parliamentary History 260
  Political Register 260
  State Trials 260
Cocks, Michael 291
  Sir Richard 130
commission, royal 347
commissioners to perambulate royal
  forests 11
Commonwealth Games 353
Commonwealth Parliamentary
  Association 353
Compton, James see Northampton, earl of
  James, styled lord 110
  Spencer see Wilmington, earl of
Conference on Security and Cooperation
  in Europe 284
convocation 56, 60, 79, 89
Conway, Edward, 2nd viscount 44
Cook, Robin 293
Cooke, Edward, colonel 60
Cooper, Anthony Ashley
  see Shaftesbury, earl of
  Cropley Ashley see Shaftesbury, earl of
  Duff 217
  Thomas 50
Copley, family 90
  John Singleton 159
Cosin, John, bishop of Durham 56

Cottington of Hanworth, Francis,
  baron 44
Cotton, Sir Robert 96
council 6, 11, 19, 77, 322
  great 3
  of officers 112
  privy 34, 35, 91, 93, 134, 355
  protector's 49, 116
  regional 91
  of state 49
  of war 103
Council of All Ireland 346
Council of Ireland 339
Courtenay, Edward see Devon, earl of
  Thomas see Devon, earl of
Coventry, Warws. 20, 83
Cowper, Henry 65
  William, 1st earl 156, 157
Craig, Sir James 341, 345
  William 348
Cranborne of Essendon, Robert Arthur
  James Cecil, baron 222
Cranfield, Lionel see Middlesex, earl of
Cranmer, Thomas, archbishop of
  Canterbury 38
Craven, William, earl of 61
Creed, Mr 122
Crew, John 50
Crewe, Ranulph 106, 111
Crick, Bernard 221, 283, 298
Cripps, Sir Stafford 218
Cromwell, Henry 50, 330
  Oliver, lord protector 26, 62, 88, 93, 110,
    112, 116, 118, 314
  Richard 50, 110, 112, 115
  Thomas (d. 1540), baron 91, 93, 94, 96
  Thomas (d. 1610/11) 96
  Thomas (d. 1687), 4th baron 44
Crossman, Richard 226, 244, 283, 291–3,
  296
crown, prerogative of 39, 42, 107, 108,
  152, 153
Cumberland, Prince Rupert, duke of 44
Curzon of Keddleston, George Nathaniel,
  marquess 216

Dacre, Francis Lennard, 14th baron 49
Dalyell, Tam 285
Danby, Thomas Osborne, 1st earl of
  57, 60, 64, 66, 67, 68, 134–6, 139,
  140, 142
Darcy, Patrick, *An Argument* 324
David II, king of Scots 307, 310, 312
David III, king of Scots 312
David of Wales 12
Davies, Sir John 328
Debrett, John 189

Declaration of Right (1689) 127
De Clifford, Edward Southwell Russell, 26th lord 219, 220
Delamer of Dunham Massey, George Booth, 1st baron 56, 67
De La Warr, Herbrand Edward Dundonald Brassey Sackville, 9th earl 218
Democracy and Devolution: Proposals for Scotland and Wales 258
Dempster of Dunnichen, George 174
Denbigh, Basil Feilding, 2nd earl of 55
Dennison, John Evelyn, Speaker of the House of Commons 253
Derby, Charles Stanley, 8th earl of 69
  Edward Stanley, 13th earl of 203, 206, 208
  James Stanley, 10th earl of 353
Despencer, family 16
de Valera, Éamon 346, 356
de Vere, Aubrey *see* Oxford, earl of
  Robert *see* Oxford, earl of
Devereux, Robert *see* Essex, earl of
Devon, Edward Courtenay, 3rd earl of 18
  Thomas Courtenay, 5th earl of 19
Devonshire, William Cavendish, 4th earl of 44
  William Cavendish, 4th duke of 156
D'Ewes, Sir Simonds 95, 96, 114, 115, 121
  The Journal of All the Parliaments during the Reign of Queen Elizabeth 96
Digby, George *see* Bristol, earl of
  John *see* Bristol, earl of
Digby of Greashill, Kildare, 2nd baron [I] 44
Disbrow, John 50
Disraeli, Benjamin
  see Beaconsfield, earl of
Domville, Sir William, 'Disquisition' 324
Dorset, Edward Sackville, 4th earl of 44
  Richard Sackville, 5th earl of 54, 56, 57, 63
Douglas, Isle of Man 353
Douglas, James *see* Queensberry, dukes of
  William *see* Queensberry, earl of
Douglas-Home, Sir Alex *see* Home, earl of
Dover, Henry Carey, earl of 44
Drogheda, Co. Louth 329
Dublin, Co. Dublin 321, 329, 330, 339, 364
  Blue School, Oxmantown 329
  Chichester House 329
  Dublin Castle 328–30
  King's Inns 331
  Leinster House 356
Dublin, archbishop of 197
Dudley, John William Ward, 4th viscount 201
Duffy, Michael 178

Dundas, Henry *see* Melville, viscount
Dunsmore, Francis Leigh, baron 44
Dupplin, George Hay, styled viscount 152
Durham, bishops of *see* Cosin, John; Langley, Thomas; Tunstal, Cuthbert
Durham, palatinate of 88
Dursley, James Berkeley, styled viscount 57

Eden, George *see* Auckland, baron William 178
Edgar, king, charters of 3
Edinburgh, Midlothian 197, 307, 311
  Canongate 307
  General Assembly Hall of the Church of Scotland 359
  Holyrood House 150
  Parliament Building 359
  Parliament House 150, 307
  tolbooth 307
Edward, the Black Prince 19
Edward, prince of Wales 341
Edward I, king 11, 12, 22
Edward II, king 16, 24, 75
Edward III, king 20, 76
Edward IV, king 83
Edward VI, king 97
Egerton, John *see* Bridgwater, earl of
Eldon, John Scott, 1st earl of, lord chancellor 195, 250
Eliot, Sir John 102
Elis-Thomas, Dafydd, baron 362
Elizabeth I, queen 30, 90, 91, 93, 97, 98, 148
Ellenborough, Edward Law, 1st baron 160
Elliot of Minto, George 183
Elsynge, Henry 30, 114
England 5
  union with Scotland 107, 158, 363
  'union' with Wales 87, 363
Essex, Arthur Capel, 1st earl of 70
  Robert Devereux, 2nd earl of 38
  Robert Devereux, 3rd earl of 33, 38, 44, 45, 113
Eure, George 6th lord 49, 50
  Sir Sampson, Speaker of the House of Commons 113, 113
European Convention of Human Rights 284, 355
European Court of Justice 284
European Economic Community 284
European Union 283, 284, 354, 364
  commission of 364
  parliament of 364
Ewens, Ralph 101
exchequer 140, 344
  senior officials of 11

Eynns, Thomas 89

Fagg, Sir John 68
Fauconberg, Thomas Belasyse, 1st viscount 49, 50
Faulkner, Brian 348
Feckenham, John, abbot of Westminster 30
Feilding, Basil *see* Denbigh, earl of
Fell, John, bishop of Oxford 55
Fenwick, Sir John 66, 67, 140
Ferrers, George 90
Fiennes, John 50
   Nathaniel, Speaker of the 'Other House' 49, 50
   William *see* Saye and Sele, viscount
finance 21
Finch of Fordham, John, baron, Speaker of House of Commons 44, 46, 108
Fitzalan, Thomas *see* Arundel, earl of
   William *see* Arundel, earl of
Fitzroy, Augustus Henry *see* Grafton, duke of
Fitzwilliam, Sir William 96
Fleetwood, Charles 50
   Sir George 50
   William 96
Foley, Paul, Speaker of the House of Commons 135
Fortescue, Sir John 311
Foster, John 89
   John Leslie 252
Fox, Charles James 168, 175, 180
   Richard Henry *see* Holland, baron
Fraser, Simon *see* Lovat, lord
Frederick, prince of Wales 161

Gandon, James 329
Gardiner, Stephen, bishop of Winchester 38
Gascony, subjects in 13
Gash, Norman 149
Geddington, Northants. 5
General Chamber of Manufacturers 182
General Strike (1926) 217
George, prince of Wales 65
George I, king 155
   creation of peerages 149
George II, king 155, 161
   creation of peerages 149
George III, king 159, 161, 162, 193, 194, 197
   creation of peerages 149, 163
George IV, king, previously prince of Wales 65, 200, 201, 202
   creation of peerages 201

George V, king 216, 341
   creation of peerages 211
Gerrard, Sir Gilbert 50
   Sir Thomas 101
Gibbs, Graham 177
Gilbert, Thomas 172
Gladstone, William Ewart 206, 207, 208
Glasgow, Dunbartonshire 181
   Strathclyde Regional Council 359
Gloucester, Glos. 5, 12, 20
   abbey 76
Gloucester, Gilbert de Clare, 6th earl of 12
Glynn, John 50
Godolphin, Francis 70
   Sidney, 1st earl of 60
Goffe, William 50
Good Friday Agreement (1998) 349
Goodwin, Francis 101
Gordon, George *see* Aberdeen, earl of; Byron, baron
   William *see* Byron, baron
Grafton, Augustus Henry Fitzroy, 3rd duke of 188
Grand Remonstrance (1641) 46
Grant, James 249
Great Britain, union with Ireland 160, 187, 324, 325, 363
Great Contract (1610) 105, 106
Greenwood, Anthony 276
Gregory, Arthur John Maundy 215, 215
Grenville, George 178, 188
   William Wyndham, baron 150, 197, 198, 200, 208
Grey, Charles Grey, 2nd earl 165, 196–8, 200, 208
   Lady Jane, queen 147
   Thomas *see* Stamford, earl of
Grey of Codnor, Richard, 4th lord 19
Grey of Warke, Ford, 3rd lord 65
Griffin, Edward, 1st baron 55, 56
   Edward, 3rd baron 56
Guest, Frederick 215
Guilford, Francis North, 1st baron 69
Gunpowder Plot (1605) 101

Hailsham, Douglas McGarel Hogg, 1st viscount 220
Haldane, Richard Burdon, viscount 216, 217
Halifax, Yorks. 184
Halifax, Charles Montagu, baron 61, 67, 68, 137, 140
   George Savile, marquess of 63, 69
     Some Cautions offered to the Consideration of those who are to Chuse Members to Serve in the Ensuing Parliament 130

Halifax of Monk Bretton, Edward
    Frederick Lindley Wood, 3rd
    viscount 219
Hall, Arthur 90
    Edward 79, 95
    Chronicle 95
Hamilton, Douglas, 8th duke [S] of 153
    James, 4th duke [S] of 151
    John 220
Hampden, Richard 50
Hansard, Luke 260
    Thomas Curson (d. 1833) 259, 260
    Parliamentary Debates (Hansard) 260
    Thomas Curson (d. 1891) 260
Hanworth, Ernest Murray Pollack, baron
    219
Hardwicke, Philip Yorke, 1st earl of
    155, 159, 159
Harley, Robert, Speaker of the House of
    Commons see Oxford, earl of
Hastings, Henry see Huntingdon, earl of
    Theophilus see Huntingdon, earl of
    Warren 158, 179, 180
Hatton of Kirby, Christopher, 1st baron 44
Haxey, Thomas 18
Hay, George see Dupplin, viscount
    James see Carlisle, earl of
    William 172
Hay-Drummond, Robert Auriol
    see Kinnoul, earl of
Hayton, David 174
Heath, Edward 241, 348
Henchman, Humphrey, bishop of
    Salisbury 56
    diary of 69
Henderson, Arthur 276
    Tommy 346
Henry II, king 6
Henry III, king 11, 12, 354
Henry IV, king 77, 353
Henry V, king 20
Henry VI, king 19, 20
Henry VII, king 24, 57, 75, 83
Henry VIII, king 30, 79, 83, 87, 89, 90,
    93, 97, 148, 195, 325, 326
Herbert, A. P. 272
    Sir Edward 111
    Philip see Pembroke, earl of
Heron, Sir Robert 258
Hertford, Edward Seymour, earl of 88
    Maria Emily Seymour, marchioness
    of 201
    Willliam Seymour, 1st marquess of 44
Hesilrigge, Sir Arthur 50, 123
Hewson, Sir John 50
Hitler, Adolf 219
Hobart, Sir John 50

Hogg, Douglas McGarel
    see Hailsham, viscount
Holand, Thomas de see Kent, earl of
Holland, Richard Henry Fox, 1st baron 65
Holles, Denzel, 1st baron 57
Hollis, Christopher, Can Parliament
    Survive? 283
Holmes, Geoffrey 148
Home, Sir Alex Douglas-Home, 14th earl
    [S] of 207
Honywood, Sir Thomas 50
Hooker alias Vowell, John 95, 96
Hopkins, Douglas George 220
Horton, Wilmot 258
Hoskins, Bennett 120
Hotham, Sir John 46
household, royal 83, 94, 134, 165
    comptroller of 94
    lord chamberlain of 69
    treasurer of 94
    vice-chamberlain of 94
Howard, family 38
    Henry see Mowbray and Maltravers,
        lord; Surrey, earl of
    Thomas see Norfolk, duke of; Suffolk,
        earl of
    William see Stafford, viscount
Howard of Charlton, Charles, baron 44
Howard of Escrick, Edward, 1st 49, 111
Howard of Morpeth, Charles, viscount 50
Hunt, Thomas 57
Huntingdon, Henry Hastings, 5th earl of,
    diary of 37
    Theophilus Hastings, 7th earl of 55, 64
    father of 64
Husbands, Edward 116
Hyde, Edward see Clarendon, earl of
    Henry see Clarendon, earl of
    Laurence see Rochester, earl of

Ibbs, Sir Robert 297
Ilay, Archibald Campbell, earl [S] of 151
Inglis, Sir Robert 257
Ingoldsby, Richard 50
Instrument of Government (1653) 110–12,
    117, 118
Ireland 103, 213, 252, 364
    Bank of Ireland 329
    clerk of the crown 197, 213
    Confederation of Kilkenny, general
        assembly of 330
    council 322, 323, 328, 343
    crown, prerogative of 307
    direct rule 347–8
    governor of 322
    lord chancellor of 213
    lord lieutenant of 198, 342

Index 371

[Ireland *continued*]
  president of 357
  subjects in 13
  union with Great Britain 160, 187, 324, 325, 363
  see also Northern Ireland
Isaacs, Stella *see* Swanborough, baroness

James, prince *see* James II, king
James Francis Edward, the Old Pretender 148
James I, king 97, 100–3, 104, 106, 107, 148, 323; *see also* James VI, king of Scots
James I, king of Scots 303, 307, 308, 310
James II, king, previously prince 44, 58, 59, 127, 140, 147, 148, 332
  as duke of York 44, 58, 64, 136
  chaplain of 64
  creation of peers 55
  see also James VII, king of Scots
James III, king of Scots 312
James IV, king of Scots 314
James VI, king of Scots 307, 312, 314
  see also James I, king
James VII, king of Scots 304, 312
  see also James II, king
Jenkinson, Robert Banks
  see Liverpool, earl of
Jennings, Ivor 279
Jermyn of St Edmundsbury, Henry, 1st baron 44
Jersey, isle of 88
Jobson, Sir Francis 97
John, king 6
Johnstone of Warriston, Sir Archibald 50, 314
Jones, Inigo 32
  John 50
  Philip 50
  Richard *see* Ranelagh, earl of
justice 21, 22
justices 11
  of the forest 11
  of the peace 116

Kenilworth, Warws. 12
Kennedy, John *see* Cassilis, earl of
Kent, Thomas de Holand, 3rd earl of 19
Kilbrandon Commission 347, 358
Kildare, Co. Kildare 329
Kilkenny, Co. Kilkenny 329, 330
Kilmorey, Francis Charles Adelbert Henry Needham, 3rd earl [I] of 214
Kingston, Sir Anthony 95
Kingston-upon-Hull, Henry Pierrepont, 2nd earl of 44

Kinnoull, Robert Auriol Hay-Drummond, 10th earl [I] of 65
Kit Cat Club 137
knights 5

Lamb, Ernest Henry *see* Rochester, baron
  William *see* Melbourne of Kilmore, viscount
Lambarde, William 95
Lambeth, Surr. 12
Lancashire, palatinate of 88
Lancaster, Thomas of Lancaster, earl of 16
Langford, Paul 174, 184
Langley, Thomas, bishop of Durham 19
Lansbury, George 276
Lansdowne, Henry Petty, 3rd marquess of 196
  Henry Charles Keith Petty-FitzMaurice, 5th marquess of 208
Large, David 165
Laski, Harold 228
Latimer, William, 4th lord 23
Laud, William, archbishop of Canterbury 42, 46, 48
Law, Andrew Bonar 215
  Edward *see* Elleborough, baron
lawcourts 91, 130
  chancery 35, 91, 101, 142, 204
  common bench, justices of 12, 30
  common pleas 35
  ecclesiastical 46
  exchequer 35
    chief barons of 30
  high commission 46
  king's bench 11, 35
    judges of 30
  star chamber 46
Lawrence, Henry 50
  R. J. 344, 346
Lawrence committee 289
Lechmere, Nicholas 121
Lee, Charlotte *see* Lichfield, countess of
Leeds, Yorks. 184
Lees-Smith, H. B. 276
Lefevre, Charles Shaw, Speaker of the House of Commons 253
Leicester, Leics. 20
Leicester, Robert Sydney, 2nd earl of 44
Leigh, Francis *see* Dunsmore, baron
Leigh of Stoneleigh, Elizabeth, baroness 67
  Thomas, 1st baron 44
  Thomas, 2nd baron 67
Lennard, Francis *see* Dacre, baron
Lennox, Charles *see* Richmond, duke of
Lenthall, William, Speaker of the House of Commons 50, 113, 114

Lichfield, Charlotte Lee, countess of 55
Lilburne, John 47
Limerick, Co. Limerick 329
Lincoln, Lincs. 13
Lincoln, bishop *see* Neile, Richard;
  Williams, John
Lindsey, Montagu Bertie, 2nd earl of
  44, 69
  father of 69
Lisle, John 50
  Philip, viscount 50
Littleton of Hounslow, Sir Edward, baron
  43, 44
Liverpool, Lancs. 181
Liverpool, Robert Bankes Jenkinson, 2nd
  earl of 198, 200
Llandaff, bishop of 87
  see also Van Mildert, William
Lloyd George, David 208, 215, 215, 274
Lockhart, Sir William 50
London 4, 12
  apprentices of 43, 44
  Bedlam 159
  Blackfriars 20, 86
  Bridge Street 297
  Carlton Club 276
  Church House, Dean's Yard 281
  coffee houses 186
  Custom House, clerks of 116
  East India Company 135, 141, 162, 179
  Gold and Wire Drawers' Company 141
  Guildhall 59, 59, 94
    clerks of 116
  inns of court 116
  Millbank 297
  Newgate 119
  Norman Shaw Building, Embankment
    297
  Parliament Street 297
  Portcullis House 297
  St James's Palace, Queen's Presence
    Chamber 59
  St Margaret's Westminster 101
  Savoy, the 94
  Serjeants' Inn 94
  Skinners' Company 68
  Tower of 42, 56, 62, 119, 153
  Westminster 2, 4, 5, 12, 20
  Westminster Abbey, chapter house of
    21, 76
    refectory of 21, 76, 86
  Westminster Palace 20, 59, 118, 281
    Chamberlain's 23
    coffee houses 122
      Alice's 122, 251
      Carter's 122
      Wagham's 251

[London *continued*]
  [Westminster Palace *continued*]
    Court of Exchequer 121
    Court of Requests 122, 193, 194, 195,
      251
    Court of Wards 33, 94, 104, 122
    fire (1834) of 36, 193
    House of Commons 220, 221,
      251, 253, 259, 281, 297; Grand
      Committee Room 294; offices
      for 297
    House of Lords 193, 281; Library 219;
      Royal Gallery 220; Royal Robing
      Room 221, 281
    Houses of Parliament 193
    Jewel Tower 36
    Marcolf's Chamber 23
    Painted Chamber 20, 32, 34, 59, 60,
      76, 193
    Parliament Chamber 31, 32, 193
    Prince's Chamber 32, 49
    Prince's Lodgings 60
    Queen's Chamber
      see below White Chamber
    St Stephen's Chapel 86, 92, 94,
      100, 133, 175, 249; dining room
      (*Bellamy's*) 250, 251, 252;
      Lobby 250, 250
    Speaker's House 253
    Star Chamber 94, 103
    Stone Building 251
    Tally Office 122
    taverns:
      Heaven 122
      Hell 122
      Paradise 122
      Purgatory 122
    Treasury Chamber 121
    Westminster Hall 67, 122, 159, 180
    White Chamber 21, 23, 31, 32, 59, 76
  Whitehall 59, 94, 97
    Council Chamber 112
    lodgings 121
    Lord Keeper's Lodgings 60
    offices 59
    see above Westminster Palace
London, bishop of *see* Tunstal, Cuthbert
London County Council 205
Londonderrry, Co. Londonderry 340
Longueville, Henry Yelverton, viscount de
  63
lord chancellor 21, 26, 30, 32, 68, 69, 154,
  160, 205
  secretary of 195
lord great chamberlain 69
lord keeper 30, 68, 117, 154
lord president of the council 30

lord privy seal 30, 69
lord treasurer 30
Lovat, Simon Fraser, 10th lord [S] 158, 180
Lovelace of Hurley, John, 2nd baron 44
   John, 3rd baron 56
Lowther, Henry 257
   James William *see* Ullswater, viscount
   Sir James 186
Luttrell, colonel 188
   one 55
Lyons, Richard 23

McBirney, R. M. 345
Macdonald, Ramsay 216–18
McGuinness, Martin 349
Mackenzie, William *see* Amultree, baron
Mackworth, Humphrey, colonel 122
   Margaret *see* Rhondda, viscountess
Maclean, Sir Donald 276
Macmillan, Harold 241, 295
   Hugh 220
   Hugh Pattison, baron 219
Magna Carta 6, 7, 38, 39
Mahon, Philip Henry Stanhope, styled viscount 185
Major, John 289
Manchester, Lancs. 184, 185
Manchester, Edward Montagu, 2nd earl of 50, 54, 61, 68
   George Montagu, 4th duke of 195
   Robert Montagu, 3rd earl of 54
Mandevile, Henry Montagu, lord 47
Manners, Anne *see* Roos, lady
   Henry *see* Roos, lord
Mansfield, William Murray, 1st earl of 159
March, Roger de Mortimer, 1st earl of 16
Markievic, countess 272
Marlborough, John Churchill, 1st duke of 60, 152
Marshall, Peter 171
Marvell, Andrew 131, 134
Mary, queen consort of George V 341
Mary, queen of Scots 38, 89, 97, 98, 307
Mary I, queen 30, 31, 93, 97
Mary II, queen, previously princess 59, 90, 127, 127
   creation of peerages 55
Masham of Otes, Samuel, 1st baron 65
master of the rolls 30
Matilda, daughter of Henry I 5, 147
Matthew, Colin 206
Merton, Surr. 12
Melbourne of Kilmore, William Lamb, 2nd viscount [I] 165, 251
Melville, Henry Dundas, 1st viscount 158, 165

Middlesex, Lionel Cranfield, 1st earl of 105
   Lionel Cranfield, 3rd earl of 54
militia 46, 116
ministry of justice 354
Mohun of Okehampton, Charles, 3rd baron 66, 67, 68
   Warwick, 2nd baron 44
Molyneux, William, *The Case of Ireland's Being Bound by Acts of Parliament in England, Stated* 324
Monck, George *see* Albemarle, 1st duke of
Money, John 185
Monmouth, James Scott, duke of 63, 67
Monmouthshire 87
Montagu, Charles *see* Halifax, baron
   Edward 50; *see also* Manchester, earl of; Sandwich, earl of
   George *see* Manchester, earl of
   Henry *see* Mandevile, lord
   John *see* Sandwich, earl of
   Robert *see* Manchester, earl of
Montagu of Boughton, Edward, 1st baron, diary of 37
   Edward, 2nd baron 54
Montfort, Simon de 12
Montgomery, Sir Graham 257
Mordaunt, Henry *see* Peterborough, earl of
More, Sir Thomas, Speaker of the House of Commons 79
Morley and Monteagle, Thomas Parker, 15th lord 67
Morrice, Sir William 126
Mortimer, Roger *see* March, earl of
Mowbray and Maltravers, Henry Howard, lord 44
Moyle, Thomas, Speaker of the House of Commons 87
Mulgrave, Edmund Sheffield, 1st earl of, proxy of 45
   Edmund Sheffield, 2nd earl of 50
Murray, Charlotte *see* Atholl, duchess of
   David *see* Stormont, viscount
   James *see* Atholl, duke of
   William *see* Mansfield, earl of
Murrow, Ed 281

National Union of Farmers 233
Nayler, James 49, 118
Neadler, Culverwell 69
Needham, Francis Charles Adelbert Henry *see* Kilmorey, earl of
Neile, Richard, bishop of Lincoln 104
Neville, Henry *see* Abergavenny, lord
Newark, Notts. 86
Newcastle-under-Lyne, Henry Pelham, 4th duke of 201
Newcastle-upon-Tyne, Northumb. 12

Newcastle-upon-Tyne, Thomas Pelham, 1st duke of 155–7
Newdigate, Sir Roger 175
Newmarket, Suff. 61
New Model Army 45, 47, 113
Newport, Mountjoy Blount, 1st earl of 44
Newport of High Ercall, Richard, baron 44
newspapers, journals and magazines:
   Caledonian Mercury 189
   Gentlemen's Magazine 186
   London Magazine 186
   Morning Chronicle 188
   Parliamentary Register 259
   The Times 259
New Zealand 363
Nicholas, Edward 102
Nicolson, William, bishop of Carlisle 148
Noel, Baptist *see* Campden, viscount
Norfolk, John de Mowbray, 4th earl of 19
   Thomas Howard, 2nd duke of 195
   Thomas Howard, 3rd duke of 93
Norham, Northumb. 12
Normandy 4
Norris, John Bertie, 5th lord 65
North, Francis *see* Guilford, baron
   Frederick, styled lord 162
   Roger 135
Northampton, Northants. 12
   abbey 76
   assize of 5
   council of 5
Northampton, James Compton, 3rd earl of 44
North Atlantic Assembly 44
North Atlantic Treaty Organisation (NATO) 283, 284
Northern Ireland 285
   governor 342, 343
   Royal Ulster Constabulary 340
   see also Ireland
Northumberland, Algernon Percy, 4th earl of 50
Northumbria, noblemen of 3
Nowell, Alexander 89

Oates, Titus 64
O'Connell, Daniel 261
Ogilvy, James *see* Seafield, earl of
Oliver, John 343
Omai, the Tahitian 159
O'Neil, Terence 347
Onslow, Fulk 95
   Sir Richard 50
orders in council 345
Orford, Edward Russell, earl of 67, 68, 137, 140

Organisation for Security and Cooperation in Europe (OSCE) 284
Ormond, James Butler, 1st duke [I] of 60, 139
Orrery, Roger Boyle 1st earl [I] of 139
Osborne, Thomas *see* Danby, earl of
Oxford, Oxon. 2, 4, 12, 13, 108, *113*, 133
Oxford, bishop of *see* Fell, John
Oxford, university of 11
   Christ Church 55, 113
   Geometry School 59
Oxford, Aubrey de Vere, 20th earl of 69
   Robert de Vere, 9th earl of 19
   Robert Harley, 1st earl of 135, 152, 153, 158, 159

Packe, Sir Christopher 50
Paget of Beaudesert, William, 1st baron 38
   William, 6th baron 44
Paisley, Ian 349
Palmer, William Waldegrave
   see Selborne, earl of
Parke, James *see* Wensleydale, baron
Parker, Thomas
   see Morley and Monteagle, lord
parliament (*parlement, parliamentum*):
   (1232) 11
   (1234) 11
   (1236) 11
   (1237) 16
   (1244) 11
   (1254) 11
   (1255) 11
   (1258) 11, 13
   (1262) 11
   (1267) 11
   (1268) 11
   (1269) 11
   (1270) 11
   (1278) 11
   (1280) 11
   (1285) 13
   (1290) 11
   (1292) 11
   (1295) 16
   (Nov. 1296) 11
   (1297) 11
   (1300) 13
   (1301) 11
   (1322) 87
   (1327) 87
   (Oct. 1339) 77
   (1376), the 'Good' 23, 76
   (1378) 20
   (1387) 21
   (Feb. 1388), the 'Merciless' 23, 81

[parliament *continued*]
  (Sept. 1397) 19
  (1406) 18, 76
  (1407) 20
  (1422) 81
  (1423) 19
  (1425) 19
  (1439) 18
  (1442) 18
  (1447) 18
  (Nov. 1449) 19, 81
  (1453) 83
  (1459) 83
  (1461) 25
  (1512) 36
  (1523) 36, 79, 92
  (1529) 30, 36, 79, 91
  (1536) 30, 32
  (1539) 30, 32
  (1542) 32, 87, 88
  (1545) 32
  (1547) 91
  (Apr. 1554) 36
  (Nov. 1554) 31, 92
  (1558) 30
  (1559) 30
  (1571) 31, 92
  (1572) 31, 89
  (1584) 31
  (1593) 31, 30
    'journal' of 96
  (1597) 31, 106
  (1601) 32
  (1604) 31, 101, 105–7
  (1614), the 'Addled' 105–7
  (1621) 31, 32, 35, 103, 105, 107
  (1624) 31, 32, 35
  (1625) 31, 35, 107
  (1626) 31, 34, 35
  (1628) 31, 35, 108
  (1640), the 'Short' 45, 116
  (1640), the 'Long', the 'Rump' 113, 115, 115, 116–19
    ephemera printed for 116
  (1644), royalist, 'Oxford' 43, 44
  (1653), the 'Nominated Assembly', 'Barebones' 111, 112, 120, 330
    writ of summons to 112
  (1654) 120, 314
  (1656) 120, 314
  (1659) 110, 112, 115, 119, 314
  (1660), the 'Convention' 128, 130
  (1660), the 'Cavalier' 132, 140, 141
  (1679), the 'First Exclusion' 130, 135, 140
  (1680), the 'Second Exclusion' 69

[parliament *continued*]
  (1681), the 'Third Exclusion', the 'Oxford' 62, 69
  (1685) 143
  (1689), the 'Convention' 55, 59, 59, 69, 140, 141
  (1705) 147
  (1707) 147
  acts 26, 31, 105, 115–17, 345
    abortion (1967) 294
    administration of justice (appeals) (1934) 219
    administration of justice in Wales (1536) 87
    American stamp duty (1765), repeal of 161
    appellate jurisdiction (1876) 204
    (1913) 219
    attainting the earl of Strafford (1641) 46
    banning clergy from being MPs (1640) 110
    Catholic emancipation (1829) 327
    corn laws (1816) 200, 203
    corporation (1661) 181
    corrupt and illegal practices (1883) 288
    criminal justice (1948) 219
    dissolving the Knights Templars (1540) 30
    elections (1770) 188
    emergency powers (1940) 280, 345
    enabling (1942) 345
    enfranchising County Durham (1673) 128
    equal franchise (1928) *see below* representation of the the people
    established church (Wales) (1914) 212
    European assembly elections (1977) 284
    European communities (1972) 284, 286
    (amendment) (1986) 284
    (1993) 284
    excluding office holders (1694) 135, 174
    (1700) 135, 174
    (1701) 135, 174
    for continuing expiring statutes (1628) 106
    government of Ireland (1914) 212, 285
    (1920) 339, 340, 343
    honours (prevention of abuses) (1925) 215, 215
    House of Commons (administration) (1978) 297

[parliament *continued*]
  [acts *continued*]
    human rights (1998) 285, 286
    Ireland (1949) 345
    Irish declaratory (1720) 158
    Irish Free State (agreement)
      (1922) 339
    labourers (1349) 26
    landed qualification (1711) 131, 172
    life peerages (1958) 243
    ministers (1926) 275
    ministers of the crown (1937) 276
    municipal corporations (1835) 205
    musters (1558) 92
    navigation (1661) 58, 315
    Northern Ireland (1973) 344
      (1998) 349
    Northern Ireland (confirmation of
      agreement) (1925) 340
    Northern Ireland parliament 344-5
    occasional conformity 153
    parliament (1911) 152, 207, 208,
      211-13, 223
      (1949) 211, 213, 223, 228, 242
    peerages (1963) 150, 243
    political parties, elections and
      referendums (2000) 288
    poor law (1834) 205
    private 26, 140, 141, 160
    public 160
    redistribution of seats (1885) 262,
      263, 266, 364
      (1994) 287
    re-election of ministers (1919) 275
    reform (1832) 152, 202-3, 259, 262,
      364
      (1867) 262, 364
      (1884) 262, 263, 364
    regency (1706) 135, 174
    regulating (1773) 179
    regulating elections (1413) 81, 82
      (1430) 81, 82, 128
      (1445) 81, 82
      (1696) 129
    representation of the people
      (1918) 211, 271, 272, 364
      (1928) 211, 271, 364
      (1945) 272
      (1948) 272, 364
      (1970) 364
    restoring first fruits and tenths
      (1555) 26
    reversal of Cardinal Pole's attainder
      (1554) 31
    schism (1714) 153
    Scotland (1978) 285
      (1998) 286, 287, 358

[parliament *continued*]
  [acts *continued*]
    septennial (1716) 153, 176, 183
    sex disqualification (removal)
      (1919) 214
    sexual offences (1967) 294
    succession (1536) 90
      (1545) 90
    supremacy (1534) 90
    test (1673) 58
      (1678) 58, 64, 142, 181, 182
    treason (1571) 92
    triennial (1641) 100, 126
      (1694) 58, 127, 129, 170, 183
    uniformity (1559) 92
    union with Ireland (1800) 128, 197
    union with Scotland (1707) 128, 150
    union with Wales (1536) 87
      (1543) 87
    Wales (1978) 285
      (1998) 286, 358, 361
      (2006) 361
    see also below bills; legislation
  addresses 132, 140, 142
    of thanks 163
  assent, royal 26, 30, 39, 58, 93, 105, 126,
    147, 148, 212
  authority of 117, 118
  ballot, secret 129
  bicameral 1
  bills 22, 89, 92, 93, 94, 102, 103, 105,
    108, 185, 195, 196, 207, 212, 213,
    218, 233, 255, 256, 272, 279, 280,
    293, 294
    abolishing the episcopacy (1641) 42
    abrogating the oath of supremacy in
      Ireland (1691) 333
    against monopolies 108
    allowing peeressses to sit in the
      Lords 214
    attainder 24
    attainting Sir John Fenwick (1696)
    bishops' exclusion (1641) 42
    Catholic emancipation 193
      (1821) 200, 201
      (1825) 201, 202
      (1828) 202
    coal mines (1930) 221
    corn laws (1816) 200
      repeal (1846) of 203, 291
    defining Lords' judicial powers 142
    disestablishment of the Irish Church
      (1869) 206
    dissolving colleges and chantries
      (1545) 89
      (1547) 89

Index   377

[parliament *continued*]
  [bills *continued*]
    dissolving the greater monasteries
      (1539) 30
    Elizabethan church settlement
      (1559) 89, 97
    emergency powers (1930) 218
    enabling 294
    ending MPs' wages (1677) 132
    enfranchising Cheshire (1543) 88
    enfranchising County Durham
      (1624) 100
      (1673) 88
    English education (1870) 206
    European communities (1972) 291
    government 228
    habeas corpus (1679) 65
    India (1783) 161, 162
    Indian constitutional reform (1934–5)
      221
    in restraint of annates (1534) 97
    in restraint of appeals (1533) 93, 97
    Irish church (1833) 202
    Irish corporation (1836) 194, 203
    Irish home rule (1893) 206, 207
      (1912) 207
    Irish tithe (1834) 203
    lace importation (1698) 141
    land tax 142
    limit slave trade (1799) 65
    London orphans (1695) 135

    money 212, 222
    nationalizing iron and steel industry
      222
    New Shoreham 163
    pains and penalties (1820) 200
    parliament (1911) 207, 211, 221
      (1931) 218
      (1947) 222
      (1948–9) 221, 223
    peerage (1719) 153, 153, 186
    penalising exiles (1555) 95
    prayer book (1927) 221
    preventing bishops interfering in
      state affairs (1641) 42
    preventing dangers arising from
      disaffected persons 64
    preventing stockjobbing (1734) 154
    private 58, 69, 135, 187, 227, 233, 294
    protecting MPs from assault (1404)
      82
    providing for the alternative vote
      (1931) 272
    public 160, 187, 221, 227, 228
    Quaker tithe (1736) 154

[parliament *continued*]
  [bills *continued*]
    reform (1832) 193, 194, 202
      (1867) 206
      (1884) 206
    regency (1811) 195
    restrictions on MPs (1694) 148
      (1696) 148
    reversing Cardinal Pole's attainder
      (1554) 93
    reversing Henrician and Edwardian
      ecclesiastical legislation 89
    Scottish education (1869) 206
    Scottish militia (1708) 147, 148
    subsidy (1523) 92
    supply (1671) 142
    test (1675) 64, 68
    Thomas Haxey's (1397) 18
    treason (1554) 92
    triennial (1693) 58, 148
    unemployment insurance (1930) 218
    see also above acts *and below* legislation
  Channel Islands 1
    bailiffs of 354
    Guernsey, states of delegation 354–5
      committees 354
    Jersey, assembly of states 355–6
    Sark 354–5
    states of 1, 2
    subjects on 13
    wardens of 354
  commissions 286, 287
  committees, joint 33, 45
    of both kingdoms 45, 121
    see also below Commons, House of;
      Lords, House of
  Commons, House of 21, 22
    anxious to participate in legal
      proceedings 46
    archives (muniment room) of 36, 86
      see also below records
    assumption of judicial power 49, 68
    attendance in 43
    broadcasting of 298
    business and functions of
      176–8, 255–7
    committees 92–4, 133, 179, 272,
      278–81, 287–9, 292–7
      external 289
      for returns 91, 94
      'general' 94
      of supply 176
      of the whole House 94, 12, 103,
        120, 299
      of ways and means 176
      on the state of the nation 146
      Osmotherley rules 296

[parliament *continued*]
  [Commons, House of *continued*]
    [committees *continued*]
      select 94, 179, 180, 256, 279, 280, 289, 295–7
      standing committees 102, 120, 256, 279, 293
      sub-committees 102, 280
    composition of 11, 16, 79, 80, 108, 111, 134, 170, 172–6, 249–50, 287, 292, 315
    decision of, to abolish House of Lords 48
    divisions 79, 92, 188
    elections to 16, 26, 81, 90, 91, 102, 112, 128–31, 160
      broadcasts 287
      by-elections 91, 129, 275
      cost of 287
      disputed 68, 91, 101, 158, 183–4, 188
      entertainment 131
      general 130, 149, 170, 188, 203, 206, 221, 275, 276, 287, 290
      A Guide to the the Elections of Great Britain 186
      poll books 129
      votes 287; alternative (AV) 272, 274; single transferable (STV) 274
    executive of 283
    factions in 119, 136, 156, 183–4, 206
    franchise 90, 110, 111, 128–30, 258–9, 267, 271–3
    freedom (liberty) of speech 82, 89, 103, 104
    Great Contract (1610) 106
    initiation of money bills 68
    leaders, of the House 297
      shadow 297
    A List of One Unanimous Club of Voters 143
    management of 105, 134–5, 253–7, 267
    MPs 131–3
      biographies of 262
      Irish 244, 271, 314, 334
      letters and memoirs of 262
      ministerial control of 253–5
      nomination of, by nobility 38, 166
      payment of wages to 90, 132, 274, 289–90
      Scottish 151, 170, 183, 314
      speaking 252–3, 257–60, 267
      reports by 103
      role of 274
      war service of 280

[parliament *continued*]
  [Commons, House of *continued*]
    modernization of 292–9
    oath 90
      of supremacy 101
    officers of 86, 94
      serjeants at arms 94, 119
      under-clerks 36, 92, 95, 114
    opposition, leaders of 276, 277
      allowance for 291
    orders 115, 133, 139
      standing 133, 134, 256
    party 138–7, 265–7, 290–2
      leaders of 276, 277
    peers sitting in 49, 111
    placemen in 134, 164
    prayers 92
    privilege 82, 90, 101, 102, 118
    procedure 79, 91, 92, 281
    Protestation (1621) of 104
    questions and question time 295
    records of 95, 96, 114, 115, 172
      book of orders and usages 95
      book of ordinances 114
      Commons journal 27, 30, 36, 94, 95, 96, 101, 102, 104, 114, 186
      Hansard 157, 257, 259
      lists of MPs' names 103, 186
      register of leave of absence 95
    reform of 292, 298
    relations with crown 103–8, 143–4
      with Lords 46, 47, 48, 68, 104, 105, 119, 141–3, 200, 212, 223, 228
    reporting of 142, 143, 185–90, 260
    reports on 298
    right to assent to taxation 76, 82
    right to legislate 82
    A Seasonable Argument to Perswade all the Grand Juries in England to Petition for a New Parliament 143
    Speaker 81, 89, 91, 94, 97, 1–3, 104, 113, 114, 135, 154, 276, 297
      presentation of 26, 31
      see also Abbot, Charles; Denison, John Evelyn; Eure, Sir Sampson; Finch, John; Foley, Paul; Harley, Robert; Lefevre, Charles Shaw; Lenthall, William; More, Sir Thomas; Puckering, John; Rous, John; Russell, John; Seymour, Edward; Trevor, Sir John; Turnor, Edward
    submission to Lords 82
    tactics 134
    times of business 91, 92, 293
    visits to, by monarch 97, 98
      by distinguished personnel 98, 179

[parliament *continued*]
  [Commons, House of *continued*]
    Votes and Proceedings 143
    West Lothian Question 285, 361, 364
    whips 277–9, 291, 292, 294
  conferences 222
    of the two Houses (joint conferences) 34, 44, 60, 65
    Speaker's 271, 272
  constituencies 80
    Antrim 273
    Ashburton 111
    Aylesbury 130
    Beaumaris 86
    Blackburn 273
    Bolton 273
    Brighton 273
    Bristol 86, 129
    Calais 86
    Cambridge University 100, 273
    Canterbury 11
    Cheshire 88
    Chester 88
    Cockermouth 111
    Combined English Universities 273
    Cork 334
    Coventry 101
    Cricklade 183
    Derby 273
    Down 273
    Dublin 334
    Dublin University 273, 334
    Dundee 273
    Durham City 112, 128
    Durham County 112, 128
    Edinburgh and St Andrews Universities 273
    Exeter 86
    Fremanagh and Tyrone 273
    Gatton 90
    Glasgow and Aberdeen Universities 273
    Grampound 128
    Halifax 112
    Haverfordwest 87
    Helston (Helleston) 184
    Honiton 111
    Huntingdonshire, knights for 18
    Kingston-upon-Hull 132
    Lancashire 88
    Leeds 111
    London 11, 128, 188, 273
    London University 273
    Merioneth 87
    Middlesex 160, 174, 188
    National University 273

[parliament *continued*]
  [constituencies *continued*]
    Newark 128
    Newborough 86
    New Shoreham 163, 183
    Norfolk 91
    Northallerton 111
    North Wales 87
    Norwich 86, 129, 273
    Okehampton 111
    Oldham 273
    Old Sarum 100, 129, 131
    Oxford University 100, 273
    Plympton Erle 91
    Preston 273
    Queenborough 128
    Queen's University, Belfast 273
    Sandwich 91
    Scottish Universities 273
    Seaford 111
    Southampton 273
    Southwark 129
    Stockbridge 130
    Stockport 273
    Sunderland 273
    Wendover 173
    West Looe 91
    Welsh Universities 273
    Westminster 129
    Whitehaven 186
    Yorkshire 128
  declarations 115, 117
  diaries 36, 37, 96, 102
  dissolution of 26, 113, 117
  duration of 75, 126, 117, 212
  England 1, 2, 147
    meeting places of 2, 12, 18, 20, 100, 133
    origins of 3, 10
  finance 137, 171
  frequency of 11, 75
  Great Britain 2, 147, 170
  Iceland, Althingi of 1
  impeachment 23, 24, 66, 67, 68, 82, 104, 105, 139, 140, 158, 159, 179, 180
  intercommuning 21
  Ireland, pre-1800 1, 321
    (1460) 322
    (1494) 322
    (1557) 325
    (1560) 325
    (1613) 323, 325, 327
    (1634) 323
    (1640) 323, 324, 326
    (1660), the 'Convention' 326, 330–1
    (1689), the 'Patriot' 331–3

[parliament *continued*]
  [Ireland, pre-1800 *continued*]
    acts 324, 331
      against papal authority (1537) 325
      banishing all papists exercising ecclesiastical jurisdiction (1697) 327
      Catholic relief (1778) 327; (1782) 327; (1792) 327; (1793) 327
      customs (1662) 326
      declaration (1460) 325
      disarming and dismounting Catholics (1695) 327
      enabling Catholics to testify their loyalty (1774) 327
      excise duties (1662) 326
      explanation (1665) 326
      faculties (1537) 325
      hearth tax (1662) 326; (1665) 326
      in restraint of first fruits and 20ths (1537) 325
      kingly title (1541) 326
      legislation 322, 315–7
      Newtown (1748) 333
      octennial (1768) 327, 334
      place (1793) 334
      Poynings's Law (1495) 322, 323, 325, 326, 331; amending (1557) 322
      preventing the further growth of popery (1704) 327
      procedure 323
      prohibiting foreign education (1795) 326
      regulating elections (1542) 333; (1728) 333
      settlement (1662) 326
      statute of Kilkenny (1366) 325
      succession (1537) 325
      supremacy (1536) 325; (1560) 325
      taxes and taxation 323, 325
      uniformity (1560) 325
      union (1800) 325, 332, 334
      Yelvertons' (1782) 324
    bills 322, 323
      supply 323
    Commons, House of 327, 328, 330
      Speaker of 327–8
    committees 328–9
      of the whole House 328
      standing 328
    composition of 321–2, 331
    conferences 328
    constituencies 331
      Cashel 329
      Clonmel 329

[parliament *continued*]
  [Ireland *continued*]
    [constituencies *continued*]
      County Down 333
      Drogheda 329
      Dublin University 332
      Naas 329
      Ross 329
      Trim 329
    'Declaration' (1644) 324
    elections 334
      general 334
    franchise 331, 333–4
    judicial powers and work of 322, 324
    licence or hold parliament 322
    Lords, House of 158, 197, 322, 328
      legal assistants in 328
    meetings of 321, 324
    origins of 321
    records of 329–30
    reporting on 329–30
      The Journal of the House of Lords of the Kingdom of Ireland 330
      The Journals of the House of Commons of the Kingdom of Ireland 329
      The Parliamentary Registers: or, History of the Proceedings and Debates of the House of Commons of Ireland 330
      The Statutes at Large passed in the Parliament held in Ireland 330
    votes 330
  Ireland, post-1922 (Oireachtas) 2, 356–7, 364
    Dáil Eireann 356, 357
    legislation 356
    Seaned Eireann 356, 357
  language of 25–7
  lawsuits:
    Annesley v. Sherlock 158
    Ashby v. White 68, 130, 142–3, 158
    Bishop of London v. Ffyche 158
    Goodwin v. Fortescue 130
    Rosebery v. Inglis 158
    Shirely v. Fagg 142
  legislation 4, 5, 12, 13, 21, 22, 35, 58, 78, 79, 93, 94, 96, 102, 116, 126, 140, 141, 160, 171, 172, 179–85, 213, 227, 242, 255, 284, 285, 293, 294
    provisos 97
    see also above acts; bills
  lord chancellor 21, 26, 32
  Lords, House of 16, 17, 21–3
    abolition of 30, 48, 216, 218, 221
    absence from 196

Index

[parliament continued]
  [Lords, House of continued]
    attendance in 31, 43, 44, 193, 200, 221, 222, 229, 230
    attitude to Catholic emancipation 200–2
    committees 32, 33, 56, 57, 60, 63, 160, 179, 230, 231, 233
      appellate 220
      for petitions 45
      journals 161
      of privileges 204, 214
      of the whole House 33, 155, 160, 196
      on the state of the nation 160
      select 155, 160, 179, 230, 231, 245
      standing (great) 33, 233
      sub-committees 231
    composition of 17, 30, 30, 42, 43, 54–6, 57, 149–59, 198, 207–8, 211, 213–18, 226, 234–42, 315
    'factions' in 38, 43, 212
    'Fane Fragment' 21, 22, 25
    functions of 227–9
    judicial powers and work of 34, 35, 45–7, 66–8, 142, 158–60, 204–6, 219–20, 220, 227, 284
    judges in 32
    knight marshal, men of 70
    legal assistants 30, 32, 69
    management of 60–1, 63
    meeting places of 59, 60, 76, 194, 250
    oaths 64, 196
    officers of 68–70
      black rod 70
      clerk of the parliaments 25, 27, 32, 34, 36, 69, 70
      clerks 69, 70
      serjeants at arms 70
    pairing 196
    parties and party affilations in 61, 161–3, 165, 172, 197, 199, 203–4, 206, 221, 23, 237, 239, 241–3
    peerages, hereditary 211, 212, 214, 216–19, 236, 237, 243, 244, 246
      life 204, 223, 226, 236–9, 241, 244–6
    placemen 164
    powers of, legislative 203, 212, 227
    privilege 30, 47, 48, 70
    procedure 44–5, 195–6, 227
    protests 45, 156–7, 157, 163
    proxies 17, 18, 27, 34, 64, 65, 150, 162, 163, 196, 197
    rank and precedence in 19

[parliament continued]
  [Lords, House of continued]
    records of 36, 161
      Lords journal 22, 26, 27, 30, 31, 36, 70, 157, 161; draft 36
      main papers 36
      manuscript minutes (scribbled books) 36
      proxy book 34
    reform of 212, 218, 219, 221–3, 226–8, 241–5
    relations with Commons 46, 47, 48, 68, 141–3, 200, 212, 223, 228
    relations with government 216–19, 221–6, 233–4, 239, 241
    reporting 161, 199–200
    representative peers, Irish 197, 198, 201, 201, 250, 334
      Scottish 150, 162, 198, 201, 243
    restoration of 54
    right to legislate for Ireland 322
    Salisbury convention 222
    seating in 18
    sittings of 229, 230
    sovereignty of 283–6
    standing orders 34, 64, 70, 157
    summonses to 11, 16, 26
    survival, reasons for 245–6
    veto 48, 203
    voting 45, 64, 65, 66, 196, 201
      divisions 65, 66, 70, 162, 163
    whips 196
  Man, Isle of 1
    lieutenant governor of 353
    Tynwald (*Tinvaal*) of 1, 2
      act, House of Keys election (1866) 353
      functions 353
      House of Keys 352, 353
      Legislative Council 352, 353
      legislation 352, 353
      origins of 352
      statute book 354
      taxes and taxation 353
      votes 353
  management 126
  Modus Tenendi Parliamentorum 75
  Northern Ireland 1, 2, 285, 286
    acts, education (1930) 344
      prolongation of parliament (1943) 345; (1944) 345
    Commons, House of 340
      composition of 340
      Speaker 341
      standing orders 341

[parliament *continued*]
  [Northern Ireland *continued*]
    constituencies:
      Queen's University, Belfast 340
      (South) Down 346
    elections 345–6
    franchise 340
    functions 343
    legislation 343, 347
    parties 345–6
    relations with Westminster 343–5
    Senate 340
  opening of 26, 31
  opposition in 119
  ordinances 26, 93, 115, 116
    declaring invalid titles conferred since May 1642 (1646) 43
    self-denying (1645) 46, 48
  'Other House' 49–51, 314, 220
    committee of the whole House 49
    committees 49
    divisions 49
    Speaker of *see* Fiennes, Nathaniel
    summons to 50, 314, 330
  parties 156–60
    Conservative 213, 214, 221, 227
      Conservative Private Members (1922) Committee 277, 278, 280
    Democratic Unionist (DUP) 349
    Fainna Fáil 346
    Independent Labour (ILP) 278
    Labour (PLP) 213, 216–18, 221, 227, 244, 246, 275, 277, 278, 280, 285, 287, 292
      Tribune Group 291
    Liberal 212, 214
    Nationalist 346
    Northern Ireland Labour Party (NILP) 346
    Plaid Cymru 285
    Scottish National 285
    Social and Democratic Labour (SDLP) 349
    Social Democratic (SDP) 287
    Sinn Féin (SF) 349
    Ulster Unionist (UUP) 341, 345, 349
  petitions 13, 21–4, 34, 35, 45, 46, 77, 78, 132, 184, 258
    Additional Petition and Advice (1657) 110
    Humble petition and Advice (1657) 110
    Petition of Right (1628) 38, 39, 105, 137
  receivers of 33
  triers of 25, 33

[parliament *continued*]
  prorogation of 26, 113, 117
  referendal theory 207
  rolls of parliament 13, 21, 25
  Scotland, pre-1707 1, 2, 48, 285
    (1290) 305
    (1469) 305
    (1540) 305
    (1560), the 'Reformation' 304
    (1571) 307
    (1681) 305
    (1689) 307
    (1703) 307
    acts, anent feuding (1598) 312
      private 310
      public 310
      shire representatives (1428) 304; (1587) 304
      triennial (1640) 307
      Union (1707) 315
    Acts of the Parliament of Scotland 313
    assent, royal 309
    attendance 305
    chancellor 308
    clerk register 309, 311
    commissioners, from the royal burghs 303; election of 303, 304
      from the shires 304–6
      royal 307–8
    committees 308, 309, 311
      lords of the articles 308–9
    composition of 301–2
    constituencies:
      Clackmannan 304
      Cromarty 303
      Edinburgh 303
      Kinross 304
      Orkney 306
      Shetland 306
    franchise 306
    judicial powers and work 309–10, 313
    legislation 308, 310, 314
    meeting places of 307
    origins of 1, 301
    procedure 308–9
    records:
      division lists 311
      registers 311
      rolls of parliament 311
    riding 307–8
    summonses to 306–7
    voting 309
    sovereignty 311–13
    taxes and taxation 310, 312–4

Index 383

[parliament *continued*]
  Scotland, post-1999 (*Parlamaid na h-Alba*) 2, 286, 301, 359–61, 364
    committees 360
    composition of 358
    constituencies 360
      Orkney 360
      Shetland 360
    debating chamber 359
    elections 360
    presiding officer 359, 360
    voting 360
  sermons 26
  Sewel convention 286
  speech from the throne 177
  statutes *see above* acts
  taxes and taxation 6, 11, 21, 22, 75–8, 79, 82, 88, 126, 239, 141
    subsidies 39
    trials 67
  United Kingdom 1
  veto, royal 147, 148
  Wales 286, 364
    National Assembly (*Cynulliad Cenedlaethol Cymru*) 2, 361–2
    elections 361
    composition 362
    franchise 361
    functions 361
    presiding officer 362
    taxes and taxation 361
  West Lothian question 285
  What's Wrong with Parliament? 226
  white papers 277
  writs, of summons 26, 30, 112
    ordering elections 26
Passfield, Sidney Webb, baron 250, 250
Pearce, Edward Lovett 329
Peel, Sir Robert 203, 291
Pelham, Henry (d. 1662 or later) 113
  Henry (d. 1754) 156
  Henry (d. 1851) *see* Newcastle-under-Lyne, duke of
  Thomas *see* Newcastle-upon-Tyne, duke of
Pembroke, Philip Herbert, 4th earl of 38, 49, 111
Penn, William 132
Pepys, Samuel 56, 122
Perceval, Spencer 250, 250
Percy, Algernon
  see Northumberland, earl of
Percy of Alnwick, Henry, baron 44
Perth, Perthshire, Blackfriars 307
Peterborough, Henry Mordaunt, 2nd earl of 44
Pethwick-Lawrence, F. W. 276

Petty, Henry *see* Lansdowne, marquess of
  John *see* Shelburne, earl of
Petty-FitzMaurice, Henry Charles Keith *see* Lansdowne, marquess of
Philip, prince 31
Philipson, Mabel 272
Pickering, Sir Gilbert, bt 50
Pierrepont, Henry
  see Kingston-upon-Hull, earl of
  William 50
Pigott, Christopher 101
Pitt, Robert 131
  Sir Thomas 131
  William, the Elder *see* Chatham, earl of
  William, the Younger 162, 164, 165, 166, 171, 175, 178, 185, 194, 197, 251, 324
Plunket, William Conyngham 253
Pole, Michael *see* Suffolk, earl of
  Reginald, cardinal 26
  William *see* Suffolk, duke of
Pollock, Ernest Murray
  see Hanworth, baron
Popham, Alexander 50
Popish Plot (1678–9) 63, 66, 67
Portland, Jerome Weston, 2nd earl of 44
  Thomas Weston, 4th earl of 67, 68
  William Henry Cavendish Bentinck, 3rd duke of 198
Potenger, John 63
Poulson, John 289
Poynings, Sir Edward 322
Pride, Sir Thomas 50
'Pride's Purge' (1648) 44, 122
Primrose, Archibald *see* Rosebery, earl of
printers, king's 115
Prior, James 348
provisional government (1688–9) 59
Provisional Irish Army 342
Prynne, William 121, 133
Puckering, John, Speaker of the House of Commons 89, 94
Pugin, Augustus 251
Pulteney, William 156
Pym, John 102, 119

Queensberry, James Douglas, 2nd duke [S] of 151
  James Douglas, 3rd duke [S] of 153
  William Douglas, 8th earl [S] of 312

Ramsay, Sir Archibald 280
Ramsey, abbot of 18
Ranelagh, Richard Jones, 1st earl [I] of 140
referenda 286, 287, 358
Reichenbach, Benjamin 178
Review Body of Top Salaries 289, 290

Rhondda, Margaret Mackworth, 2nd
    viscount 214
Rich, Edward *see* Warwick, earl of
    Robert, styled lord 44
    Robert *see* Warwick, earl of
Richard, Ivor Seward, baron 280, 361
Richard I, king 6
Richard II, king 18, 19, 24, 75
Richard III, king 24
Richardson, Thomas 106
Richmond, Surr. 97
Richmond, Charles Lennox, 3rd duke of
    163
    James Stuart, 1st duke of 44
Rivers, John Savage, 2nd earl 44
    Thomas Savage, 3rd earl 54
Roberts, Sir William 50
Robinson, Sir Joseph 215
Rochester, Ernest Henry Lamb, baron 218
    John Wilmot, earl of 67
    Laurence Hyde, 1st earl of 59, 63, 69
Rockingham, Charles Watson-Wentworth,
    2nd marquess of 159, 161
Roger of Howden 5
Rolle, John 101
Roos, John Manners, styled lord 67
    Anne Manners, lady 67
Rosebery, Archibald Primrose, 5th earl [S]
    of 207, 208
Ross, Co. Cork 329
Ross, George 181
Rous, Francis, Speaker of the House of
    Commons 50, 113
Rupert, prince *see* Cumberland, duke of
Russell, Conrad 117
    Edward *see* Orford, earl of
    Edward Southwell *see* De Clifford, lord
    Francis *see* Bedford, earl of
    Sir Francis 50
    John, Speaker of the House of
        Commons 19
    John Francis Stanley, 2nd earl 220

Sackville, Edward *see* Dorset, earl of
    Herbrand Edward Dundonald
        Brassey *see* De La Warr, earl
    Richard *see* Dorset, earl of
St Alban, Francis Bacon, viscount 105
St Andrews Agreement (2006) 349
St Asaph, bishop of 87
St David's, bishop of 87
St John, Oliver 50
St John Stevas, Norman 296, 297
Salisbury, James Cecil, 3rd earl of 62
    Robert Arthur Talbot Gascoyne-Cecil,
        3rd marquess of 206, 207, 208

[Salisbury *continued*]
    Sir Robert Cecil, 1st earl of 38, 94, 97,
        106
    William Cecil, 2nd earl of 49, 111
Sandwich, Edward Montagu, 1st earl of
    50, 54
    John Montagu, 4th earl of 163
Sankey, John, viscount 218
Savage, John *see* Rivers, earl
    Thomas *see* Rivers, earl
Savile, George *see* Halifax, marquess of
    Thomas, viscount 44
Saye and Sele, William Fiennes,
    viscount 33, 38, 45, 50
Scobell, Henry 116
Scone, Perthshire, abbey 307
Scotland 12
    Church of Scotland 182, 359
    comptroller of 306
    convention of estates 307, 309, 313
    convention of royal burghs 181, 304
    councils, general 307, 313
        privy 309, 313, 314
    court of session 309, 310
    crown, prerogative of 312
    Declaration of Arbroath (1320) 312
    general assembly 314
    lieutenants, king's 307
    lord advocate 359
    solicitor general 359
    subjects in 13
    treasurer of 306
    union with England 107, 158, 314, 315
Scott, Francis *see* Buccleuch, duke of
    Giles Gilbert 297
    James *see* Monmouth, duke of
    John *see* Eldon, earl of
    Sir Richard 295
Scottish Office 358
Seafield, James Ogilvy, 1st earl [S] of 291
seal, great 43, 46, 117, 322
    commission of 117
Segrave, Nicholas 12
Selborne, William Waldegrave Palmer, 2nd
    earl of 207
Selby, abbot of 18
Senior, Nassau 264
Senior Salaries Review Body (SSRB) 289
serjeants at law, king's 30
Seymour, Edward *see* Hertford, earl of
    Edward, Speaker of the House of
        Commons 135
    family 38
    John 95
    Maria Emily *see* Hertford, marchioness
        of
    William *see* Hertford, marquess of

Index

Seymour of Trowbridge, Francis, 1st baron 44
Shaftesbury, Anthony Ashley Cooper, 1st earl of 54, 60, 62, 63, 64, 67, 68, 70
Cropley Ashley Cooper, 6th earl of 196
Shaw, Thomas 219
Sheffield, Edmund see Mulgrave, earl of
Shelburne, John Petty, earl [I] of 161
Sheldrake, John 69
Shell, Donald 230, 238
Shepheard, Sir Samuel 131
Shirley, Thomas, Dr 68
Shrewsbury, Salop 12
Shrewsbury, Charles Talbot, duke of 58, 140
John Talbot, 10th earl of 44
Skinner, Thomas 68, 141
Skippon, Philip 50
Smith, Frederick Edwin see Birkenhead, earl of
Robert 164
Smyth, Charles see Carrington of Burford, viscount
Snowden, Philip 218
Society of the Supporters of the Bill of Rights 188
Society of West India Merchants 181
solicitor general 30
Somers, Sir John, baron 67, 68, 137, 140
Southampton, Henry Wriothesley, 3rd earl of 33, 38, 44
Thomas Wriothesley, 4th earl of 60
Speck, Bill 171
Spencer, Charles see Sunderland, earl of
Robert see Sunderland, earl of
Stafford, William Howard, viscount of 66, 67
Stamford, Thomas Grey, 2nd earl of 63
Stanhope, James, 1st earl 154, 155
Philip Henry see Mahon, viscount
Stanley, Charles see Derby, earl of
Edward see Derby, earl of
James see Derby, earl of
Sir John 353
state trials 12, 16, 23
Steele, William 50
Stewart, Robert see Casltereagh, viscount
Stillingfleet, Edward 57
Stormont, David Murray, 7th viscount 195
Strafford, Thomas Wentworth, 1st earl of 43, 46, 67
Strasbourg 364
Stratford, John, archbishop of Canterbury 16
Strickland, Walter 50
Sir William 50
Stronge, Sir Norman 342

Stuart, James see Richmond, duke of
John see Bute, earl of
Suffolk, Charles Brandon, duke of 195
Michael de la Pole, earl of 82
Thomas Howard, 1st earl of 104
William de la Pole, duke of 82
Sunderland, Charles Spencer, 3rd earl of 61, 153, 154, 155, 157
Robert Spencer, 2nd earl of 60, 140
Sunningdale Conference 346
supreme court 227
Surrey, Henry Howard, styled earl of 93
Swanborough, Stella Isaacs, baroness 243
Sydenham, William 50
Sydney, Robert see Leicester, earl of

Talbot, Charles see Shrewsbury, duke of
John see Shrewsbury, earl of
Tayler, Richard 250
Taylor, A. J. P. 275
Ann 293
Tebbit, Norman Beresford, baron 157
report 298
Temple, Sir Richard 111, 134
Temys, Thomas 89
Tenison, Thomas, archbishop of Canterbury 154
Thesiger, Frederic John Napier see Chelmsford, baron
Thomas, Edmond 50
J. H. 278
Peter 71
Thomas of Lancaster see Lancaster, earl of
Throckmorton, Sir George 97
Thurlow, Edward, 1st baron 159
Tichborne, Sir Robert 50
Tomlinson, Sir Matthew 50
Touchet, James see Audley, lord
Townshend, Charles, 2nd viscount 155
Trades Union Congress 217
treasury, the 297, 344
treaties:
 Birgham (1290) 301
 Lisbon (2007) 286
 Maastricht (1992) 284
 Paris (1259) 354
 Union (1707) 150, 170, 315
 (1800) 356
 Utrecht (1713) 152, 152
Tresham, Sir Thomas, prior of St John of Jerusalem 30
William 18
Trevor, Sir John, Speaker of the House of Commons 135
Trim, Co. Meath 329
Trimble, David 349
Tuam, archbishop of 197

Tucker, John 186
  Richard 186
Tunstal, Cuthbert, bishop of London, of Durham 26, 86
Turnor, Edward, Speaker of the House of Commons 135

Ullswater, James William Lowther, viscount 272
Ulster Workers Council 348
United Nations 283

van der Meulen, Pieter 342
Van Mildert, William, bishop of Llandaff 201
Venice, ambassador of 48
Verney, Ralph. 2nd earl [I] 173
Vernon, James 61
Villiers, George see Buckingham, duke of
Vorontsov, Simon 178

Wales 12, 285
  prince of 32
  secretary of state for 361
  'union' with England 87, 363
Walker, Clement 47
Walpole, Horace 177, 179
  (Sir) Robert 153, 154–6, 170, 171, 174, 177, 180
Walsingham, Thomas de Grey, 2nd baron 160
Ward, John William see Dudley, viscount
Warwick, Edward Rich, 8th earl of 155
  Richard Beauchamp, 13th earl of 19
  Robert Rich, 2nd earl of 50
Waterford, Co. Waterford 329, 330
Watson-Wentworth, Charles
  see Rockingham, marquess of
Webb, Sidney see Passfield, baron
Wellington, Arthur Wellesley, 1st duke of 165, 198, 201–3, 206, 208
  grandson of 205
Welsh Office 358
Wensleydale, James Parke, baron 204, 205
Wentworth, Peter 89
  Thomas, 5th lord 44
  Thomas see also Cleveland, earl of; Strafford, earl of
Western European Union (WEU) 284
Westminster see London
Weston, Jerome see Portland, earl of
  Thomas see Portland, earl of
Wexford, Co. Wexford 329

Whalley, Edward 50
Wharton, Philip, 4th lord 50, 61, 62
  Thomas, 1st marquess of, previously 5th lord 61, 62
Whig Club 175
Whitelocke, Sir Bulstrode 50
Wilberforce, William 258
Wilkes, John 187, 188
William III, king 59, 60, 119, 126, 127, 143, 147, 148, 177, 307, 313, 342
  creation of peerages 55
William IV, king 251
  creation of peerages 202
William of Malmesbury 4
Williams, David 187
  John, bishop of Lincoln 30
Williamson, Philip 216
Wilmington, Spencer Compton, earl of 156
Wilmot, John see Rochester, earl of
Wilmot of Adderbury, Henry, baron 44
Wilson, Harold 241
Winchester, Hants. 5, 12
Winchester, bishop of
  see Gardiner, Stephen
Windham, William 187
Windsor, Thomas, 7th lord 69
Wintringham, Margaret 272
witan 3
Wolsey, Thomas, cardinal, lord chancellor 26, 92
Wolseley, Sir Charles 50
Womack, Lawrence 57
Wood, Edward Frederick Lindley
  see Halifax of Monk Bretton, viscount
Woodfall, William 'Memory' 189
Wootton of Abinger, Barbara Frances, baroness 243
Wright, John 101
  Robert 220
Wriothesley, Henry
  see Southampton, earl of
  Thomas see Southampton, earl of
writs of error 45
Wyatt, James 251
Wyndham, William see Grenville, baron
Wyvill, Christopher 181, 189

Yelverton, Henry
  see Longueville, viscount de
York, Yorks. 12, 20, 43
Yorke, Philip see Hardwicke, earl of